Indispensable and Other Myths

Indispensable and Other Myths

Why the CEO Pay Experiment Failed and How to Fix It

Michael B. Dorff

HD4965.5.U6 D67 2014
Dorff, Michael, 1970–
author.
Indispensable and other
myths : why the CEO pay
experiment failed and how to
fix it

UNIVERSITY OF CALIFORNIA PRESS
Berkeley · Los Angeles · London

University of California Press, one of the most
distinguished university presses in the United States,
enriches lives around the world by advancing scholarship
in the humanities, social sciences, and natural sciences. Its
activities are supported by the UC Press Foundation and
by philanthropic contributions from individuals and
institutions. For more information, visit www.ucpress.edu.

University of California Press
Berkeley and Los Angeles, California

University of California Press, Ltd.
London, England

Library of Congress Cataloging-in-Publication Data

Dorff, Michael, 1970-
    Indispensable and other myths : why the CEO pay
experiment failed and how to fix it / Michael Dorff.
        pages cm
    Includes bibliographical references and index.
    ISBN 978-0-520-28101-1 (cloth : alk. paper)—
    ISBN 978-0-520-95859-3 (e-book)
    1. Chief executive officers—Salaries, etc.
    2. Executives—Salaries, etc.—United States.
    3. Compensation management—United States.
    I. Title.
        HD4965.5.U6.D67 2014
        658.4'072--dc23   2013040333

Manufactured in the United States of America
23 22 21 20 19 18 17 16 15 14
10 9 8 7 6 5 4 3 2 1

In keeping with a commitment to support
environmentally responsible and sustainable printing
practices, UC Press has printed this book on Natures
Natural, a fiber that contains 30% post-consumer waste
and meets the minimum requirements of ANSI/NISO
Z39.48–1992 (R 1997) (*Permanence of Paper*).

*To my parents, Elliot and Marlynn Dorff, for
teaching me a love of learning*

Contents

Acknowledgments

I am deeply grateful to all the wonderful, supportive, and kindhearted people who made this book possible. This project began when my father, Elliot Dorff, told me I had written enough articles about CEO pay, and it was time for a book. Had I known how many years of work would be required to finish it, I probably would never have started. So it's just as well that he greatly underestimated the time and effort that would be necessary. Sometimes parents are right for the wrong reasons. The author of countless scholarly books himself, my father patiently guided me through the process and assured me that I *would* reach the end . . . eventually. My mother, Marlynn Dorff, was also an unceasing source of support and encouragement.

I owe a special debt to Carl Albert, chairman of Boise, Inc. Carl was an early believer in this project and has given me invaluable feedback throughout. He has also been tireless in advancing the book's ideas and finding new people for me to persuade and places for me to speak. He is an ideal mentor and role model.

I was fortunate to have many talented and accomplished scholars provide comments on the manuscript. My close friends Russell Korobkin and Douglas Lichtman were among the first to read it. Their suggestions greatly improved the final product and gave me the courage to show the manuscript to others. They were both especially helpful in coming up with the title, as was Michael Grunwald. Stephen Bainbridge, Charles Elson, Jesse Fried, Kevin Murphy, Elizabeth Pollman,

Lynn Stout, and David Walker have all taught me a great deal about CEO pay and corporate governance. This book has profited hugely from their outstanding scholarship and insightful comments. Gary Bass, Noah Feldman, Kim Ferzan, Paul Horwitz, Dan Markel, Carrie Menkel-Meadow, Dennis Patterson, Nate Persily, and Adam Winkler patiently guided a neophyte through the labyrinthine publication process and led me through to the other side. I am very lucky to count them as friends. I am also thankful for Debbie Gershenowitz's guidance and publication advice.

Closer to home, Southwestern Law School provided financial support over several summers and a sabbatical that enabled me to complete the book. Even more important, my Southwestern family—Ryan Abbott, Mark Cammack, Bryant Garth, Priya Gupta, Danielle Hart, Roman Hoyos, Hila Keren, Caleb Mason, Art McEvoy, David Fagundes, Gowri Ramachandran, Kelly Strader, John Tehranian, and Dov Waisman—critiqued countless drafts and participated in endless office conversations about them. And my Drucker School of Management teaching partners, Jay Prag and Hideki Yamawaki, provided a much-needed management perspective. I feel privileged to have such wonderful and supportive colleagues.

Southwestern also supplied me with a number of hardworking and talented law students who provided exceptional research assistance: Natalie Lee, Meredith Lierz, Justin Nash, and Grant Savoy. Another student, Joshua Roberts, provided helpful feedback. Thomas Harvey also gathered material for the book before his untimely death; I wish he were here to celebrate its completion with us.

Peter Richardson at the University of California Press saw the book's potential immediately and guided the manuscript through the approval process in record time. Along the way, he patiently introduced me to the world of academic publishing and made sure my missteps were few and quickly corrected. Christopher Lura ensured that all the technical aspects of production went smoothly. Sheila Berg, my copy editor, ensured that the text clearly and grammatically conveyed my meaning. I hope this is just the first of many projects we all work on together.

Cindy Kazan and Leslie Steinberg have helped me reach out to a much wider audience than I could possibly find on my own. If the book influences the public policy debate, it will in large part be due to their energy and enthusiasm.

Finally, and most important, I want to thank my children, Zoe and Miles, and my wife, Tanya, for their tolerance and loving understanding. I know they have heard far more than they want to about CEO pay, and I'm sure they are greatly looking forward to other topics of conversation. We can now move on to (respectively) Percy Jackson, the Teenage Mutant Ninja Turtles, and the impact of fasting on oxidative stress markers in patients taking gemcitabine and cisplatin for advanced solid tumors.

CHAPTER 1

Introduction

The year 2008 was a tough one for most public corporations. The stock market collapsed, diving 38 percent. The broader economy sank into the deepest and longest recession since the Great Depression. The financial markets froze, blocking companies from their usual ability to borrow when in trouble.

Even against this depressing backdrop, some companies' suffering stood out. American International Group (AIG) endured cataclysmic losses in 2008, over $13 billion in just the first six months. Annual losses grew to a staggering $99 billion by year's end. From a high of over $70.00 per share, AIG's stock price fell to $1.25 per share in September, a drop of over 98 percent. To keep AIG afloat, the federal government ultimately loaned the company over $180 billion.

Few companies have imploded as dramatically as AIG. But other companies' shares also dropped much further than the market as a whole. The stock price of Abercrombie and Fitch sank 71 percent, for example, and the oil and gas company Nabors Industries saw its share price cut in half.

When a company performs as dismally as these three did, we expect the board to fire the CEO. We might also envision (even a little gleefully) that the CEO's assets would be confiscated in lawsuits by angry shareholders. Images of brave captains going down with their ships spring to mind. After all, these CEOs led their companies into disaster, causing mayhem for employees, customers, suppliers, the economy generally, and, most important, the companies' owners—the shareholders. In a Darwinian economy, we expect the weak to be, well, eaten.

AIG's CEO, Martin Sullivan, was, in fact, fired. Then AIG's board of directors paid him $47 million severance as a reward for a job well done. Abercrombie's CEO, Michael Jeffries, not only kept his job, but received $71.8 million in total pay, roughly equivalent to $1 million for each percentage point *decline* in the company's value. The total included a $6 million retention bonus to persuade Mr. Jeffries to stay, even though he had been with the company for seventeen years and showed no signs of leaving. Nabors's CEO, Eugene Isenberg, also made out pretty well, taking home $79.3 million, including a $58.7 million bonus.[1]

These sorts of stories of CEOs receiving enormous rewards for dismal corporate results anger almost everyone, from pundits to presidents.[2] They seem like clear signals that something is wrong with the way the corporations are governed. You'd be hard-pressed to find someone who thinks these CEOs deserved the pay they got. When a company does poorly, even defenders of the current system tend to agree that it's wrong for the CEO to take home a huge paycheck.

But what about success stories like that of General Electric's legendary CEO, Jack Welch? Welch became GE's CEO in 1981, when its market capitalization was $14 billion.[3] By the time he retired twenty years later, GE's market capitalization had skyrocketed to $415 billion, making it the largest corporation in the world by that measure.[4] In 1999, *Fortune* named Welch "Manager of the Century." (Not everyone agrees that Welch deserves all this praise, but the dominant narrative describes Welch as a superstar.)

GE compensated Welch richly for his leadership. To give some sense of the wealth Welch—who comes from a humble background—accumulated during a lifetime of employment at GE, the year of his retirement *Forbes* estimated his net worth as $680 million (equivalent to almost $900 million in 2012 dollars).[5] Is there anything wrong with Welch earning huge sums for expanding GE's worth nearly thirtyfold?

Many people believe that when a corporation does poorly, its leader should suffer commensurately. That CEOs such as Sullivan, Jeffries, and Isenberg receive eight-figure compensation packages understandably offends shareholders who are suffering staggering losses. Employees losing their jobs at these companies no doubt feel similarly outraged. Conversely, many would support the notion of rewarding excellent performance like Welch's with superior pay.

Is it possible that both these ideas are wrong? Is blaming the CEO for a corporate meltdown unfair? And is rewarding the CEO for a company's outstanding performance wrongheaded? Could basic ideas like (1) the CEO determines the company's performance and (2) tying the CEO's pay to the company's performance will motivate the CEO to excel be completely off-target?

Our notions about pay and performance and the link between the two are based on a number of deeply held ideas that are difficult to question. What ideas am I talking about? The least controversial of these is our sense of what's normal. For the past few decades, CEO pay has risen dramatically, even after accounting for inflation. There have been a few off years, but we are typically treated to a steady diet of news stories about the latest enormous increase in CEO compensation. Because this trend has continued for so long, we tend to think that this is how things have to be.

We also have a strong intuition about how CEO pay should be structured. We are used to hearing about million-dollar salaries that are dwarfed by large bonuses, huge baskets of restricted stock, and enormous options packages (sometimes in the tens of millions). The key, we believe, is to tie CEO pay to the company's performance so the CEO will be incentivized to run the company well and boost the stock price.[6] Like our beliefs about having consistent increases in the amount of pay, the conventional wisdom about the structure of CEO pay has lasted for several decades, long enough that most of us have trouble conceiving of any other method than tying pay to performance.

Many of us also think of corporations in a sense as people. The comparison of a corporation to a person can seem apt in important ways; corporations are entities with interests and motives of their own that act aggressively to increase their wealth and power. Some of us may be suspicious of corporations; we may fear that they have far too much power in our society, that they have the money, sophistication, and connections to get what they want from the political system in a way most of us cannot. But I suspect few of us worry that corporations are vulnerable, that they are too easily taken advantage of in some of their most important deals. To most of us, corporations—especially the type of large, publicly traded corporation I discuss in this book[7]—are the epitome of power. We might need protection from them, but they are perfectly capable of looking out for their own interests.

Our faith in corporations seems especially well placed when they are negotiating their CEOs' payment packages. What could be a more important decision than how a company motivates its leader? Surely with so much at stake, and with so much sophistication and intelligence applied to the task, corporations and their CEOs must negotiate the most effective and efficient compensation packages possible, designed to inspire just the right actions. The market for CEOs (including their pay packages) must be incredibly efficient.

There is a split in popular thinking at this point. While many people wholeheartedly agree that CEO pay is set efficiently, others feel that the directors who run corporations do not bargain at arm's length with their CEOs. These critics suspect some version of crony capitalism must be at work. The directors and the CEOs move in the same social circles; many directors actually are CEOs or senior executives at other companies. Whether out of affinity for one of their own or outright corruption, the directors may funnel as much corporate wealth as they can to their friend the CEO.

There is little overlap between those who think CEO pay is efficient and those who believe it is the product of cronyism or corruption. Most people will agree with one of these ideas and disagree violently with the other. It's hard to imagine a sane person simultaneously believing that CEO pay is highly efficient *and* corrupt. Whichever theory you believe, though, you likely believe quite strongly, to the point that you have trouble entertaining seriously the possibility that the other might be true.

If you're in the efficiency camp, you will almost certainly agree with two additional statements: (1) it is imperative that companies hire the very best CEOs they can find, because the right leader can make all the difference to a company's performance; and (2) boards of directors are well equipped to figure out who that right person is. For the CEO labor market to be efficient, both statements must be true. If it doesn't matter who runs the company, then there is not much incentive for it to work out the best possible pay package. And if directors can't choose the best CEO from a pool of candidates, then we can't have much faith that there's a market in which buyers bid for the best CEO talent; you have to be able to recognize talent before you can bargain for it. Most folks in the cronyism/corruption camp will also agree that leadership is important, though perhaps they will feel less sanguine about directors' ability to spot talent.

With that brief detour into dissension, I think we can safely return to unanimity with the last two ideas. First, people are motivated by pay. If you're hiring a real estate broker, your broker's compensation should depend on the sale price of your house. That way, your broker will share your incentive to get as much money for the house as possible, and you're much more likely to maximize your profits. CEOs should be paid the same way. The more closely companies tie CEO pay to the company's results—the more sensitive CEO pay is to performance—the more successful the company should become. Well-managed companies will apply this principle throughout the organization, making everyone's paycheck depend on how they do their jobs. But it's especially important for the CEO.

Second, the CEO works for the corporation's owners, the shareholders. Since it's the shareholders' company, it's their well-being (which you can read as "wealth") that matters. Ultimately, then, the goal of a good CEO pay package is to motivate the CEO to earn as much money as possible for the shareholders. Other groups with ties to the corporation—such as employees, bondholders, customers, and the communities in which the company operates—are important only to the extent that meeting their needs furthers the fundamental goal of maximizing shareholder wealth.

If these ideas sound right to you, if you've been nodding your head, maybe thinking "of course" as you read, then it may surprise you to learn that *none* of these ideas has strong empirical support. In fact, the evidence weighs against most of these notions, in some cases quite strongly.

One of the central purposes of this book is to unpack these supporting intuitions and reveal just how flimsy the evidence for them is. But it's not enough to show that the common understanding of CEO pay is wrong; I will also explain how CEO pay really works. The defense that CEO pay is efficient and the critique that it is the product of corruption have something in common: both assume that boards are acting purposefully and achieving their aims, whether those aims are to motivate the CEO or to line the CEO's pockets. But the evidence suggests that something quite different—something much less calculating and much more human—is likely going on in corporate boardrooms. I call this explanation the "behavioral theory" because it is based on empirical studies of how people actually act (behavioral economics rather than the rational actor theory).

To understand the dynamics of CEO pay in public companies, we need to start with a preview of the history (chapter 2). The experience in recent decades of rising CEO compensation and increasing use of equity as performance pay is a radical departure from prior decades' practice. For the first few decades after World War II, CEO pay at the largest U.S. public companies remained flat in real terms (controlling for inflation) and consisted mostly of salaries and short-term bonuses. Companies used very little equity in pay packages. Some companies began to include stock options in CEO pay packages during the 1950s, but the majority did not until the 1970s. And even when companies did award options, they didn't amount to much; salary and bonus accounted for 93 percent of total CEO compensation during the 1950s and 87 percent of the total during the 1960s. (The rest consisted of stock options, restricted stock, and other long-term incentive plans.) The current norm of rapidly rising pay and heavy use of performance pay began only in the late 1970s and didn't really take hold until the 1980s.[8]

This major shift provides an opportunity to probe the inner workings of CEO pay. What caused these two radical changes in the amount and structure of CEO pay? As I explain in later chapters, neither the efficiency nor the cronyism/corruption theory can explain these changes satisfactorily. But my behavioral theory can.

The behavioral theory suggests that the switch to performance pay was the product of emerging economic ideas about how employees should be motivated (known to economists as agency cost theory). Beginning in the mid-1970s, economists (most prominently Michael C. Jensen and William H. Meckling) argued that people who worked for corporations—even as the companies' chief executive officer—would not automatically act in the companies' best interests. Instead, they would, as all good economic agents do, pursue their *own* well-being to the extent they could get away with it. To get the most out of their employees, companies had to harness their workers' self-interest by tying pay to their performance.[9]

As Cornell Law School's Lynn Stout and University of Southern California economist Kevin Murphy have separately recognized, boards were influenced by academic theories about the optimal structure of CEO pay.[10] Increasing numbers of companies began to comply with academics' advice, relying more heavily on forms of pay that tied CEOs' remuneration to the companies' stock price—especially through stock options. As more and more companies adopted performance pay, the notion that performance pay was key to good corporate governance amassed greater credibility. Eventually, the extent to which the CEO's pay was sensitive to corporate performance became the central metric by which shareholders judged whether the company had structured the pay package appropriately.[11]

Just as companies were adding stock options to the CEO pay mix, along came the longest bull market in U.S. history, making those options incredibly valuable. In August 1982, the Dow Jones Industrial Index stood at 777. Over the next eighteen years, the Index rose a jaw-dropping 1,500 percent to reach 11,722 in January 2000. There were some bumps along the way—most notably on October 19, 1987 ("Black Monday"), when the Index suffered a 508-point collapse—but for the most part, the market's rise was not only astronomical but also remarkably stable. The combination of heaps of stock options and other equity incentives and this historic bull market raised CEO pay to previously unimagined heights.

Nevertheless, despite the fact that the rising stock market was making options far more lucrative than boards likely anticipated when they issued them, directors couldn't seem to break themselves of the habit of giving options to CEOs. To the contrary, they kept issuing more, catapulting CEO pay into the stratosphere.

Why? Why would some of our smartest and most sophisticated businesspeople, entrusted with managing our largest and most important companies, continue to offer stock options when they were clearly leading to unprecedented growth in CEO pay? It's hard to imagine those same directors would have stuck voluntarily with a pricing structure for any other important input when that structure resulted in dramatically higher prices without apparent justification.

Suppose, for example, that a company that sold oil agreed to pay its sales force on commission, a percentage of the gross sales each salesperson brought in. If the price of oil suddenly skyrocketed, so that a salesperson could earn five times as much for selling the same volume of oil, would we expect the company to keep the same compensation strategy? Of course not. The oil company would reduce the commission percentage or switch to a fixed compensation amount per volume of oil sold. And if the salespeople didn't like it, the company would replace them.

Corporate CEOs may be more difficult to replace than salespeople. And boards might have been reluctant to drive off a successful CEO by suddenly cutting off the supply of profitable stock options. But we should still have seen boards make some attempt to pare back, to switch to less explosive forms of pay. Instead, boards doubled down, relying more and more heavily on equity-based compensation. At their peak in 2000, stock option awards made up about half of CEOs' total pay.[12]

My behavioral theory argues that directors' failure to rein in CEO pay was not due to some market force that suddenly made a different form of pay—and much higher pay—the compensation system best calculated to improve shareholders' welfare, nor were directors seduced by CEOs' promises of corporate largesse. Directors stayed with equity-based pay because they believed that was the best way to motivate their chief executive officers to focus on boosting the stock price.

This seems a perfectly appropriate motivation. Under the dominant theory of corporate governance, it's exactly what directors are supposed to do—raise the stock price. (I have some doubts about the desirability of making this the paramount goal, as I discuss in chapter 9, but it is the prevailing understanding of directors' central task.) The problem with directors' strategy of using equity-based performance pay to achieve that goal is this: there is no convincing evidence that it works.

There are two conditions that must prevail for equity-based pay to result in higher stock prices: equity-based pay must improve CEOs' performance, and CEOs must have the power to raise their companies' stock prices. The best evidence is that neither of these conditions holds true.

Scholars have produced surprising results when testing the impact of performance pay. Most empirical studies have found little to no link between a company's use of performance pay devices such as stock options or bonuses and subsequent increases in the company's stock price (or earnings or any other measure of corporate success). Some studies have even found that corporate results *degrade* as boards rely increasingly on performance pay to motivate their executives.

These results, though shocking, are consistent with psychological experiments in the laboratory. Psychologists have discovered that performance pay erodes intrinsic motivation for the sort of high-level cognitive tasks CEOs perform. They have also found that individual performance deteriorates on these sorts of tasks (i.e., those that require creativity or analytical reasoning) when subjects know they will be rewarded for their success, especially if the rewards are very high. Although not quite conclusive, the evidence points strongly against the utility of performance pay.

As to the second condition, CEOs' ability to have a positive impact on the companies they lead is unclear. Some leaders like Berkshire Hathaway's Warren Buffett or Apple's Steve Jobs seem to have transformed their companies, but others like AIG's Martin Sullivan appear to have sunk them. Salient examples like these support people's view that leadership (whether good or bad) is important.

When scholars try to validate this instinct empirically, though, they run into serious trouble. Part of the problem is that there are a slew of factors that may influence a company's success besides its leader, from the price of oil to interest rates to government regulation to fashion trends. To isolate the effect of CEOs in particular, scholars need a lot of statistical power, which in turn requires hordes of data points. But there simply aren't enough leadership shifts to generate that statistical power without including many decades of data. And going that far back in history just compounds the problem by adding even more variables that could affect the results.

These difficulties have not prevented scholars from trying to design tests that will work with the data they have. Their studies have generally found that CEOs do not make much difference to corporate results on average. The paucity of data might caution us not to rely too heavily on these studies, but the fact that most of them come to the same conclusion should give us serious pause. Maybe CEOs don't typically have the kind of monumental impact on their companies that people generally assume.

There is an important caveat to note here: these studies compare the impact of different people who were all sufficiently qualified to persuade a board to hire them as the CEO of a public company. No one is claiming that some random person off the street could run Apple as well as Steve Jobs did. But when we compare members of that rarified group of *actual* public company CEOs, it's hard to see differences among them by looking at changes in their companies' stock prices. Perhaps because these CEOs are so similar to one another in training and background, or perhaps because environmental effects constrain most CEOs to make parallel decisions, the board's decision to hire one hyper-talented candidate over another seems largely irrelevant.

Performance pay is much more expensive than guaranteed compensation because boards must offer executives higher expected pay to make up for the significant chance that they will fail to meet the performance targets and receive little or nothing. Advocates of performance pay therefore bear a heavy burden to demonstrate that its enormous costs are offset by improved corporate results. The best evidence, though, indicates that this is not the case; performance pay is more likely to *lower* a business's profits than to raise them.

What the evidence tells us, then, is that equity-based pay such as stock options is highly unlikely to result in higher stock prices, both because equity-based pay does not seem to produce better performance from executives and because executives generally have little influence over share prices. Yet directors' enthusiasm for equity pay has if anything only intensified over the past few decades. In recent years, they increasingly have been substituting restricted stock for stock options, but their fondness for equity-based performance pay remains as strong as ever.

This contradiction is mind-boggling. Public company directors continue to spend literally billions of dollars on equity pay annually on the strength of an academic theory that has little empirical support. How could such smart, sophisticated businesspeople spend so much money on an unsupported theory? Perhaps at first directors relied on the credibility of the academics who were advancing these theories. But once it became clear that equity-based compensation was having a tremendous impact on the amounts companies were paying their CEOs, why didn't directors begin asking tough questions about what benefits the companies were getting in exchange for all this money?

The answer begins with an epistemic problem: it is impossible to measure a CEO's contribution to the firm, even years after he or she has retired. Directors never find out whether they overpaid the CEO or got a terrific bargain. How much was Jack Welch really worth? General Electric certainly prospered during his tenure as CEO, but how much of that was due to Welch as opposed to GE's preexisting personnel, intellectual property, factories, market position, and brand reputation? How much was due to general market conditions or fortuitous circumstances? There is no way to answer that question with any confidence. Crediting Welch alone with the rise in GE's stock price seems an extreme position. Surely other factors played at least some role in helping GE grow so dramatically. But how much? We will never have a definitive answer to this question.

Directors nevertheless need to find a way to determine how much they should be willing to pay a CEO. On the one hand, they don't want to pay more than the CEO will produce for the firm. Businesses that make a habit of spending more on assets than those assets produce in income don't tend to survive very long. On the other hand, they don't want to miss out on a CEO who could radically improve the company's fortunes because they balked at the cost. Imagine if Apple's directors had failed to hire Steve Jobs because of a pay dispute. Figuring out how much is too much is an intractable problem, and yet getting the answer right is very important.

Although it is impossible to find the *correct* valuation for a CEO's services, directors persuade themselves that they have come up with a *reasonable* valuation. Even approximate valuations of CEOs' services are likely impossible, given the host of variables that affect a company's fortunes. But the interaction of some well-documented phenomena of human behavior creates the *illusion* for directors that they have hit the mark. These include the illusion of validity, the illusion of control, groupthink, and social cascades.

The illusion of validity persuades directors that the information they have about CEO candidates is far more predictive of those candidates' future performance than it really is. The illusion of control encourages directors to discount the role luck has played in candidates' careers, causing directors to give the candidates too much credit for their successes. Groupthink induces overly cohesive boards to avoid dissent when hiring a CEO by reaching consensus quickly and then protecting the consensus choice. Once a leading contender has emerged, groupthink encourages boards to give short shrift to arguments against the leader and discount negative information. Social cascades act to justify the amount of compensation companies pay their CEOs as the product of the market. Social cascades can occur when participants lack sufficient private information to outweigh the apparent value of publicly available information.

Together, these behavioral dynamics encourage boards to believe that their chosen candidate is far superior to the competition and therefore worth a premium price. And since other companies are paying a similar amount, the premium is not viewed as excessive.

Unfortunately, measuring a CEO's future impact on the company is next to impossible, and directors' faith in their ability to divine who will be the next Steve Jobs is almost entirely misplaced. Because directors believe they can predict a CEO's future success, though, they also reasonably believe they would be breaching their duty to the shareholders if they failed to hire the best CEO the company could afford. If a board thinks it has the opportunity to hire a game changer—a Steve Jobs or a Warren Buffett—then just about any amount of pay can be justified.

This is why directors failed to stop the equity pay–inspired avalanche of CEO compensation during the 1980s and 1990s. They thought it was crucial to hire the best person to head their companies, and they were confident they knew who that person was. And in terms of pay, directors' best information came from what everyone else was doing, and everyone else kept using equity pay and raising compensation.

Convinced? You shouldn't be, at least not yet. Like a good trial lawyer, I have laid out my argument in my opening statement, but I still have to present the evidence. I'll do that in three parts.

Part I explains why the dominant theories of efficiency and cronyism/corruption do not conform to the available evidence. It starts in chapter 2 with some background on the changes that have occurred in the form and amount of CEO pay. Chapters 3 and 4 then take on the notion that CEO pay is efficient. Chapter 3 explains that the underlying premise of market efficiency—that there are sophisticated buyers and sellers bargaining at arm's length—is highly suspect in the public corporation context. Chapter 4 takes on the different efficiency arguments directly, one at a time, and demonstrates their theoretical and empirical weaknesses. Finally, chapter 5 sets out the dominant critique of CEO pay—that directors are allied with CEOs in attempting to raise CEOs' pay—and uncovers its flaws.

Part II explains my behavioral theory of CEO pay. I begin in chapter 6 by looking behind the nearly universal consensus that CEOs' pay should be tied to their performance to motivate them to act in the shareholders' interests. There I show that the empirical evidence—both from laboratory experiments and from empirical studies of companies' use of different payment structures—demonstrates that equity-based performance pay has failed in its purpose of producing better corporate performance. Chapter 7 explores the evidence that CEOs matter to corporate fortunes. It argues that CEOs do not matter very much on average, at least as compared to other CEOs with comparable training, experience, and ability. Chapter 8 rounds out this part by explaining why directors have clung to performance pay even when it produced dramatic increases in compensation without comparably dramatic improvements in corporate performance.

Part III presents my thoughts about reform. Chapter 9 questions whether the stated goal of CEO pay embraced almost universally by both sides of this debate—to align CEOs' incentives with those of the corporations' owners, the shareholders—is the best policy if our aim is to maximize social welfare. I conclude that there is insufficient evidence to come to a definitive answer to this question and recommend encouraging directors to experiment transparently with different priority weightings. Chapter 10 critiques some common reform proposals and contends that we should be much more modest in our aspirations for CEO pay. Pay is unlikely to act as an automatic motivator for CEOs. We should end our decades-long experiment with incentive pay and explore other methods of inspiring our corporate leaders, such as harnessing reputational desires, creating motivational cultures, and cultivating internal drives.

I also recognize, though, that there are serious barriers that will make it very difficult to abolish performance pay. We should work to eliminate those barriers, but while they stand, directors can still improve the *way* they use performance pay. Directors should design a bonus structure that ties CEOs' payments to factors that are (a) largely within officers' control, (b) hard to manipulate, (c) easy to measure, and (d) important to the corporation's long-term goals. When applying these bonus triggers, boards should set thresholds that are reasonably attainable, and then the bonuses should increase as performance improves. Also, no single bonus component should be too large in either absolute or relative terms. I provide a case study to demonstrate how this would help us provide less distortionary incentives to executives while curbing the growth in CEO pay. We can and should have not only better motivated but also cheaper chief executive officers.

PART ONE

What's Wrong With the Dominant Theories?

CHAPTER 2

The Puzzles of CEO Compensation

Why all the fuss over CEOs' compensation? CEO pay has become something of a national obsession in the United States. There are countless newspaper and magazine articles, television stories, and blog posts on this topic every year. In part this attention is a natural fascination with the lives of the rich, no different from our interest in gossip about the salaries of professional athletes, actors, or rock stars. But there is something deeper, more caustic in public reactions to executive pay. When the stories concern celebrities, they may elicit envy but also admiration. There often seems to be a sense that the celebrities deserve the pay they receive, that they have earned it. The same is not true of stories about CEO compensation. It is rare to see a story about executive pay that does not contain quotes from critics or that suggests the CEO is worth the price.

Public attitudes can be misguided, based on a few salient stories that shape opinion. But even academics who study this topic for a living agree there are a number of perplexing aspects of CEO compensation. To understand them, we need a bit of background on the history of CEO pay in the United States.

For a generation, from the 1940s through the 1960s, the CEOs of the largest U.S. corporations received pay that was more or less static. In constant dollar terms (year 2000 dollars), median CEO pay for this group remained at around $1 million throughout this period. In fact, this group's pay actually sank during the 1940s, from $1.1 million in the first half of the decade to an average of $900,000 in the second half. During the 1950s, median pay rose slightly, back to $1 million, where it essentially remained during the 1960s.[1]

During the 1970s, however, the rate of change increased significantly, with median CEO pay (again, for the fifty largest U.S. corporations by sales) rising by some 20 percent, to $1.2 million.[2] The pace of change sped up even more during the 1980s. That decade saw median CEO pay in the fifty largest corporations reach $1.8 million, a 50 percent increase from the 1970s. To put that growth rate in perspective, from the 1940s through the 1960s, CEO pay in the largest companies remained effectively flat. From the 1960s to the 1970s, real pay rose quite fast, by about 20 percent. But during the 1980s, executive pay skyrocketed almost three times as fast as during the prior decade (which itself had seen pay rise much faster than in the previous generation).[3]

Yet somehow the increase in pay accelerated even more during the 1990s. That decade, median CEO pay for the largest firms rose to $4.1 million, a rise of over 125 percent. Again, these are constant dollar numbers; a dollar from the 1950 figures buys (roughly) the same goods and services as a dollar from the 1990 figures (excluding iPads, of course). The purchasing capacity of CEOs' compensation packages more than doubled from one decade to the next.

During the most recent decade, CEO pay trends in the largest U.S. corporations reversed, experiencing significant average declines for the first time in decades. Nevertheless, these reversals came after the record increases in the 1990s. As a result, median pay for the CEOs of the fifty largest U.S. corporations from 2000 to 2005 was $9.2 million, more than double the median during the 1990s (though less than the peak achieved at the end of that decade).[4] Taking a broader sample of large U.S. corporations—those in the S&P 500 Index—we see that median CEO compensation declined at the start of the decade but then largely stabilized. Median pay for this group of CEOs was $7.1 million in 2001 (itself a 24 percent increase from the $5.8 million median pay in 1999).[5] Median pay then dropped to $6.2 million in 2002 and remained between $6 million and $7 million through 2008.[6] At the time of this writing, CEO pay seems to be rebounding. Median pay for S&P 500 companies was about $7.2 million in 2010 and $7.7 million in 2011.[7] (Again, all these figures are stated in year 2000 dollars.)

The *average* compensation numbers are considerably higher for all these years because the top-paying companies in this group pay much more than the lowest-paying. Newspaper reports tend to focus on the higher average numbers and to state the numbers in current year (nominal) dollars, so the figures you may have seen are likely considerably higher than these. But the median numbers provide a more accurate picture, without the distortion created by a few outliers at the top.

The past decade was the worst for CEOs' compensation in a generation. Chief executives have had some stellar years, but they ended the decade about where they were when it began. Still, when considered from the perspective of the past seventy years, CEOs as a class have done extremely well in the past generation. Their median pay in real terms is over *seven times* what it was during the 1940s and 1950s (and the difference may be even larger since the figures from the 1940s and 1950s looked only at the fifty largest corporations, which tend to pay more than smaller companies).

Perhaps, though, this increase is less remarkable than it first appears. After all, the broader economy has also grown a great deal during this period. A rising tide may float all boats. If we have all benefited equally from increasing national prosperity, then we should not begrudge CEOs their share.

To test this argument, we should see how average workers at large corporations have fared over this same period. In 1970, after CEO pay had remained more or less the same for several decades, the ratio of average CEO pay to the pay of average production workers was about 25 to 1.[8] In 1980, after a significant rise in executive pay, the ratio doubled, to about 50 to 1.[9] In 1990, after CEO had risen substantially throughout the 1980s, the ratio doubled again, to around 100.[10] Although CEO pay rose dramatically during the 1980s, worker pay clearly did not benefit as much from the economic boom. But that change pales in comparison to what happened during the 1990s. In 2000, by some accounts, the average CEO was making over five hundred times as much as the average worker.[11] That ratio has since shrunk considerably as CEO pay has fallen during the Great Recession, with even the AFL-CIO (a powerful federation of labor unions) admitting the ratio sank to about half that number in 2009 before rising again to about 380 in 2011.[12] Others put the numbers somewhat lower, peaking at around 300 in 2000.[13] Still, when we consider that this ratio was in the twenties through the 1970s, it seems hard to escape the conclusion that CEOs have gained much more than average workers over the past forty years.

Also troubling is that executive pay takes up an increasing percentage of corporate profits. In 1993, when average CEO pay had already risen sharply from its thirty-year, postwar plateau of about a million dollars a year, compensation for the top five executives at each corporation absorbed some 5 percent of corporate profits on average. That is, the compensation for just five people at each company took up one dollar in twenty of the company's profits. As big as that number seems, though, it doubled just ten years later. In 2003, companies shelled out 10 percent of their profits to buy the services of their top five executives.[14] Why did the relative price of executive talent double in such a short time?

At the same time the *amount* of CEO pay was changing, the *structure* of CEO pay shifted just as dramatically. Prior to the 1920s, incentive pay was very rare in the United States, though commonly used in Europe.[15] Some incentive pay mechanisms developed during the 1920s, but these largely disappeared during the Great Depression.[16] From the 1930s through the 1950s, executive compensation consisted almost entirely of salary and short-term bonuses (bonuses based on immediate performance rather than long-term measures).[17] Equity and option grants were negligible. There are press accounts of stock options dating to the 1950s, but options, stock awards, and long-term bonuses (based on the corporation's performance over several years) did not begin to become popular until the 1960s.[18] Performance-linked forms of pay steadily grew in importance through the 1970s and 1980s. By the 1990s, nearly all major corporations included incentive pay in their chief executives' compensation plans, generally consisting of a mix of stock options, stock, long-term incentive plans, and immediate bonuses.[19] By 2006, stock and option awards made up over half the typical CEO's pay package in S&P 500 firms.[20]

As the comparisons to average workers' salaries do not explain the rise in CEO compensation, perhaps a better justification can be found by examining CEO pay in other industrialized countries. If countries like France, Germany, Italy, Japan, and the United Kingdom pay their CEOs as much as we pay ours in the United States, then perhaps we could argue that there is some common phenomenon occurring across the globe. We might even contend that these payments are sensible, since every major industrialized country ends up paying similar amounts for their corporate leaders.

Just as with worker salaries, though, the international comparison raises questions about current CEO compensation levels in the United States. Let me begin with an important caveat: payment data for international CEOs have generally been difficult to obtain (though it's becoming easier). In the United States, publicly traded corporations have, since 1938, been required to disclose significant information about how and how much they pay their chief executives.[21] Most other industrialized nations, however, have been much slower to adopt parallel regulations.[22] As a result, much of the historical data we have for international CEO pay comes from voluntary surveys—often of compensation consultants—not from company securities filings. Also, comparisons must take exchange rates into account, so the precise figures depend greatly on which date the researcher chooses for the exchange rate.

Despite these complications, there is broad consensus among executive compensation researchers that U.S. CEOs are paid considerably more than their international counterparts.[23] According to one study of midsized public companies, in 1984, their CEOs earned an average of about $425,000 per year (in 1990 dollars).[24] That same year, CEOs of similarly sized companies in the United Kingdom earned about $225,000, and those in France and Germany about $250,000. This ratio remained fairly constant more than a decade later. In 1996, CEOs of these same companies in the United States earned about $900,000, while their colleagues in the United Kingdom and France earned $500,000 and those in Germany only about $375,000.[25] In both periods, U.S. CEOs earned about twice as much as their counterparts in other countries. That difference held true only for the chief executive; executives further down the pecking order earned about the same, regardless of country.[26] A more recent study found the U.S. premium continued to exist in 2006.[27]

These distinctions fade somewhat when we control for company size. As I discuss in chapter 3, CEOs of larger companies are paid more than heads of small companies, at least currently. And U.S. companies are, on average, larger than foreign corporations. Thirty-three of the world's largest fifty companies are found in the United States.[28] So perhaps it should not surprise us that U.S. companies—which tend to be larger—also pay their chief executives more. But size only moderates the difference. Even after controlling for size, U.S. CEOs receive a significant premium for heading a U.S. company; controlling for company size and industry only reduces the premium from 100 percent to 79 percent.[29]

In addition to this difference in pay *volume,* there is also a sharp contrast in pay *structure.* In the United States, performance-linked pay—especially various forms of equity such as options and restricted stock—makes up the majority of CEO compensation. Historically, other countries have not made equity a significant portion of their executive compensation packages. One study of thirty-seven countries in the period 1996–2004 found that twenty-one (57 percent) used equity for less than 10 percent of their CEOs' total pay.[30] This equity-averse group includes countries such as Germany, Japan, Italy, India, and South Korea. The United States is the only major economy where over half of CEO pay packages consist of equity.

This difference seems to be narrowing, however. A recent study found that international corporations are relying more heavily on options and restricted stock than they have in the past. While U.S. companies still lead the pack in their use of equity, international practice seems to be trending toward convergence with the United States.[31]

The premium apparently commanded by U.S. CEOs does not give us much comfort, but perhaps it is not a cause for great concern either. Cultures, laws, and circumstances—especially companies' capital structures—vary widely across countries, so perhaps it should not surprise us that companies have responded to their different environments with very different payment strategies. A small group of scholars, including Kevin Murphy, has argued that the U.S. pay premium largely disappears once sufficient variables are controlled for. Most significantly, in order to eliminate (or nearly eliminate) the pay premium U.S. CEOs receive, the authors control for the use of performance-based pay.[32]

The key lesson of the international comparison, then, may be that the difference in the amount of pay is driven by the difference in pay structure. U.S. CEOs are paid more because their compensation packages include much more performance pay than that of their colleagues in other industrialized countries. Why would structure make such a difference in the amount of pay?

Performance pay is risky by its very nature. By way of illustration, take the pay package of Home Depot's CEO, Francis Blake. In 2011, Blake's compensation included just over $1 million in salary, about $4.5 million in stock, $2.6 million in options, and $2.4 million in bonuses, for a total of about $10.8 million.[33] (There was also about a quarter of a million dollars in "other compensation," which mostly consisted of retirement benefits, various forms of insurance, and use of the company airplane.) As Home Depot proudly reported, some 88.5 percent of Blake's pay was contingent on performance; only his salary and retirement benefits were guaranteed. The stock, options, and bonuses all depended on the performance of either Home Depot or its stock. For example, Blake would have lost half his stock award had Home Depot's operating profit not been at least 80 percent of the target set by the board. The rest of his stock award depended on how much Home Depot's share price rose.[34]

Home Depot performed well in excess of the targets the board set for it, so Blake (and his fellow senior executives) received a great deal of pay. But if the company had not done as well, his compensation would have been less generous. In the extreme case—if Home Depot and its stock had both done quite badly—Blake would have earned almost 90 percent less.

I was not present when Blake negotiated his package with the board, and I don't have any private information about that discussion. (I wouldn't be able to write about Home Depot if I were privy to its private information.) But we can imagine that Blake might have had some hesitations about making almost all his pay contingent on how well the company and its stock did. Although most of us would be very happy to earn over $1 million per year, that's still a far cry from earning over $10 million. And as I discuss in chapter 7, Home Depot might suffer for reasons totally outside of Blake's control. The failure of the housing market to recover, for example, would hurt Home Depot's sales and most likely also its share price. Blake has no control over the demand for new housing; he can't control interest rates, the unemployment rate, or banks' willingness to lend money to buy homes. Blake's inability to affect these things, though, would not prevent his being punished with lower pay if they lowered Home Depot's sales.

Even a very self-confident Blake, then, might reasonably have some hesitations about accepting a compensation package that could vary so much based only partly on his own actions. Let us assume for the moment that Blake is perfectly rational. (We'll relax that assumption just below.) Guaranteed pay is still worth more than pay that is contingent on future events. Suppose Blake was highly confident that Home Depot would hit all its targets, say, 90 percent certain. His expected payout (again, assuming he's perfectly rational) would still be only nine-tenths the promised amount.

To compensate for this discounting, the Home Depot board could increase the amount of the payoff, so that after discounting Blake ended up in the same place. For example, instead of promising a bonus of $1.4 million for hitting profitability targets, Home Depot could promise a bonus of $1.55 million. Then if Blake is 90 percent confident of hitting the targets, his expected payment will be back up to $1.4 million (or just about).

This calculation assumes Blake is a rational actor who can determine probabilities with some certainty. These two conditions rarely obtain, however. People are often risk-averse. Risk-averse people prefer a certain payoff to a contingent payoff with the same expected value. In other words, someone who is risk-averse will prefer a 100 percent chance of winning $10 to a 50 percent chance of winning $20, even though the expected payout for both promises is $10. In addition, people can rarely be confident in their estimates of the probability of success.[35] Uncertainty about the odds compounds people's aversion to risk more generally, inflating the price people demand to bear risk. In fact, a recent international survey found that executives discounted long-term incentives by at least 50 percent compared to their risk-neutral value.[36] A risk-averse Blake might demand a bonus with an expected value of, say, $2.8 million to substitute for guaranteed pay of $1.4 million, because his subjective expected pay—taking into account his risk aversion—may be much lower than his rational expected pay.

Because of risk aversion, most people in Blake's position would prefer to have a straight salary, all else being equal. But most people in the board's position would prefer to make at least a chunk of Blake's pay contingent on success. If the board really wants Blake to take on risk, in all likelihood (depending on a number of bargaining factors such as the board's belief about what Blake can do for Home Depot and Blake's other opportunities) it will have to agree to larger expected pay. That promise will likely make both parties better off. Blake receives higher pay (at least on average), and Home Depot succeeds in incentivizing Blake to run the business well. But if Home Depot *does* perform well, Blake won't get his *expected* pay, or even his rational, expected pay; he'll receive the full potential bonus of $2.4 million.

This is how performance pay can lead to higher realized pay, and it may help explain why European and Japanese companies of comparable size still pay their CEOs less than U.S. companies do. If U.S. boards insist on making a much bigger portion of CEO pay contingent on companies' success, CEOs may be responding by demanding higher expected pay to compensate them for their risk.

That performance pay can lead to higher realized pay may clarify the apparent CEO pay gap between the United States and other industrialized countries. But we are still left with two troubling questions. First and most saliently, what accounts for the enormous changes in the *amount* companies paid their CEOs? After remaining more or less constant throughout the 1940s, 1950s, and 1960s, why did CEO pay begin to rise during the 1970s, rise faster during the 1980s, and truly accelerate during the 1990s? Why did that growth trend stop during the past decade in favor of some vacillation? And second, why did the *structure* of CEO pay change beginning in the late 1970s? Why did boards suddenly decide that performance pay was important?

The trend in CEO pay amounts bears no apparent relation to real growth in the U.S. economy. In fact, there is almost an inverse relation between the growth rate of the gross domestic product (GDP) and the growth of CEO pay. While CEO pay was stable in real terms during the three decades from 1940 to 1969, real GDP growth averaged a little under 5 percent.[37] During the 1970s, as CEO pay began to rise, average GDP growth shrank to 3.3 percent. GDP growth continued to average only a little over 3 during the 1980s and 1990s, while CEO pay skyrocketed. The 2000–2009 period saw a different pattern, with much slower GDP growth, about 1.8 percent, and some declines in CEO pay (Figure 2.1).

But the underlying point remains: higher CEO pay seems to be neither the result of greater economic growth nor a driver of greater economic growth. Why have corporate boards been paying so much more for their CEOs these past few decades while their businesses have been growing more slowly? The net result is that boards are shelling out an increasing percentage of their profits to pay for managers. Why are they willing to do this?

Before the 1970s, performance pay formed a negligible portion of executive compensation. Today, the various performance-based mechanisms

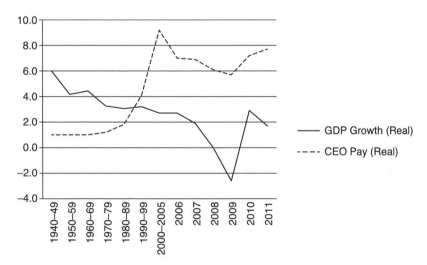

FIGURE 2.1. Real Growth in GDP and CEO Pay in 2000 Dollars.

SOURCE: Data on GDP from the U.S. Department of Commerce's Bureau of Economic Analysis, www.bea.gov/national/index.htm#gdp. Data on median CEO pay from Frydman and Jenter, "CEO Compensation," 38, 41; and Wall Street Journal/Hay Group Surveys of CEO Compensation.

far outweigh straight salary. In 2008, CEOs of S&P 500 companies received only 17 percent of their compensation as salary, while bonuses and long-term incentive pay made up 21 percent, options accounted for another 25 percent, stock for an additional 32 percent, and a few miscellaneous categories for the remaining 5 percent.[38]

Performance-based pay may motivate CEOs efficiently, or it may not. (I discuss this question in chapter 6.) But why would paying for corporate performance motivate the CEOs who worked after the 1970s but not the CEOs who ran companies in the decades prior? And why have options in particular swelled in importance so dramatically? It is hard to imagine a reasonable explanation for why the negotiated composition of managers' pay changed so radically over time. This question, too, demands deeper analysis.

Conventional wisdom (perhaps even corporate mythology) provides some answers to these questions, answers that I test rigorously during the course of this book. One answer begins by arguing that corporations are large, sophisticated entities that have an enormous stake in choosing the right leader and motivating that leader properly. Therefore, the market for CEOs' labor must be efficient, and that efficient market must be producing an optimal outcome; we just have to look hard enough to understand why patterns that appear problematic are actually sensible.

This answer assumes that corporations do a good job of looking out for their own interests. It looks at corporations as a whole as though there were such a thing as a corporate personality that made its own decisions in its own interests.

In the next chapter, I look into the heart of the corporation to find out if this assumption of corporate self-interest is a reasonable one. Who makes decisions for the corporation? Do these decision makers' interests coincide with those of the corporation's owners, the shareholders? Just who is the "corporation"?

CHAPTER 3

The Corporate Personality Myth

"Corporations are people, my friend." Former Governor Mitt Romney made this statement during the Republican presidential primary elections in 2011 at the Iowa State Fair.[1] Romney's comment was decried by critics as demonstrating his misplaced priorities, putting corporations before flesh-and-blood human beings. By emphasizing corporate personhood, the critics said, Romney was showing he just didn't get it, didn't realize that it was people who mattered and not businesses. The clip of Romney uttering those five words played over and over again on television.

In fact, Romney's point was precisely the opposite. Romney was expressing concern for people, in particular, for their tax burdens. He was trying to explain why he was opposed to raising taxes on anyone, including corporations.

Romney was responding to a comment from the crowd urging him to raise taxes on corporations. Romney's answer was that it was impossible to tax corporations without also taxing human beings. Hence, "Corporations are people, my friend." When someone in the crowd cried out that they were not, Romney replied, "Of course they are. Everything corporations earn ultimately goes to people."[2]

In the CEO pay debate, many defenders of the current system treat corporations as though they really were "people" in the sense of acting purposefully in their own interest. They fall victim to what I call "the corporate personality myth," the perception that corporations pursue their self-interests as though they were people. When we look more deeply at how corporations work, it's far from clear why we should believe this is true, especially in the CEO pay context. And if it's false, what becomes of the central justification of CEO pay—that it's produced by an efficient market?

CEO compensation is frequently defended by pointing to its source: the market. The latter term is spoken of with such reverence that it almost demands capitalization: The Market. Does the pay seem high? Well, that's because the market demands lucrative compensation. Do the rewards seem divorced from performance? Nothing could be further from the truth. After all, the market designed the pay package.

But what is the market, really? A market consists of a group of individuals and/or entities that trade in something. In this case, the market participants are buying and selling the CEO's labor. On the production end, CEO candidates bargain for the highest price they can obtain. On the demand side are corporate employers. The particular buyers I am concerned with—large, publicly traded U.S. corporations—are enormous, complex, and sophisticated entities. The market for CEOs' labor includes highly educated and intelligent CEO candidates bargaining with wealthy, artificial entities. It is no wonder, then, that observers readily believe that this market produces efficient results. With so much sophistication on all sides and with so much money at issue, the parties must be choosing the best possible solutions.

When we dig a little deeper, though, the situation becomes murkier. To state the obvious, the public corporations that are buying CEOs' labor are not human beings. They are legal fictions, created for the purpose of organizing capital and labor efficiently. Because corporations are *not* people, they cannot think or act for themselves. To understand the corporate side of the market for CEO labor, we need to understand who has the right to make corporations' decisions. Who is in charge?

At one level, the answer to this question is simple. The corporation's board of directors is empowered to make the corporation's decisions about CEO pay.[3] As Delaware's General Corporation Law states,[4] "The business and affairs of every corporation organized under this chapter shall be managed by or under the direction of a board of directors."[5] But this legal answer tells us very little about what really interests us: what are the directors' interests, and how do they differ from the corporation's? For the corporation to bargain effectively on its own behalf, the directors must choose to pursue its interests. Will they?

The answer depends on what mechanisms are in place to align directors' interests with those of the corporation. (I'm going to assume for purposes of this chapter that the shareholders all have the *same* interests and that the corporation's interests are synonymous with the shareholders' interests. Given the diversity of shareholders and the importance of nonshareholder constituencies, these assumptions are not necessarily correct, as I explain in chapter 9. But they will suffice as a simplification for the purposes of this chapter.) There are a number of ways directors' interests might be aligned with those of shareholders.

First, directors might act in the corporation's interest to persuade shareholders to let them keep their seats. Directors are elected by the shareholders, and an electorate disappointed with how much the directors had paid the CEO might replace them in the next election.

Second, directors' pay packages might motivate them to act in the shareholders' interests. If the directors are paid based on the company's success, they might watch the bottom line carefully, including when they are deciding how much to pay the CEO.

Third, directors might pursue shareholders' interests out of fear of liability. Shareholders might sue directors for overpaying the CEO—especially if the CEO provided the directors with benefits in exchange. Fear of such suits might keep the directors in line.

Fourth, directors' psychology might encourage them to act in the company's best interests. Even without a direct, pecuniary incentive, directors might try to contain CEO pay for shareholders out of altruism or because they believe their role on the board requires them to do so.

But before exploring these possible motivational tools, I want to discuss boards' institutional limitations. Even if directors *want* to act on shareholders' behalf for one of the four reasons outlined above, they may lack the time or information to do so or may face difficult compositional or cultural challenges. Let's start with these questions of the boards' institutional capacity and then move on to their possible motivations.

INSTITUTIONAL CAPACITY

The law grants boards of directors almost unlimited authority over their corporations. Outside of a few categories of major changes, the board may act as it pleases. The approval of the corporation's putative owners, the shareholders, is required for only a handful of corporate actions, such as mergers and amendments to the corporation's articles of incorporation (a sort of constitution for the corporation).[6]

Despite having such enormous formal power, as a practical matter directors only occasionally exercise significant influence over the company's day-to-day affairs. The board instead delegates authority to make most corporate decisions to the company's management team, led by the CEO. The CEO will return to the board for approval of major decisions, but the board generally approves the CEO's recommendations. To do otherwise in many cases would be the effective equivalent of demanding the CEO's resignation. The board is empowered to fire (and hire) the CEO, and about 2 percent of the largest U.S. public companies fire their CEOs each year.[7] But as long as the company is performing reasonably well, the board is highly unlikely to reject the CEO's chosen course of action. Outside of a crisis, the board's role is generally reduced to monitoring the company's progress and offering advice.

Why have boards accepted this subservient role? Why would directors voluntarily give up the bulk of their power over the vast resources owned by publicly held companies? Why don't directors take a more active role in running the company's business? One part of the answer to these questions lies in the institutional constraints on directors' actions, which can be divided into four major categories: time, information, composition, and culture.

Time

Time is probably the least important constraint on directors' ability to act on the company's behalf in negotiating the CEO's pay, though it plays a critical role in other corporate decisions. Directorships are part-time positions. The time directors spend on their duties has risen in recent years, especially after the passage of the Sarbanes-Oxley Act, but they still typically report spending only around 240 hours per year on board activities.[8] That number includes time spent traveling to board meetings. In other words, directorships require about 8 percent of the time of a full-time executive. And it bears noting that what we know about time spent comes from the directors themselves, from self-reported survey data. It is entirely possible that the surveys exaggerate directors' actual time commitment.

Part-time directors simply cannot hope to manage a major corporation without relying heavily on the full-time executives. As a result, boards have long adopted a monitoring rather than managing model of their role. With some exceptions, which typically involve a crisis, boards are relegated to approving or disapproving the course that management has already set. Boards may reject management's advice, but then they may need to start searching for a new management team.

Time is likely a less important constraint when it comes to the CEO's pay than it is for other corporate decisions. The CEO and the corporation's employees cannot usually devote a large percentage of their time to the question of the CEO's pay, and the board may often deem the question sufficiently important to take up quite a bit of the time they dedicate to the company's business. But the directors' general monitoring approach to the company's other affairs could influence them on pay decisions as well.

Information

An important consequence of the limited time spent by directors on the company's behalf is that they may face limited information when they make corporate decisions. The law provides directors with the tools to demand essentially any corporate information they want. In Delaware, for example, the law provides, "Any director shall have the right to examine the corporation's stock ledger, a list of its stockholders and its other books and records for a purpose reasonably related to the director's position as a director."[9] Once a director has requested information, the corporation has the burden of proving that the director is seeking the information for an improper purpose.[10] As the Delaware Chancery Court has written, "The Court works from the presumption that a sitting director is entitled to unfettered access to the books and records of the corporation for which he sits."[11]

Although directors have powerful legal rights to obtain corporate information, in most circumstances they will simply accept whatever materials the senior management team provides. As a practical matter, the board is responsive, not proactive. Directors respond to the concerns raised by the CEO and other senior executives; they rarely initiate their own inquiries, and when they do, those inquiries generally begin and end with the senior managers. Directors do not share in the flow of information from middle management as the CEO does. They therefore are in a much less advantageous position from which to spot emerging problems or promising new trends. The senior management team, in contrast, sits squarely in the information stream. The lead executives regularly review enormous volumes of information from middle management and have much more detailed knowledge of the company's operations.

CEO compensation represents a particular informational challenge because much of the most important information does not even belong to the corporation. Directors typically want to know how much CEOs make at other companies before deciding how much their CEO should earn. Although this information is publicly available in securities filings, boards generally hire outside compensation consultants to gather and analyze the relevant data.[12] Consultants compile a table of CEO compensation at "comparable" corporations, which boards can then use to evaluate whether their own CEO is paid appropriately. Some commentators have suggested that these comparables may be chosen strategically in order to make the CEO seem underpaid.[13] Consultants may try to please the CEO to land the corporation's other consulting business. Even if the comparables are chosen objectively, however, the tables themselves tend to produce a Lake Wobegone effect.[14]

Lake Wobegone is a fictional town invented by the author Garrison Keillor where all the children are above average.[15] Directors naturally believe that their own CEO is also above average, even exceptional; why would such an august board have hired and retained anyone who wasn't extraordinary? And if the CEO nevertheless turns out to be less than stellar, the board should replace him or her with someone better.

Exceptional talent deserves an exceptional reward. If the compensation tables show the CEO is paid less than the average for comparable companies, the board may feel compelled to boost his or her compensation. But that increase produces a larger comparable for the next company's compensation table, which in turn pushes that company's board to increase its own CEO's pay. This dynamic may easily produce a strong, one-way ratchet for executive pay, with each company's decision to bring its CEO's pay above average driving its competitors to raise their own CEOs' compensation.

Perhaps the most important piece of information in determining CEO pay, though, is not available. This gap has nothing to do with boards' institutional constraints; it stems from universal human limitations. As I discuss in chapters 6 and 7, what directors should want to know is how much the CEO will produce for the company as compared to the board's second choice for the position. That is the number that represents the true value of the CEO to the firm, not the price that other companies are paying for their CEOs. Both because CEOs' impact on their companies is unclear (chapter 7) and because any effect they *will* have is unpredictable (chapter 8), this critical information is not available.

Composition

A third institutional challenge that boards face is their composition. Who sits on corporate boards? The plurality of directors consists of current or retired senior corporate executives, such as CEOs and chief operating officers (COOs).[16] These directors' personal and professional lives may ordinarily constrain their ability to intervene actively in the corporation's affairs in a number of ways.

First, directors may have conflicts of interest. Directors' outside positions may be with companies or organizations that have business relationships with the corporation. A director may be a partner in a law firm that represents the corporation, an executive of an investment bank hoping to underwrite the company's next bond issue, or the CEO of a corporate supplier or customer. For example, Microsoft's board of directors includes (as of 2012) Charles H. Noski, vice chairman of Bank of America. If he pushed to reduce the pay of CEO Steve Ballmer, Ballmer might retaliate by refusing to hire Bank of America the next time Microsoft issued new shares to the public or sold bonds. As committed as directors may be to the corporation, they can still be expected to put the welfare of their full-time employers first. Even if the corporation might benefit from a more actively managing board, directors in this position seem unlikely to jeopardize their primary livelihoods by irritating the CEO.

Second, a director may have a personal and professional relationship with the CEO or some of the other board members. Directors tend to come from the ranks of the friends and acquaintances of existing directors or the senior managers. Those friendships give the board confidence that the new members are worthy of the position and likely make for a much more pleasant and congenial work environment. But those relationships may also hamper directors from raising difficult questions. Directors may censor their comments in board meetings to avoid embarrassing or irritating their friends and colleagues who want to reward the CEO richly.

Third, the current and former executives who sit on corporate boards are accustomed to large pay packages and have every interest in seeing they continue. If IBM director Andrew Liveris successfully argues that CEO Virginia Rometty's pay should be lower, he may have trouble resisting a similar move by his own board at Dow Chemical, where he is the CEO.

Corporate Culture

A final institutional constraint that limits directors' likelihood of managing the corporation actively comes from corporate culture. Because directors have a monitoring—rather than active managerial—role in the corporation, they are culturally conditioned to defer to the senior management team. Just as they defer on issues of corporate strategy, they may also defer on compensation questions.

This cultural norm of deference to management is also consistent with the self-interest of the senior executives who typically serve as directors. Executives, especially CEOs, naturally would want as much autonomy as possible in their managerial roles. When they act as directors, they may defer to management just as they would want their own boards to defer to them.

For example, Millard Drexel sits on Apple's board and is also the CEO of J. Crew. If Drexel takes an aggressive stance as a director of Apple, he will have trouble squaring that attitude with the deference he expects from the board of J. Crew for his decisions as J. Crew's CEO. Wanting J. Crew's board to follow his lead as CEO, Drexell may naturally—though perhaps subconsciously—respect the decisions of Apple's CEO Tim Cook when acting as an Apple director. Drexell would likely justify this deference—to the extent he questioned it—as simply what constitutes proper conduct for directors, a norm of corporate culture.

Directors who are not also corporate executives may also become culturally conditioned to defer to the CEO, especially on compensation questions. Directors who come from other professions, such as academia and politics, may naturally look for guidance to their more experienced corporate colleagues. Think, for example, of the theoretical physicist Shirley Ann Jackson, president of Rensselaer Polytechnic Institute and a director of IBM. When deciding CEO Rometty's compensation, wouldn't it be natural for her to look to experienced colleagues such as W. James McNerney, CEO of Boeing, for cues as to appropriate behavior in a foreign environment? Academics and politicians may start out with their own notions of what level and type of pay is appropriate, but it seems unlikely that they would insist on those notions in the face of their colleagues' assured statements about what is normal and proper in the corporate world.

What should we take away from all this? The conception that markets are efficient is rooted in the sense that the participants act independently and in their own interests in (ideally fierce) competition with one another. When we personify the corporation, we can easily imagine that the labor market for public company CEOs is highly efficient. After all, public corporations are wealthy, sophisticated organizations that should be perfectly capable of protecting their own interests. And in many contexts, they are. For example, when the corporation faces a competitor trying to take away its market share, it will likely behave just as a sophisticated person in that position would.

But the corporation is not a real person. To understand how a corporation behaves, we have to look deeper into its internal dynamics. In the CEO compensation context, the "corporation" is the board of directors. And the board of directors faces serious constraints in trying to negotiate with the CEO. In most contexts, the board is accustomed to deferring to the CEO, and perhaps rightly so. In fact, for the most part the board has little choice given the limited time and information it has. The directors may also have little desire to do otherwise when we consider who sits on corporate boards and why. When it comes time for the board to negotiate with the CEO over his or her pay, though, the directors must stand up and negotiate at arm's length with the very person they normally follow. This sudden shift in roles presents a serious challenge, one that boards may not be institutionally designed to meet.

I am not claiming that we can draw firm conclusions on this basis. The kind of sophisticated and experienced people who sit on public company boards might find a way to rise to the challenge. But the fact that boards are designed primarily to monitor and assist the CEO should at least raise serious questions about their ability to bargain against that person on an issue that matters enormously to the CEO (and perhaps not very much to the directors, for reasons I discuss in subsequent chapters). The deck is stacked in the CEO's favor in terms of both incentive and institutional capacity. We should not be surprised if the outcomes tilt heavily in the same direction. When one side of the market is a group that normally defers to the other side, we should at least be skeptical that the market is producing an efficient result. Still, other factors may outweigh these institutional constraints by giving directors a strong motive to bargain vigorously with the CEO. The leading candidates for such influences are considered in the next few sections.

ELECTORAL CONSIDERATIONS

Corporations are governed as plutocratic democracies. Shareholders elect directors to the board, with each share counting for one vote. (More complicated capital structures are possible, but let's keep it simple for purposes of this discussion.) The more shares one owns, the more power one has to influence the election. In theory, directors who want to keep their jobs (and candidates who want to gain a board seat) can only do so by pleasing the shareholders, especially those with the most shares. Like politicians in the governmental arena, directors might cater to those who elect them, voting in board meetings according to their perceptions of their constituents'—the shareholders'—interests.

The desire to win election to the board might push directors to act in shareholders' best interests when negotiating the CEO's compensation. After all, a similar dynamic seems to work pretty well with politicians (at least some of the time). To understand if this really happens, though, we need to take a closer look at how corporate elections work to see if directors face a realistic threat of being replaced if they overpay the CEO or choose payment mechanisms that are inefficient. The risk to directors depends on who the shareholders are and how much power they have to replace the board.

Who Are the Shareholders?

Historically, most shares were owned by relatively small shareholders, individuals who had insignificant percentages of a company's stock. As recently as 1970, households and nonprofits (who are combined by the Federal Reserve when it gathers these data) owned 78 percent of publicly traded U.S. stock.[17] That capital structure led to rational shareholder apathy. A single shareholder rarely owned enough stock to have much impact on the corporation's election, so there was little point in the shareholder learning enough about the issues to cast an informed vote. Instead, the rational (and even reasonable) approach was to vote as the board recommended, or even to abstain from voting altogether. Becoming informed didn't pay. As a result, directors faced very little danger of being voted out by disaffected shareholders, even if they made an unpopular decision to, for example, vastly overpay the CEO. For the most part, outside of unusual events like an attempted hostile takeover, the shareholders were simply not paying attention.

This dynamic led the landmark corporate governance scholars Adolf Berle and Gardiner Means to declare that public corporations experienced a separation of ownership from control.[18] What they meant was that the people who owned the corporation, the shareholders, exercised very little meaningful control. Instead, the board of directors and the professional management team made all the decisions. For the most part, the shareholders went along with whatever the board and senior managers decided.

In the past few decades, however, the capital structure of U.S. public corporations has shifted significantly. By 1990, individuals' and non-profits' share of U.S. public equities had shrunk to 56 percent and by 2008 had fallen to 36 percent.[19] A majority of the outstanding shares of U.S. public companies are now owned by a class of large stockholders known as institutional investors.[20]

Institutional investors include companies such as banks, mutual funds, pension funds, arbitrageurs, hedge funds, and insurance firms. What these entities have in common is that they have enormous sums of (usually other people's) money to invest. Unlike the typical individual investor, who rarely owns more than a tiny fraction of a percent of a company's outstanding shares, institutional investors have the resources to buy significant ownership stakes in even the largest public companies. As a result, they arguably have the appropriate incentives to play an active role in governing corporations. They also have the necessary expertise (or the resources to hire those who do). Institutional investors could be the sort of shareholder constituents that directors must please or face ouster from the board. Certainly many corporate governance scholars have argued that they play such a role.[21]

There are reasons to be skeptical, or at least to leaven our enthusiasm. Institutional investors have not eliminated the separation between ownership and control. This is true for a variety of reasons, but one of the most important is that each investor still owns too little stock to exercise significant influence over the election of directors and therefore over the company. In fact, institutional shareholders seldom own more than a few percentage points of a company's stock.

For example, Bank of America has about 10.8 billion shares outstanding, and a little more than half of those are owned by institutional investors. But those 5.7 billion shares are divided among some 1,200 institutions, so that the shareholder with the largest stake (as of this writing), State Street Corporation, owns only about 4 percent of the company.[22] Most of Bank of America's institutional shareholders own far less. A few percentage points are not sufficient for State Street to exercise control over Bank of America's board by itself.

Still, institutional investors may help narrow the gap between ownership and control because they are less likely to be rationally apathetic. State Street's 4 percent of Bank of America may not be a sufficient stake to exercise control, but it is enough to make State Street care a great deal about Bank of America's fate. Institutional investors are likely to monitor the corporation's affairs and to vote when offered a chance.

There are other problems with institutional investors—they may suffer from conflicts of interest with their core business, for example—but at least they're paying attention.

How Much Power Do Shareholders Have?

Today a majority of public companies' shares are owned by investors who are sophisticated and who have a sufficient stake to make monitoring those companies worthwhile. Directors are *elected* by the shareholders, so they would seem to have a powerful incentive to *please* shareholders, namely, their desire to remain in office. Any director who does not avidly pursue the shareholders' goals should quickly be replaced, right?

It turns out that shareholders' practical ability to oust directors is less straightforward than one might think. By state law, public corporations must hold a shareholder meeting at least once per year.[23] The actions taken at a shareholder meeting bind the corporation only if a minimum percentage of outstanding shares—a quorum—are "present" (more on this last point in a moment).[24] The quorum is set by the corporation's governing documents, the certificate of incorporation and the bylaws, but is generally fixed at a majority of the outstanding shares (and cannot be set below one-third of all outstanding shares).[25] As a consequence, in order to have an effective shareholder meeting—which, again, must take place at least once a year—generally a majority of outstanding shares must be "present."

If being "present" meant the owner was physically at the meeting, few public corporations would ever manage a quorum, much less manage one annually. For small, individual shareholders, it does not pay even to vote, much less to pay for a plane ticket and hotel to attend the shareholders' meeting. These shareholders have almost no chance of influencing the outcome of a vote. Even if their vote mattered, small shareholders own too little stock for the benefit of voting to outweigh the travel costs.

In order to allow corporations to function, the law permits voting by proxy.[26] Public corporations solicit their shareholders' proxy and supply them with a proxy form they can use to vote by mail or electronically. The solicitation process is heavily regulated by federal law and supervised by the Securities Exchange Commission (SEC).[27] Proxy solicitation is not cheap. Estimates vary, but expenses can easily exceed $1 million.[28]

While shareholders regularly vote on other issues as well, the key element of the proxy form for our purposes is its use to elect the board of directors. The director selection process is cloaked in the language of democracy. We speak of elections, voting, candidates, as though this were a political election. The truth is something quite different. Most obviously, in corporate elections the usual rule is one vote for each share of common stock (though this can vary). One person (or one institutional investor) can own many (even many millions of) shares. We count the number of shares voted, not the number of owners. Corporate democracy is more like a plutocracy. In short, money talks.

More important for our purposes, though, usually there are exactly as many candidates running for the board as there are open seats to fill; shareholders' only choice is whether or not to vote in favor of the board's nominees. Take a moment to let this sink in. It is as though precisely 435 people ran for the seats in the House of Representatives. Think what that sort of election would look like, with absolutely no opposition in any district. Imagine how the lack of competition would eviscerate representatives' incentives to act in their constituents' interests. Why bother addressing voters' concerns if you're going to be reelected regardless?

In addition, the default rule in corporate law is that only a plurality of votes is required for a director to win a seat on the board.[29] As a result, even if a majority of shares are voted *against* a candidate, as long as there are no competing candidates and *at least one share* is voted in the candidate's favor, the candidate is elected. It is as if all a member of Congress had to do was vote for herself in order to secure reelection.

A corporation can change the default rule for itself and require a majority vote to elect a director by passing a bylaw. Many corporations have done this.[30] The default rule remains plurality voting, though. Also, many of the companies that have adopted a majority vote requirement leave the final decision in the board's hands, not the shareholders'. Under these "Pfizer-style" or "plurality-plus" provisions, a director who did not receive a majority of the votes cast would still be elected but would be required to tender his or her resignation to the board. The board would then decide whether to accept the resignation (in which case the director's term would end) or reject the resignation (in which case the director would be reelected despite having received only a plurality of votes). Nike's majority vote provision, for example, states: "Any nominee for director in an uncontested election who receives a greater number of votes 'withheld' from his or her election than votes 'for' such election shall tender his or her resignation for consideration by the Nominating and Corporate Governance Committee. The Committee shall recommend to the Board the action to be taken with respect to the resignation."[31]

The Delaware courts seem willing to enforce these provisions. They have permitted boards to reinstate directors who have received only a plurality—not a majority—of votes.[32]

Capitalism is, at its heart, about the freedom to make choices. Apple or Microsoft? Cable or DSL? French fries or salad? Paper or plastic? Why, then, do public corporations, the engines that drive capitalism, offer so little choice when it comes to electing their leaders? Why are there so seldom opposing slates of candidates running for seats on boards?

The reason there is rarely any opposition in corporate elections is that it is very expensive to propose an opposing slate. Any shareholder who wanted to nominate an alternative director—or an entire set— would have to solicit his or her own proxies. That means the insurgent would have to create a new form, file it with the SEC, obtain the SEC's approval, and mail copies to every registered shareholder. In addition, the insurgent would have to persuade the other shareholders to vote for her slate rather than the corporation's nominees. A successful proxy fight (in which the insurgent asks shareholders to vote for a different slate of directors than the one the incumbent directors favor) generally requires an advertising campaign, which is even more expensive. To take one recent example, when Hewlett Packard (HP) proposed merging with Compaq (a transaction that required shareholder approval) and Walter Hewlett, the son of one of HP's founders, staged a proxy fight to oppose the merger, the total expense for both sides was estimated at $100 million.[33] The HP proxy fight involved a shareholder vote on a merger rather than a board election, but the mechanics and expenses of the proxy fight are the same in either case.

Insurgents must bear their own expenses. The incumbent board, in contrast, uses the corporation's money to fund its proxy solicitation (and, if necessary, the accompanying advertising campaign). The incumbents have the twin advantages of effectively infinite resources (better yet—access to someone else's effectively infinite resources) and the inherent credibility of representing the corporation. Outside of a takeover contest (when the buyer stands to make a fortune if successful in taking over the company), few shareholders own a sufficient stake in the vote's outcome to make this investment worthwhile. The net result is that the directors, who decide who the corporation will nominate for the following year, effectively choose their own successors.

Although the board's election process is full of democracy-speak, in essence the board is a self-perpetuating body. The electoral mechanics rarely provide much incentive to directors to please the shareholders. Their reelection is secure as long as a majority of their colleagues on the board are willing to renominate them.

The SEC recently promulgated a regulation that might have shifted this dynamic, at least to a degree. Adopted under the explicit authority of the Dodd-Frank Wall Street Reform and Consumer Protection Act, Exchange Act Rule 14a-11 required companies to include shareholders' nominees in the company's own proxy form under certain circumstances.[34] But in a suit by the U.S. Chamber of Commerce and the Business Roundtable, a federal appeals court overturned the regulation.[35] The court's decision left room for the SEC to try again, but so far it hasn't. Even if the court had affirmed the regulation, the rule was so restrictive that some commentators argued it would have had little impact.[36] Directors remain pretty secure in their seats and have little electoral motivation to worry about shareholders' reactions when negotiating the CEO's pay package.

DIRECTORS' COMPENSATION

In the previous sections, I have assumed without discussion that directors want to keep their seats. This seems like a safe assumption. After all, any director who did not like the job could quit. The *reason* directors want these positions is a separate question, and the answer may tell us a great deal about how directors are likely to act. If the appeal of a board seat is financial, then structuring directors' compensation appropriately may motivate board members to act in shareholders' interests, including when they negotiate executive compensation. But if directors covet board positions for other reasons, their behavior may be much more difficult to shape.

The most obvious reason someone might be interested in gaining a position on a board of directors is monetary. Directors might act in shareholders' best interests to keep earning their salaries. But in the previous section we saw that there is very little chance that shareholders will fire directors for the decisions they make. Directors do not generally face a realistic threat that they will be cut off from their position and its associated compensation, as long as they retain the good opinion of their colleagues on the board. The possibility of losing their pay cannot be expected to do much work in the board of directors context (or at least it cannot be expected to induce directors to oppose CEOs on behalf of the shareholders). Instead, if pay is to have any impact on directors' behavior on the job, it must be the design of their compensation that matters.

One can imagine compensation schemes that might have the desired effect. For example, if directors earned more as the company's stock rose, they might make the decisions they thought would have the best chance of boosting the stock price. Directors' compensation packages, though, tend to use the same tools that we see in CEO compensation packages, such as stock options and restricted stock.[37] I analyze these devices in chapter 5 and argue that they are not terribly efficient motivators. More troubling, promising directors large payments when the corporation does well is not an effective way to wring better work from them, a point I make in chapter 6 with regard to CEOs.

But let's leave that aside and assume for the moment that compensation structures like stock options and restricted stock do motivate CEOs effectively. Directors present a more difficult challenge. CEOs' pay packages are enormous, often breaking eight figures in large companies and sometimes even nine. Apple paid its CEO Tim Cook, for example, some $378 million in 2011, though most was in the form of restricted stock that could not be sold for five to ten years. (Cook may not get any additional shares for a while, but as of May 2012 his stock's value had already risen to $530 million.)[38]

Directors earn a small fraction of that amount. The median director of a large public company earns about $190,000 per year.[39] That is easily enough income from that position alone to put directors in the top 5 percent of household income in the country.[40] To most of us, that seems like a lot of money, especially for a part-time position. If we use the 240-hour figure as an estimate of how much time directors spend on their board duties per year, that amount breaks down to about $800 per hour.

As large as that number seems, for the kind of people who become directors of major corporations, it's fairly trivial. As discussed above, the most common full-time job of corporate directors is as a CEO or other senior executive of another major corporation. As chapter 2 explained, CEOs of large public corporations earn an average of about $10 million per year (in 2013 dollars) and perhaps many times that amount. Someone who earns $10 million per year seems unlikely to care very much about an additional $190,000.

Even on an hourly basis, for such an individual a job as a director is a huge step down. Suppose that CEOs typically work about seventy hours per week every week of the year (with no vacations). A $10 million compensation package then amounts to roughly $2,750 per hour. That is almost $2,000 more per hour than directors earn. For those corporate executives who earn $50 million per year, the hourly compensation rate jumps to about $13,750, or nearly $13,000 more per hour than what they would earn as director.

To get a concrete sense of what a major corporate board looks like, consider Target, Inc., a Fortune 100 company that operates a line of retail stores. In 2010, Target's board consisted of twelve directors who earned between $134,000 and $250,000 from that position.[41] Target's board then included the CEO of Move Networks, Inc., an Internet television services provider; the chairman of Darden Development Group, LLC, a real estate development company; an executive vice president of McDonalds; the vice chairman of Perseus, LLC, a merchant banking private equity firm; the former chairman of the Board of Wells Fargo & Company, a major bank; the then-current chairman and CEO of Wells Fargo & Company; a partner in Lion Capital, a private investment firm; the chairman and former CEO of Xerox Corp.; an executive vice president and chief financial officer of Eli Lilly & Company, a pharmaceutical company; the retired chairman and CEO of General Mills, Inc., a consumer food products company; and the chairman and CEO of Target.[42]

We can find out how much some of these directors earned at their full-time jobs. (The salaries of those who work at private companies is . . . private. And some of the senior officers of public corporations were not among those executives whose compensation must be disclosed in public filings.) The CEO of Wells Fargo earned over $21 million in 2009.[43] The CEO of Xerox earned about $4.8 million in 2009 but received $13.6 million in 2008 and $14.6 million in 2007.[44] The CFO of Eli Lilly earned over $7.6 million in 2009.[45] And, not to be left out, the CEO of Target itself earned over $16.1 million for his work as CEO.[46]

If the *total* amount directors earn is trivial to them compared to the sums they earn from their day jobs, the differential from growing the company's stock price is entirely insignificant. Suppose, for example, that a director received all of her compensation in company stock. Suppose further that the director receives compensation that is well above the average for large corporations, $300,000 per year. If the director is wildly successful and the company's stock price rises by 20 percent, that will yield him or her an extra $60,000. This amount is unlikely to have much effect on someone who earns $10 million per year. For them, $60,000 is about two days' pay. And changing the CEO's pay package is unlikely to move the company's stock price nearly that much.

In sum, directors' positions are generally very safe, so the threat of losing their annual compensation in the future is largely empty. In addition, for most directors, the amount they earn as directors is a very small fraction of their total annual income. Even if pay packages are tied closely to performance, the difference between a great year and a terrible one is still going to be only a fraction of the director's total pay. If the entire package is not significant to a director, a fraction of the package is very unlikely to shape behavior.

This discussion raises the question of why directors serve at all. If the pay is so poor by their standards, why bother? Answers no doubt vary for each director, but I can suggest a number of possibilities. Some may like the idea of being a director because the position carries a great deal of prestige. Others may become directors because the job can create connections for them personally or for their full-time businesses that can lead to lucrative business deals. Still others may take the post out of a sense of duty and service.

Some may actually want the money. Not all directors are senior corporate executives; some are academics or former politicians or others whose primary occupation is less fiscally rewarding than business and for whom the directors' pay package seems very generous. For example, Microsoft's board currently includes Maria M. Klawe, president of Harvey Mudd College; and Michael J. Boskin, a professor at Stanford, sits on ExxonMobil's board, as does William W. George, a professor at Harvard. Former secretary of state Henry Kissinger served as a director of American Express, and former vice president Al Gore sits on Apple's board.

Only this last group—a small minority of directors in large publicly held corporations—are likely to be motivated by their compensation to act in a particular way (assuming they are not independently wealthy like Vice President Gore). And even they will be influenced in regard to CEO pay only if a sufficient amount of their compensation depends on the company's performance *and* CEO pay strongly affects the company's results. For the most part, then, directors' compensation packages are unlikely to prove a useful means of persuading directors to act in shareholders' interests when negotiating the CEO's pay package. Directors' pay may even have the opposite effect: it may pressure directors to fall in line with the CEO (see chapter 5).

DIRECTORS' LIABILITY TO SHAREHOLDERS

Although the carrot of compensation is not likely to be much of a motivator for directors, they might respond to the stick of liability. Directors who fear significant personal liability for their actions might protect themselves by making decisions favoring shareholders' interests. They might take care to act carefully and thoughtfully, researching each decision thoroughly and generally doing everything possible to keep shareholders happy and nonlitigious.

If shareholders were empowered to sue directors and hold them personally responsible for any damage to the corporation for their negligence or malfeasance, directors would have a powerful incentive to take due care. Damages in such an action based on overpayment of the CEO could well be astronomical. For example, a board that overpaid its CEO by $20 million a year for five years could face liability of $100 million, a powerful deterrent against negligent or self-interested behavior.

This logic depends on directors' personal vulnerability to shareholder suits over the way they compensate the CEO. That vulnerability, however, is almost entirely lacking. State law and private contractual arrangements combine to provide almost complete protection to directors from bearing personal liability for their actions as directors. State law mounts substantive and procedural hurdles that are very difficult for any shareholder to overcome. Many corporations also provide in their certificates of incorporation that directors are immune from liability for acts—even negligent acts—taken in good faith.

If shareholders persevere and succeed in obtaining a judgment against the directors, it is likely to be satisfied by a combination of insurance (whose premiums are paid by the corporation) and the corporation itself (through indemnification agreements). Although there are exceptions, for the most part directors face at worst some inconvenience and embarrassment from shareholder suits; they rarely bear personal liability.

Directors' legal protections begin with the substantive law governing overpayments and general mismanagement by the board. These rules make it very difficult for a shareholder to prevail. Courts do not want to run corporations. Judges have neither the expertise nor the mandate to scrutinize every decision made by a corporate board. To avoid becoming drawn in to internal corporate disputes, courts have adopted a highly deferential standard of review of corporate actions—the business judgment rule.[47]

The business judgment rule has its roots in the statutory principle that the board of directors governs the corporation.[48] The rule is essentially a strong presumption that the board acts properly in making business decisions. The complaining shareholder must rebut the presumption that the board employed a reasonable procedure in considering the issue; that the board made the contested decision in good faith, while reasonably informed and without suffering from a conflict of interest. If the plaintiff fails to rebut these presumptions, the court will test the directors' actions only under a rationality standard of review, also known as the waste test. Courts find waste only when the corporation received essentially nothing in exchange for its assets.[49]

A shareholder plaintiff who does successfully rebut one of the procedural presumptions—say, by showing the board was not informed when it made its decision—will receive much less deferential review of its actions under the entire fairness test. Under that test, the board has the burden of proving that the transaction was entirely fair to the corporation.[50] The entire fairness test is far more advantageous for the shareholder-plaintiff, and directors subject to that test may well face liability.

But in the absence of a conflict of interest or a desire to harm the corporation, a shareholder plaintiff is left only with the possibility of proving the board was insufficiently informed when it made its decision. The presumption that the directors were informed is very difficult to overcome. The standard the directors must meet is gross negligence, meaning that if they were not grossly negligent, they have satisfied the rule's requirements.[51] As a result, directors are extremely unlikely to be found liable for making a decision about compensating the CEO.

A recent and famous case demonstrates this point.[52] Michael Eisner, then CEO of the Walt Disney Company, hired his good friend Michael Ovitz as president of the company in 1995. Ovitz's hiring package included a hefty grant of stock options. He also was promised a lucrative severance package as long as he was not fired because of gross negligence or malfeasance (a "non-fault termination"). The package included his full salary for the five-year term of the agreement at $1 million per year, a $7.5 million bonus for each year remaining on the contract at the time of termination, the immediate vesting of millions of stock options, and a $10 million termination payment.

Ovitz struggled at Disney and ultimately left a little over a year after he started work. As part of the agreement about his departure, he was given a nonfault termination. In consequence, he received an estimated

$130 million for about a year's (unsuccessful) work. Although the board and Eisner had approved this package, including the severance arrangements (which arguably paid Ovitz more if he were fired than if he remained for the duration of his contract), the Delaware courts ultimately found that the board was not liable. The directors were not interested, were sufficiently informed, and acted in good faith, and Ovitz's contract was not a waste of corporate assets. The case presented strong facts for the shareholders, but the Delaware courts still protected the board from liability for approving Ovitz's compensation package.[53]

Shareholders must often fight even to get a hearing under the business judgment rule; there are substantial procedural hurdles that can make it very difficult to mount a suit against the directors. In order to sue directors for paying their CEO too much, shareholders must launch a special type of action called a derivative suit. Derivative claims belong to the corporation itself, so the decision about whether to bring suit should be made by the board. A shareholder who brings a derivative claim is really suing the corporation to force it to launch a lawsuit that it is reluctant to bring itself. Courts are understandably hesitant to allow shareholders to force the board's hand, so they require a preliminary showing that the board's judgment cannot be trusted before allowing the suit to proceed. They also have qualification standards for the shareholder bringing suit. Even after the court has allowed the suit to go forward, it will permit the board to establish an independent committee to evaluate the suit and move to dismiss the case if the committee finds the suit is not in the company's best interests.[54]

For those directors who are not satisfied with the protection they receive from the substantive protection of the business judgment rule or the procedural requirements of derivative actions, corporations have another shield to offer. Delaware law permits corporations to put a provision in their certificates of incorporation that immunizes directors from liability for their actions.[55] This immunity has some limits: directors will still be liable for breaches of their duty of loyalty (which generally involve some self-interest) and for actions or omissions that were not made in good faith. But outside of these broad limits, directors who serve corporations with these provisions receive very powerful liability protection. Disney had such a provision in its certificate of incorporation, which is part of the reason its directors were not held liable for how they compensated Ovitz.[56]

Despite all these layers of protection, some directors may *still* be found liable to the corporation or its shareholders. For these rare instances, corporations have devised two additional shelters. First, corporations are permitted to purchase (and most do purchase) directors' and officers' insurance to protect their board and senior executives from personal liability in shareholder suits.[57] This insurance also has some limits: the coverage may not be sufficiently extensive; it is typically on a "claims-made" basis, which may leave directors uncovered for past conduct; there is often an "insured versus insured" exclusion for when the corporation is the plaintiff suing its directors or officers (though derivative suits do not come under this exclusion); and breaches of the duty of loyalty are usually excluded. But within those limits, the directors are well protected.

Second, corporations may often—and sometimes must—indemnify directors and officers for liability they incur as a result of their position. Corporations have the power to indemnify officers and directors so long as they acted in "good faith and in a manner such person reasonably believed to be or not opposed to the best interests of the corporation."[58] (Note that although directors must have acted in good faith to be entitled to indemnification, there is no such limitation on the corporation's power to insure them. Corporations may purchase insurance policies that will reimburse directors for their liability even for bad faith conduct.)[59] Corporations *must* indemnify directors and officers when they have been successful "on the merits or otherwise" in defending against a lawsuit that involved their corporate role.[60]

When we take a step back and examine the full panoply of protections the law and corporate contractual arrangements provide for directors to shield them from personal liability, it becomes hard to imagine that they ever end up writing a check. In fact, a 2006 study found only one case since 1980 in which a verdict against outside directors resulted in their personal liability for breach of their fiduciary duty.[61] In that case, *Smith v. Van Gorkom,* the Delaware Supreme Court found the directors had breached their duty of care by failing to gather sufficient information before approving a merger.[62] The case subsequently settled for $23.5 million. The company's insurance covered $10 million of this, leaving $13.5 million for the directors to pay out of their personal assets. In the end, though, they escaped without paying. The acquirer in the merger that was the subject of the suit voluntarily paid the balance, asking only that the directors each donate $135,000 to charity.[63]

Most shareholder suits settle, so the story about reported verdicts may not be representative of directors' actual exposure. But the same 2006 study found that only about a dozen of these settlements resulted in personal liability for the directors, even when we include suits for violations of federal securities laws.[64]

Directors may be somewhat deterred by the threat of becoming a defendant; lawsuits are time consuming and potentially embarrassing. In rare cases, they may even result in personal liability. To the extent directors are extremely risk-averse, they may act to avoid liability. But the thick protections that surround directors probably make it unrealistic to rely too heavily on the threat of liability to influence their behavior as they negotiate the CEO's pay package.

ROLE INTEGRITY AND ALTRUISM

The final set of influences on directors' behavior may be the most important, but it is also the most overlooked. All the prior possibilities—institutional constraints, electoral considerations, compensation, and potential liability—essentially treated directors as rational agents acting purely in their self-interest. In the world of business and economic theory, the self-interested and rational agent is a familiar and comfortable lens through which to view human behavior. It connotes hardheadedness, realism, pragmatism, a true understanding of how the world works. But it fails miserably as a complete description of how people actually behave.

Self-interest is a powerful motivator, but it is not the sole motivator, at least not as narrowly described. People often behave in ways that are difficult or impossible to explain as a product of self-interest. Here I am not referring to the cognitive errors that behavioral economics explores, heuristics and biases such as the optimism bias, cognitive dissonance, or the endowment effect (though I make good use of some of this literature in chapter 8).[65] What I mean is that often people act purposefully in ways that at least appear to be against their self-interest such as giving gifts or making charitable donations.

Frequently this behavior can be explained as a sort of second-order strategic self-interest. Even gift giving has been explained this way, as a signal to potential contracting partners that one is reliable.[66] But we must strain, sometimes quite hard, to find self-interest in these cases, and it is far from clear that self-interest is the most accurate explanation. We may give charity out of enlightened self-interest, recognizing that if we all band together to do good works we can build a society that ultimately is healthier and safer for all of us. We might alternatively give charity in order to impress our potential business partners by demonstrating our great wealth and general trustworthiness.[67] But don't we at least sometimes give charity because it makes us feel good to do so? Isn't our largesse often motivated by a feeling of duty to the schools that educate our children, the churches that nourish our values and community, the institutions that feed and shelter our community's hungry and homeless?

Feelings like generosity or duty are difficult to explain and impossible to quantify. They are also much harder to predict than self-interest, making them challenging to model or test. But they are nonetheless real and often quite powerful. Why did Bill Gates and Warren Buffett, two of the wealthiest individuals this planet has ever seen, pledge the bulk of their fortunes to helping the world's most impoverished?[68] Was it really out of a desire to impress their potential business partners? Surely just about anyone would have been thrilled to do business with these two before they decided to give away their fortunes. What reputation benefit could they possibly have gained that was worth the billions they have given away?

Gates and Buffet are far from the only examples of such apparently selfless acts. People perform countless acts of self-sacrifice every day, often anonymously, with no real thought of personal gain. There are two explanations for this type of behavior that may aid our understanding of corporate directors: role integrity and altruism.

Role Integrity

I am borrowing the term *role integrity* from Ian Macneil and his innovative work on relational contracting.[69] Macneil used the term to refer to the behavior a person was expected to exhibit given his or her social role in a particular context.[70] He quoted the British philosopher Dorothy Emmet's discussion of roles in moral thinking:

> What people think they ought to do depends largely on how they see their roles, and (most importantly) the conflicts between their roles. It may be a bridge notion between myself as an individual, with my proper name and my personal responsibility, and "my station and its duties" in the institutional world of the society in which I have to live.[71]

Like Macneil, I believe that role playing is universal in human behavior.[72] We often act in ways we think are expected of us based on the particular role we are taking on at that moment. Firefighters run into burning buildings because that is their role. Soldiers advance into enemy fire because that is their role. And perhaps senior corporate executives take on positions as directors of other corporations—and attempt to represent shareholder interests the best they can while serving as directors—because that is their role.

The most famous demonstration of people's tendency to act according to their assigned roles is the Stanford prison experiment. The Stanford psychologist Philip Zimbardo set up a mock prison in the basement of Stanford's psychology building. Twenty-one male college students, all of whom were prescreened for their physical and mental stability, were randomly assigned a role as either a guard or a prisoner. The prisoners had to remain in the "prison" twenty-four hours a day for the full duration of the experiment, which was expected to be two weeks. The guards worked eight-hour shifts and were allowed to return home after their shifts were over.[73]

The experimenters told the subjects assigned to be guards that they should act like real prison guards the best they could and also maintain order in the prison. The students chosen to be prisoners were unexpectedly arrested by real police officers, processed, and taken to the prison. There, the warden read them the rules of the prison and told them they were required to memorize them. The prison was made as realistic as possible, down to requiring both prisoners and guards to wear appropriate uniforms.[74]

The subjects were educated, well-balanced young men. Dressing up and taking on a role should not have seriously changed their behavior. Yet it did. Guards quickly became abusive, while prisoners became passive. For example, the guards would drag prisoners' blankets through a thorn bush and then force the prisoners to pick out the thorns. They would also make prisoners do push-ups with a guard on their back. One guard—who described himself as a pacifist at the start of the experiment—by the fifth day tried to force a sausage down the throat of a prisoner who refused to eat and justified his conduct as necessary to maintain the guards' authority. The situation deteriorated so rapidly that Zimbardo called off the experiment after only six days, less than half the planned interval.

The prisoners were badly affected by this treatment. One had to be released after only thirty-six hours because of uncontrollable crying and fits of rage. Three more prisoners had to be released early because of severe depression. Even Zimbardo was drawn into his role as warden and found himself excusing the guards' bad behavior. Only when a graduate student intervened did Zimbardo terminate the experiment.[75]

The Stanford experiment demonstrated that taking on a role can change people's behavior, even in shocking ways. That experiment put subjects in a setting that may have been unusually intense, though, so it may not say very much about whether people pursue shareholders' interests because they have taken on the role of a director.

Another experiment, by the Wharton marketing professor J. Scott Armstrong, tested the impact of role playing in a boardroom setting. Armstrong set up an exercise in which he placed subjects in the role of directors of the Upjohn Company, a pharmaceutical firm. Armstrong based his experiment on a real decision made by Upjohn's board. Upjohn manufactured a drug called Panalba. The drug was associated with serious side effects and even fatalities. Some of Upjohn's competitors made drugs that apparently had therapeutic properties similar to Panalba's but with much less dangerous side effects. Upjohn's board had to decide whether to remove Panalba from the market.[76]

First, Armstrong provided audiences of students, faculty, and managers with this information and then passed out a questionnaire asking what the audiences would do if they were chair of the board of Upjohn. Only 2 percent of respondents answered that they would do what the actual Upjohn board did, which was to use political and legal pressures to try to keep Panalba on the market. Without role playing, people thought keeping the drug on the market was highly inappropriate.[77]

In his role-playing experiment, subjects were told to act as though they were directors and that the board had passed a resolution saying that the directors' duty was to represent the stockholders. The experimenters gave the subjects five possible actions the company could take in regard to the drug: (1) take it off the market immediately; (2) stop production but sell the remaining supply; (3) continue production but cease marketing efforts; (4) continue making and selling the drug until it was banned; or (5) exert legal and political pressure to prevent the drug from being banned.[78]

The experimenters also gave the subjects accounting information that listed the expected loss to shareholders (from lost profits), customers (from illness and death), and employees (from lost wages) for each of the five possible actions the company could take. For the shareholders, the best option was #5 (preventing the drug from being banned), with each option above it becoming progressively worse. For the customers, precisely the opposite was true; the best option was #1, and the losses grew from there. Total losses to all three groups mirrored the losses to customers; choice #1 had the lowest total losses, and choice #5 imposed the greatest total loss. In other words, the losses to customers from taking the drug far outweighed the financial losses to shareholders from taking the drug off the market.[79]

Armstrong tried this experiment with fifty-seven different groups and a number of different nationalities. Remember that subjects who did *not* take on the role of a director overwhelmingly thought the best course of action was to pull the drug from the market (choice #1). Only 2 percent said that if they were the chairman of Upjohn, they would fight to keep the drug legal (choice #5). Within the role-playing exercise, however, the mock directors made a radically different choice: nearly 80 percent of the groups concluded that they should fight to keep the drug legal (choice #5).[80] And again, that was the choice that the actual Upjohn directors made. Taking on the role of directors not only changed the subjects' views about what was appropriate behavior, but it also made their views much more consistent with those of the real-life directors.

The subjects in Armstrong's experiment—like the subjects in the Stanford prison experiment—behaved very differently when they assumed a role. Both experiments exhibit the possibility that real-world directors might pursue shareholders' interests because they believe that is their role, separate and apart from any pecuniary incentive they have. (As we have seen, the tangible incentives for directors to protect shareholders seem quite weak.) But we have no direct evidence that directors' conduct is actually driven by role taking, just that it might be. Alternatively, directors' behavior might be shaped by some other—perhaps still undiscovered—cause. Still, role integrity does have some explanatory power in the corporate context, and the experiments show that people can behave differently when placed in a particular role. Role integrity is a theory worth investigating further.

Altruism

Altruism is an alternative, or perhaps overlapping, explanation for why directors might pursue shareholders' interests even without a pecuniary incentive to do so. Perhaps boards try to protect shareholders because they feel altruistically toward them.

Before we proceed, I need to explain how I'm using the word *altruism*. What I mean by altruism is not the emotional need to help someone else even at one's own expense. Such emotions may well exist,[81] but claims about them tend to run into unanswerable questions about what should count as a selfish benefit. Suppose I drop a dollar into the hat of a street performer. My act appears altruistic, as though I paid the performer out of empathy or kindness. After all, I can enjoy the performer's music without paying for it. But when we look more deeply at my motivation, questions arise. Perhaps I paid the performer because my boss or spouse or child was watching, and I wanted to present myself as a kind and generous person (a selfish motive). Or perhaps no one I knew was watching, but I reasoned that street musicians would no longer perform if audiences failed to pay them. My desire to support a form of art that I personally enjoy could be described either as selfless or as strategic selfishness. What about my internal emotional rewards? If for some reason I *enjoy* paying the street musician, perhaps because the payment alleviates some guilt or anxiety I might be feeling about enjoying the music for free, should my action still count as altruistic?

I want to avoid these internal motivational questions altogether because I don't think they're terribly helpful for our purposes. What matters here is not so much what emotional state directors are in as what they actually *do*. For that reason, I want to focus only on observable actions. Altruism for my purposes is behavior that requires the actor to bear costs that exceed the value of any direct, personal benefit, where both the costs and benefits are material, not emotional.[82]

By that definition of altruism, mounds of experimental evidence has demonstrated that people behave altruistically quite frequently.[83] Remarkably, they behave altruistically even toward strangers whom they never expect to see again.

Directors' interests may well conflict with shareholders' in the CEO pay context. For example, a director may value staying on good terms with the CEO over minimizing an important corporate expense such as executive compensation. In such a case, directors will likely lavish pay on the CEO to preserve their relationship. But if directors faced with such a conflict are in an environment that makes altruistic behavior more likely, they may choose the shareholders' interests over their own and fight to minimize CEO pay.

Research has identified a number of factors that make altruistic behavior either more or less likely.[84] The factors with the most potential to affect directors' behavior in negotiating CEOs' compensation include corporate governance norms, the cost of helping shareholders versus the rewards of doing so, the extent to which external forces try to coerce directors to put shareholders first, and the directors' personalities.[85]

Norms can be tremendously powerful. People sometimes obey strong social norms even when doing so goes against their selfish interests. For example, people often leave tips in restaurants even when traveling in a strange city they never intend to visit again, and even when eating alone. There is no rational reason to tip someone who will never serve you again. The point of a tip is to encourage good service. Since tipping isn't done until the end of the meal, you've already received whatever service you're going to get at the time you decide whether or not to tip. If you're never going to be served by this person again, there's no purely selfish motive to tip. But people do it time and again. The social norm that requires tipping is very strong and difficult to overcome. Skipping the tip would make most of us feel a little embarrassed, maybe even guilty. We might fear that the server and—if they find out—the other people in the restaurant will think we are rude or cheap.

At a restaurant full of people we will never see again, why should we care? It's very hard to come up with an economic rationale for tipping under these circumstances. We're not trying to persuade the server to give us good service in the future, and it's hard to believe we're trying to signal our good character to people we don't know and will never get to know. The norm is engrained in us, though, so, probably without much thought, we leave a tip. The *norm* may be efficient, in that it preserves a system that perhaps improves restaurant service. But without a direct, personal benefit, there is no selfish motive to obey it.

Norms' impact on CEO compensation will depend on the norms' substantive content and on their power to overcome any countervailing selfish interests. If directors widely embrace a norm that just about any amount of pay is acceptable to get the best person for the job (at least when the job is as CEO), then directors' norms will tend to inflate pay. Directors who feel the cost of pay is trivial compared to the cost of losing out on the best leader will naturally take lightly concerns about the amount of pay. In other words, for directors to behave altruistically toward shareholders they first have to see a need. If shareholders are being helped rather than harmed by huge executive pay packages— because the benefits of hiring the right person far outweigh any costs— then they are very unlikely to try to change the status quo.

On the other hand, if the dominant norm is to watch the bottom line carefully and to weigh every expenditure rigorously against its expected benefits, directors might be more reticent to approve a large package. Instead, they might think carefully about the costs and benefits of hiring an alternative candidate as CEO, one who would not demand as much compensation and might lead almost as well as the more expensive choice. Norms are likely to vary from company to company, so it may not be possible to predict norms' impact across corporations.

The personal costs and benefits of helping also play a large role in determining whether someone will behave altruistically. Not surprisingly, altruistic behavior that is easy or cheap is more likely. Similarly, altruistic acts that also produce a large benefit to the actor (such as a boost to the altruist's reputation) are more likely to occur.

For executive compensation decisions, the cost of pushing for a smaller package or asking to tie the CEO's pay more tightly to performance is that the aggressive directors may irritate the CEO. If pushed far enough, the CEO may seek employment at another corporation, one where the pay is more generous and less risky. In addition, some theorists have argued that directors jeopardize their board seats by advocating for smaller pay packages or more contingent compensation structures. (I discuss this theory in detail in chapter 5.) Irritating the CEO may also damage any business relationship a director may have with the CEO outside the corporation. A further risk is that focusing on the costs of CEO compensation may inculcate a norm of lower pay whose logic spreads to director compensation as well, resulting in reduced remuneration for directors (which, remember, is already low by the standards of people who are offered seats on a board). More threatening, the parsimony norm may spread to the corporations where the directors serve as senior executives, lowering the pay at their full-time jobs.

The benefit of reducing CEO compensation or of improving the package's incentive structure may be more efficient and cost-effective compensation. The corporation may both save money by paying less and earn more money by using more sensible incentives. (Note that in chapter 6 I challenge the notion that linking pay to performance induces better performance.) There may also be some more generalized benefits to the corporate system as a whole. As more corporations restrict executive compensation, boards will have a progressively easier time hiring an excellent CEO for a more modest sum. Lower comparables at other companies will mean that CEOs will have a correspondingly more difficult time arguing that their compensation is below market.

Directors personally, though, will likely see little direct benefit from fighting for lower or more efficient compensation. They may enhance their reputations as good stewards. On the other hand, they may instead develop a reputation as a troublemaker and lose the opportunity to serve on other companies' boards. And, as already mentioned, they may find that reducing the CEO's pay indirectly produces reductions of their own pay as executives of other corporations. As a result, the cost-benefit analysis to directors personally may weigh pretty strongly against acting altruistically toward shareholders on executive compensation.

The final altruism factor is personality type. Some personalities are more likely to behave altruistically than others. People who exhibit greater sympathy, empathy, personal responsibility, and docility tend to be more altruistic.[86] These are not necessarily traits found in an ideal director. Docility in particular would tend to prevent a director from standing up to other directors or the CEO in pursuit of the shareholders' interests.

More important, the danger in seeking out altruistic personalities is the uncertainty about where their altruism will be directed. Altruism is more likely when the beneficiary and the altruist are similar or have some relationship, leading to greater empathy.[87] Directors meet with the CEO regularly but are likely to have much less frequent contact with shareholders, especially small shareholders. While directors may have much in common with representatives of institutional shareholders, they should have at least as much in common with the CEO, and perhaps quite a bit more. Those directors who are themselves CEOs of other corporations seem especially likely to empathize with the CEO rather than the shareholders. Altruistic directors, then, are at least as likely to aim their altruism at the CEO as they are at the shareholders.

Overall, role integrity and altruistic impulses may help shape directors' decisions about CEO compensation, but there are many reasons to be skeptical. There is little direct empirical support for the theory of role integrity, though it meshes well with our intuitions about human behavior and laboratory studies. Altruism has been studied much more closely, but the lessons of that research often argue against altruism having a significant impact on directors' decisions about executive pay. Norms likely vary across corporations and may well support buying quality at any price. Directors are likely to face a high cost for altruism toward shareholders at the CEO's expense, with little offsetting personal benefit. And directors with personalities that foster altruism seem more likely to direct that altruism at the people they know best—the CEOs—rather than the more distant shareholders.[88]

Both role integrity and altruism are worth studying more closely in the executive compensation context. But for now, the empirical support for the proposition that either exerts much influence on directors' decisions about executive pay is sparse.

CONCLUSION

Directors are institutionally limited; are largely self-perpetuating and unlikely to be voted out by shareholders; have little financial incentive to work hard as directors or to actively pursue shareholders' interest; are unlikely to be found liable (and even less likely to bear liability) for their decisions; and probably do not champion shareholders' interests out of altruism. Yet as Steve Bainbridge has pointed out, somehow U.S. public corporations seem to have done pretty well, with U.S. stock markets generally outperforming stock markets in other countries.[89] If boards' conduct affects companies' share prices, the performance of U.S. stock markets seems an endorsement of U.S. corporate governance. Directors also seem to be willing to take steps (like firing the CEO) to protect the corporation when necessary.[90] And shareholders are apparently pleased with how directors are compensating CEOs, at least based on their recent voting behavior. In 2011, shareholders for the first time gained the right to a nonbinding vote on the CEO's compensation.[91] Shareholders overwhelmingly approved the packages directors had negotiated, passing 98 percent of them in that year and in 2012.[92]

All this makes me feel a bit like a physicist claiming that bumblebees are incapable of flight. Clearly they are; perhaps it is my physics that is wanting. Nevertheless, to the extent directors run corporations effectively and selflessly on behalf of shareholders, this behavior is difficult to explain on a pure self-interested rational actor model. They may act out of some less direct form of rational self-interest, such as a desire to enhance their reputations. Alternatively, they may behave responsibly out of a sense of duty to maintain the corporate governance system, a desire for public service, or some other motivation outside the canon of rational self-interest, such as role integrity or altruism.

We badly need direct observations of boards to help us figure out what directors think they are doing and why they generally seem to pursue shareholders' interests. But we are out of luck in this area. Boards rarely allow outsiders into meetings, so objective, empirical evidence about directors' behavior is difficult or impossible to obtain.

Still, for purposes of understanding CEO compensation, it is very helpful to understand that the employer—the board—has opaque interests and incentives. Public company boards are not the kind of arm's-length players that would be ideal to form an efficient labor market. There is likely a lot going on beneath the surface here, some good, perhaps some bad. But all of it is murky. At a minimum, the lesson we should draw from this chapter is that we should be suspicious of a market where one side is represented by these strange bodies we call corporate boards.

This chapter has provided one reason to be skeptical of arguments that the CEO labor market is efficient: the directors who run corporations may not have interests that align with the companies they represent. Nevertheless, scholars have advanced a number of arguments for why we should believe the CEO labor market *is* efficient. I discuss these arguments in the next chapter.

CHAPTER 4

Market Mythology

Boards of directors are mysterious entities. We don't have a solid understanding of how or why they function. U.S. public corporations are led by a group whose members—the directors—have little direct financial incentive to invest much time or energy in furthering the corporation's interests. Still, these businesses seem to have managed pretty well over the past century, delivering remarkable growth and contributing greatly to an economy that is now the largest in the world, by an enormous margin.[1]

As a result, many—perhaps most—scholars who study executive compensation have been skeptical that anything serious can be wrong with the system. Defenders of the status quo have written countless articles stating that the puzzles discussed in chapter 2—the sudden, rapid growth in pay volume and the comparably precipitous increase in reliance on equity-based compensation—can be explained as the outcome of an efficient market. In fact, Kevin Murphy has argued the number of articles written about executive compensation may have grown faster than executive pay itself.[2]

In this chapter, I discuss the seven major arguments justifying the amount of CEO pay on grounds of efficiency. Although there are many variants, and new ideas are being developed all the time, these justifications are as follows: company size, advances in technology, company image and self-image, tournament competition, superstardom, government regulation, and behavior modification. Together, these arguments—sometimes referred to as optimal contracting theory—represent the conventional wisdom among academics that the system is somehow getting it right. Yet, while many scholars have marshaled data to support these theories, we will find a surprising lack of convincing empirical support for any of them. To the contrary, there are important reasons to doubt that these theories really explain the puzzles we have observed in executive compensation. Although most academics believe strongly in the efficiency of the CEO labor market, the evidence that supports this belief is startlingly underwhelming. We will take the arguments each in turn.

FIRM SIZE

Perhaps the most popular recent justification involves the size of the employing company. The most influential advocates for this explanation are the economists Xavier Gabaix and Augustin Landier. They looked at the past few decades and found a remarkable correlation between a company's size and the amount the company pays its chief executive officer.[3] The larger the company, the more the business pays its CEO. Although CEO pay has grown remarkably quickly since the 1970s, so has the size of publicly traded companies. In fact, if CEOs must be paid more to run a larger company, and if the amount of this hypothesized premium is directly proportionate to the size of the firm, then the growth of U.S companies over the past few decades accounts pretty neatly for the growth in CEO pay.[4] This theory seems to have a lot of potential to explain the recent explosive growth in CEO pay. Perhaps CEOs are being paid more because the companies they run are much larger.

But we are still missing an explanation for *why* there should be a relationship between firm size and CEO pay. Why do CEOs of larger companies get paid more? And why should the same CEO of the same company receive more pay just because the company grows over time?

The connection between company size and executive pay is not obvious. One could imagine, for example, that *smaller* firms might pay more because they have a greater need for executive talent to help them grow. Large firms are already established, so perhaps they can get by with executives who are merely very good rather than stellar. But small firms need truly exceptional talent if they are to break through all the barriers that stand in the way of their becoming industry leaders.

Alternatively, there might be *no* consistent relationship between firm size and CEO pay. Firms might pay for the talent they think they need. Some skill sets could be scarce relative to demand and therefore command a high price. Other skill sets might—at some given point in time—be relatively plentiful and therefore cheap. Why should we think that large firms would always need the skill sets that happen to be most expensive, especially since the expense of different skill sets should vary over the years?

Those scholars who have advanced the firm size explanation have not relied solely on the remarkable correlation between company size and executive pay. They understand that correlation does not always indicate causation and have thought carefully about reasons why this relationship might exist.

One possibility is that larger companies are more difficult to manage.[5] The larger the firm, the more difficult the management task, and the more executives must be paid to persuade them to take the job. If large firms paid the same amount to their executives as smaller firms did, the large firms would have a great deal of trouble hiring chief executives. Who, after all, would take on a more difficult task for the same amount of money?

Another possibility is that talent is worth more to large firms than to small ones.[6] The intuition here is fairly straightforward: it takes money to make money. The more assets the CEO controls, the greater his or her ability to generate wealth for the firm. A hotshot CEO who runs a $10 million company might double or even triple the company's value over the course of a few years. But all that effort and talent would only generate a few tens of millions of dollars. (The irony of this statement is not lost on me.) Now suppose that same CEO instead ran a company worth $10 billion. If the CEO doubles or triples the value of this larger company, the result is new wealth in the tens of *billions* of dollars. The larger company should therefore be more than willing to outbid the smaller company. If CEO talent is transparent to the market and if a talented CEO really can generate more wealth for a large company than a small one, then we should expect larger companies to pay their CEOs more. We should also expect to see a distribution of talent in which the best CEOs run the largest companies. CEO talent is most valuable to the largest companies, and they are also able to bid the highest price.

A third possibility is a bit counterintuitive. Larger firms may face more difficult agency problems. They likely have more shares outstanding, and therefore their capital structure is probably more diffuse. Because large firms generally have more shareholders, it is harder for those shareholders to monitor the firm and restrain management from acting in their own interest. As a result, larger firms must implement more extensive corporate governance to compensate. They need more activist and involved directors and must use compensation packages that more closely tie executives' pay to the firm's performance. Under this line of reasoning, the executives of these larger companies ironically face *greater* monitoring than they would in a smaller firm. They therefore must work harder to impress their directors with the job they are doing and face a greater risk of being fired. To compensate managers for having to work harder and bear a larger risk of termination (as well as a greater proportion of contingent pay), big companies must pay their executives more.[7]

While each of these explanations has some appeal, none is entirely convincing. There are particular problems with each theory, and there are more comprehensive issues with them all. I will start with the theory-specific problems.

The firm complexity theory suffers from a lack of empirical evidence. While at some level it seems likely that larger firms are more difficult to manage, there is no apparent method of comparing the work involved. Anecdotally, CEOs of midsized firms often seem to work the same long hours as CEOs of larger companies. If CEOs were like lawyers and billed by the hour, we would have some means of testing this theory.

Conceptually, though, it is not clear that larger firms necessarily require their CEOs to work harder. Larger firms likely have more layers of executives, to help manage the greater number of employees. Some large companies may therefore require less of their CEOs in terms of management of day-to-day issues. They may have sufficient executive staff—and sufficiently talented executive staff—to relieve their CEOs of the burden of day-to-day management, freeing them to focus on more important, strategic concerns. From this perspective, larger firms may be more interesting to lead, because they have the resources to permit their CEOs to spend their time doing only what they think is most important. CEOs can more easily delegate the grind of company minutia in a large firm than a small one.

For the same reason, it is not at all clear that larger firms require rarer skill sets for their executives than do smaller or medium-sized firms. Certainly an executive running a large corporation needs a different sort of talent and experience than someone running a small local store. But does running a $5 billion company require fundamentally different skills than running a $15 billion company? I am not claiming smaller firms are more difficult to manage, just that logic does not conclusively say anything about a link between a company's size and its leader's workload or required skill set. In the absence of hard data, the firm complexity theory is not terribly persuasive.

Similarly, the theory that talent is more valuable to larger firms is difficult to support empirically. If we had a reliable measure of CEO talent, we could test this theory.[8] We could compare the total wealth gain of different-sized firms that were led by similarly talented CEOs to see whether larger firms made better use of leadership talent than smaller firms. But then again, if we had a reliable measure of CEO talent, we probably wouldn't have a problem with executive compensation, and this book wouldn't need to exist. Without such a measure, there is no way to determine the relative impact of leadership talent on firm wealth.

In fact, this relative impact theory may have it precisely backward. Smaller firms may have greater growth potential than larger firms. Big companies already have a sizable chunk of the market, making it hard to increase their sales. But small firms have much greater capacity to improve, since they are beginning with so little. A talented CEO might then only be able to increase a large firm's earnings by a small percentage but could quickly double or triple the sales of a small company.

Moreover, this theory depends on boards' ability to discern CEO talent, perhaps with remarkable precision. In Gabaix and Landier's study advocating this relative impact theory, the authors concluded that the difference in talent between the best CEO and the 250th best would have an impact of .016 percent on the company's market capitalization.[9] That is, if the firm led by the 250th best CEO replaced that person with the very best, it could expect its market capitalization to rise by a whopping .016 percent. This suggests that the differences in talent among the top few hundred CEOs are vanishingly small. (Gabaix and Landier concede this point but argue that even this small difference in talent justifies very large differences in pay between the CEO of the largest company and the 250th.)

Can directors really perceive such fine distinctions among CEOs? If they can't, the theory collapses. The theory argues that CEOs of larger firms are paid more because their talent can be better leveraged to produce wealth when managing more assets. But if directors are unable to distinguish between the most talented CEO and the 250th most talented CEO, how can we believe that the most talented CEO is running the largest company? The directors of the largest company might quite understandably have made a mistake, and hired a CEO that is only the 100th best, or the 200th best. If so, the largest company ends up paying top money for talent that does not justify the premium. If CEOs are not allocated to firms so that the best ones are running the largest firms, then the justification fails. And as I discuss in some detail in chapter 8, there is good reason to believe that directors are not able to predict which CEOs are the most talented.

Carola Frydman and Dirk Jenter have pointed out that there is also an empirical problem with this theory. If company growth really explained the rise in CEO pay, we would expect to see a fairly active market in CEOs. As information developed about the relative talents of executives, we should see the largest companies actively bidding to replace their CEOs with those revealed to be superior. But no such active market exists. To the contrary, even though average CEO tenure has shrunk considerably in the past decade or so, CEO turnover remains quite infrequent, and CEOs rarely transfer directly between firms.[10] Charles Elson and Craig Ferrere confirm that "particularly for the large firms comprising the S&P 500, CEOs are rarely traded in any market for their talents."[11]

Moreover, the notion that talent is worth more to larger firms suggests that managerial talent is one-dimensional and fungible. A good CEO can run any firm; a poor one will bring any firm down. Does this really mesh with our experience of business leadership? Perhaps this theory conflates talent with charisma. Even charisma may not be equally appealing at every firm; not everyone finds the same people charming. Managerial skills seem even less likely to be portable. Different industries—and different companies within an industry—may need different skill sets. Imagine a manager of a national grocery chain who has succeeded in lowering costs through her excellent connections with agricultural suppliers. She seems unlikely to thrive equally as the head of an investment bank, an automobile manufacturer, or a real estate development firm. These different businesses require different knowledge bases and separate—if perhaps overlapping—skill sets. Yet this theory treats all managerial talent as homogeneous and readily transferable. This view seems increasingly fashionable among boards of directors as well, as I discuss below. But it seems unlikely to prove correct.

The third argument for the correlation between firm size and CEO pay ties the relationship to agency costs, arguing that larger firms face greater agency costs and respond by imposing tighter corporate governance. CEOs must therefore work harder to impress their boards and also face a greater risk of termination. The larger the firm, the better the corporate governance, and the more CEOs must be compensated to work harder and take on a greater risk of being fired.

There is some empirical support for the idea that corporate governance has become more rigorous since the 1970s. Boards now draw on outsiders, people who do not work full-time for the company, for a much larger fraction of their directorships. Shareholdership has also become more concentrated in the hands of sophisticated institutional investors, who are better able to monitor the company's affairs and intervene when the business goes awry.[12] Perhaps as a result of these changes, CEO turnovers have become more frequent since the 1970s, when CEO pay began to rise.[13]

But the relationship between these increased CEO turnovers and company performance is disputed.[14] Plus, the change in corporate governance is one that has occurred across time; it is not as clear that larger companies have stricter governance than smaller ones. More important, there is no direct evidence that the shift in governance has caused the increase in CEO pay, especially given the enormous magnitude of the change in CEO pay levels.[15]

All this suggests that efficiency may not be the most persuasive explanation for the recent link between company size and CEO pay. Firm size may not be clearly related to firm complexity, and there is little empirical evidence that supports the theory that CEOs of larger firms work harder than those of mid-sized firms or require a noticeably different or rarer skill set. More talented CEOs may be more valuable to larger companies, inducing the behemoths to pay more for a resource that is worth more to them. But empirical evidence is lacking for this theory, and logic indicates the reverse might often be true. Also, the differences in talent among the elite CEOs appear likely to be quite small and hard for boards to distinguish, making the enormous premiums larger companies are paying for their CEOs difficult to justify. And executive talent is unlikely to be so interchangeable that CEOs can compete meaningfully on a single dimension. Instead, different companies probably need different combinations of skills, again calling into question boards' ability to rank CEOs by ability and pay them accordingly. The tightening of corporate governance standards has not correlated closely to company size, as would need to be true if tougher governance was the reason larger companies seem to pay their executives more.

In addition to these critiques, there is an overarching problem with all three arguments for the correlation between company size and executive compensation. Frydman and Jenter have argued that the correlation seems to date only to the beginning of the dramatic rise in CEO pay.[16] Firm size and CEO pay march closely together starting in the early 1970s but wander separately before then.[17] If so, we have to wonder whether some other factor that began in the 1970s caused both the increase in CEO pay and the new correlation between executive pay and company size. Otherwise, we have to find some explanation for why larger firms paid more for CEOs after 1970 but not before. None of the explanations advanced above for the link between company size and CEO pay answer this question.

More troubling, even in recent decades the apparent correlation between company size and CEO pay may just be the accidental product of flawed data selection.[18] Gregory Nagel has found that when inadvertent data selection biases are removed, firm size accounts for only a tiny fraction of the growth in CEO pay.[19] He has argued that the apparent correlation between firm size and pay is the product of accidental biases in choosing which companies to examine. Gabaix and Landier's study—the primary source cited for the connection between companies' growth and the increases in CEO pay—contained a number of such data biases. For example, Gabaix and Landier relied on a data set that excluded 19 percent of the smallest S&P 500 firms in 1980, the first year of their study, but all S&P 500 firms after 1991. Another data set they rely on provides average compensation data for the top three executives at each firm but does not break out the CEO's pay. That data set also values options using a different term than another data set they use, making comparisons inaccurate. There were other, similar, problems. When Nagel ran the analysis with a corrected data set, he found that—with conservative measures of firm size (such as sales)—only about 9 percent of the over 600 percent increase in CEO pay since 1980 could be explained by changes in companies' size (and at most about one-third using more aggressive measures of company size).[20]

If the correlation between firm size and CEO compensation is a phenomenon that began suspiciously at the same time as the rapid growth in CEO pay or if the correlation is actually just a phantom of data selection, then the competition-based explanation for the rise in CEO pay utterly fails. More in-depth examinations of the data are required before we can draw firm conclusions on these questions.

In the meantime, since explanations rooted in efficiency seem to have failed us, we will have to cast a wider net to find an explanation for the puzzling correlation between CEO pay and firm size (if such a correlation really exists). One possibility has to do with outrage costs, a concept that comes from the legal economists Lucian Bebchuk and Jesse Fried and one I will explore in depth in chapter 5.[21] The basic idea is that directors want to please the CEO in order to retain their positions on the board. They face an important constraint, though, in the form of outrage costs. Although shareholders typically exercise little power in public corporations, they may rise up and punish directors who too obviously pursue the CEO's interest at the shareholders' expense. Shareholders may be less sensitive to CEO pay in larger companies because the same amount of compensation represents a smaller percentage of the companies' profits. Directors of larger companies, then, may be less constrained by outrage costs in raising their executives' pay.[22]

This is not an efficiency theory; the claim here is that directors are pursuing their own interests at shareholders' expense, not that larger firms have a good reason for paying more for executive talent. This explanation shouldn't make us feel reassured that larger companies are right to pay their CEOs more. It also depends on a particular view of board behavior—the managerial power view—which has some serious flaws of its own that I address in the next chapter. And I'm not entirely convinced that shareholders consistently respond to percentages of profits rather than to the absolute amount of pay, though they may sometimes react this way.

Although little work has yet been done in this area, group psychology may furnish some more promising leads. The link between firm size and CEO pay may be a sort of self-fulfilling prophecy. Larger firms may pay more because everyone expects them to. They have the resources, and part of the story their boards tell themselves is that they are buying the best talent and therefore need to pay the highest price. Plus, consultants look for peer companies when advising boards about pay. Implicitly, consultants are *telling* directors to pay executives based on the company's size. Such a dynamic may have begun to arise in the 1970s with the increased use of consultants. But this explanation indicates that any link between executive pay and company size is a product of · social norms, not an efficient market.

TECHNOLOGY

As scholars have searched for an explanation for the changes in CEO pay that began in the 1970s, they have looked for some other factor that has changed at more or less the same time that might have influenced executive compensation. If two trends occurred at the same time, they speculate, perhaps one trend caused the other. In the last section, we saw scholars looking at one candidate: growth in firm size. Although that is the current hot theory, we have strong reason to doubt the idea that the larger a company grows, the more it will rationally pay for CEO talent.

Another, more obvious candidate is technology. In particular, two areas of technology have combined to produce a revolution in how we do business in the past forty years: computers and communications. The extraordinary growth of cheaply available computational power, combined with the development of e-mail, smart phones, and the World Wide Web, has transformed the way we conduct our personal and professional lives. Not surprisingly, some scholars have pointed to technology as the reason CEOs are paid so much more now than they were in 1970.

The core idea is this: CEOs are worth more now because technology has allowed them to leverage their talents more efficiently. Companies pay CEOs more because technology has made them worth more.

How might this work? Luis Garicano and Esteban Rossi-Hansberg, the two scholars who originated this theory, postulated that knowledge is an important component in any production process. They also hypothesized that workers are organized hierarchically and at each level can choose to invest more or less effort in learning or investing in new production-related information. Those at higher levels in the hierarchy know more than those below them. As communication technologies improve, leaders are better able to direct workers. As a result, lower-level workers have less need or incentive to learn. Leaders become more important because they can exercise greater control over larger teams of workers. Leaders' knowledge gets applied to more people and to more production processes, making that knowledge more valuable. Conversely, workers' knowledge becomes less important. The workers do not need much knowledge because communications technologies now allow the leaders to direct them more pervasively. The result? The differences among leaders becomes more important and valuable, leaders receive commensurately higher pay (especially those with the most knowledge), and workers' pay becomes more homogenized.[23]

At first glance, Garicano and Rossi-Hansberg's theory does a pretty good job of describing what has happened in public corporations over the past forty years. Communication technologies—e-mail, the Internet, and cellular telephones—have radically improved. At the same time, CEOs' compensation has risen dramatically and workers' compensation has stagnated or even declined slightly.

But when we look more closely, we find a few serious problems. First, the timing of these technological developments does not match up very well with the increase in CEO pay. Cell phones began to come into widespread use in the mid-1980s but did not achieve deep market penetration until the 1990s. Similarly, consumers did not widely embrace e-mail and the Web until the 1990s. CEO compensation, on the other hand, began to rise in the early 1970s and increased dramatically in the 1980s. Executive pay did rise even faster during the 1990s, and perhaps communications technology played some role in that acceleration. But it seems difficult to credit improved communications for a secular pay trend that predated popular adoption of the new technologies by some two decades.

Second, improved communications do not explain the sudden popularity of equity and other forms of incentive compensation. Even if technology improved the value of a good CEO, why would the *method* of payment change? If incentive pay works—if it induces better performance—then it should have worked well before these technologies came on the scene as well as after. Why did companies increasingly include equity in their executive compensation packages beginning in the 1970s? There is no apparent explanation that links technology to payment methods.

Third, there was another technology that developed at around the same time as cellular telephones and e-mail that may have had the opposite effect. Garicano and Rossi-Hansberg themselves point out that database technologies also developed rapidly during the past few decades.[24] Database technologies make it easier for workers to search for and access information. They therefore make leadership *less* important for problem solving. If workers can easily access the information they need to solve production problems, they do not need the help of a leader who has mastered that same information.[25]

The vast improvements in storage and search capabilities and computer processing power tend to counteract the effect of better communications. Enhanced communications make leaders more useful, because they can more easily control their workers. Database technologies make leaders less necessary, because they enable workers themselves to acquire information cheaply and easily. Since both sets of technologies improved in a similar time frame, any impact of the new communications tools would be at least somewhat offset by the new database technologies. Garicano and Rossi-Hansberg acknowledge the potential impact of database technologies but do not satisfactorily resolve the net result of these opposing forces. It seems hard to deny, though, that this dilution of the impact of improved communications technologies makes them a far less likely explanation of the powerful shifts in executive pay.

Fourth, the theory suffers from a conceptual flaw. When we think about how we use e-mail and cell phones, it becomes hard to believe that CEOs are using them to solve workers' problems. Do factory workers or line managers pause when perplexed and e-mail or call the CEO? When faced concretely, that view of the technology seems a little far-fetched. E-mail may help CEOs manage their immediate subordinates, but those have always been—and continue to be—relatively few in number. E-mail and cell phones make communication faster and cheaper. Little evidence exists, however, to suggest they have enabled managers to manage more people or to manage their workers more comprehensively.

In some ways, these technologies may actually impede efficiency. E-mail, for example, is often a little too easy to use to reach large numbers of people. As a result, most of us receive many e-mails a day we could easily have done without. At my own law school, a few colleagues have struggled unsuccessfully to persuade everyone to avoid the "reply all" function when, say, sending a congratulatory response to an e-mail about a new book or a moot court team's victory. How many "nice job" e-mails do we all have to suffer before we develop a norm that protects us? Even if we delete these e-mails without reading them, the filtering process requires more and more time as the sheer volume of e-mail increases. And let us not forget about the spam that bombards us daily, requiring us to install and then monitor junk filters that are chronically both overinclusive (filtering out e-mails we need to see) and underinclusive (permitting unwanted e-mails to pass through). When we consider the way we actually use cell phones and e-mails, as well as the timing issue, the failure to explain the shift in pay structure, and the impact of database advancements, technology seems an unlikely explanation for the changes we have witnessed in executive pay over the past few decades.

RATCHETING/COMPANY IMAGE

Male peacocks are famous for their bright, beautiful, and enormous tail feathers. These same tails that delight zoo visitors have long posed a dilemma for evolutionary biologists. Evolutionary biologists believe the impersonal forces of evolution slowly but inevitably cause species to adopt traits that help individuals pass on their genes, often by making it easier to survive in their environment. The tails sported by male peacocks present a serious challenge to this belief. Bright, beautiful tails may be lovely to look at, but they also seem maladaptive to survival in the wild. The same bright colors that attract a mate may also attract predators, and the long feathers that show off those bright colors make it harder for the peacock to escape. Why, then, do male peacocks have such long, beautiful tail feathers?

One answer, proposed by Amotz Zahavi, is the handicap principle.[26] Suppose you are the genes that make up an extraordinarily healthy and fit male peacock. You would like to let all the female peacocks know this so they will mate with your peacock, replicating you many times in the next generation. That is how genes win the evolutionary game, by being copied into as many offspring for as many generations as possible. (Note that it's the *genes'* perspective we care about here, not the individual peacock's.) You could just have the male tell the females he's fit. But the females are unlikely to take him at his word, and besides, peacocks have a very limited vocabulary.

Instead, one strategy the genes might adopt is to add some very obvious and very obviously maladaptive trait. That trait then serves as an advertisement to the females of the species that the male's *other* traits must be outstanding. Otherwise, how could he possibly have survived so long with, for example, an enormous, brightly colored tail that must read to predators like an "all you can eat" sign? This is the handicap principle, the idea that maladaptive traits might actually help genes replicate themselves by serving as a credible signal to the opposite sex of general health and fitness.

A similar principle has been used to explain CEO compensation. Corporations and healthy male peacocks face a similar challenge. They both need to signal to the outside world that they are unusually fit and healthy. Corporations, unlike peacocks, have a host of verbal tools at their disposal, including some pretty credible ones. Federal securities laws require extensive disclosure of public companies' financials and also impose severe penalties for lies and misleading statements or omissions in those disclosure forms.[27] Even so, financial statements are sufficiently complicated, and necessarily incorporate so many judgment calls where reasonable people could differ, that investors might not trust them as much as companies would like. More important, these disclosures are long, complicated documents and do not make for easy reading. As a result, they are not particularly salient; they don't jump out at investors and scream "buy me" the way a peacock's tail might scream "eat me."

One strategy corporations might adopt to help investors see their underlying value is to pay their CEOs an extraordinary sum of money, in line with the amounts spent by the leading corporations on their own chief executives. By assumption, the industry leader must have an excellent CEO, otherwise how could it have achieved its position? Directors may reason that investors will believe CEOs who are paid the same amount are similarly capable. CEO pay is a highly visible statistic, something the financial press—and even the popular press—is likely to notice. Paying an executive in line with the very best in the industry may be a way for a company to signal credibly that it too is an industry leader (or will soon become one under its expensive—hence valuable—CEO's leadership).[28]

If this theory is correct, we should observe a one-way ratchet in CEO pay. That is, we should see companies raise their executives' salaries each year to match those companies at the very top of the pay scale (at least within the same industry). If companies do this consistently, CEO pay should rise rapidly across the board. And, from 1970 through 2000, that's just what CEO pay has done. But, as we continue to see with each of these efficiency-based explanations, this theory does not explain why CEO pay was more or less stagnant from the mid-1940s through 1970, nor does it help us understand why executive compensation took a nosedive in 2001 and 2002 and then stabilized during the following decade before beginning to rise again in 2010. And of course, it also does nothing to help us understand why the structure of executive pay changed so markedly beginning in the 1970s. Overall, this explanation does not appear particularly convincing.

TOURNAMENTS

Imagine a marketing professional for a large manufacturer of computer servers. Her job is to help develop a national marketing campaign to assist the direct sales team in persuading businesses to buy the company's servers. Although the campaign will be an important determinant of the following year's sales, the efforts of the direct sales team will also be critical. Plus, she is only one of a team of fifteen marketing professionals at the company working on this campaign.

The company offers the marketer two choices for the bonus component of her compensation. The first option is pay for performance, in which the company will look at the total server sales for the year, attempt to determine the marketer's individual contribution to those sales, and pay her a bonus that is a fixed percentage of her contribution to the company's revenues. In all likelihood, this bonus will amount to roughly 20 percent of her base pay. The second option is a tournament. Rather than pay the marketer a bonus, the company will choose the best performing member of her marketing team for a promotion. The promoted member will earn a salary three times the marketer's current pay. Which option would motivate her to work harder?

Tournament theorists argue that, at least for some types of jobs, a tournament is a better motivator than paying for performance. When individual performance is not transparent, the employer may underestimate the employee's contribution. The marketer in our example might reasonably fear that the company will underestimate her contribution to total sales. Sales revenue itself is probably a visible and credible number. But there is a lot of wiggle room in determining the contribution of marketing to the total sales effort relative to the other teams involved—direct sales, design, customer service, and so on. There is even more uncertainty in trying to figure out the value of one member of the marketing team to the team's effort as a whole. Even if the company is acting in good faith, it might well shortchange the marketer in rewarding her contribution. The marketer, aware of this risk, might not put forth her best efforts. Instead, she might divert her energies into ensuring her superiors know about whatever contributions she does make, and perhaps even into fooling them into thinking she has done more than she really has.[29]

A tournament might solve this incentive problem. Advocates of the theory argue that it is considerably easier to rank employees than it is to determine their contributions with any precision. And, in theory at least, a tournament for a prize can provide the same motivation as paying for performance. Employees competing for a prize will rationally discount—and, if risk-averse, excessively discount—the chances they will win. To provide the same motivation as a direct payment, then, the prize must be quite large. Tournament theory therefore predicts that each level in the hierarchy will be paid considerably more than the level below, with gaps between levels increasing in size as we move up the ladder.[30]

Tournament theory may explain why we see such a wide gulf between the compensation the CEO receives and the amount the company pays the executives on the tier just below.[31] Companies may be setting up tournaments to motivate their executives, with the CEO slot as the top prize. And there is some empirical support for the notion that tournaments can motivate people. For example, one study looked at professional car races. The reward for professional races differs from race to race, so the researchers were able to compare drivers' performance in races where the prizes were more closely clumped together with those races where the top finishers received much more than those who drove more slowly. The study found that drivers had faster times when the spread between prizes was greater. This is the result predicted by tournament theory.[32]

But, as the study's authors readily acknowledge, studying the impact of tournament theory is a bit like looking for a lost wallet under a lamppost because that's where the light is, when you really lost it down the block. Tournament theory suggests that tournaments are useful when it is difficult or impossible to measure an individual's contribution.[33] But the effect of tournament theory can be studied only in contexts where individual performance *can* be measured. Otherwise, how can we know whether or not the tournament is affecting individual performance? It's unclear how useful it is to look at contexts that are not really appropriate for tournament theory to measure its power to motivate. Quite possibly, in those contexts where individual performance can be observed easily, what is really motivating competitors is some version of pay for performance.[34]

Still, there is empirical data that are consistent with tournament theory in more appropriate contexts. The pay gap between the CEO and the level just below seems to change based on the probability that anyone in that second tier will succeed to the position. As tournament theory predicts, the pay gap is widest when the likelihood of succession seems smallest, such as when a new CEO has just been hired, especially if the new leader came from a different corporation.[35] Also, some studies have found that companies with larger pay gaps perform better, suggesting that tournaments are effective motivators (though other studies have found the opposite result).[36]

This evidence, though, is at best indirect, and may be the result of a number of factors other than tournaments. Pay gaps may be widest when a new CEO is hired, especially from outside, because new, external CEOs are generally able to negotiate higher pay packages. The lower officers, who are staying in their previous positions, presumably see their compensation remain static while the new CEO receives considerably more than his or her predecessor did, thus producing a larger gap. Once the new CEO is in place, the CEO's raises tend to be smaller, allowing the pay gap to gradually shrink during the CEO's tenure.

The relationship between the pay gap and performance is more intriguing. Since the gap is largest when a new CEO comes on board, one possible explanation is that the new CEO tends to improve the company's performance. Over time, the new CEO settles in and stops making dramatic changes. Performance may therefore hit its nadir as the new CEO nears retirement, just as the pay gap is smallest.

At any rate, even if tournaments work as motivators, that does not mean boards are intentionally using them. Strikingly, directors themselves do not justify CEO pay with tournament theory. All public corporations must annually file an explanation of the rationale for the CEO's pay package, the "Compensation Discussion and Analysis" section of the proxy form. Federal law requires boards to describe honestly and accurately their rationale for the CEO's pay. A company typically points to its performance and the need to align the executive's interests with those of shareholders. But I have never seen a public filing justify the CEO's high pay as an inducement to lower-level officers to work harder.

For example, in explaining CEO Jeffrey Immelt's 2010 compensation of over $21 million, General Electric's 2011 proxy form touted the company's excellent performance over the prior decade and past year; the company's stellar growth in earnings; the company's enormous size (one of the ten largest companies in the world as measured by the past decade's earnings); the substantial changes the executives had steered the company through in recent years; the fact that the CEO had taken no bonus for the prior two years; the conditions on compensation that tied executives' pay to the company's performance; and the need to align executives' interests with those of shareholders.[37] Despite this long list of justifications for what can only be described as substantial compensation, there was not even a hint that part of the board's rationale was to inflate Immelt's pay so that his senior executives would feel greater motivation to succeed him.

If tournament theory correctly describes the rationale for executive compensation, we would certainly expect directors themselves to be self-conscious about its use. Otherwise, what mechanism would produce the predicted effects? How would the tournament be set up, if not by the purposeful action of the board? This is not something we could expect the invisible hand of the market to produce automatically, without conscious knowledge of the major participants. And if directors are using tournament theory as a self-conscious strategy, they are legally obligated to disclose that strategy. But they don't. There is an undeniable gap between the CEO's pay and that of the next tier of executives. But we likely have to look elsewhere—such as a widespread perception that the CEO is much more valuable than lower-ranking executives—for an explanation.

Just as importantly, tournament theory does not explain any of the core puzzles of executive compensation. How would a tournament have produced the rapid rise in compensation that began in the 1970s? Why would a tournament lead to the sharp increase in the use of performance-based compensation that also began in the 1970s?

There are other critiques of tournament theory as well, some of them acknowledged even in the pioneering article by Edward Lazear and Sherwin Rosen that first advanced the theory.[38] First, how can tournament theory motivate the CEO? The tournament is designed to encourage lower-level executives to compete for the top spot. There seems little incentive for the winner to keep trying hard once the contest is over. Second, tournament theory depends on being able to pick out the winner from a group of competitors. The very condition that makes tournament theory useful—that it is difficult to evaluate an executive's individual contribution to the company—may make it just as difficult to pick a winner from the crowd of competitors. Third, it seems difficult to square tournament theory with the powerful trend recently for boards to look outside the corporation for their CEOs instead of promoting from within. And fourth, as Derek Bok pointed out some decades ago, tournaments may discourage cooperation among lower-tier executives, interfering with the functioning of the essentially cooperative exercise of running a major corporation.[39] But others have raised most of these arguments elsewhere, and the critiques above should suffice for our purposes.[40]

SUPERSTARDOM

The legend of Midas tells the story of a Phrygian king who turned all he touched to gold. In Ovid's version of the tale, some Phrygians captured the satyr Silenus while he was drunk and brought him before their king, Midas. Midas recognized Silenus and rescued him from his people. Midas feasted Silenus royally for ten days and nights, then returned him to the god Bacchus, who was Silenus's foster child. Bacchus rewarded Midas for the return of his beloved foster father by agreeing to grant him one wish, and Midas responded by wishing that all he touched would turn to gold.[41]

Midas's story then took an unpleasant turn. Since everything he touched turned to gold, Midas found himself completely unable to drink or eat and—in some versions of the story—even turned his own daughter to gold. Not to worry, though, after Midas repented, Bacchus told him the curse could be removed by bathing in the source of a particular stream. Midas went on to a number of other misadventures, including judging Apollo in a music contest (with unfortunate results for Midas's ears).

Midas's story is hardly triumphalist. But the phrase "Midas touch" has taken on a strongly positive connotation. In American culture, we respect, even idolize, those with the "Midas touch" who succeed at anything they try. The superstar explanation for CEO compensation argues that such people exist but are rare and therefore can command a premium price for their services.[42]

Recently, the renowned scholars Kevin Murphy and Jan Zabojnik have advanced a much more sophisticated version of this theory.[43] The story they tell is that the past few decades have seen an increase in the demand for generalized managerial talents, at the expense of firm-specific knowledge. They offer several possibilities for why firms might rationally prioritize general skills. Because of the rising importance of institutional investors and external capital markets, CEOs must focus more on communicating with the outside world and less on managing the company's internal dynamics. Communication skills are general, not firm-specific. Also, Murphy and Zabojnik hypothesize that the advances in managerial science over the past few decades have made it more broadly applicable to any organization. Finally, database technology has also advanced, making it much easier for outside CEOs to acquire firm-specific knowledge after they have joined the company.

Murphy and Zabojnik's theory is consistent with much of the empirical evidence. As their model predicts, CEO pay rose sharply for several decades. Also as predicted, boards have increasingly turned to outsiders to replace departing CEOs. During the 1970s and 1980s, an average of only 15 percent and 17 percent, respectively, of CEO positions were filled by outsiders. This portion increased to 26 percent during the 1990s and to nearly 33 percent in the first half of the following decade. External candidates receive higher pay than those promoted from within, perhaps arguing that they are worth more. There is some additional, more incidental empirical support as well, such as an increase in the percentage of CEOs with MBA degrees, arguing for an enhanced emphasis on formal mastery of managerial science.

What is missing, as Murphy and Zabojnik themselves point out, is any direct evidence of an increased emphasis on generalized skills.[44] We also lack direct evidence of a causal link between any such new emphasis and the observed rise in CEO pay. And the theory fails to address the change in pay structure—a dramatic rise in the use of stock options and other performance-linked pay—for CEOs over this period. Perhaps CEOs with more generalized skills need greater alignment with shareholders' interests, but on the surface it is unclear why this should be the case. One might even suppose the opposite. Managers who have invested in firm-specific skills might fear the loss of the firm more than those who can readily transfer elsewhere. Firm-specific managers might therefore need greater incentives to take the risks diversified shareholders desire.

There are other questions this theory leaves unanswered. The fortunes of external CEO candidates did not begin to improve until the 1990s, or at least the very late 1980s. But CEO pay began rising during the 1970s and accelerated during the 1980s. If the pay increase was driven by a new desire to hire external CEOs, why did pay begin rising a decade or two in advance of the new hiring trend?

Also, how can this theory explain what happened to CEO pay from 2000 to 2010? During that period, remember, CEO pay fell sharply before stabilizing and remaining more or less stagnant for several years. The stock market crashed during this period, which eviscerated the value of many executives' stock options and restricted stock. But nothing prevented boards from making up these losses with new options or some other form of compensation. If Murphy and Zabojnik are correct, boards seem to have voluntarily missed out on a wonderful buying opportunity for managerial talent. Those companies who refused to reimburse CEOs for their devalued options should have lost their chief executives to companies more willing to open the corporate purse. That is generally how markets respond to sudden external shocks such as a stock market collapse. Participants take advantage of others' mistakes until the market reaches its equilibrium price. Why didn't this happen? Why did average pay drop so much? Why did pay then take so many years to regain its upward momentum?

Finally, as I argued in discussing the firm size explanation, it seems hard to credit that the same skill set—in this case, communications skills—could matter equally to all firms in all industries. Murphy and Zabojnik offer some interesting explanations for why some skills might be valuable to all firms, but I am not sure they can explain why these talents should consistently dominate other, firm-specific or industry-specific skills. Some companies might, at some points in their development, badly need access to external capital markets. Those firms might well pay a premium for communications skills. Other firms—or even those same firms at different developmental stages—might prefer cost-cutting skills, which might involve greater technical knowledge of the industry (and probably not the sort of knowledge one can acquire sufficiently by conducting a Google search). Still others might need the ability to spot inventive talent, or to chart a course through changing technologies, or to spot bargains in the raw materials markets. There is just no obvious reason to believe general skills are consistently trumping those more specific to a firm's needs.

A recent empirical study supports my skepticism here. Martijn Cremers and Yaniv Grinstein examined nearly two thousand CEO replacements from Fortune 1500 firms between 1993 and 2005. They found that the vast majority—86 percent—of CEOs came from companies in the same industry as the company they were hired to lead. This percentage holds pretty much constant throughout the period.[45] These results strongly suggest that even when directors hire CEOs from outside their own company, they still believe industry-specific skills are critical (even if not firm-specific knowledge). The Cremers and Grinstein study indicates boards are not looking for generalized managerial talent when they search outside the company to hire a new CEO.

Charles Elson and Craig Ferrere similarly conclude that the superstar theory fails to explain the rise in CEO pay. They argue that the superstar theory requires that there be a market for CEO talent in which companies bid against one another to hire the best CEOs. If such a market exists, we should see CEOs moving from company to company with some frequency. But we don't. They point out that only a small percentage of CEO transitions involved a "raid" of one company by another of its sitting CEO.[46]

Why then do external CEO candidates receive higher pay than internal candidates? Most simply, perhaps external CEOs must be compensated for leaving behind their long-term compensation packages and workplaces where they are already valued and feel comfortable. Or, as Bebchuk and Fried might argue, perhaps they must be compensated for leaving behind their power over their former directors.[47] (I discuss Bebchuk and Fried's theory in great depth in the next chapter.)

Alternatively, boards that are increasingly dominated by outside directors may feel more pressure to justify their hiring choices. Promoting from within may not generate the same credibility with institutional investors or the financial press as finding someone with a proven track record, even if that track record took place at another company in a different industry. Harvard Business School professor Rhakesh Khurana has argued convincingly that boards search for a "savior" who will persuade external constituencies that the directors have chosen the perfect person as CEO.[48] Khurana's explanation fits nicely with the psychological explanation of CEO pay that I present in chapter 8.

Still, Murphy and Zabojnik have captured what I suspect is a widely held intuition that some people can succeed at anything. This intuition may very well be driving the recent trend toward hiring external CEOs, and external candidates may, for a variety of reasons, be more expensive than promoting from within. What remains to be proven convincingly is whether this intuition—that external candidates with proven track records make the best CEOs—is actually true or just comforting and popular. Directors who try to hire Midas may risk having their daughters turned to gold.

GOVERNMENT REGULATION

Sir Ernest Benn, a confirmed capitalist, once said, "Politics is the art of looking for trouble, finding it everywhere, diagnosing it wrongly, and applying unsuitable remedies."[49] Like Benn, economists and finance scholars are naturally suspicious of governmental interference with the free market. Not surprisingly, then, some have pointed an accusing finger at the government to explain the puzzles of CEO pay, arguing that government policy has distorted the market and generated unintended consequences. Two policies in particular draw their ire: the favorable accounting treatment until recently afforded certain stock options and the special income tax rules that govern how public companies must treat the compensation they provide their senior executives.

Until 2004, public corporations could grant employees stock options and not charge the expense of those options against their earnings. The option grant was still disclosed in public filings but generally in a footnote. Because the options were disclosed, most economists agreed that the market took option grants into account when valuing the company's stock. Options reduce the value of a share of stock through dilution. Essentially, the same pie (the corporation) is being divided into more pieces (the shares of stock), making each slice (share of stock) smaller.

Nevertheless, Kevin Murphy has argued that directors (probably irrationally) focused on the company's accounting earnings.[50] These directors might—incorrectly—perceive that the options were effectively free to the corporation because they did not affect the reported earnings. Directors' misguided perception that options were costless to the company might account for the enormous use of options as compensation, even for employees too far down the ladder to have an impact on the company's share price.[51] The Financial Accounting Standards Board changed this rule in 2004, requiring companies to report the estimated current value of the options as an expense to the company.[52] Still, the former rule may have encouraged corporations to substitute options for other forms of compensation, if boards really did perceive options as cheaper. And the rule change may help explain why companies in recent years have started replacing options with restricted stock.[53]

The second legal rule often blamed for increasing executive compensation is section 162(m) of the Federal Tax Code.[54] This provision was adopted under the Clinton administration in 1993 in an effort to curb executive pay. The statute limits public companies' ability to deduct the compensation for the CEO and certain other senior executives to the extent a covered executive's pay exceeds $1 million per year. The first million paid to each executive may be deducted, but every dollar after that must be counted in the company's income (even though the company is really paying that money as salary to the executive).

How could a provision that *limits* executive pay be blamed for *increasing* it? As so often is true about the law, the key is in the exceptions. The statute contains an exception for performance-based pay, compensation that is conditioned on the employee's success. Conventional options count as "performance-based," so companies are free to award their executives as many options as they like (even if total compensation far exceeds the $1 million cap) and still receive a tax deduction for the options' full value.[55] For this reason, many experts have blamed the dramatic increase in the amount of options companies awarded their executives during the 1990s on the enactment of this rule.[56]

Reasonable people might differ on when the government should intervene in the market, or even whether it should ever do so. But most of us probably share the intuition that the government's intervention will have a powerful impact, even if not always achieving the end result policy makers intended. These two examples, though, should make us question that intuition.

The law on expensing options changed in 2004, yet options remain an enormously important component of executive pay packages—an average of 25 percent in S&P 500 firms.[57] There are plenty of other forms of pay that count as performance-related for tax purposes, yet companies continue to use substantial numbers of options. Options do seem to be decreasing in importance, consistent with the perceived cost theory. On the other hand, the decline may also be due to the long-struggling stock market. When a company's stock price stagnates or falls over a prolonged period, options will generally remain worthless. Restricted stock, on the other hand, holds at least some value even in the face of sharp falls in the company's stock price. Restricted stock is in this way less risky than options. The decade from 2001–2011 saw little net growth in the stock market, which may have encouraged executives to shift to a less risky form of compensation.

Consistent with this stagnant market hypothesis, restricted stock had already doubled in 2004 as a percentage of the average CEO pay package in S&P 500 firms, before the accounting rule changed.[58] Restricted stock continued to grow quite dramatically and made up nearly one-third of the average pay package in 2008 (up from about 7 percent earlier in the decade and 15 percent in 2004).[59] The stock market continued to struggle during this period, perhaps encouraging executives to seek the comparative safety of stock over riskier options. Further empirical testing is necessary to determine which of these factors played the decisive role, though perhaps both had some effect.

The impact of § 162(m) is similarly unclear. Careful empirical studies have concluded that § 162(m) had little if any effect on executive compensation as a whole, though it may have had an impact on salary levels at some firms.[60] Certainly the statute could not have affected compensation during the 1980s, before it was passed. Since executive pay levels and the use of options both rose dramatically during that decade, we may need to look elsewhere for an explanation.

More fundamentally, government regulation may push the market in certain directions, but the market has demonstrated a remarkable ability to push right back. Advocates of perceived cost theory such as Murphy argue that boards and CEOs have responded to government regulation strategically, so that the regulations have often produced the opposite of their intended effects. But this leaves open the root question of what creates directors' perceptions of appropriate pay. Murphy may be correct (despite some contrary evidence) that exempting stock options from the $1 million salary cap on deductibility led to a dramatic rise in the use of options. He may also be correct about the many other problematic government policies we have adopted through history, which I unfortunately do not have the space to discuss here.[61]

Why, though, when increasing options led to rapid growth in pay, did boards refuse to reverse course? Why did they go along with spiraling pay? They certainly had the tools to cut back, even though encumbered by admittedly clumsy federal laws such as § 162(m). They could have given fewer options, for example, or capped their value or at least limited other forms of compensation to make up for their increased use of options. Yet directors did none of these things. Government policy may have influenced the form pay took, and may even have helped justify some forms of pay such as stock options. Ill-advised regulations may also help explain some of the apparent inefficiencies in the structure of CEO pay that I discuss in the next chapter. But government policy cannot explain the heart of the mystery: boards' willingness to keep increasing CEOs' rewards. Murphy himself recognizes that government regulation can at most be a contributing factor and that some other theory—such as market efficiency or board corruption—is also necessary for a complete understanding of CEO pay.[62]

To those who, like Benn, have their doubts about government's ability to manage the market effectively, indications that the government has trouble influencing the market may prove reassuring. However inept one may think it is, though—and I am somewhat more optimistic about government than Benn—the government and its policies seem an unlikely source for a convincing explanation of the changes in executive pay over the past few decades.

SHAPING BEHAVIOR

In the former Soviet Union, there was a popular joke: "They pretend to pay us, and we pretend to work." Workers generally had lots of cash, but there were no goods available to buy in the stores. Soviet rubles were not convertible, so Soviet citizens could not use rubles to buy products abroad either. Not surprisingly, a population of workers who were paid in a currency that couldn't buy very much had a legendarily poor work ethic.

The point of paying someone is to motivate them to work. A fixed salary can often suffice to ensure someone shows up to work each day, but what they do once they arrive will depend on a host of factors. For example, an employer who closely supervises the employees may find they rarely shirk. Close supervision is not really a viable strategy for directors of a public company, for reasons covered in chapter 3. Compensation experts have therefore focused on the structure of pay, hoping to motivate CEOs to act in shareholders' best interest by paying them more for achieving the shareholders' goals (which generally involve raising the stock price). In particular, scholars have argued that compensation packages might incentivize executives to take greater risks.[63]

Coming on the heels of the financial crisis, which has been blamed in large part on banks taking on too *much* risk, the notion that shareholders might need to push executives to risk more may seem a bit, well, insane. But this is actually conventional wisdom among finance theorists. The core idea is this: with risk comes reward. Business opportunities compete for investment dollars. Holding all else equal, investors prefer larger returns and less risk. These preferences produce a trade-off between risk and reward; riskier opportunities have to offer a greater expected return to induce investors to buy them.[64]

Most people—and therefore most investors—are at least somewhat risk-averse. They are willing to sacrifice some expected return for an increased certainty of earning some reward. For example, imagine three investment opportunities: Safe, Moderate, and Risky. After one year, Safe has a 100 percent chance of earning a 5 percent return; Moderate has a 50 percent chance of earning a 12 percent return; and Risky has a 10 percent chance of earning a 90 percent return. To keep the math simple, we'll assume that that the other possibility is just the return of capital without an investment gains, or a 0 percent return. Which opportunity would attract your investment dollars? Pause for a moment to consider.

The moment's thought (and perhaps a glance at the last note) shows you the expected return for Safe is 5 percent; for Moderate, 6 percent; and for Risky, 9 percent. Nevertheless, when I present questions like this as a class exercise, most students choose Moderate (even if I've just explained expected return).

Why would anyone choose Moderate when Risky clearly offers a much higher expected return? The usual answer (though it may not hold true for you) is risk aversion; most people are uncomfortable with the chance of earning nothing or losing money. They may be willing to take a chance, but they must be compensated for it more than mathematics would predict. (It's also true that when offered three choices on a spectrum, people tend to choose the middle one. But that's a story for another day.) Most people see this question as involving a single investment. If they only get one roll of the dice, they are not willing to accept a 90 percent chance of earning nothing.

Investors, on the other hand, can afford to be risk-neutral, or at least a lot less risk-averse. They can invest in many companies that adopt a particular strategy, effectively giving them multiple rolls of the dice. Imagine if I told you that for a $1,000 investment, we would roll a hundred-sided die one thousand times, with each roll determining the outcome for a single dollar. Which investment would you choose now? Risky seems a lot less scary if the entire outcome does not depend upon a single roll.

Senior executives are likely risk-averse about the company that employs them. Unlike investors, senior executives cannot diversify their investments in the company. They have tremendous human capital tied up in the business; if the corporation fails, they will lose their job (and may have difficulty finding another one if the failure is seen as their fault). Also, because of the way compensation packages have been structured in the past few decades, they likely have a large portion of their wealth tied up in the company's stock, either directly or through options or other long-term incentive plans. Much as they would love to see the company earn outsized returns, they may fear failure too greatly to bet the company's money on Risky. This is bad news for diversified shareholders, who would like to earn the highest expected return.

The challenge for directors, then, is to find a compensation mechanism that encourages CEOs to take risky bets when those bets offer the highest expected returns. (This assumes the risks are diversifiable, but that discussion is beyond the scope of this book.) Most experts agree (though I challenge this belief in chapter 6) that executives will lead companies into riskier, higher expected-value projects if companies reward them for doing so.[65]

Options are considered by some to be particularly fit for this purpose. The economists Ingolf Dittmann and Ko-Chia Yu argue that high stock price growth is an unambiguous sign that the CEO is investing in risky, high-reward projects. Low stock price growth, on the other hand, is an ambiguous signal. Low growth could mean the CEO is sticking to safe investments, which earn relatively low returns for the company. Alternatively, low stock price growth could mean the CEO is taking on the right kind of risky investments, but the company has been unlucky. After all, high-risk investments by definition will often fail. Options work very well as a motivational tool, then, because they appropriately reward executives for successfully raising the stock price but do not punish executives when the stock price sinks. Options are superior to restricted stock in this way, since restricted stock awards do punish executives when the stock price sinks, even though executives may have done precisely what shareholders want them to do.[66]

The wrinkle here is that options are themselves risky. They may turn out to be worth a fortune, but they may also turn out to be completely worthless. Executives, remember, are risk-averse, just as most of us are. To the extent boards substitute options for less risky forms of compensation like salary, they will generally have to pay executives more than they otherwise would.

For example, suppose a CEO negotiated a total pay package—all in salary—of $2 million. The board then decided it preferred to substitute options for half the package. To persuade the CEO to agree to accept this substitution, the board likely could not just offer $1 million worth of options. Even though options are priced at their expected value, so that a purely rational person would be indifferent between $1 million worth of options and $1 million worth of cash, executives are risk-averse. The board must therefore offer more—likely quite a bit more—than $1 million worth of options. The board may find this extra cost worthwhile; if options motivate the CEO to perform a lot better than he or she otherwise would, options may be more than worth the additional expense.

The extra cost of options may account for some of the increase in CEO compensation. As boards have shifted to options, perhaps they have had to increase the expected value of executives' pay packages to compensate them for taking on the extra risk options bring.[67]

There is a lot to be said for this theory. Although, as I discuss in the next chapter, options have come under increasing fire lately, for several decades they were considered the ideal form of executive compensation. And they continue to attract passionate defenders. But while the theory may work as a normative explanation for why boards *should* include options in executive compensation packages, it does not do a good job of describing what boards actually have done.

If directors want executives to invest in riskier projects, and if options are an effective tool to motivate executives, why didn't boards include options in executives' pay packages in significant numbers in the decades before the 1980s? Companies were certainly aware of options in earlier decades; some even used them (though in relatively small amounts). Also, why are boards now turning away from stock options?

Worse for the theory's descriptive prowess, boards seem to be replacing options with an inferior vehicle—restricted stock. Remember that under this theory's view, restricted stock does not induce risky behavior as well as options do because executives who receive restricted stock suffer losses when risky investments fail. Yet the current trend is clearly toward a much wider use of restricted stock, accompanied by a significant decline in the use of options.

In addition, this theory struggles to justify the enormous increase in CEO pay overall. Executives' risk aversion should not vary widely over time, at least not on average. But when we look at how options and total pay have changed over time, they do not seem to have risen proportionately, as we would expect under this theory. During the 1970s, stock options made up about 11 percent on average of the pay packages for executives of S&P 500 companies. During that decade, average executive pay was $1.2 million. During the 1980s, the proportion of stock options increased by 8 percent, and total pay increased by $600,000, amounting to $75,000 per percentage increase in the use of options. During the 1990s, the proportion of options rose another thirteen points, and the total average compensation package jumped by $2.3 million, amounting to $177,000 per point of increase. During the period 2000–2005, the proportion of options increased far less—only five additional points. Yet total pay rose by $5.1 million, over $1 million per point.[68]

The impact of options on total pay seems wildly inconsistent. Why would the premium demanded by executives to take on risky options have varied so widely over time?

There may be an argument that as options have become a larger and larger portion of the total package, the risk faced by executives has risen exponentially, not arithmetically. That argument would be more persuasive, though, if the less risky components of executives' pay had shrunk as options increased. They did not. Salaries and bonuses have risen in absolute terms along with options, though not as quickly. Executives have actually received larger risk-free payments along with their much larger option grants.[69] It is difficult to escape the conclusion that risk inducement cannot explain very much of the increase in total pay executives have enjoyed, nor does it effectively explain the pattern of option awards over time.

CONCLUSION

CEO pay is in many ways the linchpin of our economy. Most economists and finance theorists believe CEOs' motivations stem primarily from the way corporations pay them. Fortunately, we have entrusted some of our smartest and most sophisticated citizens with setting up CEOs' compensation systems. We have given a crucial task to those with the best capacity to fulfill it. We *should* feel confident that the task is being performed in the best way possible.

And yet, we have some concerns. CEO pay exhibits some deeply troubling characteristics. Pay has ballooned since the 1970s in real terms. At the same time, CEO compensation has transformed radically in structure. And executive pay is absorbing an increasing percentage of corporate profits. Should we nevertheless trust that all is well in America's executive suites?

Many leading scholars—especially in the fields of economics, finance, and, to a somewhat lesser extent, law—have suggested that we should. They have marshaled powerful, sophisticated arguments to reassure us that directors have set up efficient compensation schemes, optimally designed to motivate CEOs appropriately (and sometimes with remarkable subtlety). The basic intuition these scholars share is that the CEO labor market is efficient. With so much at stake and with such sophisticated participants on both sides of each transaction, how could the market be otherwise?

This chapter has demonstrated that these justificatory theories fall short. They explain only some aspect of CEO pay over some time period. This limited success should not surprise us. As Frydman and Jenter have pointed out, the theories were mostly designed to explain recent events, so we should expect the theories to fit well with recent data. When we look further back into history, though, especially to the period before 1970, the theories have great difficulty explaining why boards then took such a markedly different approach.[70]

These theories also treat directors as though their interests were perfectly aligned with those of shareholders. As I explained in chapter 3, however, this is an assumption that requires closer examination. Corporate law has not done a very good job of setting up pecuniary incentives for directors to pursue shareholders' interests. Directors may be trying to help shareholders—I believe that they are—but they have very weak financial incentives to do so.

Finally, these theories rely on the market to produce efficient results. But markets work only when the conditions are right. Most relevant for our purposes here, there must be a feedback mechanism that tells the participants whether their predictions were right or wrong. For example, the market in wheat futures periodically has real crop data to grade traders' guesses about future crop yields. Those who guessed right make fortunes, and those who guessed wrong lose them. The CEO labor market has no such correction mechanism. A board never finds out if its CEO was worth his or her pay. It does learn whether the corporation did well or poorly while the CEO was at the helm, but—as I discuss in chapter 7—it can never quantify the CEO's role in generating the corporation's profits. Without any later correction to punish those who guess wrong, the market's pricing mechanism must remain inherently unreliable.

Khurana has detailed other serious flaws in the CEO labor market. He argues that an efficient market would have a large number of buyers and sellers. In contrast, the CEO labor market has only a few buyers at any given time, and these buyers believe that only a small number of sellers (CEO candidates) are worth serious consideration. The process of identifying potential sellers is also problematic; it's not the fluid, transparent process we would expect in an efficient market. Sellers are already employed and may face adverse consequences from their current employers if they publicly apply for a position leading another firm. Similarly, the buyers are generally concerned that if their first offer is refused, analysts and employees will discount whomever they ultimately hire as a second-tier choice. The resulting secrecy is a far cry from the transparency we see in efficient markets.

Moreover, Khurana argues that boards' driving concern is often legitimacy more than talent; the most important consideration is not whether the candidate can do the job but whether important constituencies will *believe* that the candidate can do the job. As a result, the market is "socially constructed"; the market participants' perceptions of other actors' positions are important influences on market outcomes. Again, this is a far cry from the essentially anonymous transactions in an efficient market.[71] A market that departs so far from the ideal should be approached with a healthy dose of skepticism.

In the next chapter, I discuss some theorists who take a radically different view of directors' motivations. Unlike the defenders of executive compensation, these theorists harbor deep suspicions that the system is not only inefficient, but rigged. They argue that directors' incentives are primarily to remain directors. The surest way to keep a board seat, they contend, is to stay in the CEO's good graces, in large part by showering the CEO with compensation.

CHAPTER 5

Incentives Mythology

Picture a room with dark, wood-paneled walls. There is a hint of smoke in the air, as though cigars have just been put out, or are about to be lit. A group of (mostly) men sit around a large conference table. The door is shut, the room is private, and the men are slapping each other on the back, telling each other how wonderful they are, and writing one another checks drawn on someone else's account.

This scene is the nightmare of corporate governance critics, and has been for centuries: the specter of the backroom deal where those without a personal stake sell out those whom they are supposed to be protecting. This is what we fear. The efficiency advocates discussed in chapter 4 mostly assumed directors would act in the shareholders' interests. Few if any of these theorists even addressed the question of what incentives directors have and how well those incentives match up with shareholders' interests. Instead, they seemed to accept unquestioningly the incentives mythology, the notion that directors are one with the corporation and the shareholders.

ORIGINS OF MANAGERIAL POWER THEORY

Not all scholars—not even all economists—share this view. At least since Adam Smith in the eighteenth century, many scholars have believed the nightmare vision of backroom deals is the reality, not the idealized vision of directors implicitly adopted by the efficiency theorists. Smith, one of the founders of modern economics, worried greatly about directors' incentives. While discussing publicly traded companies, Smith wrote:

> The directors of such companies, however, being the managers rather of other people's money than of their own, it cannot well be expected that they should watch over it with . . . anxious vigilance. . . . . Negligence and profusion, therefore, must always prevail, more or less, in the management of the affairs of such compan[ies].[1]

Nearly two centuries later, in the early 1930s, Adolph Berle and Gardiner Means built on Smith's concerns by drawing attention to the separation of ownership and control in public corporations. Berle and Means pointed out that most shareholders owned very little stock in any one company. As a result, shareholders were rationally apathetic, with little incentive to pay much attention to corporate affairs and even less ability to influence them. Directors and officers, who did not own the company, were nevertheless left in almost complete control.[2]

Berle and Means harbored deeper suspicions about directors' conduct than did Smith. Where Smith's concerns were limited to directors' negligence, Berle and Means worried about their malfeasance. They highlighted a few possibilities for executives and directors to profit at shareholders' expense, such as issuing misleading financial statements or trading on the basis of inside information.[3] More generally, they warned, "Where the bulk of the profits of enterprise are scheduled to go to owners who are individuals other than those in control, the interests of the latter are as likely as not to be at variance with those of ownership and . . . the controlling group is in a position to serve its own interests."[4]

A generation later, during the late 1950s, Joseph Livingston, financial editor of the *Philadelphia Bulletin,* applied these suspicions to executive compensation. Livingston argued that executives were paid too much and that this excessive pay was in part the result of self-dealing. Livingston cited a study that had found that corporations that were not controlled by large shareholders paid more to senior managers. He argued that this study "supports the theory that those who are beholden to nobody become generously disposed toward themselves."[5]

In 1980, the University of Chicago economist Eugene Fama, certainly a fan of markets, warned of the possibilities that senior executives might take advantage of their power over the company. While arguing that a company's executives are in many ways ideally suited to act as its directors (since they compete actively with other executives for advancement and have a great deal riding on the firm's success), he also issued a warning. Fama wrote, "Having gained control of the board, top management may decide that collusion and expropriation of security holder wealth are better than competition among themselves."[6] To ameliorate this problem, Fama advocated leavening the board with a few outside directors, who could act as referees overseeing the managers' competition.[7]

In the early 1990s, an insider of the process, the compensation consultant Graef Crystal, published what can only be described as an exposé. Crystal's book blasted the executive compensation system. As a major player in that system, Crystal brought instant credibility to his critique. Although not a scholar, he provided the insights that only a practitioner who has seen the process from the inside can bring. He was particularly harsh on the role consultants (such as himself) played in aggravating the problems. He was also highly critical of compensation packages that did not tie pay closely to performance and particularly opposed the repricing of option strike prices and the widespread use of executive perks.[8]

Around the same time, the law professor and executive compensation expert Charles Elson warned that boards of directors had been "captured" by management. He argued that boards were not really selected by shareholders, since individual shareholders seldom owned a sufficient stake in the company to exercise meaningful control. Instead, he said, "corporate management controls the business."[9] The corporation's senior executives, not the shareholders, chose the directors, so the directors answered to management. The predictable result: directors overcompensated managers. Elson argued that paying directors primarily in company stock would solve this problem by aligning directors' pecuniary incentives with those of shareholders.[10]

Also during the 1990s, former president of Harvard University, Derek Bok, penned *The Cost of Talent*.[11] In a remarkably accessible and prescient work, Bok examined corporate executives, doctors, lawyers, university professors, teachers, and federal officials and how their relative compensation had changed. Bok pointed out that elite lawyers, doctors, and executives had managed to raise their incomes considerably since 1970, yet university professors, teachers, and federal officials had not. He argued that this difference was not caused by an increase in the value the more highly paid professions contributed to society but rather by flaws in the market.

We need an elite doctor, lawyer, or executive because we have some critical task to perform, whether it is saving a life, defending a company's fortunes, or managing a large corporation. Understandably, in such situations we want the very best person available. Yet there are seldom clear and reliable measures of quality for any of these positions. In addition, we rarely know the entire field of available candidates, so we search only the narrow subset of professionals who are familiar to us or our contacts. Moreover, these professionals do not compete on price. To the contrary, offering a lower price is often seen as a sign of a lower-quality provider. Even so, the cost of these services is small compared to what is at stake—a company's fortunes or a person's life. Once hired, the results the professionals obtain are difficult to evaluate accurately. Patients do not readily understand why they have been healed (or why they continue to suffer).[12]

With regard to corporate CEOs, Bok pointed out that CEOs exert significant influence over their own pay. At the time, a CEO typically served as chair of the board and his or her views on who should be appointed to the board had great weight with the other directors. CEOs also had the most to say about both directors' pay and the choice of the compensation consultant who would advise the board in setting the CEO's compensation.[13] Also, Bok argued, corporate boards lacked the resources to police accounting manipulations that may mask mediocre performance as a remarkable achievement. In an insight that foreshadowed later thinking, Bok concluded, "Because few directors will wish to incur the burdens and risks of searching for a new leader, and because they cannot be sure how well potential replacements would perform, the easiest course is simply to recommend increases that are comfortably within the upwardly spiraling norm for top executives."[14] Bok's solutions for these dilemmas—greater transparency, more independent directors, empowering directors to hire independent advisers—have by now all been tried but have had little success in constraining the growth of CEO pay.[15]

BEBCHUK AND FRIED'S ARGUMENT FOR MANAGERIAL POWER

As these examples demonstrate, critics have expressed skepticism about directors' motives for almost as long as there have been corporations.[16] Not until Lucian Bebchuk and Jesse Fried expressed similar views, though, did these concerns receive widespread scholarly attention and credibility. In a groundbreaking article with David Walker and then in a landmark book, *Pay without Performance: The Unfulfilled Promise of Executive*

Compensation, Bebchuk and Fried provided the best articulation for what they term the "managerial power" critique of executive pay.[17]

Directors' Incentives

Bebchuk and Fried began by unpacking directors' incentives. Why do outside directors agree to serve on a company's board? Bebchuk and Fried argued that directors receive a number of benefits, including a salary that typically breaks six figures for large companies. Some companies also provide their directors with free products or services; Bebchuk and Fried cite United Airlines as permitting its directors to fly United for free, for example. Less tangibly, board seats are prestigious and generate introductions to powerful and well-connected directorial colleagues.[18]

Because they want to continue to serve on the board, one might think that directors would take great care to protect shareholders' interests. As I explained in chapter 3, however, corporate governance law empowers directors over shareholders for most purposes. Those candidates nominated by the board almost always win; few board elections are even contested. The key to keeping a seat on the board, then, lies far more in being nominated by the current directors than in pleasing the shareholders. That nomination process, Bebchuk and Fried argue, is heavily influenced by the CEO. Although nomination committees generally consist exclusively of independent directors, the CEO may play a critical informal role both in identifying candidates and in screening those suggested by others. Under normal circumstances, a nominating committee would not select a candidate opposed by the CEO, nor would a candidate be likely to accept the nomination knowing the CEO opposed his or her election.[19]

Directors have another reason to want to please the CEO besides a desire to keep their seats: CEOs control access to a number of rewards they can choose to bestow on favored outside directors. Directors are often executives of other companies, and the CEO can often choose to direct business their way. Lawyers, accountants, consultants, and bankers also often serve as directors. They, too, want the company's business. A grateful CEO might send some of the corporation's business to their firms; an irritated CEO likely will not. For those directors who work for nonprofit organizations, the CEO might direct a portion of the company's charitable giving toward the directors' employers. Even directors who work for profit-seeking institutions may have favorite charities they would enjoy seeing receive corporate donations. The CEO can make that happen, if sufficiently pleased with the director.

A small percentage of companies have interlocking directors, where each company's CEO also serves as a director on the other company's board. Interlocking directors have particularly strong incentives to ensure that each CEO is pleased with the other, since both favors and troubles are easily traded.

Finally, the CEO may influence the directors' pay. Although by law the directors set their own pay, the CEO may affect the outcome by encouraging or discouraging an increase. There is some empirical evidence that boards who pay themselves more also tend to compensate their CEO more generously, and that high pay is associated with worse corporate performance.[20]

In addition to these tangible reasons to please the CEO, directors may have psychological incentives to lavish pay on their leader. The directors work closely with the CEO and naturally form ties of friendship and mutual respect. In that relationship, the CEO is an authority figure. Directorships are part-time positions. The directors are accustomed to deferring to the CEO on substantive business matters. They can and should ask hard questions and demand satisfying answers. But the directors do not have the time, attention, or information to run the business themselves. That is the CEO's job. For general business decisions, although the directors legally have the final say, they are likely to go along with the CEO's recommendation most of the time. If they insist on overruling the CEO very often, they will need to replace him or her with an executive who makes decisions more to their liking. Firing a CEO is considered a drastic step, and even today is not one taken very often.[21]

A group of respectful colleagues, accustomed to deferring to their leader, may understandably have trouble switching gears when it is time to negotiate the leader's pay at arm's length. Rather than jeopardize the harmonious working relationships that are critical to maintaining the business, the directors might reasonably choose to let the CEO have the pay he or she wants. Pay may be easily (in some cases perhaps correctly) rationalized as relatively unimportant when compared to the crucial task of keeping an effective leader happy.[22] (Bebchuk and Fried do not delve very deeply into the psychological mechanisms by which this sort of calculation might take place. I take up this challenge in chapter 8.)

Bebchuk and Fried emphasize that there is little downside risk for directors who choose not to fight the CEO on pay. Directors generally do not have much of their wealth tied up in the company's stock, so they stand to lose little even if they vastly overcompensate the CEO. (Where directors do have more of their wealth dependent on the company's stock price,

CEOs typically receive lower pay.) Directors who are too generous might see their reputations suffer, as Fama and Michael Jensen have argued. But Bebchuk and Fried think this unlikely, so long as the CEO's pay remains within conventional limits. Few would criticize a board for doing what most other boards have done. And even if a board does go too far and arouses a storm of controversy, the negative impact would be diluted by the fact that this was a *group* decision. Responsibility can easily be diverted to the other directors: "I didn't like it. But it was clear the others were for it, so I went along. In retrospect, I should have fought harder against it." Except in extreme circumstances, when scandals result in cases like Enron or Worldcom, directors' reputations should remain safe so long as they stick to conventional amounts and methods of payment.[23]

Information

Information also plays an important role in Bebchuk and Fried's theory. As I explained in chapter 3, CEOs have a substantial information advantage over directors, a consequence of the part-time nature of the board position. In the pay context, boards often attempt to overcome this information deficit by hiring a compensation consultant. Bebchuk and Fried point out, however, that the CEO often makes the actual hiring decision, giving the consultant an incentive to say the things the CEO wants the directors to hear. Even when the compensation committee itself chooses the consultant, the consultant is still likely to frame the information in a way that will benefit the CEO. The consultant will want to please the board, and if the board wants to enrich the CEO, the consultant will oblige. Also, compensation consultants earn a great deal of money by advising corporations' human resources department on employees below the CEO in the pecking order. The CEO has the power to advance a consultant's application to perform this work and also generally has the power to block it. A consultant who alienates the CEO—even if hired by directors to advise them—is unlikely to earn the company's business on other, more lucrative matters.[24]

For all these reasons, compensation consultants have every incentive to provide information in a way that justifies higher CEO pay. As Crystal wrote, "I acted in the full realization that if I didn't please a client, I wouldn't have that client for long."[25]

Crystal described several effective strategies available to the consultant depending on the state of the CEO's compensation and the company's performance. The consultant can perform a compensation survey, manipulating the list of "comparable companies" included in the survey to ensure that the CEO's pay appears to be well below the market average (see chapter 3). If only certain aspects of the CEO's pay are wanting, the consultant can limit the survey to one or two components of the total pay package. For example, if the CEO has been provided with ample stock options but has a relatively low salary and guaranteed bonus, the survey can be limited to salary and bonus.

Assuming the company is performing well, the consultant can highlight the dangers of losing the superstar CEO. Shareholders and the financial press are far less likely to lambaste a board for overpaying its CEO when the CEO is delivering stellar stock returns, but they may well crucify a board who loses a high-performing leader over a few million dollars in pay.

If the company is underperforming, the consultant can emphasize the need for better pay to avoid losing good executives. Stock options whose strike prices are hopelessly out of reach have little value. Talented executives may leave for more lucrative pastures if such issues are not addressed. Consultants faced with a poorly performing company can also trumpet the need to motivate the executives to do better. Boards will often be persuaded that greater pay for performance sensitivity will help boost the company's stock price and agree to provide more options to achieve this goal.[26]

With all these tools available to them and with a powerful incentive to provide information that favors the CEO, consultants are a major weapon in the CEO's arsenal. Bebchuk and Fried argue that the use of compensation consultants—no matter who hires them—boost managerial power significantly.[27]

Constraints on Managerial Power

So far, we have seen that Bebchuk and Fried argue that directors want to keep their seats, that this desire can best be met by pleasing the CEO, and that in addition to these incentive-based motivations, there are a number of psychological, social, and informational reasons the board may overpay the CEO. Nevertheless, there are two forces that might oppose the directors' tendency to favor the CEO on pay issues: shareholders and the market. Bebchuk and Fried contend that neither can successfully combat directors' pro-CEO impulses on compensation.

Bebchuk and Fried identify three methods shareholders have used in efforts to curb CEO pay: lawsuits, voting, and advancing shareholder resolutions. They are deeply pessimistic about each. Lawsuits have proven completely ineffective, for many of the reasons I discussed in chapter 3. Bebchuk and Fried cite one study that found (not very surprisingly) that between 1900 and 1992 courts nearly always upheld executive compensation in publicly traded companies.[28]

Shareholder voting has proven similarly ineffective, at least so far. Even before the SEC mandated a shareholder vote on most option plans, many corporations followed the practice, for a variety of reasons (i.e., for tax-related purposes, to acquire greater protection from shareholder suits, because some states required such votes, and because the stock exchanges required them under some circumstances). Shareholders approved the overwhelming majority (some 99 percent) of option plans put to a shareholder vote. Bebchuk and Fried suggest a number of reasons that shareholders have been so forthcoming with options. Most relate either to shareholders' relatively weak position in the process—having the power only to accept or reject and not the power to propose alternatives—or to the conflict of interest experienced by various institutional shareholders such as insurance companies and mutual funds.[29]

The SEC has recently imposed a new requirement that all public companies submit their executive compensation plans to the shareholders for a nonbinding vote at least once every three years. Early indications are that shareholders will continue to approve executive compensation plans in overwhelming numbers, perhaps for some of the reasons suggested by Bebchuk and Fried. So far, in some 98.5 percent of companies shareholders have voted to approve the executive compensation plans.[30] There have been some notable exceptions, such as Citibank in 2012,[31] but the vast majority of companies have received the shareholders' blessing for their executive compensation plans.

These results may mask the real impact of the say on pay provision. There are some hints that even this nonbinding vote is influencing boards to become a bit more circumspect in their executive pay packages to avoid the damaging publicity shareholder disapproval would bring.[32] And institutional investors may be tolerating pay practices they dislike so they can focus their energies on firms with the most egregious compensation packages.[33] But we have not seen many material changes to either the structure or the amount of CEO pay across U.S. companies, so even this behind-the-scenes impact of a shareholder vote is likely marginal, at least so far.

But perhaps we just need more time. In the United Kingdom, which has had mandatory say on pay for longer than the United States (since

2002), there is some evidence that companies have reacted to substantial negative responses by eliminating particularly controversial compensation structures—such as large severance packages—and by increasing the sensitivity of CEO pay to the company's poor performance. These changes have not decreased overall CEO pay, however.[34] More important, there is no evidence that they have produced pay structures that more effectively tie CEO pay to the CEO's own performance—rather than the company's—or that they have demonstrably improved CEOs' performance. Still, the fact that companies have responded to shareholder pressure may hold some promise for even nonbinding say on pay votes.

Shareholders have proposed resolutions aiming to reform executive compensation. Corporate law requires that these be couched in advisory form, so that even if they pass boards are not required to obey them. Nevertheless, such nonbinding proposals only occasionally pass. Bebchuk and Fried argue that so long as these proposals must remain advisory, they have little chance of reforming executive pay in any meaningful way.[35]

Perhaps shareholders hold little sway over directors, but market forces might act to shape boards' decisions about executive compensation. There are four markets that might exercise some discipline over CEO pay: the managerial labor market, the market for corporate control, the market for additional capital, and the product market. Bebchuk and Fried contend that none of these markets can be expected to restrain executive pay.[36]

The labor market can discipline employees through the promise of promotion and the threat of termination. Neither of these seems likely to have an impact on executive pay. CEOs cannot be promoted internally; they already occupy the top position in the company. And they are rarely fired. When they are, it is generally because of how the corporation has performed, not because they demanded too much pay. CEOs might be disciplined by the promise of being hired to head another, larger company. But pay seems unlikely to be affected by this possibility either. In fact, Bebchuk and Fried argue that the opposite may be the case; CEOs may try to increase their pay to ensure that their next employer has a higher package it has to meet or exceed to secure their services.[37]

The market for corporate control normally encourages management to run the company effectively through the threat of a hostile takeover. Companies with sinking stock values start to look like opportunities to acquire assets at a bargain price. To keep the sharks away, management must keep the share price up. Theoretically, at least, that means running the company well, which includes having optimal executive compensation packages. Bebchuk and Fried point out, though, that hostile take-over attempts are rare to begin with, and seldom succeed. Most compa-nies are equipped with powerful antitakeover protections, such as staggered boards.[38] These protections are generally quite effective at minimizing the risk of being acquired without the board's consent.

Even when companies lose these battles, the executives themselves are generally protected by "golden parachutes," contractual arrange-ments that provide for large payments to the senior executives in the event someone takes over the company. Plus, even highly inefficient pay arrangements are unlikely to have much impact on the company's share price, which may explain why an empirical study found that companies that overpaid their executives were not more likely to be the target of a hostile bid.[39] Still, Bebchuk and Fried state that the market for corpo-rate control has had some restraining impact on executive compensa-tion. Companies with weaker antitakeover protections do pay their CEOs less. But they contend the constraint is relatively mild and leaves ample room for inefficient contracting.[40]

The market for additional capital might hold down executive com-pensation by imposing higher costs of capital on companies with inef-ficient executive compensation. Companies that wish to raise money by selling stock to new investors must persuade those investors that the stock is a good investment. Excessive or poorly structured executive compensation would tend to lower investors' estimation of the firm's value. Companies may try to maximize the value they earn for their newly issued shares by ensuring their executive compensation packages are optimized.

Bebchuk and Fried argue that this market is unlikely to affect execu-tive pay. They point out that corporations seldom turn to stock sales to raise capital. Instead, they tend to use retained earnings or debt. Also, overcompensation or poorly structured executive compensation would not chase investors away entirely, just lower the price the company could charge for its shares. Companies would need to issue more shares to raise the same amount of money, diluting existing shareholders. Executives would suffer to the extent they owned shares of the compa-ny's stock but not nearly enough to offset their direct gains from exces-sive compensation.[41]

Finally, product markets might impose discipline on executive com-pensation. Executive compensation represents a cost the company must absorb and, presumably, pass on to consumers in the form of increased prices for the goods and/or services the company supplies. Just like paying more for steel or energy, higher costs for executive talent should translate into higher prices. In a competitive market, a company that offers the same goods for a higher price will quickly fail.

Bebchuk and Fried believe, though, that product markets are insufficiently competitive to dampen executive pay. Large companies, they argue, often operate in an environment with relatively few competitors, giving them each some market power. The companies can therefore raise prices to some degree without suffering a serious disadvantage in the product market. Alternatively, companies can keep prices the same and pay for excessive compensation out of profits. Cutting profits will hurt shareholders but probably not enough—especially given shareholders' relative lack of power—to cost executives their jobs.[42]

The Role of Camouflage

Where does this leave us? Bebchuk and Fried contend that directors have powerful financial incentives and strong psychological motives to please CEOs. Their desire to lavish pay on their chief executive officer is likely to remain unchecked by either shareholder action or the various markets that might exercise some counterbalancing influence. If Bebchuk and Fried are right about all this, what should the CEO pay universe look like? What kinds of pay devices should we expect to see, and why hasn't CEO pay risen even faster than it has? Why have boards stopped short of awarding CEOs all the company's profits?

Bebchuk and Fried argue that CEOs want to maximize their pay and minimize their risk. That is, they want as much pay as possible, and they would like to avoid having to achieve anything in order to receive their full compensation. This is a rather unflattering view of corporate executives, but we can all probably identify with both desires. Even the most driven and ambitious of us—who plan to achieve great things regardless of external rewards—would probably still prefer to receive the same paycheck even if we fail. (Not that we would ever fail.) Under the managerial power view, like doting parents, directors want to grant CEOs their hearts' desires. If CEOs want to maximize rewards and minimize risks, then that is precisely what directors will try to do for them. Boards will provide CEOs with as much pay as they can and make as little of it contingent on the CEO's performance as possible.[43]

Why, then, don't CEOs receive the bulk of their pay in straight salary? Options, restricted stock, and even bonuses generally come with some risk. Options may remain underwater, restricted stock can decline in value, and bonus targets—no matter how leniently set—may not be achieved. Bebchuk and Fried believe boards face at least one serious constraint in setting CEO pay: outrage. (Although they do not discuss this point, they would no doubt agree that corporate resources also constrain boards' ability to reward their executives, though in large companies this constraint is not terribly restrictive.) Compensation packages that go too far (though what counts as too far is heavily context-dependent) may arouse the ire of important external constituencies. Institutional shareholders may look askance at high pay when the share price and dividend yield are suffering. The company's employees may balk at pay and benefits concessions in the face of largesse for the executives. Most important, the financial and popular press may embarrass the directors by highlighting particularly outrageous compensation practices.[44]

Note that the outrage constraint is in tension with Bebchuk and Fried's argument that external constituencies—such as shareholders and the various markets—cannot effectively constrain executive pay. If directors need not fear shareholders' ability to oust them from the board, why should they care if shareholders are miffed by the CEO's compensation? And if directors are equally impregnable against shareholder lawsuits, they should have little reason to fear adverse publicity. To the extent shareholders and other outside interests can influence directors' behavior, managers' power is less, well, powerful than Bebchuk and Fried have thus far led us to believe.

This is just a tension, though, not a flat contradiction. Managers' power over directors may be considerable, even if not absolute. Some institutional shareholders—especially those with fewer or less direct conflicts of interest, such as public pension funds—may act aggressively in the face of board overreaching. If these institutional investors own a significant share of the company's stock, whether singly or as a group, their displeasure might well pressure the board to act. Similarly, directors may be influenced by reports in the press. Directors care about their reputations for their own sake, as well as for the sake of the career opportunities a sterling reputation provides (and a tarnished reputation impedes).

More troubling, Bebchuk and Fried seem to want to have the reputation issue cut both ways. This is a conceptual problem with their theory. They argue that excessive CEO compensation will not damage directors' reputations when arguing for managerial power's existence, then seem to argue precisely the opposite when making the case for outrage as a constraint on boards' behavior. But it's not too difficult to believe that directors may feel secure in doing as they please as long as no one is watching, yet exercise *some* caution to avoid attracting unwanted attention. And perhaps there is a relativity quality to outrage, so that directors can safely adopt practices within the norm of their peer firms without arousing shareholders' ire, even if all firms' practices are inefficient.[45]

True to their roots in economics, Bebchuk and Fried present a classic scenario of maximization under constraints. Their vision of the interplay between the board and the CEO is one of collusion. Executives and directors share the goal of paying the CEO as much as possible, with as little risk as possible, while still not arousing the ire of important external groups.

The strategy boards and executives have adopted to pursue these goals, say Bebchuk and Fried, is camouflage. Boards and executives want compensation packages to be as large and risk-free as possible while appearing to be reasonably sized and closely tied to executives' performance. It is the *perception* of CEOs' compensation that matters for purposes of avoiding outrage, not the reality. For that reason, say Bebchuk and Fried, "under the managerial power approach, managers will prefer compensation practices that obscure the total amount of compensation, that appear to be more performance based than they actually are, and that package pay in ways that make it easier to justify and defend."[46]

This brings us to a second conceptual problem with managerial power theory, one that Bebchuk and Fried point out themselves. (Remember that the first problem was the tension between directors who need not fear for their reputations when setting CEOs' pay—producing unconstrained managerial power—and those same directors who do fear for their reputations and therefore try to camouflage what they are doing.) To pay the CEO excessively with as little risk as possible, directors must disguise what they are doing. They must make it appear to very sophisticated institutional investors and financial journalists that the CEO's pay is reasonable and tightly related to his or her success in leading the company.

If directors can successfully hide what they are doing from such a perceptive and discerning audience, how can even brilliant theorists such as Bebchuk and Fried catch them in the act? On the other hand, if Bebchuk and Fried can detect directors' efforts to camouflage the CEO's pay, then perhaps journalists, financial analysts, and institutional investors can as well. In which case, how can Bebchuk and Fried argue that directors have successfully camouflaged what they are doing? Either directors can disguise their actions from close examination by sophisticated detectives or they cannot. Are Bebchuk and Fried somehow better positioned to discover the directors' chicanery than these other interested observers?[47]

They may well be. Those who are part of the system may be too acculturated to common practices to recognize their flaws, while outsiders may be more able to see problems in customs that are new to them. Bebchuk and Fried explain this apparent contradiction by arguing that camouflage is successful so long as it works against the target audience; it does not have to hide the truth from everyone.[48]

Although this argument can seem strained at first reading, people do often have great difficulty seeing past their cultural programming. And there are some company practices that are difficult to explain without some nefarious intent such as camouflage. Bebchuk and Fried point out that before the SEC mandated summary compensation tables, some companies would write out the pay amounts in words, arguably to make it harder for analysts to find.[49] While it's difficult to imagine this tactic would fool a sophisticated analyst, it's also difficult to understand what other reason companies could have for doing this. The backdating scandal—in which many companies were caught retroactively changing the grant date of executive stock options to the date when the stock price was most advantageous to the executives—is also hard to explain as an efficient practice unrelated to camouflage.[50] Perhaps journalists and analysts really can be fooled in ways that academics—at least *some* academics—cannot.

Direct Evidence

Even if many companies do seem to try to disguise the amounts they pay their executives, though, there may be a less disturbing explanation than managerial power. Directors may believe that they are doing what's best for the company but that shareholders, analysts, and journalists will fail to understand why their controversial practices are efficient. We need to figure out whether directors are motivated by diligent stewardship (mixed with rather troubling paternalism) or self-serving corruption. What evidence would help us resolve this question?

Direct evidence would be most persuasive. The strongest evidence to support the managerial power theory would be testimony from many directors across a host of different public companies that they purposefully overpaid the CEO in order to keep their seats on the board.

Whether or not Bebchuk and Fried have correctly described the dynamics of executive compensation, such testimony seems highly unlikely to develop. Directors engaged in this sort of nefarious conduct would surely be unwilling to admit it, for fear of the colossal damage to their reputations and enormous personal liability that would certainly result. Even the business judgment rule does not protect directors against actions intended to harm the corporation, such as using the corporation's assets for personal gain.[51]

There is some correlative evidence that managers with more power over their boards are paid more, but it is sharply disputed. Bebchuk and Fried cite studies that show that pay correlates to several measurements of managerial power: weaker boards, the absence of a large outside shareholder, a paucity of institutional investors, and stronger antitakeover protections. Larger boards are arguably weaker, since responsibility is diffused among more participants. One study found that companies with larger boards do pay their executives more.[52] Similarly, directors whose attention is divided among several boards may be expected to pay less attention to each, making the board weaker. The same study found that the more directors a company has who serve on at least three boards, the more the company tends to pay its CEO.[53] Other indications of weaker boards that correlate to higher pay are CEOs who also serve as chair of the board, having more directors who were appointed during the current CEO's tenure, and interlocking directorships. Similar relationships hold for characteristics of the compensation committee, such as the presence of an insider (higher pay) or, conversely, a member who owns a significant amount of the company's stock (lower pay).[54]

In a similar vein, Bebchuk and Fried cite studies showing that the presence of a large shareholder (generally over 5 percent) suppresses executive pay to a degree and tends to result in pay that is more sensitive to the company's performance. The theory here is that a large shareholder will more closely monitor the company's actions and ask tough questions if the directors' conduct seems questionable. This is especially true if the large shareholder does not also have a business relationship with the company and therefore does not have a conflict of interest.[55]

Another possibility is that companies with stronger protection from a hostile takeover could arguably pay their managers less, since they face smaller risks of losing their jobs. Instead, as predicted by managerial power theory, the opposite is the case. Companies tend to increase executive pay after adopting stronger protections against hostile takeovers. Without the discipline of a takeover threat, Bebchuk and Fried argue, managers feel more secure to take more of the firm's profits for themselves.[56]

Note that Bebchuk and Fried argue earlier, when explaining how markets do not significantly constrain managers, that the takeover market does not much hamper executives' ability to persuade directors to overpay them. Yet here, when looking for evidence of the link between power and pay, they argue that the takeover market does have a restraining effect. They avoid this contradiction by saying the takeover market has *some* impact on pay, just not a sufficient effect to shape pay the way an efficient market would.[57] The relatively small impact that stronger antitakeover measures have on CEO pay supports their argument that this market does not heavily restrain executive pay. But the small size of the effect also weakens their argument that the impact of stronger defenses demonstrates the relationship between power and pay.

Advocates of efficient contracting theories have countered this evidence with empirical studies of their own that show that managerial power does not seem to be an important determinant of high pay. The studies cited by Bebchuk and Fried used several indirect measures of managerial power, such as board size and the existence of large shareholders. But perhaps the best measure of managerial power is the number of independent directors on the board.

CEOs are likely to have much greater influence over other senior managers who report to them, such as chief operating officers and chief financial officers. When these insiders hold board seats, they are unlikely to oppose the CEO for fear of retaliation. The CEO is their boss; opposing the CEO could cost the inside directors their jobs. The CEO is also likely to have power over outside directors who are not truly independent because a significant portion of their livelihood depends on the company's favor. Directors who are also the company's lawyers, investment bankers, accountants, and consultants are less likely to oppose the CEO for fear of losing a big chunk of their income. If they displease the CEO, they may find that the company looks elsewhere for its outside advice. These quasi-inside directors should be more independent than inside directors, since their entire livelihood does not depend on remaining in the CEO's good graces. But they can be expected to think twice before actively opposing the company's leader.

CEOs' power should increase greatly with the number of inside and quasi-inside directors on the board, and this measure should easily trump subtler factors such as the total number of directors. Yet as Murphy has pointed out, boards' independence increased dramatically during the 1990s at the same time that CEO pay was rising rapidly.[58] Those directors were also more likely to be paid in company stock, which—according to Charles Elson—should have encouraged the directors to act in the shareholders' interests.[59] If managerial power is the most important cause of rising CEO pay, then why did CEO pay climb most steeply precisely at the same time that managerial power was experiencing its most precipitous decline?

Bebchuk and Fried have replied that takeover defenses strengthened at the same time, boosting managerial power.[60] But here again, they seek to have it both ways when it comes to the market for corporate control. They argue that the takeover market is too feeble a constraint to curb managerial power, yet they point to the weakening of that market as sufficient to offset the effect of the rise of independent directors on CEOs' power. This seems an inadequate response to Murphy's telling point.

A better reply is their view that independent directors are not truly independent. If independent directors are in fact subservient to the CEO, then they will exercise no greater restraint on CEO pay than inside directors do. In fact, they may exercise less restraint, since CEOs with purportedly independent boards can claim to have negotiated their pay at arm's length; when the board is dominated by inside directors the CEO's influence is more obvious and his or her pay harder to justify.[61] This argument is entirely logical, once we assume that independent directors are not really independent. But it depends on evidence of directors' subservience, which is hotly contested.

Stephen Bainbridge has made a parallel argument about shareholder concentration that is even harder to counter. If Bebchuk and Fried's theory is right, managers should have much less power—and a much harder time extracting excessive compensation, whether camouflaged or not—when there is a controlling shareholder. A controlling shareholder has both the power to control the board (by definition) and the incentive to ensure that executives are not overpaid. After all, the executives are being paid with the controlling shareholder's money. Yet Bainbridge has pointed out that corporations that have a controlling shareholder use the same, allegedly flawed compensation structures (such as options that are not indexed to the relevant market segment) that companies without controlling shareholders utilize. If the reason companies employ these flawed pay devices is that powerful CEOs conspire with corrupt directors to camouflage excessive pay as performance-related, why do companies where the CEO has *no* power do likewise?[62]

Yet another powerful empirical critique again comes from Murphy. CEOs' power over directors should grow over time. As the CEO gains the respect and friendship of the directors, they should become increasingly willing to defer to him or her in making business decisions and correspondingly reluctant to arouse his or her ire. The CEO's power should be closely related to his or her time in the CEO position and, perhaps to a lesser degree, to the length of time he or she has spent at the company. A new CEO hired from outside the company should have the least power; one who has served successfully for many years should have the most. If high CEO pay is caused by managerial power, then, we would expect a newly hired CEO—especially one hired from outside the company—to earn significantly less than the outgoing CEO he or she is replacing. But the precise opposite occurs. Outside hires earn significantly more than new inside hires.[63] What's more, these new outside hires earn more even than the departing CEOs they are replacing, despite the fact that the retiring CEOs have had years to develop power over the board.[64]

Bebchuk and Fried counter that directors will still want to please the new CEO, who will soon have influence over their retention and pay.[65] Still, they concede that outside candidates should have less power and therefore earn less pay, holding all else equal. They explain the discrepancy by arguing that all else is *not* equal, that outside candidates tend to be superior to inside candidates. But they provide no empirical support for this proposition.[66] More persuasively, they argue that outside candidates who already serve as CEO of another company are already enjoying the fruits of power over their company's board. To convince the candidate to leave that power behind, hiring boards must offer more pay.[67] This argument is logical and consistent, but Murphy's point remains troubling.

Overall, the direct evidence supporting managerial power is not terribly strong. Directors themselves have not confessed to bribing the CEO to let them keep their positions. The next best source of empirical evidence is the correlative studies that have been done. Although correlation never proves causation, a strong correlation would at least be suggestive that power and pay are related. But the correlative studies have had mixed results. Some studies found a strong correlation, but the studies that looked at the better measures of managerial power discovered no relationship between power and pay.

What's more, Stefan Winter and Philip Michel have recently pointed to a potential methodological flaw in these empirical studies. The studies compare CEO pay with various measures of CEO power. But they often fail to look at two potentially important mediating variables: power utilization rates and the total pool of money available.[68]

Winter and Michel point out that not all CEOs will use their power to the same degree. Some CEOs may try to maximize their pay, but others may be more restrained. Unless the degree of restraint correlates well to the amount of power, differing degrees of managerial constraint could skew the results of the empirical studies. Skeptics may doubt that CEOs exercise much self-restraint in regard to their own pay, but the authors' point is theoretically sound even if the empirical impact is uncertain.[69]

More important, some companies are wealthier than others. The CEO of a small company can only appropriate what the company owns and earns; even if she has total control over the enterprise, her pay will be limited by the company's resources. Company wealth (which Winter and Michel call "cake") may therefore also serve as an important mediating variable. CEOs with lots of power who run small companies may still earn less than much weaker CEOs of larger companies simply because there is much less money available to take. Empirical studies that do not control for company size when comparing the impact of CEOs' power on their pay may produce invalid results.[70]

Indirect Evidence: Inefficient Compensation Tools

Overall, then, the empirical data do not provide clearly persuasive, direct evidence that managerial power explains what has happened to CEO pay. Bebchuk and Fried have therefore sought support primarily from a close examination of the outcome of the executive compensation process.[71] Their proof of managers' influence over the pay-setting process is that pay is set poorly. They argue that boards structure CEO pay using incentive mechanisms that disguise overpayments as compensation for superior performance. In a lengthy, probing analysis, Bebchuk and Fried demonstrate serious flaws in the methods of compensation directors generally use.

Much of their book is devoted to unveiling the hidden inefficiencies in compensation methods in common use. They focus in particular on parting gifts, retirement benefits, bonuses, and options, though they highlight a number of other troubling aspects of CEO compensation packages as well. In each case, they argue that the mechanisms are poorly designed and have the effect of disguising low-risk or even risk-free payments as closely tied to performance. The rhetoric of each of these forms of compensation is that they reward managers only when the corporation prospers, thereby motivating managers to ensure the company's success. In reality, though, say Bebchuk and Fried, managers wax rich under each of these compensation schemes whether the corporation does well or poorly. They argue that the devices are popular because they disguise excessive payments as rewards for excellent performance or because they are harder for shareholders to detect at all.

CEOs leave a corporation for a variety of reasons: because they wish to take a position at another corporation, because a new owner takes over the company, because they are forced to leave by a disappointed board, or simply because they feel it is time to retire. Often when the CEO leaves, the board or the new owner provides a "parting gift," which Bebchuk and Fried argue demonstrates the CEO's use of power over the board.

For example, when a company is acquired, the buyer often makes a large retention payment to the CEO, to secure his or her services. Bebchuk and Fried cite a study that found that CEOs of target companies accepted lower control premiums in cases in which they were promised a position after the sale, perhaps indicating that CEOs were being bribed to use their power over their directors to reduce the purchase price. Similarly, when a board fires a CEO, the directors often provide large payments to the CEO, perhaps to persuade the CEO to accept the termination instead of using his or her power over the board to fight to stay. And at retirement, boards have sometimes awarded the departing CEO additional options or changed the method of calculating retirement benefits in the CEO's favor.

These payments were not generally required to be disclosed, hence "camouflaged" under Bebchuk and Fried's theory. Worse, they were clearly not aimed at inducing better performance, since they took place as the CEO was leaving and without a prior promise that might have encouraged stronger efforts while the CEO was in office.[72]

CEOs' retirement benefits also seem inefficient, as Crystal noted.[73] Companies generally provide some form of retirement benefits for their employees, at every level. But ordinary employees receive retirement benefits only to the extent the benefits are subsidized by a tax benefit, making them a cheap way for the company to compensate its employees. Senior executives, on the other hand, receive pensions, deferred compensation, postretirement perks, and sometimes consulting fees even when these benefits have no tax advantages. These payments are entirely independent of the CEO's performance and until recently could mostly avoid disclosure.[74] That is still true for some forms of these benefits, such as post-retirement consulting income. Bebchuk and Fried argue that boards are awarding CEOs these retirement benefits because they are a form of compensation that is less apparent to shareholders, allowing directors to reward CEOs without alerting stockholders to the overpayments.

While this argument is intuitively appealing, at least one study has found that pensions were not easily camouflaged even before the recent changes in SEC regulations required enhanced disclosure.[75] Though hardly determinative, this study casts some doubt on Bebchuk and Fried's contention that CEO power produces these retirement benefits. If they cannot be hidden from investors, they are fully subject to the outrage constraints and so are not terribly useful for directors trying to avoid shareholders' notice of their excessive compensation practices.

Bonuses should be the most direct example of paying for performance. The core of pay for performance theory is that if boards promise CEOs large sums for achieving certain goals, CEOs will be more likely to reach those goals. Bonuses implement this theory simply and directly by setting performance goals that trigger a CEO's right to large payments. Bebchuk and Fried, who advocate strongly for pay for performance mechanisms, should love bonuses.

But they don't. Instead, Bebchuk and Fried argue that boards manipulate bonuses to reward CEOs whether or not the CEOs themselves have achieved anything noteworthy. Because the payments come in the form of a bonus, they appear to be performance related (and hence deserved). But the reality is quite different. Boards set performance goals relative to the company's performance in prior years, not relative to how other companies in the industry are doing. As a result, a company that improves a bit can end up paying large bonuses to its executives even if it is the worst performer in its industry. Studies have shown that there is very little correlation between a company's performance compared to its industry peers and the senior managers' bonuses and salary increases. Instead, boards reward managers for "lucky dollars"— money the company earned because of events outside its control, such as changes in exchange rates or increases in oil prices—exactly the same as dollars earned because of superior strategy or decision making. These results are hard to square with the notion that directors are supposed to be using bonuses to motivate better performance from their executives. But they make sense to those—like Bebchuk and Fried—who believe directors use bonuses to disguise excessive payments to CEOs.[76]

Options became enormously popular in the 1990s as a way to provide CEOs with powerful incentives to focus on boosting the company's share price. An option is the right to buy a share of the company's stock for a set price, called the exercise price. Options become more valuable as the stock price rises above the exercise price. Shareholders' primary concern is to increase the stock price, so a compensation device that encourages CEOs to take that concern seriously seems like an excellent solution to the core corporate governance dilemma discussed in chapter 3: the separation of ownership and control in public corporations. During the 1990s, options became the largest component of CEO pay, accounting for nearly half of CEOs' total package by 2000.[77]

Yet options have been increasingly criticized over the past decade, for reasons Bebchuk and Fried articulate very clearly. The main problem, they say, is that options reward executives for changes in the broader stock market that have nothing to do with how the company has performed (much less how the particular executive has contributed to the company's success). During a bull market—especially the kind of historic bull market we experienced during the 1980s and 1990s—options become much more valuable even if the company is just treading water.

In fact, the bulk of stock price movements may be the result of factors having nothing to do with the company's particular situation, at least according to one careful study.[78] Changing interest rates, industry trends, new technologies, the price of oil, and the overall health of the economy all move stock market prices and together may have a larger impact on a company's share price than any particular strategic move the CEO implements. By rewarding executives for general stock market movements, options provide the illusion of paying for performance without the reality.[79]

This central problem with options could easily be avoided through a variety of relatively simple adjustments, such as indexing the options to the market as a whole or to the relevant industry segment. But few companies have used indexed options, even though they would do a much better job of encouraging CEOs to improve the company.[80]

Options may also fail to provide the close alignment with shareholders' interests that they initially promised. An option holder is not in the same position as someone who owns the company's stock. Options become more valuable when the share price vacillates more widely, because large shifts in the stock's price give the option holder more opportunities to cash out at an advantageous time. Even if the cost of increasing volatility on the high end is a larger risk of sharp declines, an option holder should prefer to gamble. Option holders face far less danger from a decline in the stock price than stock owners do because they have less invested. Stock owners have paid the full market price of the stock. They stand to lose up to the full purchase price if the stock value crashes.

Option holders have paid much less for their opportunity to share in the stock's upside potential. On the open market, options typically cost a fraction of the full price of the stock (though the precise price will vary based on the strike price, the option's duration, and a number of company-specific variables). When companies pay executives with options, the options presumably take the place of cash compensation in an amount roughly equivalent to the market value of the options, so that the executives "pay" for the options by giving up an equivalent value of cash. (Lots of hedging is required around this assumption, but it will do for present purposes.) If the stock price rises, option holders gain dollar for dollar with the stockholders. But if the stock suffers a precipitous decline, option holders lose far less (on a per share basis) than shareholders do.

Executives who hold stock options therefore have an incentive to take large chances with the company in the hope that their options will become valuable. They have much to gain and comparatively little to lose. (Though note that executives have a lot of human capital invested in the company. If they take too many risks and destroy the company, they will lose their jobs and may have trouble finding another company willing to risk hiring them. For this reason, some experts have argued that options may help offset executives' natural risk aversion, encouraging them to take the level of risks that diversified shareholders would prefer.)[81]

There is also evidence that options provide an incentive to manipulate the release of company news and to engage in other unsavory practices, such as backdating. Since strike prices are generally set at the market price at the date of the grant, executives can benefit by suppressing market prices just before they receive options. Several studies have documented that companies seem more likely to release bad news just before option grant dates and to release good news after option grant dates.[82] Another study, by Erik Lie, uncovered the widespread corporate practice of backdating the stock option grant date to pick the day with the lowest stock price in the relevant period.[83] Interestingly, the backdating scandal broke some two years *after* new SEC regulations made backdating theoretically impossible by requiring that option grants be reported within two days of grant.[84] But there is substantial evidence that many companies have violated these new rules in order to continue to backdate options.[85]

Despite all these apparent flaws, options have staunch defenders, who argue that they are an efficient form of executive compensation.[86] I discussed a number of the justifications for companies' extensive use of stock options in chapter 4, such as government regulations that make conventional options tax deductible and options' incentive effects. But Bebchuk and Fried present a persuasive case that options could be designed to be much more effective and less costly. They argue that boards like to use options as part of executives' compensation because options justify large paychecks with the (illusory) appearance that the boards are just paying for the executives' outstanding performance. Options make large pay packages easier to justify, without actually conditioning executives' pay on their performance.[87]

The evidence Bebchuk and Fried present that many of these compensation mechanisms are far from perfect is powerful and convincing. Defenders of the current system have mustered creative and interesting arguments for why the apparent flaws are really virtues, many of which I discussed in the previous chapter. But for the most part, these arguments require far more complexity and sophistication in the design of executives' compensation than Bebchuk and Fried's more direct explanations and set forth more far-reaching assumptions. Occam's razor seems to favor Bebchuk and Fried.

Alternative Explanations for Flawed Compensation Tools

Although Bebchuk and Fried make a good case that compensation packages could do a much better job of tying CEOs' pay to their performance, the next step in their syllogism is considerably weaker. Just because compensation methods are imperfect does not mean they are the product of corruption. Bebchuk and Fried's evidence works much better as a rebuttal of the theory that CEO pay is efficient than as proof of corruption. Compensation packages are not optimally designed to motivate CEOs to perform (at least, that seems the better conclusion based on the evidence available to date). The reason *why* they are imperfect, though, remains open to debate. There is nothing in particular about the ways directors have compensated CEOs that singles out managerial power as the causal force. And the direct evidence of power's impact is rather mixed. At best, the evidence seems to indicate that greater managerial power may have some effect on aspects of executive compensation packages. But the existing evidence is a far cry from persuasive proof that managerial power is the primary cause of the inefficiencies Bebchuk and Fried catalog so aptly. Managers' influence over directors may be part of the cause, or it may not.

Bebchuk and Fried acknowledge the possibility of other explanations for the use of flawed compensation methods, but they give alternatives short shrift. They identify two: norms and mistakes.

Social norms do slow change, they argue, but cannot shape the change that occurs. For that, we need some additional theory such as optimal contracting or managerial power. As I argue in the next chapter, Bebchuk and Fried greatly underestimate the power of social norms. They do not just make change more difficult; on the contrary, they can greatly accelerate changes. Bebchuk and Fried mistake social norms for tradition, arguing that all they do is make current practices "sticky."[88] As I explain in the next few chapters, this is far too narrow a view of norms. Norms such as the deeply held notion that hiring the right leader is critical, regardless of cost, can cause huge changes, especially when they combine with certain others, such as pay for performance.

Bebchuk and Fried contend that mistakes, perhaps caused by cognitive biases or directors' lack of time and information, also seem unlikely to act as the root cause of directors' use of flawed compensation structures such as options. They give several reasons. First, the flaws in such devices are not terribly complicated, so it is not credible to argue that sophisticated managers and advisers have overlooked them. Second, if mistakes were at the root of the issue, we would not expect to see the mistakes tilt consistently in managers' favor, as they do. Third, if directors' mistakes are a major reason for their use of poorly designed compensation devices, their mistakes are part of managers' power. Managers are unlikely to share directors' misperceptions, so directors are using these devices because they lack the information and time to design more effective compensation packages. Directors' lack of time and information is one of the three sources of managerial power Bebchuk and Fried have identified (the others are directors' financial and nonfinancial incentives to favor managers and social and psychological factors). Fourth, misperceptions cannot explain all the observed data. Firms have used a number of compensation devices—such as retirement plans and executive loans—in ways that seem designed to hide compensation.

Plus, there is the evidence discussed above that managerial power correlates with their pay.[89]

Bebchuk and Fried's first argument—that the mistakes are obvious—contradicts their theory that these devices are chosen precisely because they effectively camouflage compensation as performance related. Either the flaws are obvious—in which case, they can hardly be camouflaged from sophisticated institutional investors and financial journalists—or they are not—in which case, directors and even managers might reasonably use them in error. Their other arguments mostly consist of incorporating mistakes into their managerial power theory. To the extent that managerial power includes cognitive biases and other psychological phenomena, the theory is consistent with the view I will present. But much of their theory—especially the argument that directors try to camouflage excessive pay—seems to depend on purposeful acts of corruption by directors. This kind of strategic betrayal of shareholders' interests cannot be explained by well-meaning mistakes. At heart, then, their theory conflicts strongly with my perspective.

Note also that their conception seems to require that only directors—in particular, independent directors—fall prey to these errors and other psychological influences. Managers presumably understand fully that devices such as options and retirement plans act to disguise excessive compensation as performance related. In fact, Bebchuk and Fried state as much.[90] The CEOs then take advantage of directors' mistakes or psychological weaknesses to persuade them to adopt these devices as part of the CEOs' compensation packages.

This, too, contrasts sharply with the view I will present. I do not believe managers stand above directors, somehow able to see what directors cannot. The independent director of one firm is often the CEO of another. Does the same person understand the flaws in compensation when acting as a CEO but lose that understanding when acting as a director? The psychological dynamics that I will argue are the true root cause of the behavior we observe in the executive compensation system are powerful precisely because they produce views that are widely shared by executives and directors alike.

CONCLUSION

Managerial power theory has contributed two important insights to our understanding of CEO pay. First, the theory points out that optimal contracting scholars have fallen victim to what I call the corporate personality myth, the illusion that the board and the corporation are synonymous. Directors are human beings with interests that sometimes align and sometimes diverge from those of the corporation itself (to the extent we can identify what it means to say the disembodied corporation has interests). Managerial power scholars conclude that directors are choosing their own interests over the corporation's, using the corporation's money to bribe the CEO to keep them on the board.

I disagree with this conclusion for a number of reasons, including skepticism that the rewards are sufficient to tempt generally wealthy directors and some faith in directors' integrity. As I pointed out in chapter 3, board members' pay generally pales in comparison with the compensation they receive for their full-time positions, making it difficult to believe that their directors' salaries could suffice as a bribe to sacrifice their integrity and risk their reputations. Also, the empirical evidence for this theory is rather weak. But the argument may be correct in some unfortunate instances, and the larger point that we need to pay attention to directors' own incentives is important and valid.

Managerial power theory's second contribution is the observation that existing compensation structures are often deeply flawed. If we take optimal contracting theorists' view as correct that the goal of executive compensation should be to tie executives' compensation to their job performance (though as I explain in chapter 6, I strongly disagree with this goal), then the most popular devices such as stock options and bonuses are not serving this function very well. The theory's arguments about the flaws in popular compensation devices such as stock options and bonuses seem cogent and correct.

I am less sanguine about the conclusions managerial power theorists such as Bebchuk and Fried draw from these observations. Boards may be using subpar compensation devices for a number of reasons, not necessarily in an effort to camouflage excess pay. It seems most likely to me that directors *and* executives may simply be mistaken about the utility of these devices, for reasons I explore in chapter 8. And even if camouflage is part of directors' purpose, the desire to hide or disguise pay may also be due to reasons other than managerial power. For example, directors may sincerely (though perhaps incorrectly) believe executives are worth a great deal but worry that outsiders will not understand the enormous benefits of hiring the right person. They may harbor particular concerns about the judgment of groups like the popular press and employee labor unions. Directors may therefore try to disguise pay out of a (likely misguided) sense that they are doing the right thing for the company. Directors may be trying to prevent those with less understanding of the corporation's needs from inhibiting their efforts to run the corporation properly.

Managerial power theorists have taught us that the CEO labor market is probably not producing an efficient result, either in terms of the amount of pay or in terms of the compensation devices that try to tie pay to managers' performance. But the theory is less successful in identifying the reasons the market has failed. In the next three chapters, I present an alternative theory rooted in individual and group psychology that offers a better explanation of the flaws in the CEO labor market.

PART TWO

What's Really Going On?

CHAPTER 6

Performance Pay Mythology

Hewlett-Packard was once one of the most well-respected corporations in the country. Famously founded in a one-car garage just before World War II by Bill Hewlett and Dave Packard, the company eventually grew into the largest computer manufacturer in the world. Hewlett and Packard utilized a management style that became deeply ingrained in the company's identity, one focused on hiring the best people and then trusting them with as much authority as possible.[1]

HP's people-centered management philosophy, combined with its colossal success, helped build its reputation as one of the best-managed firms in the world.[2] The company has struggled more recently,[3] but the story I want to tell here took place in the early 1990s, during its heyday. Despite a widespread belief that the company's management style was the bedrock of its success, senior management decided to permit some small-scale experimentation with an alternative—paying workers based on their performance.

It's not surprising that HP's executives would be attracted to this management strategy. Paying for performance was an idea that already had a long and distinguished pedigree when HP decided to try it out. Frederick Taylor popularized the idea of incentive pay in the early twentieth century.[4] Taylor theorized that workers paid according to their output would be more productive than if they were simply paid by the hour or the day. His theories were enormously influential, and today Taylor is widely regarded as the father of scientific management.

Taylor's theories received indirect academic credibility some decades later through the work of the psychologist B. F. Skinner. Skinner developed the theory of operant conditioning, the notion that behavior that is followed by positive reinforcement is more likely to be repeated (and the inverse).[5] Skinner developed empirical support for this theory through animal studies, demonstrating that animals could be taught certain behaviors if the behaviors immediately resulted in rewards. Like Taylor, Skinner believed that rewards motivated behavior.

These behavioral theories seeped into the corporate governance world in the mid-1970s with the work of the economists Michael Jensen and William Meckling. In a paper that has been cited over thirty thousand times, Jensen and Meckling developed the theory of agency costs. As Berle and Means recognized in the 1930s, executives run public corporations but do not own them, while shareholders own public corporations but do not run them.[6] The central problem in corporate governance is finding a way to bring these two conflicting groups together, to persuade executives to pursue shareholders' interests and not their own.

Jensen and Meckling theorized that principals (such as shareholders) must bear costs to persuade their agents (such as corporate executives) to act in the principals' interests. "Agency costs" include these monitoring costs as well as agents' bonding costs (costs agents bear to persuade principals they are trustworthy) and the residual loss from agents' remaining departures from ideal behavior. Jensen and Meckling emphasized that one way executives and shareholders can minimize agency costs is to set up an executive compensation scheme that creates incentives for executives to act in the shareholders' interests.

Jensen and Meckling mentioned stock options as a device that is particularly useful in reducing executives' risk aversion. Economists presume that shareholders diversify their investments, buying stock in different companies to minimize the risks associated with each individual firm. Diversified shareholders should want companies to take big risks—so long as the expected payoffs make the risks worthwhile—because the profits they earn from companies whose risky investments succeed will more than offset the losses from those that fail. (Again, we are assuming these risky investments have high expected returns.) Options are useful because they allow executives to share stockholders' gains from the sort of high-risk, high-yield investments that diversified shareholders want the corporation to make.[7]

Just before HP began fiddling with pay for performance incentive mechanisms, the U.S. government gave the theory its implicit blessing through an amendment to the tax code. While running for president, Bill Clinton had railed against excesses in CEO pay and vowed to pass a law that would bring executive compensation back down to earth. After his election, Congress passed and President Clinton signed a bill that barred public corporations from claiming tax deductions for chief executive pay in excess of $1 million. But the law had a critical exception: pay that was performance related could be deducted in any amount.[8] The rationale for this exception presumably was that unlike salaries, which were guaranteed and could reflect cronyism, compensation that was tied to performance was beneficial because it would induce better performance. Even if executives still became wealthy, performance pay would guarantee that the rest of the country (or at least shareholders) benefited also.[9] So the HP executives who approved the experiments in performance pay were in very good company.

HP executives approved over a dozen pay-for-performance programs at the request of local managers. The programs were spread throughout the United States and five other countries but were almost entirely limited to blue-collar workers. As I discuss later in this chapter, blue-collar work is often much better suited to this sort of motivational tool than more creative or analytical tasks. Note also that the local managers asked for these programs; they were not imposed by fiat from above.

With enthusiastic managers implementing the program for blue-collar workers, the circumstances were ideal for a pay-for-performance mechanism to succeed. Yet, within a year, all the local managers had canceled their programs. They derided them as time-intensive, expensive, and, worst of all, ineffective.[10]

What went wrong? This was a well-managed company implementing a time-honored incentive scheme under ideal circumstances. One possibility is that there may have been some implementation problems unique to these experiments. For example, many of the pay-for-performance programs were aimed at teams rather than individuals. These systems raised mobility barriers as successful teams resisted adding members from teams that were struggling.[11] But the core problems went much deeper than this, to the very notion of paying for performance.

Promising rewards for improved performance is a highly intuitive way to persuade someone to do better. It resonates with popular child-rearing techniques, such as conditioning a weekly allowance on chore completion or cajoling children to focus on their homework by promising gifts for better grades. It also corresponds to economic theory, which has at its core the axiom that incentives motivate behavior. And it meshes well with our sense of how people operate. Wouldn't you work harder if someone promised you a big payday for success?

Pay-for-performance theory is intuitive, experiential, theoretically sound—and quite likely wrong.

How could this be? Doesn't money motivate? And if we're motivated, don't we work harder and smarter? Questioning pay for performance is rather like questioning gravity. It's a theory that encompasses our daily thought so completely—especially among businesspeople—that it's hard to conceive that it might be steering us in the wrong direction. The appeal of pay-for-performance mechanisms is not limited to directors; shareholders and scholars have also embraced the strategy. In fact, Institutional Shareholder Services, the leading proxy voting adviser to institutional shareholders, says in its proxy voting guidelines, "Pay-for-performance should be a central tenet in executive compensation philosophy."[12] Even the leading critics of CEO compensation plans, Lucian Bebchuk and Jesse Fried, strongly advocate tying pay more closely to performance.[13] But when we look for empirical evidence that will validate the theory, as applied to CEOs, we come up short.

Before I plunge into the mountain of research on this topic, it's worth pausing a moment to try to understand why conditioning rewards on outcomes might *not* produce better results. Let me start by narrowing the field a bit. My concern in this book is how we pay senior executives, not workers on the assembly line. Motivational techniques that might work beautifully when the task is boring and repetitive—say, soldering a component to as many circuit boards as possible—can have perverse effects when the task is creative or analytical, like developing a marketing plan. Paying for performance seems to work quite well for mechanical tasks but may actually impede performance when the task requires high-level thinking.

Intuitively, this may be true for a number of reasons. First, the people who rise to the highest executive ranks may be so internally driven that extra motivation is unnecessary. Performance pay may be like using a treat to persuade a dog to leave the house when the dog is already impatient to go outside. Second, executives may experience performance pay as controlling, even condescending; it may transform a collegial relationship between the board and the CEO into one that is more hierarchical. Third, it may encourage executives to focus on improving the metrics that trigger higher pay even when doing so harms the company. For example, an executive might try to boost this year's profits by cutting back on research into new products. Fourth, tying pay to performance may induce some executives to cheat. And fourth, conditioning a lot of pay on achieving certain goals might prove distracting. Rather than focusing on achieving those goals, executives might spend too much time thinking about how their lives would change if they earned all that money, or they might worry excessively about how badly they would feel if they missed this chance at a small (or not so small) fortune.

Raising these possibilities should not suffice to persuade anyone that one side or the other in this debate is correct. The utility of performance pay is an empirical question, and only empirical evidence can definitively answer it. Fortunately for us, many economists and finance scholars have tackled this issue from a variety of perspectives, producing mounds of data.

ECONOMETRIC STUDIES

Economics and finance are disciplines that firmly believe in the power of incentives to produce behavior, so we could be forgiven for expecting some bias in these studies in favor of performance pay's efficacy. Yet these studies—produced by scholars whose training should predispose them to believe in the power of incentive pay—fail to find convincing evidence that paying executives for performance produces better corporate outcomes. To the contrary, the weight of the evidence suggests that performance pay either produces no effect—in which case it is a waste of corporate resources—or actually hurts corporate performance.

A number of studies do find that performance pay acts just as advertised, boosting the company's results. For example, John Abowd examined data on over 16,000 managers at 250 large corporations to determine whether conditioning pay on performance enhances corporate outcomes. He found that a performance bonus of 10 percent was associated with an extra 4 to 12 percent growth in share price, though only a much smaller (less than 1 percent) increase in net profits.[14] Barry Gerhart and George Milkovich took a similar approach, studying 16,000 upper- and middle-level managers at some 200 companies. They, too, found that incentive pay was associated with better corporate results.[15]

Neither study was restricted to CEOs, however, raising serious causality questions. As I discuss in chapter 7, it is far from clear that even CEOs can have much impact on corporate results; subordinate managers would have an even more difficult time changing the company's fortunes.

Some studies have taken a very different approach. Instead of looking at corporations' use of performance pay in the field, these studies designed laboratory experiments to measure the impact of pay-for-performance incentives. For example, C. Bram Cadsby, Fei Song, and Francis Tapon compared the effect of fixed salaries with performance pay and found that subjects working under the performance pay condition were more productive.[16]

Although some studies like this found a positive effect from performance pay, many others—both real-world studies and experiments conducted in the laboratory—have found that performance pay either has no effect or even hurts corporate results.[17] One of the most recent of these (by Harald Dale-Olsen) examined Norwegian corporations and compared results across firms that used performance pay with those that did not. The study found no connection between a company's use of performance pay and its productivity. Executive pay was higher in firms that used performance pay, but the companies' performance was no better as a result of the extra compensation.[18]

While the Dale-Olsen study found essentially no relationship, some studies have found that performance pay *harms* performance. For example, H. Young Baek and José A. Pagán looked at S&P 1500 firms and checked for a relationship between the firms' use of performance pay and their technical efficiency (their ability to produce goods and services using as few resources as possible). They found that the more firms relied on restricted stock and stock options, the worse the firms' technical efficiency.[19] Similarly, Matt Bloom and George T. Milkovich examined companies that had to deal with unusually high risks. Among these firms, those that rewarded their executives with performance pay performed worse than those that did not.[20]

Respected scholars who have carefully combed through the literature on this question—including some who favor performance pay—have concluded that there is no empirically demonstrable relationship between firms' use of performance pay and their success in the marketplace. Kevin Murphy, although a strong advocate of performance pay, agrees: "Unfortunately, although there is a plethora of evidence on dysfunctional consequences of poorly designed pay programs, there is surprisingly little direct evidence that higher performance sensitivities lead to higher stock-price performance."[21]

Former Harvard University president Derek Bok also concluded that performance pay does not result in better corporate outcomes, as have a number of other prominent scholars.[22] A survey of international senior executives found that the executives themselves did not believe that performance pay shaped their behavior.[23]

Some scholars have responded to the lack of evidence that performance pay is effective by challenging the testability of the question.[24] They argue that for a variety of reasons, it is not possible to determine whether performance pay works. If empirical data are inherently indeterminate, we are left only with our intuitions about human behavior, and the advocates of performance pay seem to think they can win on those grounds.

Since performance pay is almost universally lauded as key to improving corporate performance, advocates may be correct that taking empirical evidence out of the equation will result in a victory for performance pay. As I discussed earlier in this chapter, performance pay has enormous intuitive appeal. In the absence of empirical evidence, our pro–performance pay intuitions may carry the day.

Making the case that a proposition is not empirically testable is a difficult challenge to meet. Nevertheless, scholars on both sides have made a wide variety of arguments to show why empirical tests are meaningless in this arena. Although the arguments are diverse, we can usefully group them into three categories: (1) confounding variables; (2) efficient capital markets; and (3) difficulties in measuring individual performance.

To understand the first problem, that of confounding variables, we have to delve into how scholars test for a relationship between pay and performance. Precise methodologies vary widely, but the central idea is to compare the results of companies that use performance pay with those that do not. This seemingly simple idea becomes enormously complicated in application. Scholars cannot just ask whether a company uses performance pay, because most companies use at least some performance pay. So they have to ask instead about the *extent* to which companies use performance pay. The extent question requires researchers to make judgments about what counts as performance pay, an issue I discussed in chapter 5 (and will revisit briefly below). Then researchers have to come up with some sort of metric (such as a percentage score) to rate the degree of performance pay employed. Any such judgment— whether a policy counts as performance pay, and if so, how much—is necessarily contestable and to some degree arbitrary.

These difficulties pale by comparison to the other side of the question: the causal link to the success of the company. First, researchers need a metric of corporate success. Surprisingly, there is relatively little agreement about what constitutes corporate success. Scholars can measure success by a number of different variables: earnings, earnings per share, growth in share price, change in market share, price-to-earnings ratio, change in Tobin's Q ratio,[25] firm productivity, firm efficiency, or a number of others, some of them industry-specific. These metrics do not always track one another, so results will vary depending on which metric of success the researcher chooses.

Once they have a measure of success, they have to determine how the success is related to performance pay. This is very difficult. A firm's outcomes are influenced by an enormous variety of external and internal factors: the quality of the goods and services it offers, the competitiveness of its markets, the changing costs of the materials and labor it needs to make its products or supply its services, prevailing interest rates, shifting demand, fashion trends, general economic conditions, changing technology, among a host of other factors. The motivation of its executives is only one of many possible causes for a change in the company's bottom line. Statistical tools can tease out the impact of particular variables, but the more variables there are, the harder this becomes. As the number of possible causes increases, researchers need more and more data points to empower them to distinguish the relative influence of each cause.

But the number of data points for the question of the impact of performance pay on corporate results is limited. Scholars can only investigate public corporations, because privately held companies are not required to disclose the kind of compensation and performance data they need. Plus, researchers tend to be most interested in the largest companies, especially those in the S&P 500 Index; these companies pay their CEOs the most and are those most frequently criticized for overpaying their executives. The most comprehensive data are readily available only for 1992 and forward, the period covered by the ExecuComp database.[26] (Even better data became available in 2006, when the federal government enhanced its disclosure requirements for executive pay.)

All of which is to say that the number of available data points is limited, but the number of potential causes of a company's success or failure is vast. There are too many factors that affect a company's success to let us discern with any confidence what impact performance pay has. Perhaps it's unsurprising, then, that many studies have found performance pay had little to no effect on a company's success; whatever impact performance pay had was overwhelmed by the multitude of other variables that together determine a company's success or failure.

The second challenge, that capital markets are efficient, at first glance does not seem like much of a problem. For most purposes, we want capital markets to be efficient. In fact, much of securities law is specifically designed to make capital markets more efficient. But when it comes to testing the impact of performance pay, efficient capital markets are a major headache.

Researchers would like to be able to use capital markets as a metric for the usefulness of performance pay. Precisely because capital markets are efficient, scholars could use them to measure companies' success. By comparing stock price appreciation of companies that use performance pay more to those that use it less, academics should be able to determine how effective performance pay is at boosting a company's stock price, an important measure of a company's success. But here's the problem: capital markets may be *too* efficient, or at least the finance theorists who conduct these sorts of studies tend to believe they are.

To see why this is such a problem, imagine we have two companies that use different levels of performance pay. High Inc. insists that three quarters of its executives' pay depends on the company's performance, while Low Inc. makes only one quarter of its executives' pay depend on performance. Researchers would like to compare the share price appreciation of the two companies and then draw a conclusion about the impact of performance pay on companies' results. I just discussed one major problem with using this comparison as a test: the excessive number of influences on a company's performance other than the structure of executives' pay packages. But let us assume this problem away and say that the two companies are identical except for their different uses of performance pay. We still have another obstacle to using relative share price growth as a yardstick: an efficient market's ability to anticipate.

Murphy has argued that an efficient market will bid up a company's share price in anticipation of the positive impact of the company's current actions.[27] He contends that investors understand that performance pay is a more efficient motivator and that therefore companies that use performance pay will have faster profit growth than those that do not. If Murphy is right, then investors will anticipate that High Inc., which has a more efficient compensation system, will experience faster earnings growth and so bid up its stock price even before that growth materializes. (This reasoning is akin to the old Wall Street maxim, "Buy on the rumor, sell on the news.") High Inc.'s stock will not increase in price faster than Low Inc.'s stock because it will start from a higher level. In fact, the market will bid up High Inc.'s stock to the point where its expected share price growth becomes *the same* as Low Inc.'s; until that point, High Inc.'s stock will be a bargain because investors can purchase a faster growth rate without any accompanying increase in risk. (Again, assuming the companies are identical except in terms of how much performance pay they use.)

Only once the anticipated growth rate is the same for both companies does this opportunity for easy money disappear. Since market participants are smart, they will almost instantly buy High Inc.'s stock until the company's stock price reaches this equilibrium level. As a result of this characteristic of efficient capital markets, we cannot divine anything from the relative speed with which the two companies' stock prices increase.

The astute reader may note a flaw in this line of argument. Even if the argument is basically sound, there will be a difference between the way the market treats High Inc. and Low Inc. In order to equalize the two companies' anticipated share price appreciation, the market must pay a higher premium for High Inc.'s earnings than it does for Low Inc.'s. The ratio of market price to earnings per share will be higher for High Inc. than for Low Inc. Although Murphy may be correct that the capital markets' efficiency is an important obstacle to using growth in share price as a metric of the efficacy of different compensation packages, we should be able to use price-to-earnings ratios of otherwise similar companies to accomplish the same goal. But we would still be stuck with the difficult challenge of finding otherwise similar companies, as I discussed just above.

Another way around this problem is to conduct event studies. Researchers could look for companies that change their executive compensation packages, making CEO pay either more or less sensitive to the company's results. The efficient market's immediate reaction to these changes might tell us a great deal about the utility of tying executive pay to firm performance. As Murphy points out, the problem here is discerning the moment the market credibly learns that the company plans to redesign its executive compensation structure. Is the relevant time the date the company makes a public announcement of its intention? The day the new plans are actually included in executive contracts? The day rumors of the company's intentions begin circulating? Event studies work only if the event can be clearly identified, a condition that may not be met for changes in executive pay.[28]

To be useful, event studies would also require the market to make the correct judgment about the utility of different types of pay. The market's reaction is just the aggregation of the individual market partici-pants' beliefs about which types of executive pay are most effective. If the buyers and sellers in the stock market are wrong about the useful-ness of, say, stock options, then their reaction will not validate options; it will tell us only that the investors like them. There isn't any reason to suppose that institutional investors know more than anyone else does about performance pay's utility. But again, these studies have *not* shown that the market gets especially excited when a company adopts more performance pay.[29]

The final problem with empirical studies that try to measure the use-fulness of performance pay is that *individual* performance is difficult to measure. Without a valid measure of *executives'* success, it is impossible to determine how closely pay is tied to performance and therefore impossible to measure the effectiveness of performance pay. Many stud-ies measure the sensitivity of pay to performance by asking about the degree to which companies use compensation devices such as options, bonuses, and performance shares. These studies reason that such devices necessarily tie executive pay to performance, however measured.

But as Bebchuk and Fried have cogently argued—and as I discussed in chapter 5—these devices often deliver only the illusion of performance sensitivity, not the actuality. Options are seldom indexed to the market as a whole, much less the relevant industry segment of the market. That is, companies could tie the options' exercise price (and therefore their value) to some measure of how the stock market as a whole is doing to avoid rewarding executives for increases in stock prices that were due to factors beyond their control. When the broader market has risen 10 percent, for example, and the CEO's company's stock has risen 12 per-cent, only some of the increase could reasonably be attributed to the CEO. The 10 percent increase enjoyed by the entire market was most likely caused by general economic conditions, not the CEO's efforts. Options that are not indexed to the market (or better yet to the share prices of companies in the same industry) reward (or punish) executives for general increases (or decreases) in the market that have nothing to do with the company's performance. For example, a decline in interest rates may raise stock prices across the board, rewarding executives who hold options even though they had nothing to do with setting interest rates.

Similarly, bonuses and performance stock can deliver the illusion of performance sensitivity without the reality. Both often have triggers that are set very low, at least for a partial payment. And like options, these triggers are seldom indexed to the performance of the industry as a whole, allowing executives to profit from broad, external trends they did not create.[30]

Studies that look beyond the use of these compensation devices still overwhelmingly measure some characteristic of *corporate* performance, not the performance of the individual executives. Studies look to share price, earnings, number of patents created, or some other measure of the company's success. But they rarely examine the CEO's performance as something separate from the company's performance. Instead, they implicitly assume that the company's successes and failures must be due to the CEO's actions. This is a logical and factual fallacy, as I explain in chapter 7. Sometimes the company's results are because of actions the CEO took, but often they obtain from internal resources that existed before the CEO took charge of the company or from external events beyond the CEO's control.

Any causal nexus between companies' use of performance pay and their relative success must run through the impact of performance pay on executives' motivations to act. If the resulting actions have only an occasional impact on corporate results, then we should not expect empirical studies to demonstrate a strong link between the use of performance pay and better corporate outcomes.[31]

Although the first two arguments—that there are too many variables to account for with the statistical power we have and that capital markets are efficient—may serve as a defense of performance pay, the latter is difficult to square with the contention that companies should tie pay more closely to performance. Under the first two arguments, we might disregard the absence of a clear empirical connection between performance pay and corporate performance. But the third argument, that individual performance is difficult to measure, explains the empirical lacuna by saying that the reason it is difficult to measure is that it may not cause better corporate outcomes. Since that is the very question we care about, performance pay's defenders cannot take much comfort here.

Even the first two arguments (too many variables and the efficiency of capital markets) at most take the empirical studies out of the discussion; they do not flip the empirical evidence into proving performance pay's virtues. And neither is powerful enough to make us discount the empirical studies altogether. There are many factors that affect corporate results, but if performance pay's effects were really powerful, they should emerge in the studies. Performance pay may have some positive effect, but if so, it is likely quite subtle if the studies have failed to detect it consistently. And while capital markets are efficient in many senses, it is hard to credit them with the ability to anticipate perfectly the effect of performance pay. A company's market price represents a sort of weighted average of investors' best guesses as to the company's future earnings. For the market to cancel out the effect of performance pay by raising share prices in anticipation of performance pay's impact, market participants would have to predict with some precision what that effect will be. Scholars specializing in performance pay cannot quantify its effects. It is difficult to believe that market participants know what specialists in the field do not.

Many studies using different methodologies have failed to find consistent evidence that performance pay significantly improves outcomes for corporations. This failure seems like a powerful indictment of performance pay. And performance pay is expensive—more expensive than straight salaries—because executives understandably demand higher expected pay to compensate them for taking on the risk that they will fail to hit the trigger points.[32] (For a more in-depth discussion of this point, see chapter 2.) In light of these two facts, companies' continued use of performance pay—and shareholders' insistence that they do so—seems deeply puzzling.

But let us set these arguments aside for the moment and assume that evidence of performance pay's efficacy is impossible to find for the reasons discussed above: there are too many influences on corporate performance to isolate the effects of performance pay; efficient capital markets make this search even more difficult by anticipating performance pay's effects in advance; and isolating individual performance—as opposed to corporate performance—and its effects on corporate outcomes is a difficult if not impossible task.

If we buy the argument that the empirical evidence is inconclusive, we must look elsewhere for evidence of performance pay's efficacy. Advocates of performance pay might point to our common experience of human nature that people respond to incentives. If executives can earn more money by improving the company's outcomes, they will try hard to do so. Advocates might also argue that the widespread use of performance pay devices in private company settings—where the owners do not face the sort of agency problems that arguably prevent shareholders in public firms from optimizing executives' pay structure—validates their use in public companies as well. If smart, sophisticated people with lots of money at stake choose to motivate their executives using performance pay, the logic goes, they must have a good reason.[33]

Intuitions are pretty flimsy support for such an expensive policy. In the absence of persuasive evidence that performance pay works, that's exactly what we're trusting when we defer to the practices of sophisticated businesspeople. Why do smart people with their own money at stake use performance pay? Is it because they are aware of data that haven't been published that prove performance pay works? Or, as seems more likely, is it because performance pay feels intuitively sound and everyone else uses it too? I have a lot more to say in chapter 8 about the psychological dynamics I think are really behind the conventional wisdom on executive pay.

PSYCHOLOGICAL STUDIES

There is an alternative to turning to intuition or deferring to business practices. Psychologists have investigated the impact of performance pay in laboratory experiments. Admittedly, laboratory experiments are far from perfect; they necessarily mimic real-world circumstances but cannot duplicate them. They are therefore always vulnerable to the criticism that they have omitted some important aspect of corporate life that would have changed the results.

While experiments are imperfect, they are superior to the sort of purely intuitional or faith-based approaches we would otherwise have to adopt in the absence of convincing direct, empirical evidence. Instead of assuming the answer, experiments test to see if our intuitions are grounded in fact. And unlike intuitions, experiments' flaws can be exposed and their impact on outcomes debated.

For the past forty years, psychologists have investigated the impact of rewards on people's motivation and performance, a body of work that recently received popular exposure in Daniel Pink's excellent book, *Drive*.[34] For some types of tasks, the conventional wisdom about performance pay turns out to be entirely accurate. When people are given dull, repetitive tasks like assembly line work, they perform faster and better when their rewards depend on their productivity. The results are much different, though, when the tasks are interesting, especially if they involve creative or analytical thought. For these high-level tasks, performance pay actually *weakens* motivation and results in lower-quality work.

Performance pay is supposed to operate by motivating people to work harder and smarter. All of that hard and smart work should produce better results. The psychological studies undermine this theory in two ways: by demonstrating that performance pay counterintuitively *degrades* motivation for certain types of tasks and by showing that the outcomes for those tasks are *worse,* not better, when workers are compensated with performance pay.

In the 1960s, Sam Glucksberg began noticing a surprising phenomenon: for some types of tasks, performance weakened when subjects' rewards were conditioned on their achievements.[35] Glucksberg was experimenting with an exercise first developed by Karl Duncker, the "candle in the box" problem.[36] Subjects are given a candle, a box of tacks, and matches. The task is to attach the candle to the wall in a way that the wax will not drip onto a table below when the candle is lit. Most subjects try to attach the candle to the wall with the tacks or to melt the side of the candle and adhere it to the wall with the hot wax. Few subjects manage to come up with the correct solution, which is to pin the box to the wall and then put the candle on the box.

Duncker was trying to illustrate a principle called functional fixedness, the notion that people tend to use objects only in the conventional way. The box was presented to the subjects as something used to hold tacks; it was difficult for people to conceive that it might also be used as a platform for the candle. But Glucksberg discovered something else with this experiment. People who were paid based on how quickly they solved the problem were less likely to solve it than those who were told they were being timed.[37]

Edward Deci explained these surprising results by developing cognitive evaluation theory. When a person does something of her own volition, she feels that she is intrinsically motivated, that she is choosing this activity because she finds it pleasurable. But when she works for a reward—an external motivation—she perceives the task as unpleasant; she is working for the reward, not because she enjoys the task.[38] It turns out that irrespective of the inherent nature of the task, the way it is framed—whether as recreation we enjoy or work for which we demand pay—has a profound effect on how we feel about doing it.

One experiment Deci performed to demonstrate this phenomenon involved puzzles. Deci placed subjects in a room in which a number of activities were available, including magazines and puzzles. The experiment consisted of three sessions. In the first and third sessions, no reward was promised or given; subjects were free to engage in any activity they wished. Subjects often chose to work on the puzzles in the first phase, demonstrating that the puzzles were intrinsically interesting (at least as compared to the other available activities). In the second phase, some subjects were promised a dollar for every puzzle they solved, while others were not promised anything.

Deci then compared how much time subjects spent on the puzzles in the first and third phases. He found that subjects who had been promised money for completing the puzzles—performance pay—in the second phase spent less time on the puzzles in the third phase, when there was no longer a possibility of payment. Performance pay had transformed the puzzles from an inherently interesting activity into one that was only worth doing for pay. The control group—those who never were paid for working on the puzzles—maintained a stronger interest in the puzzles.[39] Deci performed a similar experiment in which one group was paid merely for participating, while the other was paid based on the number of puzzles they completed. Again, only the performance pay group's intrinsic motivation declined.[40]

Researchers have since performed hundreds of variations of these experiments. While some results differed, most meta-analyses of these studies have concluded that Deci was right: performance pay reduces intrinsic motivation for interesting or creative tasks.[41]

These studies have added nuance to our understanding of the impact of different types of compensation on intrinsic motivation. The impact of an award on intrinsic motivation depends on the signals the award conveys along two dimensions: autonomy and competence. When a worker feels that the award is controlling his behavior, he is more likely to attribute his performance to the award rather than to an internal desire to engage in the task. When this occurs, the worker's intrinsic motivation declines because he believes he only performed to get the reward.

However, rewards for performance do not always dampen enthusiasm for a task. In some contexts, subjects can see the reward as a signal of competence. The resulting ego gratification enhances intrinsic motivation. Depending on the type of reward, these two dimensions can push in the same direction or can oppose one another.[42]

Unexpected rewards and rewards that are promised with no strings attached ("task-noncontingent" awards) have no effect on intrinsic motivation. The workers will receive these awards regardless of whether they perform the task, so they do not attribute their desire to perform the task to the reward; they have no impact on the autonomy direction. Similarly, since the awards are not contingent on either completing or excelling at the task, the awards do not communicate anything about the workers' competence.[43]

Rewards that are contingent on completing the task but not on the quality of the work are seen as controlling. The worker will receive the reward only if she finishes the assignment; she is therefore likely to attribute her desire to work to the promised reward, not to the task's inherent desirability. Task-contingent rewards also signal competence, though; the worker cannot receive the reward without demonstrating some ability by finishing the work. For this type of reward, then, the two dimensions work at cross-purposes, with the autonomy dimension weakening intrinsic motivation but the competence dimension strengthening it. Both theoretically and experimentally, the net impact is to decrease intrinsic motivation. These awards are quite controlling but convey very limited competence information. The only requirement to receive the reward is to finish the task, not to exceed some level of excellence.[44]

The most dangerous type of rewards are performance-contingent rewards, where the worker receives the reward only if he not only completes the task but also meets some standard of excellence. From a theoretical perspective, it is far from clear that these rewards should decrease intrinsic motivation. They are the most controlling, since they demand high levels of performance. They therefore weaken intrinsic motivation on the autonomy dimension. But they are also strong signals of competence for the same reason, so they should strengthen intrinsic motivation on the competence dimension. When performance-contingent rewards have been tested, though, they have turned out to have the most harmful effect on intrinsic motivation.[45]

These laboratory experiments demonstrate quite convincingly that—at least under the conditions tested—performance pay damages intrinsic motivation. The studies therefore cast serious doubt on the usefulness of performance pay, since the whole idea behind paying for performance is to increase motivation.

But the studies are not conclusive on their own. These experiments ask what impact performance pay has on intrinsic motivation once the extrinsic motivation of promised rewards is taken away. If a company plans never to take away the rewards, it's possible that it doesn't need to care about intrinsic motivation; the extrinsic motivation furnished by the promised rewards may entirely suffice. A danger still lurks; extrinsic rewards are rather like a drug. Employees become addicted to the promise of rewards, and their ability to function at the same level without them quickly deteriorates.[46]

Nevertheless, for companies willing to continue to use performance pay indefinitely, the danger of undermining *intrinsic* motivation may be offset by the promise of predictable *extrinsic* motivation. For these companies, the central question is whether the decline in intrinsic motivation harms performance. What is the best way for companies to achieve their ultimate goal of maximizing performance? Does the extrinsic motivation provided by performance pay result in better outcomes for the company? Or do executives work harder and smarter when companies focus on inspiring intrinsic motivation?

Here, too, the news is troubling for performance pay in regard to the types of tasks most relevant to corporate executives. Studies have found that incentive pay can help subjects in memory tasks, such as learning strings of letters, and in solving easy problems. For these sorts of tasks, the incentives induce greater effort, and that greater effort produces better results. But when the tasks involve bargaining, risk taking, or solving more difficult problems, incentive pay has no effect on results. And for more complicated tasks involving judgment or creativity, especially when the task requires subjects to think in new or unusual ways, incentive pay undermines performance.[47]

Incentive pay therefore seems most useless—or even harmful—for precisely the sort of tasks senior executives perform. Few CEOs spend much of their time memorizing random numbers or solving simple problems. Instead, what distinguishes an excellent CEO is the ability to think outside the box about difficult business challenges. The experimental evidence pretty clearly demonstrates that incentive pay does not produce better outcomes for these sorts of tasks.

A troubling flaw in most of these studies is that subjects are paid fairly small sums even under what the studies describe as the high compensation phase of the trial. Few experimenters have a sufficient budget to provide meaningful incentives, the sort that boards routinely offer to CEOs. Dan Ariely, Uri Gneezy, George Loewenstein, and Nina Mazar recently conducted a study offering very high incentives to test whether raising the stakes to more realistic levels would change the subjects' behavior. They conducted their study in a rural town in India, where average annual income was so low that the experimenters could (and did) offer rewards that totaled more than the average villager spent in six months.[48]

The experimenters divided the participants randomly into three groups and then asked each person to play six different types of games. One group could earn only small rewards for playing the games successfully, one group had the chance to earn moderate rewards, and the final group had the opportunity to earn very high rewards. For each game, the subject's earnings depended on performance. If the subject performed well, he or she would earn half the available payout; if the subject performed very well, he or she would earn the maximum payout. Subjects who did not obtain a specified level of good performance would not earn anything for that game, which could represent a very substantial lost opportunity.

In the high reward group, the maximum compensation for each game was about equal to the amount an average villager spent in a month. A participant in this group who earned the maximum for all six games could therefore gain in one day what villagers typically spent in six months. These rewards were still lower than those boards often offer to CEOs, which can easily run into the millions of dollars (probably more than what even a CEO typically spends in six months). But the rewards were much larger than those used in most other experiments, which often totaled less than $100 (a relatively insignificant sum for American subjects, even the impecunious college students who typically participate).[49]

The games the Indian villagers played included one creativity task, two memory tasks, and three motor skills tasks. For all these games, the villagers in the low rewards group performed indistinguishably from those in the middle rewards group. This is itself fairly surprising, since the middle reward was ten times the amount of the low reward. But most surprising were the results in the high reward group. Despite the incredibly high incentive to perform—or, the researchers argue, because of them—the subjects in the high reward group performed worse than those in the other two groups across all six games (although the extent of the difference varied based on the type of task).[50]

The same research team performed an analogous experiment with MIT students, with similar results. Again, offering very high rewards degraded performance on cognitive tasks (in this case, math problems) but boosted performance on mechanical tasks (pressing a key repeatedly).[51] (If there's a joke here about comparing MIT students' mathematical abilities to their physical coordination, I am far too kind to make it.)

These experiments provide strong evidence that very large, lottery-style incentives actually undermine performance on high-level cognition tasks. Note again that the experiments tested a different set of circumstances than the motivation studies discussed just above. The motivation experiments asked about the impact of performance pay on intrinsic motivation, once the performance pay was removed. They generally found that giving performance pay hurt subsequent intrinsic motivation.

The link to performance there was indirect, though it seemed likely that having less intrinsic motivation would lead to worse performance. And it left open the possible solution of keeping performance pay in place permanently.

The India and MIT experiments asked a different question: does the possibility of earning large payments for strong performance make that performance less likely? These experiments were a more direct challenge to the theory behind performance pay, because instead of investigating the long-term impact once performance pay is removed, they questioned the efficacy of performance pay itself. The answer, in direct contrast to economic theory and most people's strong intuition, is that offering very big rewards for some types of performance makes people's performance worse. If this finding is also true for corporate executives, then not only are companies wasting the money they spend on performance pay, but they are hurting corporate results at the same time.

How can this be true? How can large incentives to achieve make achievement less likely? There are a number of possible explanations. One theory, known as the Yerkes-Dodson law, is that there is an optimal level of arousal for any given task. We want to be alert and focused, but if we are too nervous or excited our emotions may get in the way of our performance.[52] (Imagine trying to shoot a free throw to win a basketball game with thousands of fans watching.)

Yerkes-Dodson may be particularly applicable to CEOs of major corporations when they make decisions that will have a dramatic impact on their pay, such as whether to agree to a merger with another company. Take, for example, TransUnion's merger with the Marmon Group in 1980. Although the Marmon Group paid a hefty premium for TransUnion's stock, shareholders sued, claiming the price was too low. The Delaware courts ultimately held the board—including TransUnion's CEO, Jerome Van Gorkom—personally liable for failing to strike a better deal.[53] As I discussed in chapter 3, Delaware courts almost never impose personal liability on directors in the absence of some conflict of interest. But they did in this case, and Yerkes-Dodson may help us understand why.

At the time he was weighing the merger's advantages to TransUnion, CEO Van Gorkom was nearing mandatory retirement. His excitement at the possibility of selling his 75,000 TransUnion shares at a substantial premium may well have interfered with his judgment about whether he had negotiated the best possible deal for the company's shareholders (including himself). Van Gorkom's large stake in TransUnion gave him every incentive to negotiate the best price possible; this is not a story about executives selling out the shareholders for their own interests. But the same stock that aligned Van Gorkom's interests with his shareholders may also have interfered with his dispassionate judgment. The problem may not have been that he didn't have *enough* interest in the deal but that he had *too much*.

A second reason incentives may hurt performance is that the prospect of a reward narrows people's focus, preventing them from thinking broadly about possible unusual solutions. Worrying about how important it is to come up with a new marketing campaign gets in the way of creating one. Setting goals—even without tying them to compensation—has been shown to have a similar effect.

One study asked subjects to watch two teams—one wearing white shirts, one wearing black—passing a basketball and count the number of passes by the team wearing white. Subjects became so focused on the white team that they often completely missed it when a person in a black gorilla suit came on the screen, pounded his chest, and then walked off.[54] Another study demonstrated that companies that issued more quarterly earnings guidance—and were therefore likely to be more focused on hitting quarterly targets—did succeed in meeting or beating analysts' earnings forecasts more often than those that provided guidance only about longer-term goals. But these quarterly guidance firms were less focused on the company's long-term needs, spending less money on research and development. They also experienced lower long-term earnings growth.[55]

A third explanation is that a possible reward, especially a large one, inspires thoughts about the future—either a golden future where the executive has earned the reward (and fantasizes ways of spending it) or a despondent future where the executive despairs at having missed out on this exciting opportunity. Both the fantasy and the nightmare distract from the task at hand. Think of Van Gorkom again, visualizing his upcoming retirement.[56]

Fourth and finally, the answer may return us to intrinsic motivation and its link to creativity. A painter who lives to paint sunsets is likely to produce more interesting paintings of sunsets than of mountains, even if the mountain paintings are motivated by a wealthy patron's promise of largesse. The incentives may have the effect of diverting people to work that does not move them, even if it rewards them financially. The results may turn out to be . . . uninspired. Teresa Amabile conducted a study of this phenomenon by having experts rate a number of artistic works. Some of the works had been commissioned; others were solely the product of the artist's initiative. The experts rated all the works comparably in terms of technical quality but rated the commissioned works lower in terms of creativity.[57]

More research needs to be done to better understand the root cause of this phenomenon, but its existence is well documented. The kinds of tasks companies hire CEOs to perform—high-level, creative, and analytical thinking—are precisely those that performance pay is most likely to impede.

This in itself would be a powerful argument against incentive pay. But there's more. In addition to harming performance, performance pay may have these two (perhaps related) deleterious effects: it may suppress altruistic behavior and incite cheating.

One might wonder why we care about altruistic behavior in a public corporation. Corporations are organized to make money, not perform acts of charity. But the situation is much more complex *within* the firm, as many scholars have noted. Altruism covers a wide spectrum of behaviors, some of which are highly relevant to the internal functioning of a corporation. Corporate employees are often asked (and sometimes volunteer) to perform tasks that go beyond their formal roles. These tasks frequently are not included in the employees' formal evaluations or otherwise compensated. John Deckop, Robert Mangel, and Carol Cirka cite studies that show that employees compensated with performance pay are less likely to engage in this "organizational citizenship behavior."[58]

Similarly, Lynn Stout has argued that the term *altruism* can and should be extended to include working "harder and more honestly than their formal contracts with their principals can force them to."[59] Stout also contends that performance pay undermines this sort of prosocial behavior by emphasizing selfishness and material rewards, risking a downward ethical spiral that can lead to major corporate scandals such as Enron's.[60]

Financial incentives have been demonstrated to suppress altruistic behavior in other contexts. For example, people are more likely to donate blood for free than if they are paid a small sum.[61] And lawyers who would refuse to provide legal services for $30 per hour will cheerfully represent pro bono clients for free.[62] One reason for this seemingly odd behavior may be that offering compensation undermines the social norm that tells us to behave altruistically. Instead of believing we are supposed to behave well on our own, we begin to think that we are only supposed to act in exchange for payment.[63]

Performance pay could produce the same phenomenon, encouraging corporate executives to work only for financial rewards instead of out of a sense of mission and commitment to the organization. I am not suggesting that executives should volunteer to work for free but only that their mind-set about their work matters. People whose primary goal is to earn the next bonus will approach their work very differently from people who are focused on improving the organization. Pay should be structured as much as possible to encourage executives to think about the task in front of them, not their next paycheck.

Salaries obscure the connection between carrying out a work task and earning a reward for that task. Employees are well aware that they are ultimately working for pay, but with guaranteed salaries, the pay is dissociated from individual assignments. In contrast, performance pay structures like bonuses are directly tied to particular achievements, highlighting the connection between the work and the potential pay. This is precisely why economists have long thought performance pay should enhance performance. Ironically, this salient connection may have precisely the opposite effect, in part by undermining altruism norms.

And—as Stout argues—performance pay may also encourage executives to cheat. Performance pay may unintentionally encourage the idea that what matters is hitting certain financial targets, not the overall health of the company, which could in turn focus executives on the reported numbers rather than the reality. When combined with the temptation of having so much compensation riding on the company's financial results, executives might fudge the numbers to ensure they receive the pay they expect.[64]

There is substantial empirical evidence that suggests at least some forms of performance pay are in fact linked to manipulation of companies' financials.[65] For example, Paul Healy found that when performance pay is capped at some level, senior executives choose accounting methods that reduce the company's apparent earnings.[66] Presumably, these executives wanted to keep the targets for the following year lower—and make them easier to achieve—by underreporting their current results, thereby in effect pushing this year's earnings into next year. Once they had already earned the maximum performance bonus for the year, there was no incentive to reveal that the company had done even better.

More recently, Jared Harris and Philip Bromley examined a sample of 434 companies that had issued financial restatements—corrections of the statements they originally released to the markets—between 1997 and 2002. They found a strong correlation between a company's use of options as part of its executive pay package and the likelihood that the company would have to correct its financial statements. Restatements were especially likely among companies that were most generous with their options plans, suggesting that larger payoffs were more likely to tempt executives to engage in manipulation.[67]

CONCLUSION

What it all boils down to is this: *performance pay very likely (and ironically) does not result in better performance.* The empirical evidence is somewhat mixed on how companies fare when they include performance pay as part of their executive compensation packages, but the overall picture it paints is highly cautionary. Certainly the evidence does not provide the ringing endorsement for the benefits of performance pay that we would expect based on its nearly universal acceptance and high cost.

Still, since the direct empirical evidence is not entirely conclusive, we turn to the laboratory. There we learn that performance pay may actually reduce intrinsic motivation and harm performance for the types of tasks CEOs seem most likely to engage in—high-level creative and analytical thinking. Plus, performance pay may undermine CEOs' impulses to do work beyond the scope of their job description and may even encourage them to distort the company's results so they can hit their performance targets and earn more money.

HP's managers chose to abandon performance pay. At first, their experiment in performance pay seemed to go well. In fact, it went a little too well. Workers were even more productive than their managers had expected, so they earned more money than was budgeted. Managers concluded that they had set the triggers too low and tried to raise them. But the workers had come to depend on the extra income and resented that managers seemed to be trying to take it away from them. In addition, external events such as delivery delays sometimes clogged the works, preventing employees from achieving their targets through no fault of their own. This, too, the workers resented.

At the same time, the managers began to discern that the workers' focus seemed to have shifted from the work itself to doing only what was necessary to earn the extra money. And successful teams began to resist personnel changes that might threaten their success (and their bonuses), making it difficult to spread the techniques that made these teams successful throughout the organization. Ultimately, the managers concluded they could achieve the same benefits much more cheaply and

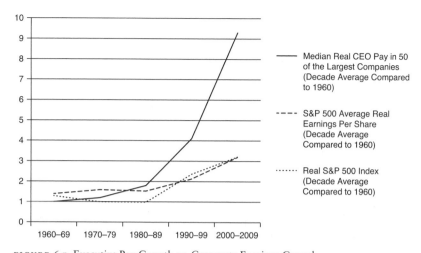

FIGURE 6.1. Executive Pay Growth vs. Corporate Earnings Growth.

SOURCE: Corporate earnings and share price data from Aswath Damodaran, "S&P Earnings: 1960–Current," http://pages.stern.nyu.edu/~adamodar/New_Home_Page/datafile/spearn.htm. Data on median CEO pay from Frydman and Jenter, "CEO Compensation," 38, 41; and Wall Street Journal/Hay Group Surveys of CEO Compensation.

without all the implementation problems by just putting in a team system and adding some training.[68]

Unfortunately, the managers' conclusion about how best to motivate their employees did not percolate up to HP's board of directors, which continued to use traditional performance pay devices to compensate senior executives.[69] Perhaps corporate boards should learn the same lesson HP's managers did and abandon their decades-long experiment with performance pay. Corporate America functioned pretty well between the 1940s and 1970s, when very little of senior executives' compensation was tied directly to the company's performance. As figure 6.1 demonstrates, executive pay has grown much more quickly than corporate earnings over the past fifty years. Executives, in other words, are taking a larger and larger share of the corporate earnings pie. It's hard to believe that rising executive pay drives corporate earnings growth when we see how little profits have risen in response to an enormous increase in CEO pay. And it's hard to understand why corporations achieved similar growth rates in the 1960s and 1970s without the supposed benefit of long-term performance pay (and while paying their CEOs much less). As figure 6.2 shows, the broader economy does not seem to have benefited from having our largest corporations spend

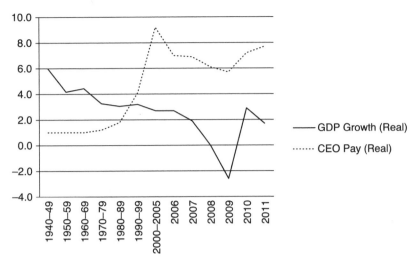

FIGURE 6.2. Real Growth in GDP and CEO Pay in 2000 Dollars.

SOURCE: Data on GDP from the U.S. Department of Commerce's Bureau of Economic Analysis, "National Economic Accounts," www.bea.gov/national/index.htm#gdp. Data on median CEO pay from Frydman and Jenter, "CEO Compensation," 38, 41; and Wall Street Journal/Hay Group Surveys of CEO Compensation.

so much more on managerial talent. Performance pay's enormous cost does not seem justified by its results. Boards and institutional investors should seriously question their faith in performance pay.

We want CEOs heading U.S. companies who are motivated by the value of the corporation's goals, by a sense of mission, by their interest in the work, and by their own ambition. The arguments for performance pay presume we are instead hiring exactly the opposite sort: executives who work for goals only when they are rewarded for achieving them. This is a terrible message to send to our most important corporate managers. What if it works? Then we will be taking intrinsically motivated, mission-driven executives and transforming them into people whose sole interest is obtaining financial rewards. CEOs are talented, experienced, and well educated; they absolutely deserve to be well compensated for their work. But the *way* we are compensating them may be undermining everything that makes them such a valuable asset.

One of the core assumptions at the heart of economists' advocacy of performance pay is that if executives are motivated properly, they have the ability to improve the company's bottom line. This is a natural assumption. The CEO is the company's leader, the boss. It's normal to think that the boss is the primary cause of whatever happens to the company. If the CEO makes good decisions, the company should thrive; bad ones, and the business should founder. Performance pay is designed to ensure the boss makes the best possible decisions, by tying his or her welfare to the company's success.

I have argued here that the empirical data show that performance pay has not succeeded in boosting corporate performance and discussed a number of psychological reasons why this might be the case (e.g., the deleterious effect of performance pay on motivation and on people's ability to solve puzzles that require creative and/or analytical thinking). The next chapter raises a very different type of explanation for why performance pay may be ineffective.

CHAPTER 7

Causation Mythology

Southwest Airlines is an astounding success story. Founded in 1971 as a small, intrastate airline in Texas with just three planes, it grew rapidly after deregulation to become one of the largest and most consistently profitable airlines in the country. Its strategy for achieving this phenomenal growth rested on providing low fares, excellent customer service, and frequent flights on short routes. The company hired personnel carefully, aiming for innovative, hardworking, and fun flight attendants to provide customers with a lighthearted experience. Southwest emphasized its joie de vivre with the corporate uniform of a polo shirt and khaki shorts.

To keep its costs low, the airline used only one type of airplane for most of its history, allowing it to save costs on spare parts and mechanic training and providing maximum flexibility to shift planes around as needed. The airline also made a practice of hedging roughly 70 percent of its fuel needs to protect itself against the possibility of rising oil prices, using common techniques such as call options and collars. These hedges allowed the airline to keep its fuel costs low while rising oil prices ground down its competitors.[1]

Unlike most rapidly growing companies and unlike airlines at any stage of development over the past few decades, Southwest was consistently profitable. Even after the tragic events of September 11, 2001, when every other major airline suffered losses, Southwest continued to earn profits.[2] In fact, it enjoyed an unbroken streak of quarterly profits for seventeen years, a feat few companies in any industry—much less any other airline—have matched.[3]

That streak ended in 2008. Southwest posted significant losses in both the third and fourth quarters that year. Part of the problem was the Great Recession, but a major contributing factor was the very strategy that had helped Southwest weather hard times before: its fuel hedges. Southwest had bet heavily that fuel prices would continue to rise in 2008. When the price of oil dropped instead, Southwest lost a fortune.[4]

Now we come to the core question of this chapter: who is responsible for Southwest's losses? This is not the way this question is usually framed in the executive compensation debate. Normally, defenders of large pay packages for chief executive officers advance the claim that since the company was successful, the CEO deserves high pay. But the central question—to what extent did the CEO cause the firm's results—is the same, whether the company earned lavish profits or suffered serious losses. To what extent can we lay corporate results—good or bad—at the CEO's feet?

Gary Kelly, Southwest's CEO in 2008, had taken the helm in July 2004.[5] He therefore had plenty of time to put his stamp on the organization. In addition, Kelly was an internal appointment; he had previously served as Southwest's chief financial officer. While CFO, Kelly initiated the fuel hedging program at issue in 2008. Southwest (and other major airlines) had long used hedging to a degree, but Kelly pushed the airline to hedge much more aggressively.[6] There are clearly many reasons to hold Kelly responsible, and conventional wisdom strongly holds that the credit (or blame) for a company's performance goes to the leader.

On the other hand, this philosophy may be overly simplistic. At the time Kelly implemented the strategy, James Parker was the CEO. Should Parker receive credit for Kelly's hedging profits? He was in charge at the time and presumably approved Kelly's plan. Similarly, since the strategy was implemented on Parker's watch, perhaps Parker should be blamed for the losses the hedges caused years later. But both the idea and its implementation were Kelly's; doesn't he deserve the lion's share of both the credit and the blame?

Or perhaps neither CEO should be blamed. Fuel prices are notoriously volatile and unpredictable. No mere human being can be expected to predict the price's future direction consistently. Blaming Kelly for unexpectedly falling fuel prices would be like blaming the CEO of an insurance firm for losses caused by a "storm of the century." The CEO cannot even predict—much less control—the changes in fuel prices, so we should lay the blame where it belongs, on the unpredictable fuel market.

Another argument against blaming Kelly is the competitive structure of the airline industry. The real price of an average airline ticket has shrunk substantially over the past ten years. While inflation generally has risen some 27 percent, airline ticket prices have gone up only 4.5 percent.[7] Because airlines compete so fiercely on price, they are generally unable to increase prices even when fuel costs rise precipitously.[8] If the industry were less competitive, rising fuel prices would be less devastating; at least some of the increase could be passed on to the consumer. It is precisely because ticket prices are so inelastic that airlines are driven to hedge the price of fuel. Should Southwest's CEO be blamed for the competitiveness of the airline industry that pushed the company to hedge the price of jet fuel?

We could go on like this for some time, trying to decide whether Kelly should bear full responsibility (or receive full credit) for Southwest's results, or whether he was so constrained by the external environment and internal limits (such as Southwest's low-cost strategy) that the results were mostly beyond his control. But intuitively, most of us feel that the leader is responsible for the firm's results. After all, as Harry Truman famously said, "The buck stops here." The CEO makes the ultimate decisions, so she or he should bear responsibility for their outcomes.

The direct corollary to this theorem is that the right leader can make a huge difference to a company. A uniquely talented CEO can take a firm from the brink of oblivion to the apex of success, as Steve Jobs did for Apple. We admire CEOs like Warren Buffett of Berkshire Hathaway, Jack Welch of General Electric, and Bill Gates of Microsoft because of the performance of the companies during their tenure. The business press similarly focuses more on the leaders of companies whose companies have performed particularly well.[9] When we pause to think about the question, we might concede that a good leader is not the *only* thing a company needs to thrive. But surely a talented CEO is the most important element in determining a company's future.

Despite this strong intuition, scholars have had great difficulty documenting what most people believe—that leadership is crucial to an organization's success. As a result, academics who study this issue generally fall into one of four camps: (1) unknowability, (2) environmental dominance, (3) situational dependence, or (4) CEO power.

UNKNOWABILITY

The first group of scholars argues that it is impossible to determine what contribution a CEO makes to a firm.[10] No matter how much we study this issue, no matter what data we gather or sophisticated analyses we perform, we will never find a determinative answer to this question. They point to at least five reasons that this search is likely to remain fruitless.

First, designing a study that can answer this question poses intractable problems.[11] There are two major ways to answer an empirical question: randomized, prospective trials and retrospective multivariate analyses. Prospective trials are by far the more reliable method. With a prospective trial, the experimenter can design the trial to test only the variable at issue, minimizing the risk that some other cause is at work. Also, with a prospective trial, the experimenter can randomly divide subjects between the control group and the experimental group, further protecting the results from being affected by some unanticipated factor.

Applying multivariate analysis to existing data presents additional challenges, since the data were created outside the lab and may therefore be subject to any number of influences. But with a large enough sample size, sophisticated statistical techniques can often isolate the impact of each factor, allowing the researcher to at least determine correlations. Causality, though, is particularly difficult to establish with post facto analysis like this.

Prospective studies are impossible in this area. Boards of directors will not permit their CEOs to be chosen by randomized selection. Directors' fiduciary duties to their shareholders forbid them from permitting the corporation to be steered by someone selected with anything but the corporation's best interests in mind. Scientific study—no matter how worthwhile to society generally—is not an acceptable reason for the board to defer to an experimenter on what is widely viewed (rightly or wrongly) as the board's most important responsibility: the selection of the CEO. Directors will be especially averse to letting the experimenter choose someone entirely inappropriate in order to measure the impact of poor leadership on the company. Researchers can set up laboratory experiments designed to mimic corporations, but these are unlikely to provide a very realistic model of real-life companies.[12]

Multivariate statistical studies, though, are almost as problematic. There are a host of factors that can influence a corporation's results other than its CEO's talent. The company's industry, culture, history, technology, branding, employees, and other officers can all play a large role. In addition, the external environment—the growth rate of the economy, interest rates, inflation, the price of oil, unemployment—also has an impact on the firm's success.

Statistical analyses require a large amount of data if they are to have the power to tease out which of many causes have the most influence on an outcome. But there aren't nearly enough data points available here. Companies typically replace their CEOs once or twice a decade. In order to have even ten CEOs for one company, the researcher would have to look back some fifty years. Over the course of such a long time span, the enormous changes in both the external environment and the firm's internal makeup would make it very difficult to isolate the leaders' impact from the host of other changes, especially with so few data points. (We will see shortly how these problems have plagued scholars trying to perform such analyses.)

Second, studying CEOs' importance poses serious measurement problems. Key to determining the role a CEO played in an organization's success is figuring out how successful the organization was under the CEO's tenure. But the success of a large, publicly traded corporation should not be measured as the company's earnings or share price growth during the few years the CEO was in office. Instead, we need to look at the firm's long-term experience. CEOs can boost corporate earnings in the short run through a variety of techniques that trade investment in the company's long-term health for a temporary boost in profits. For example, CEOs can cut the budget for research and development, skimp on major advertising campaigns, reduce the quality of the goods the company produces, or spend less on customer service. All these steps have the effect of robbing Peter to pay Paul. To truly understand the impact a CEO has had on a firm, then, we need to look at a longer time horizon, beyond the useful life of gimmicks like these. But the more years we include, especially those years after the CEO has left office, the harder it becomes to isolate the CEO's impact from other internal and external variables, including the impact of the CEO's successors.[13]

Measurement is also difficult because of the impact of luck and the environment. A business can benefit greatly from good luck, or be destroyed by bad luck. When the markets reopened after the terrorist attacks on September 11, 2001, the major indices plunged. Were the CEOs of U.S. companies suddenly worse leaders that day? Or were they just the victims of bad luck? Oil companies have enjoyed record profits these past few years as the price of oil has shot up as high as $150 per barrel. Are the CEOs of those companies geniuses because oil is more expensive? As already discussed, Southwest Airlines suffered its first quarterly losses in seventeen years in 2008. Were these losses CEO Gary Kelly's fault or the fault of the Great Recession, which also took a huge toll on the other major airlines? To really understand the impact of a CEO on a firm, we would need to isolate the influences of luck and the environment, including the impact of past leaders on the firm's position, resources, and culture.[14]

Finally, to measure accurately CEOs' effects we would need to solve the counterfactual problem; we would need to know what decisions others would have made if they had served as CEO instead. Perhaps Kelly was a genius for launching an aggressive fuel hedging program at Southwest Airlines. But perhaps any competent leader serving as CEO at that time would have done much the same. After all, most major airlines hedged their fuel costs to some extent. Kelly hedged a higher percentage of Southwest's fuel costs, but perhaps that was more a function of Southwest's unique low-cost position than Kelly's brilliance. Without the ability to go back in time and replace Kelly with someone else as CEO, holding all other conditions identical, we can never truly measure how much impact a particular CEO had on a company.[15]

The third reason (after experimental design and measurement problems) skeptics argue that we can never know how important leaders are to their corporations is that we cannot be sure there is such a thing as innate CEO talent. We expect talented musicians to perform well consistently. Anyone can have a bad day, but the audience would likely be shocked if a concert pianist, say, played a few wrong notes during a performance.

Not every talent can operate as reliably as musical virtuosity. Still, the more consistently we see the same people excelling in CEO positions, the more confident we can feel that there is an innate skill set that makes one CEO reliably better than another. Data on this question would require a reasonable measure of CEO performance, which, as I've just discussed, is problematic. But there are many examples of apparently inconsistent CEOs who have headed both very successful companies and total failures. Franklin Snyder has pointed out several such examples, including Albert Dunlap, who succeeded hugely at Scott Paper but failed at Sunbeam.[16] Even the much-lauded Steve Jobs was far from an unmitigated success during his first tenure as CEO of Apple. These examples do not prove or disprove anything, but they do cast some doubt on the commonly held notion that some executives are inherently better managers than others.

Fourth, we have an attribution problem. CEOs may take credit for actions the board hired them to pursue, so that any praise or blame should really rest with the directors. Hambrick and Mason have argued that directors frequently have a sense of what the corporation needs and hire the CEO accordingly. For example, when the company needs major restructuring, the directors may hire someone with experience restructuring businesses who, not surprisingly, proceeds to restructure the corporation. Such a CEO may deserve credit for implementing the strategy effectively (or blame for executing it poorly), but the greater praise should go to the directors for making the decision to restructure in the first place. It is difficult to determine, from public records, whether the board or the new CEO made the initial decision.[17]

The attribution problem goes beyond the directors. Publicly traded corporations are large, complex enterprises. The CEO is the most salient figure and may often play a critical role in advancing the company's fortunes. But the CEO cannot succeed on his or her own. There is a supporting cast of literally thousands whose work is also essential to the firm's success. How should we divide the credit (and more important for our purposes, the financial rewards) for a successful high-tech product launch, for example, among the shareholders who financed the operation, the senior management team who helped supervise and direct the company, the board that set broad policy, the scientists who developed the product, the sales force who sold the product, the advertising team who marketed it, and the workers who assembled it? Derek Bok articulated this issue best when he pointed out that we do not reward night watchmen with a percentage of the merchandise they rescued from a warehouse fire, nor do we reward U.S. presidents with a percentage of the gains from their foreign policy.[18]

Saturday Night Live performed an excellent sketch many years ago depicting Ross Perot offering the American people just this type of deal. The Perot character offered to serve as president for free if economic growth during his presidency was only ordinary. But he would receive billions if he achieved exceptional growth in GDP. The sketch was hilarious, *Saturday Night Live* at its very best. But the very fact that the sketch was so funny illuminates a problematic issue in CEO pay: even if CEOs are crucial to a company's success, they cannot succeed on their own. Allocating credit among the various groups who are responsible for a company's success may prove an impossible task.

Scholars who believe in the unknowability of CEOs' importance have aptly listed the daunting difficulties of measuring the impact of a CEO on a company. Nevertheless, many scholars in the area have made the attempt. Not surprisingly, given the enormous challenges of this undertaking, their conclusions have varied widely. Some believe that CEOs have little impact on average, some that CEOs' importance depends on the particulars of the situation, and some that CEOs are extremely important. Each of the next three sections is devoted to one of these groups.

ENVIRONMENTAL DOMINANCE

When Gary Kelly initiated Southwest Airline's aggressive oil hedging program, his motivation was to control a key and volatile cost. No airline can operate without jet fuel, and the cost of oil—and therefore the cost of jet fuel—fluctuates wildly. In 2008, oil peaked at over $140 per barrel. Less than a year later, the price dipped below $60 per barrel. In 2011 alone, oil topped $110 per barrel and also dropped below $80.[19] Faced with such extreme gyrations in a critical commodity, most major airlines engaged in oil hedging programs. Southwest's was more aggressive than most, but the core strategy was not terribly different from other airlines' tactics.

The external environment pushed Kelly to start the hedging program, just as the same environment prompted other airlines to do much the same. A number of population ecologists have argued that CEOs face so many external and internal constraints on their actions that there is scant room left for them to maneuver. Hemmed in on all sides, CEOs have little autonomy in making corporate decisions. The CEO's talent, personality, and experience therefore usually make only a slight difference to the company's fortunes. As long as someone competent is at the helm, the corporation will steer much the same course.[20]

CEOs face additional constraints. As Sydney Finkelstein, Donald Hambrick, and Albert Cannella Jr. have pointed out, they also desire legitimacy. The quest for legitimacy can induce CEOs to imitate one another's strategies. Imitation is safe, from a legitimacy perspective, because although a CEO may be wrong, he or she will not look foolish if reputable peers are pursuing the same tactic. Moreover, CEOs' demographics argue for a certain degree of uniformity. The CEOs of large, publicly traded corporations in the United States are overwhelmingly white, male, college educated (often with an MBA as well), and middle aged. They also have similar training, typically having served for many years as senior executives of large corporations. If CEOs tend to respond similarly to challenges, then we should not expect dramatic differences in outcomes just because one CEO rather than another happens to be in charge.[21]

The most prominent empirical study supporting this mode of thought was performed by Stanley Lieberson and James O'Connor. Lieberson and O'Connor studied a sample of 167 large corporations over a period of twenty years, 1946–65. They examined leadership changes and the subsequent shifts in the corporations' performance, as measured by sales, earnings, and profit margins. They then considered the broader economy, the industry of each company, the position of each company within its industry, and leadership shifts as possible explanations for the variance in companies' performance.[22]

Although the precise numbers depended on the performance measure (sales, earnings, or profit margins), the findings were broadly similar. Lieberson and O'Connor found that the general economic conditions had very little impact during this period, explaining only about 3 percent of the variance. This period was almost uniformly prosperous, though, so perhaps this finding should be unsurprising. Industry was far more important, accounting for about 20 to 30 percent of the variance. A company's position within its industry was the most important, explaining some 65 to 68 percent of the variance. Adding leadership changes, however, had very little impact, explaining about 6.5 percent of the variance in sales performance, 5.5 percent of the variance in net income, and 15 percent of the profit margin variance.[23]

Lieberson and O'Connor concluded from this study that CEOs were too heavily constrained to matter very much to corporate performance. They pointed out that the performance graphs for eight large steel manufacturers during this period had almost identical shapes, demonstrating the enormous impact of industry factors on corporate results. They summed up by saying, "Were General Motors and American Motors to trade all their top executives, the two companies' positions would not likely be reversed even if the quality of management were radically different (though that is, of course, an empirical question)."[24] They did acknowledge, though, that leaders in some companies might have more latitude to make changes than in others and that the importance of leadership might vary from industry to industry.

The Lieberson and O'Connor study created quite a stir in the management literature. What was the point of having business schools, after all, if even the head of an organization could not affect its success? Their methodology was criticized, but subsequent studies generated remarkably similar results.[25]

Still, these studies are far from conclusive. Even studies that examine a twenty-year period, like Lieberson and O'Connor's, end up with comparatively few leadership transformations. There are so many variables that may affect a company's performance—interest rates, unions, government regulation, industry-specific variables, international trade agreements, prevailing wages, firm culture, firm history, the company's position in the industry, the corporation's intellectual property, unemployment rates, the quality of the firm's research and development, the caliber of its marketing team and sales staff (and I could go on)—that it would require a much larger data set of leadership changes to control adequately for them all.

Critics have also argued that some of these studies use poor measures of corporate performance. Profits and sales may both be proxies for company size. The size of the company may swamp the impact of other variables and may also implicitly include CEO talent if larger companies consistently hire better CEOs.[26]

And at least one scholar has given these studies the opposite interpretation. Alan Thomas defends Lieberman and O'Connor's methodology but argues that their study and those like it actually stand for the proposition that leadership does matter. Although these studies found that changes in leadership explained only a small percentage of a company's variance in performance, Thomas contends that what matters is not the percentage of the *total* variance that leadership explains but the percentage of the *remaining* variance after company size and environment are accounted for. By that measure, leadership matters a great deal.

Some of the companies in these studies (including Thomas's own work) were much larger than others. The natural result of this size discrepancy, argues Thomas, is that company size will dominate in accounting for the variance in companies' performance, especially when performance is determined using measures (such as total profits) that vary with companies' size. But leadership may still matter a great deal internally to the company's fortunes, even though size affects the final results much more.

Analogically, it is as though the market were a race between a Ferrari and a Smart Car. The Ferrari should always beat the Smart Car. That does not mean that the Ferrari's driver is better, just that the difference in engines is more important than the difference in the drivers' skill. But the drivers' skill still matters in a potentially important way: the driver can still determine whether the Smart Car's time is better or worse. That may not matter to the outcome of the race—total profits—but it may matter a great deal in comparing the Smart Car's time across different races. If the prize is not awarded bimodally, with the winner taking everything, but in some proportion to the cars' finishing times, then having a better driver will still make a difference to the Smart Car's owner.

If Thomas is correct, then leadership is an important factor in determining a company's success but is dwarfed by both the company's size and its industry. Even an average driver could win a race driving a Ferrari against a Smart Car. If what we care about figuring out is not whether having a better driver can make a difference but whether driving skill is more important than engine size to winning races, then Thomas's argument is inapposite. The rhetoric surrounding CEOs suggests not only that a good CEO can help the company at the margin but also that talented leadership is *critical*. That rhetoric strongly suggests that leadership outweighs most other factors and that hiring the best CEO is the most important determinant of a company's success (as though the right driver could race the Smart Car to victory over the Ferrari). This theory of CEO primacy seems incompatible with the line of empirical studies that has followed Lieberson and O'Connor.

SITUATIONAL DEPENDENCE

CEOs may not greatly affect corporate performance on average, but perhaps there are particular circumstances when they can make all the difference. Our intuition that leadership is critical may stem from especially salient stories, such as those of GE's Jack Welch and Apple's Steve Jobs, in which a leader seems to have transformed a company. The lesson of these stories may not be that leadership *always* matters but that it sometimes matters a great deal.[27]

Scholars have explored a number of different ways in which CEOs' importance might be situationally dependent. One possibility is that they matter only when making certain types of fundamental decisions. Although CEOs might not have much impact in daily stewardship, perhaps better judgment matters when making strategic decisions that will determine the company's fate, such as whether to launch a new product or acquire another company.

Marianne Bertrand and Antoinette Schoar tested this theory by examining five hundred executives in six hundred large firms over a thirty-year period, from 1969 to 1999. They did not limit their study to CEOs, because there were too few cases of a CEO of one company leaving to become CEO of another. (In the study's thirty-year period, this happened only 117 times.) Instead, they included executives at the level of vice president and above who had spent at least three years at each firm. They confirmed earlier studies' findings that on average, leadership changes did not matter very much, accounting for only 3 to 4 percent of firms' variance in performance.

Most of firms' variance was due to environmental conditions and firm characteristics. But when firms made certain types of important decisions, such as acquisitions, diversification, dividends, and cost-cutting decisions, leadership mattered more. For example, when companies were acquiring other firms, leadership accounted for 11 percent of the variance in performance—three to four times the average. Similarly, senior managers mattered three to four times as much when companies were diversifying, again accounting for some 11 percent of the variance in performance. Note, though, that even for these high-impact decisions, the effect of the senior executive paled in comparison to environmental and firm-specific factors, which accounted for nearly all the variance.[28]

Another possibility is that leaders have the most impact when they are especially talented, or especially dismal. CEOs who are reasonably competent and who come from similar backgrounds might make parallel decisions, but perhaps a few CEOs stand out from the crowd. These mavericks might break from the herd and push their companies in innovative and creative directions. Some of these brave leaps might advance a firm to a whole new level; others might plummet the firm into the abyss. Either way, the truly unusual CEO matters to the company's fortunes in a way that most CEOs do not.

We have some empirical support for this theory from a study by David Denis and Diane Denis. Denis and Denis looked at CEO transitions reported in the *Wall Street Journal* between 1985 and 1988 that were not associated with a takeover attempt. Of these, 107 were forced resignations and 110 were normal retirements. Measuring firm performance as the ratio of operating income to assets, the researchers found a sharp difference in the pattern of firm performance between these two groups. Firms in which the CEO was forced out saw a substantial fall in performance before the CEO's departure and noticeable increases after the new CEO took office. Firms in which the CEO retired without pressure, however, saw no performance declines before the transition and only modest increases after.[29]

These data could support the notion that when the CEO is particularly poor—so much so that the board takes the unusual step of forcing the CEO to step down—the firm noticeably suffers. Once the incompetent CEO is replaced, however, the firm returns to normal performance. In contrast, when CEOs are of normal ability, leadership transitions are not associated with any marked change in corporate performance. Interestingly, both sets of transitions were associated with big changes such as layoffs and asset sales, but only when the board required the outgoing CEO to leave did these changes result in significant improvements in firm performance. New leaders seemed to feel a need to put their stamp on the firm right away, but in firms with normal retirements these changes had little impact.

The evidence doesn't necessarily lead to the conclusion that CEOs matter, though. The companies that fired their CEOs were performing poorly, but their tribulations may have had little to do with the CEO. By the time these companies' troubles drove them to the unusual act of firing their CEO, there may have been nowhere for them to go but up. The new CEO was then lucky enough to be there for the climb. That these companies recovered after replacing their CEOs may say more about the straits boards have to be in before they force their CEO out than the CEO's impact on corporate fortunes. Alternatively, the companies might have been suffering from problems that the old CEO would also have addressed had she or he been allowed to stay in office.

The study would tell us more if it had compared the fate of companies facing serious problems that nevertheless stuck with their CEOs to the fate of those that jettisoned them. Without that baseline comparison, there is no way to tell if the new CEO was the cause of the companies' recoveries. The former CEO might have done just as well, or the working of natural market cycles might have brought the companies back without any action by corporate leadership. Because the study looked only at leadership transitions, there is no way to tell how companies would have fared had they kept their former executives in place.

The third and final situational theory focuses on the latitude CEOs have to act. The argument that CEOs do not matter is based largely on the notion of constraint; most people in the job would end up making the same decisions because of the constraints imposed by the external environment and the firm's characteristics. A number of theorists have pursued a logical corollary of this theory, claiming that the fewer constraints CEOs face, the more the CEOs will matter. Constraints come from three sources: the external environment, the firm's characteristics, and the CEO's capabilities.[30]

The external environment may be very permissive in, for example, a new industry where different business models or technologies are vying for dominance. Or the environment may be highly constraining, as in a mature industry with a few large players. Similarly, new, small firms with light capital costs allow a CEO to remain nimble, whereas old, large, mature firms with heavy investments in machinery, infrastructure, or intellectual property restrict the CEO to a narrow range of possible strategies. And some CEOs may see branching paths where others see only one, so there is a role to play for individual talent in determining latitude as well. There are some supporting studies that seem to indicate that the CEO's predilections are better reflected in the corporation when the CEO has greater latitude to act.[31]

But a case can be made for the opposite reasoning. Noam Wasserman, Nitin Nohria, and Bharat Anand have argued that CEOs matter most precisely where opportunities are most *scarce,* directly contradicting the dominant view. They point out that in an environment where few opportunities are available, the CEO's ability to secure those opportunities that do exist becomes more important. Most theorists would argue that CEOs of firms in a mature, slow-growth industry with few players will not affect their firms' fortunes greatly. But Wasserman, Nohria, and Anand contend this is precisely the climate in which CEOs are most important. Where the dominant view would argue that in the desert, leadership is irrelevant because no one could find much water anyway, Wasserman, Nohria, and Anand counter that this is precisely when leadership is critical, when every drop is precious.[32]

They performed a study of 531 companies from forty-two industries during the years 1979–97. They found—consistent with prior studies—that leadership accounted on average for 14.7 percent of the variance in companies' performance as measured by return on assets and 13.5 percent using changes in Tobin's Q. (Tobin's Q is the market capitalization of the firm divided by the asset value.) But the averages mask a vast difference among industries. When performance was defined as return on assets, the variance explained by leadership ran from 4.6 percent (for paper mills) to 41 percent (hotels and motels); when defined using Tobin's Q, leadership explained between 2.4 percent (meat products) and 22.8 percent (measuring and controlling devices). As they predicted, the CEO's impact was higher in concentrated industries and in industries with low growth rates.

On the other hand, they also found that the CEO's impact was lower in companies with high debt levels. While they argue that this shows that high debt constrains a CEO, that explanation seems in tension with their overall notion that having fewer opportunities makes the CEO more important. They fail to explain why some forms of constraint—such as low growth rates—make CEOs more important, while others—such as high debt levels—make CEOs less important. In both cases, opportunities are scarcer. Why do some sources of scarcity exalt the CEO's importance while others minimize it?

Overall, it is hard to know how important freedom of action is in determining the importance of leadership. The empirical data are a contradictory muddle, sometimes indicating that increased latitude enhances a CEO's impact and other times indicating the opposite. In all likelihood, the core problem is the paucity of data points and the large number of variables, a combination that provides very little analytical power. The Wasserman, Nohria, and Anand study, for example, had an average of just 2.6 CEOs per company—very few transitions to use to measure the importance of leadership changes. The existing studies do not permit us to draw firm conclusions.

The same could be said for the situational dependence literature generally. While there is evidence that leadership matters more in some circumstances than others, environmental and company-specific variables nearly always far outweigh leadership in determining corporate performance. And all these studies suffer from the problems pointed out by advocates of unknowability, such as a dearth of data points and an excess of variables. Nevertheless, some theorists—especially recently—have gone even further, looking for evidence to support the intuition that leadership is nearly always critical. I turn to these theorists in the next section.

CEO POWER

The most popular view is that leadership is crucial to an organization's success. The business press certainly seems to share this view. In articles about a company's achievements, the CEO is generally the focus. We do not read about the great culture at Southwest Airlines that fosters innovation and hard work in its employees or the clever strategies implemented by its founders nearly as often or as prominently as we read about its CEO. (Even if we do hear about cultures and strategies, we hear about them in relation to the CEO's inspired leadership.) Because so many of us share a powerful instinct that CEOs not only matter, but perhaps matter more than anything else, a number of scholars have tried creative approaches to demonstrate leadership's impact on corporations.

If CEOs are critical to companies' earnings, then when CEOs die or lose close family members, the companies' profits should suffer. Three business school professors—Morten Bennedsen, Francisco Pérez-González, and Daniel Wolfenzon—examined corporations in Denmark to study whether this is true. The study found that when CEOs died or lost close family members, corporate earnings declined significantly. The authors concluded that CEOs are a critical part of corporate performance. Interestingly, not all close family members had this impact. When CEOs lost their mothers-in-law, company profits actually rose slightly.[33] (Since my wife will read this book, I'll mention that I would be entirely devastated if my own mother-in-law passed away.)

While this study suggests that having an active leader matters, it does not demonstrate that any *particular* leader is critical. Having a different, competent CEO in place who did not lose a close family member might have protected the company from the decline in performance. Two other types of studies have gone a step further, trying to reveal the importance of having an especially talented CEO at the helm. The idea here is that not just any competent leader will do; it is important to have the very best CEO possible.

One way to get at this question is to find a measure of CEO talent. If we could quantify CEO talent, at least well enough to rank CEOs by skill, we would have an easier time deciding how important it is to hire the very best CEO, as opposed to just one of several very good alternatives. Antonio Falato, Dan Li, and Todd Milbourn recently attempted to do just that. They compiled three alternative proxies for CEO talent: good publicity, career pace, and undergraduate education. The authors ranked the CEOs in their study using these proxies for talent and found that better CEOs generated superior results. In particular, CEOs one decile higher in talent generated shareholder returns that were between 0.3 percent and 0.45 percent better (depending on the talent measure). Choosing the best possible CEO could therefore pay significant (though not enormous) dividends for a company.[34]

But studies like this are only as good as the talent measure. Do we really believe these proxies for talent correlate with actual ability? A person's relative youth upon attaining his or her first CEO position may have more to do with the size of the first company led than the CEO's inherent abilities. And the frequency with which newspapers report positive stories about someone seems unlikely to correlate strongly with that person's ability to run a corporation. To the contrary, at least one study has found that the business press focuses more on leadership in companies that fall on the far ends of performance measures, whether good or bad. The more extreme the company's performance, the more the press attributes the company's performance to its leaders.[35] CEOs running companies that are doing particularly well, then, should expect a lot more favorable press, independent of whether they had anything to do with the company's performance.

Also, it is difficult to believe that even the most prestigious colleges can really pick out, primarily on the basis of a standardized test and the student's high school grades, who will be the most talented CEOs half a lifetime later. College admissions seem an ineffective proxy for CEO talent.

Perhaps more important, there is no evidence that directors look for these particular proxies in hiring a CEO. Do directors really care that much about a candidate's undergraduate education? Do they perform comparative publicity analyses on their finalists, hiring the candidate with more press mentions? To demonstrate that individual talent matters to corporate performance, we would need to study the talent proxies directors actually use in evaluating CEO candidates. It is talent *as defined by directors* that we need to assess, because that is the measure that determines who gets a chance to run major companies.

Another way to get at CEO talent directly is to look to the employment market for answers. To do this, we have to assume that CEOs can do the most good in the largest firms, that the market will therefore assign the most talented CEOs to the largest firms, and that there is an efficient market in CEO pay. (I've already explained that these are problematic assumptions, but let's suspend disbelief for just a moment.) Then economists can use the distribution of CEO pay and firm size to calculate the dispersion of CEO talent. Two recent studies that performed this analysis—both by authors who argued that CEO pay was efficient—came to remarkably similar conclusions: talent distinctions among sitting CEOs were vanishingly small.

Xavier Gabaix and Augustin Landier found that replacing the best CEO with the one-thousandth best CEO would decrease the largest company's market capitalization by only 0.04 percent.[36] Framing the question slightly differently, Marko Terviö concluded that in 2004, if the one-thousand largest U.S. public companies replaced their CEOs with the CEO of the smallest company in this group (therefore the worst CEO), the total market capitalization of these companies combined would have declined by $21 billion to $25 billion. The net gain to shareholders is actually even smaller, since $4.4 billion of this amount is paid to the better CEOs to secure their services. Although this number may sound large, it is an insignificant fraction (less than two-tenths of 1 percent) of the total market capitalization of these firms—$12.6 trillion.[37] Nevertheless, corporations earn a net gain even after spending huge sums to hire the best CEO they can afford. These studies concluded that CEOs improve corporations sufficiently to be worth their extravagant pay.

As I discussed more fully in chapter 4, the studies discussed above suffer from some important flaws. The assumptions underlying the studies—that there is an efficient market in CEO pay, that large firms benefit more from CEO talent than small ones, and (implicitly) that CEO talent is one-dimensional and fungible across firms—are likely incorrect. For example, Richard Hall has argued that the larger the organization, the less impact a new leader can have.[38] I won't revisit these issues here.

More pragmatically, if the talent dispersion is as narrow as these studies find, then the assignment model they postulate seems unlikely to exist. As highly as I regard corporate directors, I have trouble believing they could distinguish between two CEO candidates whose respective impacts on the company would be nearly identical, within a small fraction of a percent. CEOs' differential impact on corporate performance may be important, even if small. But I have to doubt that real-world directors or shareholders can reliably pick out the CEO candidates who are worth the extra money.

As small as these distinctions are, the studies may actually be overestimating them because they make no allowances for luck. In a fascinating and groundbreaking study, Seoyoung Kim calculated the variance we should expect in a company's performance based solely on luck. He then examined actual variances and discovered that luck accounted for almost all of them, leaving very little room for CEO talent to play a role. He argued quite persuasively that even accounting for industry variables is not enough to measure CEO talent; we also have to subtract out the variance we would expect just from luck.[39] Because the talent studies do not do this, they give talent too much credit for producing firms' results.

Two other types of arguments that CEOs have an important impact on corporate performance are worth a brief mention before concluding. A few scholars have tinkered with Lieberson and O'Connor's methodology to obtain sharply different results. For example, Nan Weiner and Thomas A. Mahoney changed both the measure of corporate performance and the way leadership was calculated. Their study concluded that leadership accounted for a whopping 43.9 percent of the variance in firms' performance, dramatically higher than Lieberson and O'Connor's results. But their entire model could only account for a little over half of all the variance in outcome. By comparison, Lierberson and O'Connor's model accounted for over 95 percent of the variance in sales and income data.[40] With so much variance left unexplained, Weiner and Mahoney's model is too incomplete to be very persuasive.[41]

A number of articles explore whether there is a link between corporate performance and the amount of equity the CEO owns in the firm. If companies perform better when CEOs own a significant percentage of equity, perhaps the improvement is due to the CEOs' extra efforts. By implication, the CEO—when motivated—can have a significant impact on the company's bottom line. The results of these studies are hardly persuasive. Companies seem to do better as CEOs increase their ownership stake up to about 5 percent. But then companies actually do worse as ownership increases past this point, until CEO ownership crosses the 25 percent threshold. At that point, companies improve again with increasing CEO stakes but only very slightly.[42] The studies again fail to account for the role of luck in driving variance, and the conclusions are frankly bizarre. Why would company performance ever get *worse* because the CEO owned *more* equity? These results do not provide much confidence of a strong causal link between CEO ownership and firm performance.

CONCLUSION

The belief that CEOs are the most important cause of corporate performance is deep and widespread but largely lacks empirical support. Even fervent advocates of CEO power have calculated CEOs' average impact as small and easily swamped by environmental and company-specific variables. Perhaps this small contribution is important enough to merit the sort of pay packages CEOs of the largest companies receive, if the maximalist studies are correct. But the supporting rhetoric that suggests companies will rise or fall based entirely on the CEOs' talent is entirely overblown, a mythology of causation.

Remember, though, that this research studies the *average* impact of CEOs. There are highly salient outliers who appear to have truly transformed their companies. Their stories may in part account for the causation myth's ability to survive despite all these undercutting findings. But the reality for the vast majority of companies is that one competent CEO is very much like another. This is not to say that anyone can run a Fortune 500 company. Picking a person without the requisite knowledge or experience would be a recipe for disaster. Once a board has narrowed the selection to a few highly competent candidates, though, the differences among them are almost certainly inconsequential.

The causation myth's durability is also due to our tendency to credit the leader for a group's success and blame the leader for a group's failure. A number of studies have demonstrated that subjects wrongly assign responsibility to a group's leader even when the true cause was clearly something else.[43] For example, one study divided subjects into groups and then randomly selected which groups would succeed at their task and which would fail. The groups that succeeded rated their leaders much higher than those that failed, indicating that the subjects attributed the group's results to the leader even when leadership was irrelevant.[44]

Directors should try to restrain this natural tendency to believe that the right CEO can save a flailing business. Even Warren Buffett, who may be one of the few CEOs who has made an enormous difference to the company he heads, has expressed some skepticism about a CEO's ability to save a struggling company. Buffet is reported to have said, "When a management with a reputation for brilliance tackles a business with a reputation for bad economics, it is the reputation of the business that remains intact."[45]

Still, the temptation to gamble on hiring that rare phenomenon, a truly transformative CEO, may remain irresistible to many boards. The question for them is whether it is possible to detect such a person in advance with any reliability. I take up that question in the next chapter.

CHAPTER 8

Predictability Mythology

Imagine you are a director of a publicly traded brokerage firm that specializes in derivatives trading. The company has been experiencing troubles lately and has suffered five quarterly losses in a row. Would you hire this person as your new CEO? He comes from humble origins. He is a graduate of the University of Illinois at Urbana-Champaign and the University of Chicago's Booth School of Business. After completing his MBA at Chicago, he went to work for a regional bank for a few years before becoming a bond trader at a major New York investment bank. He eventually rose to become co-CEO of the investment bank, which he helped to take public, becoming extraordinarily wealthy in the process. He left the investment bank after a dispute with his co-CEO and ran successfully for a U.S. Senate seat. Five years into his Senate term, he won election as governor of his state. He lost his bid for reelection as governor in a close election. He is now looking to return to Wall Street.

This seems like an easy decision. The board certainly thought so. The company seemed lucky to get such an illustrious figure as the CEO of a struggling brokerage company. But the CEO was Jon Corzine, and the company was MF Global. Less than two years later, MF Global was bankrupt.[1]

The company's failure began with Corzine's leveraged gamble on European sovereign debt. He had the company borrow money to buy billions of dollars of debt issued by European countries struggling with their economies and their budgets, such as Italy and Ireland, betting that the rest of Europe would bail out these governments and prevent a default. Corzine bought $6.3 billion worth of this debt, about five times MF Global's value.[2]

This was an enormous gamble and a highly risky strategy. After MF Global's auditors insisted that this trade be disclosed, regulators forced the company to set aside $200 million in capital in case the trade lost money. That changed ratings agencies' minds about the strategy, and they downgraded MF Global's ratings to just above junk. Trading partners began demanding more capital as security to do business with the firm, and MF Global's share price dropped precipitously. The company couldn't function for long under these circumstances. Under pressure, someone at the company—apparently without Corzine's knowledge—improperly used customers' funds to cover the company's losses. When the company discovered this, it had little choice but to declare bankruptcy.[3]

Interestingly, the European debt investment ultimately turned out to be profitable. But the risk involved brought down the firm before these profits could be realized. Corzine's high-stakes gamble failed, bringing down the company.[4]

In contrast to Corzine's risky gamble, the directors' decision to hire Corzine as CEO seemed like a sure thing. It's hard to imagine a better track record than the one possessed by this former CEO of Goldman Sachs. Yet the man they brought in to save the company sank it instead. What went wrong?

The core problem is that choosing the right CEO requires directors to predict the future. At first blush, this may seem a strange statement to make. Predicting the future is something we normally associate with fortune-tellers, palm readers, psychics, and similar charlatans. It is not the sort of thing we expect from public company directors. But in fact business people try to predict the future all the time. Corporate managers need to know how well a product will sell, whether commodity prices will go up or down, what direction future regulation will take, what new technologies will be developed, how fashion trends will shift, even what will happen to interest rates. Most important for our purposes, corporate directors must try to predict which CEO candidate will best guide the company to a prosperous and profitable future and how much rosier the company's fortunes will look under the chosen candidate's leadership than the runner-up's.

Predicting the future is difficult, and prognosticators are frequently wrong. The rational and sensible response to all this uncertainty is to tread carefully. Directors should treat forecasts with appropriate skepticism, bearing in mind that they are highly fallible. They should follow a rule of prudence. This rule of prudence should apply to all the board's decisions but especially to one of the most important actions directors take: hiring a new CEO and deciding on his or her compensation.

When hiring (or deciding to keep) and compensating a chief executive, directors should remember that their ability to evaluate which final candidate will best lead the company is limited. They will, no doubt, have a strong feeling about this decision. After reading resumes, interviewing candidates, and talking to people who have worked with the finalists, the directors will naturally form a firm opinion about which candidate they favor. But this opinion is based on what is essentially a guess about the future. Just as a promising athlete may disappoint, so may a promising senior executive. The sensible response to dealing with this uncertainty is therefore to discount predictions about the candidates' abilities and to keep in mind that the differences among the finalists are probably too small to allow for very accurate forecasts.

Boards are very unlikely to adopt this attitude of healthy skepticism, to follow the rule of prudence. Instead, they are likely to overestimate greatly both their ability to predict who will best lead the company and the extent to which the favored candidate is superior to his or her competitors. As a result, boards may rationalize even extremely large compensation packages as justified by the gains the corporation will garner by hiring the best executive talent. Directors may say to themselves, "Why should we care what we pay our CEO when she's going to make us all rich?" Especially when peer companies are awarding similar compensation, boards are unlikely to question common compensation strategies even if they lead to questionable results. To understand why this is the case, we need to explore a number of psychological heuristics and biases we all share.

Beginning with the groundbreaking work of the psychologists Daniel Kahneman and Amos Tversky (for which Kahneman received a Nobel Prize in Economics), the past few decades have seen a revolution in our understanding of how humans make decisions.[5] Before Kahneman and Tversky, the dominant framework for examining decision making in economics was the rational actor theory. Rational actors are purely self-interested and take the actions calculated to maximize the attainment of their desires.[6]

Although economists always understood that the rational actor theory was a simplification of human behavior, they generally argued that

departures from rationality would be random and, in a large population, cancel one another out.[7] Kahneman and Tversky demonstrated
that people's departures from rationality were not random.[8] Humans
take shortcuts in their reasoning. These shortcuts or heuristics are generally quite useful and allow us to come to reasonable conclusions while
reducing the time and effort involved in making decisions. Useful as
they may be, heuristics also produce systematic and predictable errors,
errors that people replicate in test after test.

In addition, people suffer from certain biases in how we interact with
the world. Here, I do not mean racial or gender biases, with which we
are all too familiar, but something more subtle. For example, we are
biased in our own favor and therefore tend to have too high an opinion
of our own abilities.[9] To see a dramatic demonstration of this "optimism bias," have a group of people close their eyes and then ask them
to raise their hands if they are an above-average driver. Typically,
between 70 and 90 percent of the group will raise their hands. Unless
the group is a meeting of race car drivers, it is highly unlikely that most
of the members are above-average drivers; we would expect less than
half to be above average in a random sample. Nevertheless, because of
the optimism bias, most of us believe ourselves to be better-than-
average drivers.[10]

Since our departures from rationality trend in particular directions,
the economic models that assume people will behave rationally, at least
on average, are flawed, sometimes seriously. The first two theories of
CEO compensation I have discussed—the theory that CEO pay is efficient and the critique that it is the product of corruption—are largely
based on the rational actor model of behavior. These theories can still
teach us important insights, since much of our behavior is rational. But
because they overlook the ways in which our behavior consistently
departs from rationality, the theories are incomplete. To truly understand the forces that shape CEO compensation, we must explore the
heuristics and biases that influence boards' decision making. Four phenomena concern us here: the illusion of validity, the illusion of control,
groupthink, and social cascades.

THE ILLUSION OF VALIDITY

Decisions are based on data, so ultimately our decisions depend on our
observations of the world. We perceive more information than we can
absorb. We necessarily filter out the information that seems trivial and

focus on the more important or reliable perceptions as those deserving of our attention. When we take this necessary step, though, we introduce errors. The type of errors that concern us here are termed the "illusion of validity" or "representativeness heuristic."

Suppose you heard someone described as quiet, bookish, and wearing glasses. What would you think that person does for a living? If the word that popped into your head was "librarian," you would be in good company. Studies show that is the most common response.[11] How confident are you that your assessment is correct?

The description "quiet, bookish, and wearing glasses" does not convey very much information. For one thing, it represents only one person's observation, and we know nothing about how well the observer knows the subject. The observer might have met the subject only once, perhaps in a library. In that case, the description might be based on a very small and skewed sample of the subject's behavior. Most of us are quiet in libraries, and we tend to be reading books while there. The person might not be quiet or bookish (or even wearing glasses) at, say, a party or a baseball game.

Even if the observer knows the subject well, their acquaintance might be limited to certain contexts. If the observer is the subject's professor, for example, and the two mostly interact in class, even a large sample of the subject's behavior might be skewed by the context. Or the observer might simply be a poor judge of character.

More important, the description does not contain much information. Being quiet, bookish, and wearing glasses does not require that one become a librarian. There are plenty of doctors, teachers, lawyers, plumbers, accountants, and factory workers who meet that description. If we looked hard enough, we could probably find people in almost every career who are quiet, bookish, and wear glasses. Nevertheless, most subjects felt highly confident that their prediction of this person's profession—librarian—was correct.[12]

These studies demonstrate the illusion of validity. When the information we have matches up well with our preexisting ideas—when it's internally consistent—we are more likely to have confidence in our conclusions about what the data predict.[13] We like a good story, one that confirms what we think we already know. Hearing the beginning of a familiar story gives us comfort that the ending will also be familiar. The better the story, though, the less we focus on the real predictive power of the information, the information's validity. Good stories are seductive this way; they cloak information in an illusion of validity.

The very element that makes for a good story—internal consistency—should make us most suspicious about the data. The best sources of information are independent of one another. The more one piece of information causes another to be true, the less the second piece tells us.[14] Independent sources are more likely to conflict, reducing the consistency of the story and making us less confident in our predictions.[15]

The illusion of validity may also cause us to ignore information that does not fit our preexisting ideas. This aspect of the illusion of validity is sometimes called cognitive dissonance.[16] A new observation that conflicts with the story we believe is taking place is often overlooked or rationalized away.

For example, one study gave psychology graduate students a paragraph supposedly written by a clinical psychologist about Tom.[17] The students were told that Tom was then a graduate student, but the paragraph had been written about him when he was in high school. The psychologist described Tom as intelligent but uncreative and hungry for order. The description went on to characterize Tom has having little feeling or sympathy for other people, though he did have a deep moral sense.

After reading this paragraph, the graduate students had to rank the likelihood that Tom was studying one of nine fields. The students thought Tom was most likely an engineering or computer science graduate student and least likely to be studying social sciences, social work, the humanities, or education. The graduate students were also asked their opinion of the type of tests used by the cognitive psychologist to evaluate Tom's personality. They generally agreed that these tests were not a valid predictor of a subject's future career choices.

Subsequently, the graduate students were told that Tom was actually studying education with a specialization in children with special needs, a possibility they had regarded as very unlikely. The heart of the study was this: the graduate students were then asked to explain the apparent disconnect between Tom's personality (as revealed by the clinical psychologist's tests when Tom was in high school) and his eventual career choice.

The graduate students correctly assessed that the tools used to evaluate Tom were not effective in predicting future career choices. The logical conclusion, then, in looking at Tom's career choice in special education would be that the high school assessment had not been accurate. Tom was actually a kind and caring guy, despite what the clinical psychologist thought of him in high school.

This was not the approach the graduate students took. Instead, most of them tried to explain Tom's profession as a function of some of the aspects of his personality described by the clinical psychologist. They concluded that Tom's deep moral sense or need for dominance—both traits identified by an assessment made years before with tools ill fitted to predicting career choices—explained his decision to work with special needs children.

The graduate students—like the subjects in the "quiet, bookish" study—were the victims of the illusion of validity. They had heard a story about Tom, and the story set their mental framework for any future observations about him. Even when they were exposed to convincing data that strongly contradicted the initial framework, they refused to abandon it. Instead, rather than adjust the framework, they altered their perception of the data to make the data fit the story they already knew.

The danger of the illusion of validity is not just that people may make the wrong decision; it is that they may feel unduly confident that they made the right one.[18] The illusion of validity makes often irrelevant or repetitive information seem much more predictive than it is. It also veils contradictory data as irrelevant or as somehow consistent with past observations.[19] People then make predictions feeling confident that the data support their forecasts. In truth, the information people rely on is often not very helpful at all in predicting the future and is generally much less predictive than they believe. As a result, people feel more confidence than is justified that their predictions will come true.

How does the illusion of validity apply to CEO compensation? CEO positions are prestigious, extremely lucrative, and highly desirable. A public company seeking a new CEO will not usually lack for qualified applicants. Directors are likely quite good at winnowing the applicant list to a handful of outstanding candidates. The illusion of validity does not prevent directors from eliminating those who clearly lack the required experience, education, and skills. Where problems begin to crop up is in the final stage of the selection process, when directors must choose among several closely comparable finalists. At this point, the illusion of validity can have a pernicious effect, causing directors to believe the candidates are much further apart than they are.

The final candidates will generally have very similar (highly impressive) backgrounds. All will be extraordinarily accomplished, having excelled at most tasks throughout their careers. With so many eager competitors for the top spot, only the most gifted and able will make it through to the final round. The finalists are generally so close to one another that picking one out as the most able to run the company will be a difficult and subtle task.

At the same time, choosing the right candidate is seen to be critically important. (The previous chapter argued this perception may be mistaken.) The leader of a major public company manages billions of dollars of assets. Even a small difference in talent, when leveraged across the vast resources of a large corporation, can have a tremendous impact.

Gabaix and Landier have tried to quantify this difference.[20] They developed an economic model that assumes CEO pay rises with the size of the company (as well as the size of the average company). Their model also assumes that the best CEOs are employed by the largest companies. Using these assumptions, they calculated the difference a CEO's talent can make to a company's worth (measured as the company's market capitalization, or the price of one share of stock multiplied by the total number of shares). They concluded that a company that hired the best CEO instead of the 250th best would increase its market capitalization by 0.016 percent. That number is not a misprint: sixteen thousandths of a percent. Still, that difference, when applied to a corporation worth $100 billion, amounts to $160 million. The board of such a company, then, understandably feels as though it would be letting its shareholders down if it refused to hire the very best person as CEO, even if that person demanded, say, $50 million a year. The shareholders would still profit considerably from hiring the best person, even if the 250th best was willing to work for half as much. (But as I pointed out in chapters 4 and 7, there are good reasons to be skeptical of this study.)

Directors hiring a CEO face a serious dilemma. They must choose the very best person for the job among applicants who appear virtually indistinguishable while believing that enormous sums turn on their making the right choice. One begins to wonder why anyone agrees to serve on a corporate board. What information can they use to make this decision? Broadly speaking, there are two primary sources of information available in making hiring decisions: candidates' records of life experience and directors' impressions from personal interactions, especially job interviews. Because of the illusion of validity, both are likely to be taken as more predictive of future performance than they are.

The candidates' records of past achievements are likely to be highly dependent. Success at one job creates opportunities for a position further up the chain. The opportunity to excel at a high level, one where the stakes are great enough to attract notice, will be much rarer for those who fail early in their careers. Getting into a prestigious college makes it much easier to find a good job at graduation. That job in turn, especially combined with a prestigious college degree, impresses prestigious business schools. The high-powered MBA degree again makes it much easier to get the next important job, which can lead to a series of others. Each job does provide independent information—the candidate performed well enough to keep advancing—but much of the information is highly dependent. Early successes generate a virtuous circle that continually creates new opportunities to shine.

Once candidates achieve a strongly favorable reputation, they also acquire an ability to ride out failures. Their supervisors who start out with powerfully favorable impressions, whether based on actual experience or reputation, will find it difficult to blame the candidates if things go badly. The studies of the illusion of validity demonstrate that the supervisors' initial story—that the candidates are outstanding talents—will persist even in the face of strong, contrary data (e.g., a mistake). Failures are likely to be rationalized as the result of circumstances beyond the candidates' control—a bad economy, poor expert advice, an unfortunate confluence of circumstances, some employee's unpredictable error, the supervisor's own shabby performance, or just bad luck. Several decades' worth of achievements do convey important information about a person's skills, but this information is less reliable than directors are likely to believe.

Another problem with relying on resumes to distinguish final CEO candidates is that their records are likely to be very similar. Boards might choose based on the character of a candidate's past work. For example, the directors might feel that a background in marketing is currently more useful in a CEO than one in operations. But if that is how they feel, arguably they should look for marketing experience in making cuts in prior rounds as well. If they follow the same criteria throughout the search process, all the finalists should have fairly similar backgrounds. The distinctions among them are unlikely to prove very helpful in predicting their ability to run the company, especially given the information's dependence.

The other type of information directors typically have comes from their personal interactions with the candidates, often in the form of formal job interviews. Meeting someone face-to-face conveys a strong impression of a candidate's personality and abilities, so it is not surprising that employers rely heavily on interviews. One survey of 852 organizations found that 99 percent of them relied on interviews as part of the hiring process.[21]

Our trust in personal interactions is so strong that these interactions may swamp other, more reliable information. For example, a group of psychologists gave undergraduates majoring in psychology two forms of advice in choosing their courses.[22] One group met individually with an older student to hear about the courses the older student had enjoyed. The second group saw the results of a survey of a large group of older students. The older students had ranked courses on a scale from 1 to 5, and the survey presented the average score for each course. This second group of subjects clearly received more helpful information. The first group heard from only a single student, whose tastes in courses might have been quite different from theirs. Some of the subjects may have shared similar tastes with the student adviser, but most of them likely did not. The second group got the benefit of a whole range of students' opinions. Input from many independent sources is generally much more reliable than information from only one.

Nevertheless, the subjects who met with a single student adviser took that person's advice very seriously. In fact, the first group followed the advice they received to a much greater extent than the second group did. A single adviser was much more persuasive than the group scores, even though the scores represented much better information; the scores better predicted the subjects' future reactions to the courses they were choosing. The subjects in the first group did not know their individual advisers and had no way of determining whether their tastes in courses were similar.

The adviser was more influential only because the adviser's advice was delivered in person. Subjects in the first group must have believed that simply by speaking with the adviser, they could determine that his or her preferences would be a good prediction for their own. In other words, even in the very brief interaction that subjects had with a personal adviser, they may have believed they could learn enough about the person's personality to figure out what that person liked in a psychology course. The subjects apparently placed so much faith in the value of this short conversation that they paid a great deal of attention to the guidance that resulted, much more than other subjects did to more objectively valid information.

This experiment demonstrates what other studies have shown time and again: personal interviews are much less predictive than they appear. We are very optimistic about our ability to get a real sense of a person from a short face-to-face conversation. When psychologists compare this impression to the interviewee's later performance, though, they find that the interview was not very helpful in predicting success. Interviews provide some information, but we greatly overestimate their value.[23]

I am not suggesting that there is some better predictor out there that boards should be using to screen CEO applicants. To my knowledge, there is not. But directors should bear in mind that the information they have about candidates is very limited in its ability to predict a CEO's future performance. The illusion of validity gives directors too much faith in the power of the available information to distinguish among closely competitive finalists for the CEO job.

THE ILLUSION OF CONTROL

Have you ever played craps in a casino? In craps, everything turns on the roll of the dice. There are reasonable bets and sucker bets, so smart players should do better, over time, than, well, suckers. But in the end, it all comes down to pure luck: if the dice spin the right way for you, you win.

With fair dice, most of us have no power over how they come up. Sure, you could act like my daughter sometimes did when she was four and put the dice down with the right numbers facing up. And perhaps we can even admit the theoretical possibility of someone training to be able to manipulate the dice to roll the right number. Casinos require that every throw bounce against the end of the table to prevent this very possibility, and there are books and websites that claim to be able to teach how to master "rhythm rolling" or "dice setting."[24] But barring cheating or extraordinary skill and training (and I confess to some skepticism here), dice rolls are random. That is, after all, why we use dice for games of chance.

But if you have ever actually played craps and rolled the dice yourself, you know that there is for most people a sense that they can somehow control the dice. Players hope for a "hot shooter," one who rolls a streak of the right numbers, and celebrate (even tip) a shooter whose rolls win them money. Psychology studies have demonstrated that shooters throw the dice harder when they want a high number and softer when they want a low number.[25] At some level, players seem to believe that they can control the purely random dice throw. Shockingly, even casinos—who should be sophisticated about randomness if anyone is—seem to share this belief. One study demonstrated that dealers in Las Vegas who went through a streak of bad luck were often fired for that reason.[26]

The Harvard psychology professor Ellen Langer has named this intuition the "illusion of control."[27] Langer has studied the illusion of control in a number of different settings, but one of the most telling involved lottery tickets.[28] Say what you will about the possibility of learning to control the way dice roll, no amount of skill can help you pick a winning lottery ticket. The act of choosing a lottery ticket cannot affect the chances that the ticket will win. A lottery is a random event and cares not at all who picked which ticket. Langer devised an experiment to test whether people succumb to the illusion of control even in lotteries, where it is clear beyond question that skill has no effect on the outcome.

Langer divided subjects into two groups. She gave lottery tickets to the first group. This group's tickets were assigned; the members had nothing to do with deciding who received which ticket. The second group chose their tickets. After everyone had either been assigned or chosen their lottery tickets, the experimenters offered to buy the tickets back. The tickets each had the same chance of winning the lottery prize. From a strict rationalist perspective, then, the tickets were each worth exactly the same amount of money, and we would expect the two groups to accept roughly the same price for their tickets. Certain individuals might demand a bit more, perhaps because they were more risk accepting, were better bargainers, or enjoyed the thrill of possibility that comes with a lottery ticket. Conversely, some might have demanded less, because they were more risk-averse, were less skilled bargainers, or did not particularly like lotteries. But when we average the prices across the group, these individual idiosyncrasies should have canceled each other out. The average price demanded by members of each group should have been more or less the same.

Instead, a fascinating thing happened, an event that would be very mysterious without the illusion of control. The group members who were assigned lottery tickets were not particularly attached to them and willingly traded them for a small sum of money. The other group, whose members chose their own tickets, felt more strongly about their selection. They clung to their tickets until offered *four times* the price cheerfully accepted by the other group. There was no ambiguity about the nature of the lottery; all the subjects understood it was a purely random drawing. Nevertheless, the simple act of choosing one's ticket radically changed the ticket's perceived value. The subjects in the choice group believed they could somehow affect their odds of winning, making the tickets they picked more valuable. This is the power of the illusion of control. Even when it is clear beyond question that skill is entirely irrelevant, people latch on to any possibility that their actions matter.

Langer explains that most tasks involve a mix of luck and skill and that it is often difficult to tell which has produced a particular outcome.[29] People associate games of skill with certain kinds of activities such as choice, active involvement, and competition.[30] When games involve one or more of these elements—even when they are clearly random, such as drawing the high card from a well-shuffled deck—players are more likely to feel that they can control the outcome.[31]

Outside the laboratory, too, tasks almost always involve a mix of skill and luck. A business may stand or fall because of factors beyond any of the participants' control. For example, imagine a yo-yo manufacturer. The company makes yo-yos for fifty cents each and sells them to wholesalers for seventy-five cents. The yo-yos are made from plastic, which in turn is made largely from petroleum. The business succeeds for many years, when suddenly a war breaks out in the Middle East. As a result, the price of petroleum—and therefore of plastic—quadruples in a week. At this higher price, the company is forced to triple its yo-yo prices in order to make any profit at all. Wholesalers refuse to buy the yo-yos at that price, and the company fails.

Or consider a family farm that grows pomegranates. For most of the farm's existence, it has managed a small but stable profit selling pomegranates to the small market of those who enjoyed eating them. Then medical researchers discover that pomegranates may reduce many of the risk factors for heart disease. Suddenly, the demand and price for pomegranates skyrocket, and overnight the small family farm becomes a hugely profitable enterprise.

Skill certainly played some role in both these fictional stories. Perhaps the yo-yo company's CEO should have hedged against the price of oil by securing a long-term supply contract before the price rose so precipitously. And the family farm's managers stuck with a niche product for years, perhaps gambling on an eventual rise in popularity. But there can be little doubt that luck played a huge role in both the demise of the yo-yo company and the wild success of the pomegranate farm. In business, both skill and luck influence success. Sometimes talent counts for more, but sometimes "it's smarter to be lucky than it's lucky to be smart."[32]

The illusion of control masks this reality. Luck is inconsistent. Statistics teaches us that random events tend to revert to the mean. In other words, past luck is not predictive of future luck.[33] Luck will have affected all the candidates for a CEO position. Because of the illusion of control, neither the directors nor the candidates themselves are likely to take the role of luck into account. Instead, they will all assume that the candidates have earned their success through pure talent, determination, and hard work (and their failures through lack of the same).

All those factors are critically important to success, but so is luck. In fact, at least one study has found that luck may be the most important variable in accounting for an executive's success.[34] To determine properly which final candidate is best able to lead the company, boards would have to analyze the role luck played in the candidate's careers. The executive who ran the yo-yo company and the manager who ran the pomegranate farm may be equally talented. But in evaluating them, most of us will attribute their success or failure to their own efforts. By hiding the role of luck, the illusion of control impedes our ability to assess talent properly. In a decades-long career, luck may sometimes even out. But it may not. When choosing between closely matched candidates, ignoring luck can easily lead to inaccurate judgments about talent.

GROUPTHINK

Picture the following scene. You are standing near the end of a long line with a group of strangers. A psychologist shows the group two cards. The first card has a single printed black line. The second card has three lines, all similar to the line on the first card but of different lengths. The psychologist asks each person in turn which of the lines on the second card best matches the line on the first card. The answer is obvious, yet oddly the first person in line gives the wrong answer. Then the next person in line gives the *same* wrong answer, as does the third, the fourth, and so on. Finally it is your turn. Which answer do you give? Do you reply correctly, based on what you observe to be true? Or do you go along with the group's unanimous response even though you think the answer is wrong? After all, the entire group cannot be mistaken about something so simple. Perhaps you are just misunderstanding the question or looking at the card the wrong way. You do not want the others to make fun of you for giving the wrong answer to such an obvious question, and no one will laugh if you state the same answer everyone else gave.

This experiment was actually done by Solomon Asch, and many variants have been conducted since then by Asch and others.[35] Only one person in each group is a subject; all the others are confederates who have been told to give the same wrong answer. Although 99 percent of the subjects could correctly identify the best match when asked in private, 70 percent of them gave the wrong answer—the group's answer— at least once in a group setting.

The impulse to conform to the group is incredibly powerful. Asch's experiment is remarkable because it shows that people will conform even when the right answer is easy and obvious. The subjects *knew* the answer they were giving was wrong (though some claimed when interviewed after the experiment that they believed their wrong answer). They almost always identified the correct line when asked alone, without the pressure of a group's unanimous wrong answer. Nevertheless, even though the group's answer was obviously and objectively wrong, subjects parroted the group with surprising frequency.

Boards of directors may similarly choose to follow the herd when deciding how, and how much, to pay their chief executives. It is far safer to make the same bet as peer companies than to try something new that may fail.[36]

As powerful as the impulse to conform is when surrounded by strangers, the pressure to go along with the group can be almost overwhelming when the group consists of people we know, admire, and wish to impress. When we know our fellow group members, our natural impulse to conform can cause a phenomenon identified by the well-known psychologist Irving Janis as "groupthink."[37] Groupthink consists of a number of mistakes groups make when members are too focused on cohesion.

Some cohesion is necessary for a group to function well. If the group members have no loyalty to each other or some purpose greater than self-interest, they are likely to spend too much time fighting with one another to get much done.[38] Too much cohesion, though, can be as bad as none at all and can lead to very poor decisions.

Boards of directors are very much at risk of groupthink. Groups tend to be more cohesive when their members are friends who gather together for a prestigious undertaking. Janis himself wrote that groupthink was more likely when a group's cohesiveness was "based primarily on the rewards of being in a pleasant 'clubby' atmosphere or of gaining prestige from being a member of an elite group."[39]

Few groups are more prestigious than a public company board of directors. Being selected as a member of such an elite group inflates a person's sense of both individual and group competence. A person appointed to a board might well feel flattered to be part of such an important group. The resulting ego boost comes from the group's reflected glory. It is only natural, then, to believe that all the members of the group are extremely impressive; otherwise, group membership might be less flattering and gratifying. A group that consists of very talented people must not need much by way of outside help, advice, or information. And such a rarified group must seldom make mistakes.

If a member privately disagrees with the group's consensus, then, can you blame him or her for keeping quiet? After all, if I disagree with a group that is seldom wrong, probably I am the one making the mistake. The last thing I want is to reveal my ignorance or faulty reasoning to the rest, lest they think I am not worthy of membership. Part of groupthink is this sort of peer pressure.

Also, the more similar the group's members are in terms of background and experience, the more likely groupthink is to develop.[40] Similar people are likely to think similar thoughts, so dissenting opinions should rarely crop up. Public company boards are notoriously homogeneous. They overwhelmingly consist of white, middle-aged men who have spent their careers working for large corporations.[41] They are steeped in the same corporate culture and broadly speaking have received the same sort of educations. Public company boards are elite groups of similar people. It should not surprise anyone that they are particularly susceptible to groupthink, as many scholars have recognized.[42]

Janis identified a number of symptoms groups demonstrate when they focus too much on group harmony.[43] Four of these may work together to boost directors' confidence in their ability to choose the best CEO to unrealistic levels. The fifth may inflate CEO pay by means of a different dynamic.

The first four symptoms together produce a double whammy. They degrade the quality of the group's decision while at the same time making the group more confident its decision is correct. First, overly cohesive groups limit the range of options they consider. Adding possibilities to the discussion makes it much harder to reach a consensus and risks lengthy disputes. Suppose a group is trying to choose a paint color for a room. If the only choices are red, blue, and green, they may settle quite quickly on blue as the best option. But if seventeen shades of blue are available, building consensus will be much harder.

Group unity is difficult to maintain during a long argument, so groups overly focused on cohesion will protect internal harmony by limiting options at the outset of discussion. For example, the group's leader may start the conversation by suggesting that in her mind the best two colors are cobalt and periwinkle. To avoid dissent (and for some other reasons, explored below), the group is likely to accept the limiting instruction.

Second, groupthink groups generally do not spend much time talking about their goals when making decisions. In other words, cohesive groups focus too much on the issue at hand without putting the question into a larger strategic context. Strategic questions are often more difficult and therefore more contentious than narrower issues. It is much easier to decide whether a new car model should offer Bluetooth as part of the standard package than it is to figure out whether the company should be launching this model at all. Strategic questions affect many more constituencies within the corporation and are likely to have much higher stakes. If a board values unanimity, it should try to focus on well-defined tailored questions and avoid larger issues. The danger of this strategy is that decisions are made without regard to broader goals. The corporation's strategic direction is then the accidental product of many small choices instead of being driven by a purposeful, considered plan.

Third, once a group suffering from groupthink fixes on a plan, it seldom ventures beyond the obvious when thinking about the plan's potential disadvantages. This is again a strategy designed to avoid conflict. If the group works too hard trying to anticipate problems, some members of the group may begin to think the plan should be changed or abandoned altogether. That kind of discussion can quickly become acrimonious. The group members may not be able to avoid considering obvious disadvantages, but more subtle problems are swept under the rug in the name of unity.

Fourth, groupthink groups tend to ignore information that contradicts the favored decision. Once again, the purpose here is to avoid conflict. The group is already close to reaching a decision. Information that contradicts this decision will undermine the developing consensus. The group will then have to analyze the new information and discuss whether it is strong enough to push them to a different outcome. If so, the members will then have to find a different strategy around which they can build a new consensus. At each of these steps, there is a risk that divergent opinions will prevent agreement. Worse, one of these disputes may become serious and even disrupt the group's long-term functioning. Rather than risk this kind of dispute, the group may simply discount or ignore the information that threatens the favored decision.

These four symptoms—limiting the range of considered options, steering clear of discussing goals, avoiding serious consideration of a plan's nonobvious disadvantages, and discounting contrary data— work together to artificially inflate directors' confidence in their ability to pick the best CEO candidate. Let's take these symptoms one by one to see how they might make directors feel overconfident.

Boards that limit the options they consider may think very narrowly about the field of possible CEO candidates. As a result, they may overlook excellent candidates. For example, consider a corporation that manufactures a low-margin, largely undifferentiated product like paper. Directors of a paper company might reasonably decide at the outset that they want someone with deep operations experience who can focus on reducing costs and achieving somewhat thicker profit margins. Once a groupthink board has made this decision, it is very likely to refuse to consider someone whose background is mostly in marketing. And perhaps this is a reasonable policy, for most marketers. A typical marketer might not be able to add much value to a company whose product is fungible. A true marketing genius, on the other hand, might find a way to brand the product in a way that allows the company to boost prices and profit margins considerably. (Please do not ask me how this could be done. If I knew, I would be selling paper.) A groupthink board would generally dismiss even a marketing genius out of hand, since it decided early on to look for an operations expert as the new CEO.

The directors will believe they have chosen from the top talent available. As a result, they will feel very confident that they have chosen the best possible person as CEO. But their confidence is unwarranted. The board actually missed out on an opportunity to hire someone who could change the very nature of the company's business for the better. The directors' focus on conformity led them to narrow their options too much, and groupthink prevented them from realizing their mistake.

Similarly, boards that studiously avoid discussing their long-term goals may adhere to qualifications criteria even when they have a chance to hire someone outstanding who falls outside those criteria. Consider again the paper company whose board wants an operations expert as the company's next CEO. The company's goal is to improve profits. Once the board decided on a tactic for achieving that goal, it lost sight of the goal and focused only on the tactic. As a result, it missed out on an opportunity to hire a major marketing talent who would have better achieved the company's goals, only using a different tactic. Here again the directors will be confident they made the right choice. But because they chose only from operations experts, their confidence is unfounded.

This example also highlights the impact of the third symptom, avoiding discussion of nonobvious disadvantages of the favored option. When the board made its initial decision on hiring criteria, it had good reasons for focusing on operations specialists. Paper is largely a fungible product, so any advantage in the market is likely to come from being able to offer a lower price. The disadvantages of this plan are less obvious, though still not especially difficult to see. An operations specialist is unlikely to have a revolutionary vision for the company. Someone whose career has been devoted to making incremental improvements is going to continue to make small changes. Perhaps that is for the best. Revolutionary visions often come with a great deal of risk, and perhaps the board was correct to stick to what the company knew could succeed.

But the point here is that groupthink prevented the board from even considering an alternative option, such as a marketing guru. Had the directors engaged in this debate, they might have come to the same conclusion, but doubts might have been raised that left the directors more open to consider other options that came along. Instead, by refusing to consider nonobvious disadvantages of their plan, the directors artificially inflated their confidence that the path they had chosen was the correct one.

The fourth symptom—discounting contrary data—can also provide directors with false confidence that they have made the right hiring decision. In the paper company example, imagine that the directors coalesced around a particular CEO candidate. At that stage, they hired a private detective to investigate the favored candidate more thoroughly. The detective interviewed several dozen people who at various times had worked for or supervised the potential CEO. During these interviews, the detective met a former deputy who confided that the candidate had had a practice of choosing suppliers based on their willingness to pay kickbacks. Shocked at this revelation, the detective immediately reported the allegation to the board.

A groupthink board might discount this contrary data. It has already come very close to a consensus, and it will struggle to avoid anything that disrupts that consensus. The directors could follow many strategies to discount the negative information. They could argue the deputy is the only person who has made these allegations. If the allegations were true, surely someone else would also have come forward. Or they could attack the deputy's character, perhaps on the grounds that he or she is a disgruntled former employee.

Regardless of the particular method the directors use, if groupthink is operating, they will find a way to ignore the new information and hire their favored candidate as their CEO. This decision might well be the right one. Perhaps the deputy was lying or mistaken. Or perhaps the detective somehow misunderstood. But in the absence of conclusive proof of the candidate's innocence, the directors should investigate further before finalizing their choice. Groupthink can prevent this from happening. Instead, the directors may brush the negative information aside and (too) confidently proceed to hire their chosen candidate.

The fifth (and final for our purposes) symptom of groupthink is that affected groups are unusually likely to defer to their leader.[44] The leader is generally seen as personifying the group's values. Members demonstrate that they agree with the group's values by voting in favor of the leader's proposals. Conversely, disagreeing with the leader is perceived as rejecting the group's values. The hallmark of groupthink is cohesion, so affected groups are particularly reluctant to publicly repudiate the group's core beliefs by disagreeing with the leader.

This kind of outsized deference by boards can lead to excessive pay packages for CEOs. CEOs are leaders of their corporations and by extension, of their boards. In recognition of this fact, until recently most CEOs also had the title chairman of the board. There is now a trend to split the two roles to reduce this problem, but the underlying reality often remains much the same.[45] As I discussed in chapter 3, directorships are part-time positions. The CEO, on the other hand, likely spends every waking hour working for the company. As a result, CEOs generally set boards' agendas, presenting them with the issues the CEOs believe require their attention. The board has the power to fire the CEO, so in a sense the directors as a group are the CEO's bosses. But as long as the CEO retains the directors' good opinion, the CEO leads the group.

When the CEO proposes his or her own pay package, the directors are put in an awkward position. Formally, they are the CEO's employers. They represent the shareholders and should try to bargain the CEO down to the lowest acceptable compensation. But they are also members of a board effectively led by the CEO. They would normally give great deference to any proposal the CEO put before them as the leader of the company. In the case of the CEO's pay, they should exercise much greater caution. The CEO cannot be expected to have the company's interests at heart when negotiating his or her own compensation. But boards subject to groupthink will be especially likely to defer to their leader, the CEO, even on issues of executive compensation.

The first four symptoms of groupthink combine to urge the board toward excessive optimism about the CEO. Directors who believe they have the ideal CEO may—perhaps rightly—see it as their duty to make sure that that CEO joins the company (or stays), regardless of cost. The fifth groupthink symptom inhibits tough questions about pay. When directors fall under the influence of some or all of these groupthink symptoms, the compensation package can easily grow very quickly.

In addition, the form of compensation may prove less than ideal. Groupthink discourages directors from considering serious departures from the types of compensation that peer companies are using. Groupthink pushes people to limit the range of options they consider, making it harder to adopt new or different compensation structures. Directors subject to groupthink will also avoid deeper analysis of the merits of traditional compensation tools like stock options and restricted stock and will tend to ignore or discredit data that question these tools' usefulness. As a result, not only will groupthink tend to increase compensation, but it will also hinder efforts to reform the structure of CEOs' pay packages.

SOCIAL CASCADES

Imagine a large lecture hall where two small urns sit on a desk at the front of the room. Each urn contains three balls. The first urn, which we will call Mostly Dark, contains two dark balls and one light ball. The second urn, Mostly Light, contains two light balls and one dark ball. An instructor takes the urns into another room and flips a coin to decide which urn she will use. She then pours the balls from the selected urn into a cup. She brings the cup of balls back into the lecture hall and places it on the front desk.

The students' task is to figure out which urn the instructor's coin toss chose, Mostly Dark or Mostly Light. To help, each student will have a chance to draw a single ball from the cup. Then that student must guess whether the cup comes from the Mostly Dark urn or the Mostly Light urn. Only the student whose turn it is to draw a ball from the cup will see the ball's color. Then that student will return the ball and state his or her guess out loud so that the other students can hear.

For the first student, the game is straightforward. If the student draws a light ball, the best guess is Mostly Light; with only one ball drawn, the odds are two to one that the instructor chose the urn with more balls of the same color as the drawn ball.

For the second student, the game is a bit more complicated. Since the first student guessed Mostly Light, the second student can infer that the first drew a light ball (or did not understand the game, but we can leave that possibility aside). If the second student also draws a light ball, the best guess is clearly again Mostly Light. Now presumably both draws were light balls, so the odds have risen to nearly 90 percent that the instructor chose the Mostly Light urn. If the second student draws a dark ball, though, the two draws cancel one another out. At this point, it is as though the second student has no information at all about which urn was chosen. The second student might as well flip a coin to choose which urn is correct.

Let us suppose that the second student did draw a dark ball and randomly chose to guess Mostly Light. The third student might as well stay seated; it no longer matters whether the third student draws a light ball or a dark one. Both of the first two students guessed Mostly Light. Most likely, this means that both drew light balls. (From the third student's perspective, there is a 75 percent chance that the second student drew a white ball.)[46] Even if the third student draws a dark ball, the balls in the cup would still be twice as likely to have come from the Mostly Light urn (if we assume the first two balls were light; the odds go down a bit if we allow for the small chance that the second ball was dark, but the Mostly Light urn is still about 50 percent more likely).[47]

Getting beyond the math, the bottom line for the third student—and for all subsequent students—is that his private information (what color ball he draws) sometimes becomes entirely irrelevant. The publicly available information—the prior students' guesses about which urn won the instructor's coin toss—outweighs the impact of any privately available information. No matter what color ball each student draws, the best guess is Mostly Light.

This result would not trouble us much if the public information always pointed us to the right path. Unfortunately, while the public information will often be correct, it can also easily steer us in the wrong direction. Remember that if the second student in our example drew a dark ball, there was a 50 percent chance he or she would guess the wrong urn (and sometimes this guess would agree with the first student's). More simply, the first two students might have picked the minority color. Once the first two students have made the same guess, all the other students should repeat that guess, regardless of what color ball they draw. In fact, the mathematical case for making the same guess gets progressively stronger as more and more students repeat the answer.

Social psychologists call this outcome a "social cascade," when the apparent value of public information outweighs the impact of any private information so that subsequent players repeatedly choose the same answer.[48]

Social cascades are not just theoretical. The thought experiment with the two urns was designed and tested by the economists Lisa Anderson and Charles Holt.[49] Anderson and Holt found that social cascades arose in 75 percent of the games in which they were mathematically possible.[50]

In our experiment, the social cascade was, in a sense, rational. Unlike the other psychological phenomena discussed in this chapter, this type of cascade does not depend on people acting out of emotion instead of pure reason. The cascade formed because students observed prior participants' guesses and made a rational calculation that the sum total of publicly available information was more predictive than their private information.

Cascades can arise under other circumstances, however, that may be less purely rational. Since everyone's guesses are public, people may choose guesses they privately doubt to conform with the group and preserve their reputations.[51] For example, imagine a group of teenagers asked to guess the number one rock band by sales. If the first few teenagers guess their favorite (very popular) groups, the others may be reluctant to guess a less hip band even if this is the right answer. Being wrong may seem unimportant compared to being tagged as a geek who likes uncool music.

Regardless of how the cascade forms, once it takes effect the results often take on the credibility of the market. When markets function well, they can be amazingly good at certain tasks, such as setting an efficient price. There is even some evidence that markets can be designed to do miraculous, almost mystical things like predicting Academy Award winners.[52] It is right and good, then, that in our culture markets have tremendous credibility.

For a market to work well, though, the participants must function independently. Markets' power comes in part from their ability to aggregate many individual guesses about the future, whether that future concerns the price of oil or the winner of the next presidential election. If what looks like a market is really a game of follow the leader, the outcome is not likely to be especially accurate.

The danger of cascades is that they *look* like markets. To all appearances, independent and often sophisticated players have all come to the same conclusion. In reality, though, only the first few participants made independent judgments; the remaining bets are based on the first few being correct. If the first few guesses are wrong, the "market" will reach the wrong result.

There is good reason to think CEO compensation is in part the result of a social cascade. Cascades are likely when participants do not have much private information (at least compared to the amount of publicly available information) and when each participant's actions can be observed by the others.[53] These two conditions were present in the urn experiment. Each student had only limited information—the color of the ball he or she drew—and the other students all could see each student's guess about which urn the instructor had chosen.

These same conditions exist in the CEO labor market. The most important question in hiring a CEO is the value any given candidate will add to the business. We would ideally like to know how much each applicant would add to the firm's bottom line. When it comes to measuring CEOs' past contributions, it is very difficult to separate the impact of the CEO from the host of other factors that contribute to a company's results. As discussed earlier, variables as diverse as prevailing interest rates, the price of oil, the value of the dollar, the vagaries of fashion, and of course the contributions of the thousands of other company employees all play an important role in determining whether a company has a good year or a bad one.

Projecting a CEO's future contribution is even more problematic, since it involves all these same issues with the added complication of having to predict the future. Under such conditions of uncertainty and with little private information, cascades can easily arise.

The upshot is that boards never have very good information about their CEO's value. They have their impressions from their own interactions with the CEO, chiefly at board meetings, perhaps a sense of how the other senior officers view their boss, and the company's past results under the CEO's leadership. They also have access to the various economic and environmental factors that could have skewed results in one direction or the other. But none of this is particularly precise, and certainly even the sum total does not remotely approach an accurate valuation of the CEO's services.

My point here is not that boards are somehow neglecting their duties but that no matter how diligent the directors are, they simply cannot know with any precision how much their CEO added to (or subtracted from) the company's bottom line. They may have a sense of whether the

CEO is doing a good job or a poor one. The critical information they lack, though, is just *how* valuable it is to have a great CEO. For a large company with, say, a $10 billion market capitalization, is hiring the best person available worth $1 million more than the next best person? Ten million? A billion? Without this information, it is impossible to know that the company is getting its money's worth in hiring a chief executive. As a result, boards are likely to look to other companies for guidance for an appropriate valuation range of CEO talent.

Similarly, when it comes to pay structure, directors are likely to peer at their neighbor's paper for the correct answer. As discussed in chapter 6, there is little persuasive evidence that linking CEOs' pay to their corporations' performance improves corporations' growth. But at the same time, there are so many variables that influence corporate performance that the link between any particular pay structure and corporate outcomes is hard to discern, even with very sophisticated and careful statistical analysis. If directors make more of the CEO's pay depend on the company's performance and profits rise, they may attribute the increase to a more efficient compensation structure. If instead profits subsequently fall, directors may find a host of other reasons that explain why business is weaker. There is no clear, direct feedback mechanism for the structure (or, for that matter, the amount) of performance pay that unambiguously tells directors when their experiments have succeeded or failed. They therefore have very little private information about the utility of different performance pay structures and are very likely to imitate their competitors' practices.

This brings us to the second condition for social cascades: the transparency of other participants' decisions. Like the students' guesses in the urn experiment, CEO compensation packages are largely available to the public and to other companies' boards of directors. The Securities and Exchange Commission has long required fairly extensive disclosure of CEO compensation and in 2006 broadened its requirements to apply to more forms of compensation.[54] Public corporations must include these disclosures in their public filings, which are easily available on the SEC's website, www.sec.gov. Anyone wishing to indulge their voyeuristic impulses can do so easily by looking up a company's annual proxy statement.

In addition, it is common practice for companies to hire a compensation consultant when deciding the CEO's pay.[55] The consultant prepares a comparison study that shows how CEOs at similar corporations are compensated. At a minimum, this sort of study acts as a more convenient source of the same information provided by the SEC filings, boosting transparency. But as many compensation experts have pointed out—and as I discussed in chapter 3—the compensation consultants generally are far from neutral in this process.[56] Historically, the same consultant a company hired to analyze its CEO's pay was also hired to advise on employee compensation for the company's other employees.[57] For this second, much larger and more lucrative task, it is generally the CEO who decides which consultant to hire. As a result, a consultant who wants the larger job has every incentive to make sure the CEO is pleased with his or her advice on the CEO's own compensation. The consultant can greatly influence the board's view of an appropriate level of pay by carefully choosing the "comparable" companies for the comparison study.[58] By choosing companies with relatively high CEO compensation, the consultant can make it seem as though the CEO is underpaid.

Even an unbiased comparison study, though, would produce spiraling pay. Boards hire people they believe are extraordinary to lead their companies. Certainly they should think that their CEO is above average for similar companies; otherwise, they should hire someone else. If a CEO is extraordinary, far above average, then he or she should be paid accordingly. A balanced comparison study would necessarily show that some of the CEOs in the study are paid less than others. The boards that employed these unfortunate executives would then reasonably try to repair this injustice by boosting their underpaid CEOs' compensation. The next year, a different set of CEOs in the group would appear underpaid, and their boards would similarly try to fix the problem. So even if every compensation consultant was perfectly objective, fair, and balanced, we should still expect to see companies raising average CEO pay every year.

This upward ratcheting might not occur if boards thought that other companies were acting irrationally in setting compensation for their CEOs. But few boards think this way. Instead, what other companies do is seen as the product of market forces, supply and demand generating an efficient price for managerial talent.[59] What is actually happening is probably a form of social cascade, with successive companies matching (or bettering) others' guesses as to what a good CEO is worth. What boards perceive, though, is the invisible hand of the market producing the correct result.

Boards' perceptions to some extent become a self-fulfilling prophecy. If almost everyone believes talented CEOs are worth $10 million a year, those who think CEOs should be paid less are going to be hard pressed to find a good one willing to work for them. The illusion that an efficient market values CEOs at $10 million persuades potential CEOs that they are really worth that much. As a result, they will quite reasonably demand to be paid what the "market" has said they are worth. Any company that refuses will have to hire a less qualified person (or at least a less well-credentialed person). And if that person succeeds, the company will quickly lose him or her to a competitor willing to pay the going rate.

This dynamic played out very clearly when United Airlines went bankrupt in 2006. United's bankruptcy trustee had to get the bankruptcy court's approval for United's executives' new, very generous pay packages. Some of United's creditors strenuously objected to paying such princely sums to people leading a company that was already broke.

Bankruptcy judges are federally appointed and paid by our taxes. Whatever we might think about public company directors and their tendency to want to please their CEO (see chapter 5), bankruptcy judges are not similarly amenable to the CEO's whims. Nevertheless, the judge in the United Airlines case approved the executives' pay packages. (This is not unusual. Executive pay for companies in bankruptcy looks very similar to executive pay in companies that are doing well.)[60] In explaining his decision, the judge wrote: "It may be we have a culture in this country that overcompensates management. . . . But United is just one enterprise that operates in that general environment. . . . The marketplace indicates this is a reasonable plan."[61] Such is the power of social cascades to disguise themselves as the efficient market at work.

CONCLUSION

Behavioral dynamics theory teaches us two central lessons. First, boards are primed to pay their CEOs too much. They overestimate their ability to tell which close contender will be the best CEO. Then, once they have persuaded themselves that one candidate is much better than the others, they pay whatever is necessary to hire their first choice. Boards do not ask CEOs to compete on price, only on perceived quality.

Second, boards are unlikely to look too closely at the empirical data when deciding on the structure of the CEO's pay package. So long as the structure mirrors what their peers are doing, a number of interacting psychological dynamics—the illusions of validity and control, groupthink, and social cascades—will provide comfort to the directors that they are doing the right thing.

These two lessons provide what I believe is the most convincing explanation of the past generation's transformations in executive pay. As Lynn Stout and others have recognized, during the 1970s, academics in economics and finance began propagating the idea that CEOs should not be paid in straight salaries and short-term bonuses, as was the common practice at the time. Instead, they argued that companies should reward CEOs when they have produced results, and only when they have produced results.[62]

This recommendation not only had tremendous academic credibility behind it but also rang true. Most of us share the basic intuition that people will try to achieve the goals that bring them rewards. If the prize goes to the fastest runner, competitors will work on running faster. If instead the prize goes to the person who can run the farthest, competitors will try to build endurance. Performance pay caught on like wildfire. The more companies adopted some form of performance pay, the better an idea it seemed, thanks again to the illusions of validity and control, groupthink, and social cascades. Directors' norms about pay shifted over the years, until performance pay generally (and options specifically) became de rigueur.[63]

In an arena with no real feedback available about CEOs' contribution to corporations' success, there are no obvious consequences for guessing wrong. *Any* amount of pay can be justified so long as the company is performing well (and often even when it is not). Companies are never punished by the product or services markets for overpaying their CEOs in a way that can be traced directly back to the overpayment, nor are they saliently rewarded by the product or services markets for getting CEO pay right in either structure or amount. There may be serious consequences to mistakes in this area, but there are so many confounding variables that the blame can always be laid elsewhere. There is no clear feedback about executive pay decisions.

Directors have filled this informational vacuum by looking to academics and their own intuition for guidance. As they gradually began adopting more performance pay during the 1970s and 1980s, their decisions were increasingly validated by their peers, thanks to the psychological phenomena discussed in this chapter. Even as the historic bull market of the 1980s and 1990s meshed with the new options-heavy pay structure to boost CEO pay into the stratosphere, directors continued to justify the pay. They based their judgment on the perceived importance of CEOs to company results (an importance chapter 7 argued is exaggerated), a stream of academic theories justifying every pay increase as efficient (covered in chapter 4), and the echo chamber of compensation surveys.[64] How could the emperor have no clothes when everyone—including the most learned—insisted he was splendidly dressed?

Unfortunately, the emperor is quite naked. As I discussed in chapter 6, performance pay has not boosted corporate profits. Companies have spent enormous sums to motivate executive talent without reaping commensurate rewards. Yet, far from cutting back, directors—prompted by shareholders' demands, federal tax law, and corporate governance advocates—have continued to invest in performance pay. Thanks to psychological dynamics, both directors and shareholders have ignored the evidence that performance pay simply doesn't work. We need to do something to change how companies think about executive pay.

Before we get to reform, though, there is a more fundamental question to be tackled. For the most part, I have assumed throughout this book that the purpose of corporate governance—and therefore of executive compensation—is to further the shareholders' interests. There are good reasons for this assumption. The shareholders are in important senses the owners of the corporation, so it is natural to think that their interests should trump those of other corporate constituencies such as bondholders, customers, suppliers, employees, and the communities in which corporations operate. But not everyone shares this assumption, so before I plunge into reform proposals I need to answer a foundational question: whose interests matter?

PART THREE

How Can We Best Reform the System?

CHAPTER 9

Alignment Mythology

Early in the twentieth century, the storied Ford Motor Company was owned by founder Henry Ford and a few minority investors. The minority included the Dodge brothers, who later went on to create their own line of vehicles that eventually became part of the Chrysler Corporation. Ford Motor was extremely prosperous at the time, but Henry Ford decided to stop paying dividends to the shareholders. (The corporation had paid considerable dividends up to that point.) Instead, he planned to devote the company's enormous profits to expanding the business and reducing the sale price of Ford Motor's cars.

The price reduction was not intended to reach a greater volume of buyers (and hence increase profits) but to spread the benefits of car ownership to as many consumers as possible. The price cut was expensive and would easily offset the benefit from increased sales. Henry Ford was willing to reduce the value of the company (and therefore its stock) in order to help people.

How do we know so much about Ford's motivations? He told us, under oath, in a famous court case launched by the Dodge brothers. Ford testified, "My ambition is to employ still more men, to spread the benefits of this industrial system to the greatest possible number, to help them build up their lives and their homes."[1] (Although this is the dominant version of the story, there is evidence that Ford's testimony was aimed at bolstering sales by portraying the company as the friend of the working class.)[2]

As shareholders, the Dodge brothers were outraged by this policy, which amounted to Ford giving their money away to consumers and Ford Motor's workers. In their lawsuit, they argued that the company's purpose was to enrich the shareholders, not the world at large. Policies such as the price cut that were designed with charitable, rather than profit-seeking, intent were out of bounds. The Michigan Supreme Court agreed, holding flatly:

> A business corporation is organized and carried on primarily for the profit of the stockholders. The powers of the directors are to be employed for that end. The discretion of directors is to be exercised in the choice of means to attain that end and does not extend to a change in the end itself, to the reduction of profits or to the nondistribution of profits among stockholders in order to devote them to other purposes.[3]

Despite the apparently absolute nature of this holding, the court refused to quash Ford's expansion plans and declined to order an increase in prices. The Dodge brothers had to content themselves with the court's command that Ford Motor declare a large dividend. The court explained this apparently incongruous result as stemming from its normal deference to the board's judgment in running the company. It wrote, "The judges are not business experts. It is recognized that plans must often be made for a long future, for expected competition, for a continuing as well as an immediately profitable venture."[4]

Although Henry Ford frankly admitted that his goals were not for the interests of the company over any time horizon, short, medium, or long, the court elected not to break its long-standing habit of deferring to the board's business judgment in the conduct of the corporation's affairs. Instead, it chose to believe that Ford Motor's plans could eventually redound to the shareholders' benefits, apparently in the face of management's contrary desires.

The *Dodge v. Ford Motor Company* case is puzzling in many respects and has prompted some interesting scholarly commentary.[5] But its importance lies more in symbolism than in substance. The court arguably failed to enforce its own language about the directors' duties, yet that language represents the conventional wisdom about what directors are supposed to do and is the case's most enduring legacy. The board's task is to maximize the wealth of the corporation's shareholders, a concept known as "shareholder primacy."[6]

Nowhere is the focus on shareholder primacy more evident than in executive compensation. Directors, executives, consultants, and even academics almost unanimously agree that executive compensation should align CEOs' incentives with those of shareholders. Even critics of current compensation methods, such as Bebchuk and Fried, agree that the goal is shareholder alignment.[7] Popular compensation methods such as stock options and restricted stock are justified by arguing that they will encourage CEOs to focus on what generally matters most to shareholders: boosting the company's stock price. In the compensation arena at least, the principle that executives' interests should be aligned with those of shareholders rises nearly to the level of religious dogma. It is the almost unquestioned assumption behind all executive compensation design.

In chapter 6, I questioned whether the strategies used to achieve this alignment are effective. I argued there is serious doubt whether compensation devices such as options and restricted stock successfully motivate executives to work toward shareholders' interests and even greater doubt as to whether any benefit achieved is worth these devices' enormous cost. Here I want to ask a more foundational question: are we reaching toward the right goal? Shareholders are without doubt a crucial corporate constituency. But should senior officers pursue shareholders' welfare exclusively? Or are other corporate constituencies—groups such as bondholders, employees, customers, suppliers, and communities—also worthy of some attention?

A number of corporate legal scholars have sharply criticized shareholder primacy. They tell a horror story of massive layoffs, wholesale shifting of jobs offshore, environmental degradation, the manufacture of shoddy products, suppliers left without customers, once-thriving communities left empty, bondholders holding worthless corporate debt, faltering competition, rising prices, and impoverished product choices. And all due to corporations' laser focus on increasing shareholder wealth, no matter the cost to the corporation's other constituencies or to society generally. Their solutions generally involve requiring directors and senior officers to take these other concerns into account when making corporate decisions, often by extending directors' fiduciary duties beyond shareholders to these other stakeholders.[8]

Defenders of shareholder primacy worry that distracting management's attention from the core mission of increasing profits (and therefore shareholder wealth) could weaken the company. They might point to the cautionary tale of Malden Mills.

Malden Mills was a family-owned company founded in 1906. The company's primary business was the manufacture of polar fleece, a warm, lightweight fabric used in outdoor clothing. In 1995, a fire destroyed the company's primary manufacturing facility in Lawrence, Massachusetts. Instead of retiring or moving the mill to a source of cheaper labor like the southern United States or offshore, the company's owner, Aaron Feuerstein, determined to use the $300 million in insurance funds to rebuild the mill in Lawrence. He also kept the company's idled employees on the payroll for months, at a cost of some $25 million. Feuerstein explained his actions by saying, "There are times in business when you don't think of the financial consequences but of the human consequences."[9]

A large chunk of the reconstruction funds went to rebuild a furniture upholstery facility. This business had accounted for half the company's revenues before the fire and had employed over half the company's workers. But the upholstery customers had found other sources of supply by the time the factory was rebuilt, and they did not return. Ultimately, those fifteen hundred workers lost their jobs despite Feuerstein's efforts. The polar fleece business also languished. Feuerstein asked his lenders for a $25 million loan to stave off bankruptcy—almost precisely the amount he had spent paying his idled workers after the fire.[10] His lenders refused and forced the company into Chapter 11.[11] Feuerstein lost control of the company after it emerged from bankruptcy. Eventually the company sank back into bankruptcy and its assets were sold to a private-equity firm, Chrysalis Capital Partners.[12]

At first, Malden Mills seemed an inspirational story and Feuerstein a model owner and manager. President Clinton praised him, as did the popular press.[13] Feuerstein arguably represented exactly what stakeholder theorists desire—a manager who takes into account the needs of the company's employees and the surrounding community. But as the story developed, it presented a starkly different narrative. Although the company's failure had other contributing causes—especially competition from low-priced Asian imports—Feuerstein's humanitarian actions seem the primary culprit.[14] Malden Mills now sounds a warning about the consequences for managers who pay too much attention to the needs of stakeholders other than the shareholders. Feuerstein's prodigious efforts to help his workers weighed down his company with debt that ultimately sank the firm. In the end, trying to help his workers only delayed the inevitable for them and cost Feuerstein his century-old family business.

Who's right? Could changes in corporate governance law steer corporations toward more pro-social behaviors, as stakeholder scholars claim? Or will a requirement that managers please more than one master create more problems than it solves? Corporate law scholars have debated these issues since at least the 1930s.[15] Despite the nearly unanimous support for shareholder primacy demonstrated in executive compensation policy, the answer turns out to be opaque. The muddiness of the debate does not justify the almost religious faith in shareholder primacy held by participants in the executive compensation process.

DOES THE LAW DEMAND SHAREHOLDER PRIMACY?

The law itself actually seems to tilt toward the stakeholder theory in many states. The majority of states—though not Delaware—have bolstered the stakeholder theory through legislation. Thirty states have passed "other constituency" statutes, laws that expressly permit boards of directors (and by extension, senior managers) to consider other constituencies when governing the corporation. States were generally motivated by a desire to impede hostile takeovers, but only a few of these statutes limit their effect to the takeover context.[16]

Still, nearly all these statutes are only permissive, not mandatory. They grant management greater latitude to consider nonshareholder stakeholders, but do not require that they do so. Stakeholders who feel they are being shortchanged have no remedy, since the statutes are permissive. Many of the statutes make this clear by expressly depriving stakeholders of the power to sue directors under the law. For these reasons and others, Stephen Bainbridge has reasonably argued that these statutes represent only a slight expansion of the courts' usual deference to the boards' right to manage corporations as they see fit rather than an endorsement of the stakeholder theory.[17]

Supportive of Bainbridge's thesis of director primacy is courts' tendency—in states that require directors to put shareholders' interests first—to pay lip service to shareholder primacy without actually enforcing it. In the absence of fraud, self-dealing, or grossly negligent behavior, courts generally defer to the board's decisions on how to run the company, following the business judgment rule.[18] And as I mentioned just above, in the *Dodge* case itself the court largely permitted management to do as it liked, even in the face of the company president's admitted flaunting of the shareholder primacy principle. So long as managers can provide some sincere rationale for why actions that seem targeted at helping nonshareholder stakeholders will eventually redound to shareholders' benefit, courts have deferred to their judgment.[19]

Bainbridge may well be correct, then, but these "other constituency" statutes have indisputably granted directors and officers the freedom to act for other stakeholders if they so choose. It is hard to reconcile this freedom with strict shareholder primacy, even if it does not represent a wholehearted ratification of the stakeholder theory.

Delaware, the most important state for corporate law, has not passed an "other constituency" statute. The Delaware corporations statute is essentially silent about the purpose boards should pursue, though David Yosifon has argued it obliquely hints at shareholder primacy.[20] Delaware case law contains statements that point in both directions, and respected judges and scholars have lined up on either side of this issue.[21]

The most recent statement on the issue by the Delaware Chancery Court, though—a case called *ebay v. Newmark*—clearly endorses shareholder primacy. The case involved a dispute between two of the founders of Craigslist, on the one hand, and ebay, Inc., on the other. ebay had bought a 28.4 percent stake in Craigslist from one of Craigslist's three founders, with a side payment to the other two to compensate them for certain protections ebay wanted as a minority stockholder. The remaining founders subsequently worried that ebay would try to get involved in running the company, so they put in place a strategy to ensure that they and their heirs would retain control. They expressly stated that they wanted Craigslist to focus on public service and not profit maximization and that this desire justified their actions to retain control. The Chancery Court squarely rejected this argument, writing:

> Having chosen a for-profit corporate form, the Craigslist directors are bound by the fiduciary duties and standards that accompany that form. Those standards include acting to promote the value of the corporation for the benefit of its stockholders. The "Inc." after the company name has to mean at least that. Thus, I cannot accept as valid for the purposes of implementing the Rights Plan a corporate policy that specifically, clearly, and admittedly seeks *not* to maximize the economic value of a for-profit Delaware corporation for the benefit of its stockholders—no matter whether those stockholders are individuals of modest means or a corporate titan of online commerce. (original emphasis)[22]

At the moment, then, the safest interpretation of Delaware law would seem to be that it embraces shareholder primacy. Note, though, that the Delaware Supreme Court's statements on this question have arguably shifted back and forth, and the Supreme Court trumps the

Chancery Court. We therefore cannot be entirely certain that shareholder primacy represents the law in Delaware. For most purposes, Bainbridge's point about *director* primacy is by far the most relevant.[23] Delaware grants boards so much latitude that as long as there is some sincerely intended connection between the board's decision to favor some nonshareholder constituency and maximizing shareholder wealth over some time horizon, the courts are highly likely to validate the board's action.

Whether or not CEOs and directors are legally permitted to consider interests other than shareholder wealth, there is substantial evidence that they often do so. Prominent businessmen during the 1930s spoke publicly about corporations' obligations to employees, customers, and the public.[24] Surveys of managers from the late 1960s through the 1980s have consistently demonstrated managers' belief that ethics required them to focus on employees' and customers' concerns and not solely on those of shareholders.[25] And more recent surveys tell us the same story: most directors believe that shareholders are their most important constituent but that they are ethically or pragmatically required to pursue the interests of other constituencies as well.[26]

SHOULD THE LAW DEMAND SHAREHOLDER PRIMACY?

Law and current practice, though, tell us only what *is,* and we should not try to reason from *is* to *ought.* When arguing about what officers and directors *ought* to do, the two sides have sparred over a wide field of arguments. Broadly speaking, the normative debate ranges over four major issues: conceptual arguments about the nature of shareholders' role; a debate over the best way to minimize agency costs; contentions about the most effective method to generate wealth; and disputes about the likely outcome of a bargain among the parties.

Shareholders' Role

Shareholder primacy advocates justify focusing exclusively on shareholder welfare in part by pointing to the nature of common stock. The less persuasive version of this thesis claims that shareholders own the corporation. As owners, shareholders ought to be in control and shareholders' agents (the directors and senior officers) should act exclusively in their principals' interests. The Nobel Prize–winning economist Milton Friedman advanced this theory, writing:

[A] corporate executive is an employee of the owners of the business. He has direct responsibility to his employers. That responsibility is to conduct the business in accordance with their desires, which generally will be to make as much money as possible. . . . The whole justification for permitting the corporate executive to be selected by the stockholders is that the executive is an agent serving the interests of his principal.[27]

This argument is a gross oversimplification of the relationship between common stockholders and the corporation. Shareholders do own *something,* but in a public corporation, they do not "own" the corporation in the way that a landholder "owns" real property or a sole proprietor "owns" a business. Labeling shareholders "owners" is a rhetorical move aimed at conflating wildly different situations in an effort to provide convincing, intuitive solutions to complex problems.[28]

As Stout and Bainbridge have argued separately, shareholders lack many of the core rights we generally associate with ownership. Owners control their property and have an unquestioned right to any profits the property generates. If I own a piece of land, for example, I have the right to keep others from entering my property. I also have the right to profit from any gold I discover there. In contrast, individual shareholders usually exercise little control over public corporations and have no right to corporate profits.

Shareholders have a statutory right to vote on certain corporate decisions, such as the election of directors, amendments to the certificate of incorporation, a merger with another business entity, the sale of substantially all the corporation's assets out of the usual course of business, and the corporation's dissolution. Otherwise, the business is run by the directors and senior officers. When shareholders have a right to vote, the board generally must first initiate an action to trigger that right. Even the election of directors is essentially controlled by the board, since the incumbent directors generally nominate their own successors, as I explained in chapter 3.

When the corporation earns a profit, the board may decide to pay out some of that money to the shareholders in the form of a dividend or a share repurchase. But these decisions are entirely at the board's discretion. Under modern corporation statutes, shareholders have no inherent power to sue the board to force the company to pay a dividend.[29]

Ownership consists of a bundle of different rights, and these can be divided among many different claimants.[30] Shareholders possess too few property rights in the corporation to allow us simply to defer to their interests as corporate "owners."[31]

A more refined version of this argument describes shareholders not as owners but as residual claimants to the corporation's assets. Daniel Fischel argues protecting shareholders' interests should be management's primary goal because shareholders have the best incentive to foster the firm's growth. Shareholders prosper only to the extent the company has money left over after satisfying all its other claimants, groups such as employees and bondholders whose right to a share of the firm's revenues is fixed by contract. Shareholders want to maximize the firm's value because their own returns are contingent on the firm's prosperity. The more the company keeps after paying off workers and lenders, the more money is available to reward shareholders with dividends and increased share values. Since shareholders have the best incentives to encourage growth, their interests should dominate the firm.[32]

Stout critiques this view as based on inaccurate law. Shareholders do not have a right to dividends except by the board's grace. Only when the corporation is bankrupt does the law treat shareholders as residual claimants, entitled to whatever is left over after the corporation has satisfied all other valid claimants.[33] While correct, this argument misses the larger point. Fischel cares about shareholders' rights only instrumentally, as a means to achieve economic growth.

For Fischel's conception to work, shareholders do not need a legal entitlement to dividends; they only need some incentive to act as though the company's profit growth matters to them. Dividends are one reason shareholders might care, but another is growth in the company's stock price. Many large companies seldom (or never!) pay dividends, yet their shareholders reap enormous gains because the company's stock price keeps rising. Microsoft, for example, paid its first dividend in 2003, nearly thirty years after its founding in 1975. Yet many Microsoft investors became enormously wealthy over those three decades purely from the company's share price appreciation. As long as shareholders are the group with the best incentive to push for a better bottom line, mandating that directors and management pursue shareholders' interests should be the best way to ensure public companies make every effort to grow rapidly.

The more important problem with Fischel's defense of shareholder primacy is that shareholders do not internalize all of the harms corporations cause in the pursuit of growth, nor do they internalize all the benefits corporations may bestow. A corporation's local headquarters may help a community flourish, providing an increased tax base, valuable jobs for local workers, a source of philanthropy, and a draw to other businesses. None of these benefits redound to shareholders, so shareholders have no incentive to pursue or maintain them. Conversely, if the company lays off a thousand workers, damaging the tax base and increasing the strain on local aid resources, it will not absorb these losses, so shareholders have no incentive to avoid them. If what we care about is total social welfare, and not just the welfare of a particular company, then shareholders' interests are at best a very rough and inaccurate proxy for what we really want corporations to take into account.

Agency Costs

Although the conceptual arguments for shareholder primacy are not terribly persuasive, a second type of argument may fare a bit better. Whenever those who run an enterprise are not the owners, there is a chance that the managers will take unfair advantage. We saw in chapter 3 that this separation exists in publicly traded corporations. Managers of public firms may shirk, since shareholders will often have trouble detecting how hard the managers are working. Managers may also divert the firm's resources for their own use through embezzlement, self-dealing, excessive compensation, or lavish perks. Economists refer to these harms as "agency costs."

The easier we can make it for shareholders to monitor corporate executives, the better chance we have that shareholders will be able to detect and even deter managers from engaging in these sorts of self-interested behaviors. Providing a narrow goal—shareholder wealth maximization—simplifies monitoring and thereby reduces agency costs. (Note that shareholders already have great difficulty monitoring and policing directors, as I discussed in chapter 3.) On the other hand, if we give directors and managers wide latitude to choose whose interests they should pursue, they will have a plethora of explanations available to justify almost any action.

Maximizing the welfare of all stakeholders is a problem with no clear solution. Whose interests should take priority? Suppose a company faces the possibility of firing 10 percent of its workforce to reduce costs and improve profit margins. Firing the workers will be better for shareholders and bondholders because more money will be available to pay them. But reducing costs will be terrible for the employees (both those fired and those left behind who need to work harder) and the affected communities. Either decision will help some important groups and hurt others. Stakeholder theorists have not provided a method to weigh opposing interests like these. Since we do not know the right tack for management to take, how will we detect a divergence? The company's stock price, though, is quite easy to monitor. If the share price sinks, the presumption is that managers are performing poorly and should be disciplined or dismissed. Managers will have a harder time shirking or diverting firm assets to their personal use if they are held responsible for increasing the stock price.[34]

Reducing agency costs in this way will ultimately benefit all stakeholders because lower agency costs mean greater resources for other uses. A manager induced to fly coach instead of first class, for example, frees up money that can be used to help hire more workers or pay bondholders. Managers who are free to pursue their own interests may not pursue anyone else's. But managers working to maximize shareholders' wealth will, as a necessary by-product, also improve matters for other stakeholders.

This argument may overstate shareholders' ability to monitor executives even under a strict shareholder primacy regime. Corporate strategy is indeterminate even when all agree that shareholder wealth is the only goal.[35] This is true for at least two reasons.

First, shareholders are not a uniform group. They include ten-year-olds whose parents gave them stock to help save for college and great-grandmothers living off dividends in retirement. Shareholders are multinational corporations and corner stores. They are pension funds, banks, universities, charitable foundations, churches, synagogues, mosques, governments (both foreign and domestic), mutual funds, hedge funds, and insurance companies. Shareholders include individuals and entities from Arkansas to Arizona and from Afghanistan to Australia. They are limited liability companies, general partnerships, limited partnerships, limited liability partnerships, corporations, and individuals.

Not surprisingly, this diverse group of investors has widely varied interests. They differ in their investment time horizons, their taste and tolerance for risk, and their sophistication. As a result, managers told to focus with laserlike precision on shareholders' interests will find it surprisingly difficult to identify what those interests are. A day trader prospers most from wide vacillations in stock price that will give parents heartburn as they save for their children's college tuition. A public pension fund may prefer to sacrifice some return in exchange for a lower risk profile, while a hedge fund may have an appetite for higher earnings even when the risks are substantial. A retiree may need predictable dividends to meet monthly expenses, but his working grandson may favor retaining earnings for new ventures that will manifest in higher capital gains. And a plumber may want the company to stick to investments she understands, while her sister the investment banker may push the corporation to make better use of esoteric derivatives. Shareholder primacy does not result in a determinate strategy for managers either, so perhaps this claimed advantage over stakeholder theory is overstated.[36]

The second reason corporate strategy remains indeterminate under shareholder primacy is that nonshareholder stakeholders are important for corporate results. Even a CEO trying to maximize shareholder wealth must pursue stakeholders' welfare as well. A business needs capital to thrive, but that capital can come from debt in addition to equity. The company must persuade bondholders to lend by promising attention to their concerns. Similarly, a business requires excellent employees who must often develop skills and learn knowledge specific to the enterprise. The company can more easily convince employees to work hard and develop nontransferable human capital if employees' needs are met. Customers, suppliers, and a supportive community are all critical as well, and a successful business must find a way to commit them all to the firm.[37]

Adopting shareholder primacy, then, does not exempt managers from these other stakeholders' concerns. Managers must attend to other stakeholders whether the law directs them to or not, as part of any effort to maximize the firm's value. Whether courts and legislatures mandate shareholder primacy or a broader stakeholder approach does not shift the economic reality that *all* stakeholders must be motivated to help the firm if it is to have any chance at success. Even under a shareholder primacy legal regime, managers must still have flexibility to favor other stakeholders at times; otherwise the business cannot function. The monitoring benefits of shareholder primacy fade as a result, since managers can always claim that long-term shareholder value requires that they take an action that transfers some wealth to another stakeholder group. Shareholder primacy may not simplify monitoring much after all.

The fact that managerial opportunism still occurs with some frequency supports this critique. Shareholder primacy advocates claim that shareholder primacy is currently both the law and the most widespread practice among directors and executives.[38] Yet the supposed monitoring benefits of this regime have not eliminated managers' bad conduct. Corporate scandals that reflect managerial failures still occur regularly. Did shareholder primacy prevent the meltdowns at Enron, Worldcom, Adelphia, or Tyco? Did a focus on shareholder wealth protect companies against the lending abuses that led to the current housing crisis? Some have even argued that focusing too strongly on increasing stock prices caused some of these scandals.[39] Perhaps a stronger emphasis on other, less risk-accepting stakeholders would moderate the sometimes dysfunctional pressure to increase earnings.

Wealth Creation

At this point, we see that the conceptual arguments for shareholder primacy are unconvincing and that shareholder primacy's monitoring benefits seem elusive. A third arena in which the two sides have contested is each philosophy's ability to create wealth. One argument for shareholder primacy is that managers who try to increase shareholders' wealth will often succeed. Common sense argues that managers whose sole goal is raising the company's share price will have an easier time boosting earnings than those who must also try to aid employees, customers, suppliers, and communities.

In addition, left to their own devices, managers tend to be excessively risk-averse when making corporate decisions. As much as they want the company to succeed, it is far more important to them that the company avoid failure. They have jobs now, and one sure way to lose them is to lead the company into bankruptcy. Also, they have invested time acquiring knowledge and skills that are more useful to this company than to any other. These skills will be less valuable if they have to look for work elsewhere. And having failed in their last position they are likely to have trouble finding the next one. Even one failure could ruin an executive's hard-won reputation for brilliant management.[40]

Economists express all this by saying executives have a great deal of human capital tied up in the firm. Shareholders, in contrast, are more accepting of risk. Wise shareholders diversify; they invest in a range of companies that will respond differently to shifting market conditions. This investment strategy buffers shareholders and prevents them from suffering excessive losses from the failure of any one corporation. Typically, there is a trade-off between risk and investment returns; the higher the risk, the larger the expected reward if things work out. The investment market creates this trade-off through normal market processes; riskier opportunities *must* offer higher returns to attract investors. Shareholders can afford to be more aggressive in pushing for higher returns, more willing to accept the accompanying risk of loss. Even if a company or two fail as a result of taking a few gambles, shareholders will make up these losses with the higher returns they earn in the rest of their portfolios.

Unlike managers, shareholders have no human capital tied up in any particular firm. Their jobs and reputations are not at risk, only their financial capital. Diversification makes shareholders more rational than managers, more willing to take the chances that on average will produce the highest returns, the most wealth. Left to their own devices, managers would be more timid. Shareholder primacy is the right strategy because it acts as a counterweight to managers' risk-averse tendencies and drives managers to be more accepting of the risks that produce wealth.

And producing more wealth is ultimately the best strategy for everyone. By earning more money, a business increases the wealth available to all the company's stakeholders, not just its shareholders. Bondholders are more likely to be paid in full when the company prospers, employees are more likely to continue to have work to do, customers can continue buying desirable products and services, suppliers maintain a market for their products, and communities benefit from a larger tax base and improved employment numbers.[41]

The larger society's welfare should rise with the company's as well. The more wealth businesses create, the more resources the country has to apply to solve all of society's problems, from health care to homelessness and national defense to education. Although the corporation's stakeholders have first claim on these resources, the tax system will take its share and spend the growing wealth as dictated by the democratic process. Telling managers to focus on increasing shareholders' wealth has the wonderful (if somewhat paradoxical) effect of helping not only the company's other stakeholders but also the nation as a whole.

There are several flaws in this line of optimistic reasoning. First, a rising tide does not necessarily float all boats. A seesaw is sometimes a better metaphor, with one group rising only because other groups are falling. Sometimes corporations' growth has the kind of beneficial effects just described, but shareholder wealth can also result from laying off workers, polluting the environment, buying component parts from low-cost international suppliers, and saddling the company with huge debts in order to provide a quick payout to shareholders. Increasing shareholders' prosperity does not inherently make all other corporate stakeholders better off. The reverse is too often the case. The clearest demonstration of this fact comes from the 1980s and 1990s, when an unprecedented bull market accompanied stagnant blue-collar wages, a declining manufacturing sector, and rising income inequality.[42]

The second flaw consists of the possibility that adopting a stakeholder philosophy may help managers improve corporate performance more than a narrow focus on shareholders does. This argument seems counterintuitive at first glance, but it does have an underlying logic. Businesses often need equity capital to function well, but they also depend on talented and dedicated workers, willing lenders, loyal customers, and reliable suppliers. Supportive communities may prove helpful as well. Although balancing the conflicting needs of all these stakeholders makes management more difficult, perhaps the attempt also makes management better.

Margaret Blair and Lynn Stout have put forward the most interesting theoretical framework for the stakeholder theory along these lines. They postulate that corporate law developed to solve a team production problem. Team production problems arise when a group's output is the result of its members' firm-specific investments and when the group's efforts so blend together that it is very difficult after the fact to measure each member's contribution to the final product. These situations present a difficult challenge. The group's performance can be measured, but the contribution of individuals cannot, making it very easy for each member to shirk without detection. How can the group persuade individual members to invest in creating the final product when it is so easy to shirk and not be caught?[43]

Blair and Stout argue that corporate law presents a reasonable (though admittedly not ideal) solution to this dilemma in the form of boards of directors. Boards have the independence and power to act as "mediating hierarchs," dispensing rewards as they see fit based on their perception of each team member's relative contribution. Because individuals' contributions are opaque, the board's division will not be perfect. But the board is independent of the other stakeholders, so its judgment will at least be objective. And the board's power to pronounce the final word enables it to prevent wasteful internal disputes over the fairest distribution of the company's income. The solution is far from a panacea; team members' rewards will not align perfectly with their contributions. Nevertheless, delegating the distribution decision to an independent, powerful outsider should make everyone better off than the likeliest alternative—never-ending internal squabbles.[44]

The theory is interesting, but does it work in practice? Do companies that self-consciously try to balance the needs of constituencies other than shareholders outperform those who care only about boosting the stock price?

The evidence here is mixed. Keeping some groups of stakeholders happy does seem key to enhancing the firm's performance, but devoting resources to other groups may actually hurt the bottom line. In particular, one study found that focusing on employees and customers (product quality and safety) improves the company's business. Spending money on the community, diversity, or the environment, though, either does not affect performance or has a mild negative effect.[45] A more recent study found that building good community relationships does help corporate performance, as does improving diversity. But devoting resources to social issues such as avoiding nuclear energy has a negative impact on corporate earnings.[46]

But is this really just a more strategic shareholder primacy theory? If corporate earnings are the metric we use to determine which theory is superior, aren't we really just debating the most effective approach to making shareholders wealthier? Stakeholder theory only has real bite when it demands a sacrifice from shareholders to attain better results for other groups. Otherwise, the debate is about management styles, not corporations' core purpose in society. The management debate is a useful one, but we should be careful to distinguish between arguments over means and conflicts over ends. The means debate can be influenced by a difference over ends. Those who would prefer to see nonshareholder stakeholders' interests attended to may usefully try to co-opt shareholder primacy advocates by claiming both ends are achieved by the same means (devoting resources to other stakeholders). Perhaps managers are naturally inclined to focus only on shareholders, when a broader view might ultimately prove more profitable. That is a strategic move, though, not a philosophical argument.

There are theorists who claim corporations have an ethical obligation to consider the needs of other stakeholders, even at shareholders' expense.[47] While these theorists often have some Kantian approach in mind, forbidding the pursuit of wealth at the expense of others' "right" to a job or to a clean environment, I prefer to examine this question from a utilitarian perspective. The Kantian approach depends on a theory of stakeholders' rights that these theorists tend to leave implicit. I am not convinced there could be a persuasive theory that explains why some nonshareholder stakeholders have an absolute right to see their interests pursued at others' expense. A utilitarian approach better exposes the ethical issues.

A useful way to approach the utilitarian question is to think about the Malden Mills example I described near the start of this chapter.

Suppose that favoring other stakeholders sometimes results in lower corporate earnings, or even an occasional bankruptcy. Is there still an argument that focusing on other stakeholders is the right approach to maximizing social welfare?

The answer depends on the magnitude of the impact on each group.[48] Although there is some contrary evidence, as just discussed, let us assume that shareholders are adversely affected by a decision to help other stakeholders and that helping others necessarily means putting greater strain on the business. There is no upside for investors to a strategy that at best reduces their return and at worst increases the risk of a total loss. Likewise for bondholders, a bankruptcy is usually a disaster, costing them much or all of their investment in the company and even an increased risk of bankruptcy damages their bonds' value.

For the other stakeholders, the answer is murkier. Prioritizing employees' interests and those of the community arguably helped drag Malden Mills down into the abyss. There were other contributing factors to Malden Mills's failure, such as increasing international competition and personnel issues, but there seems little doubt that keeping idled workers on the payroll for months was an expense the company was unable to bear.

But what was the alternative? Suppose that the best option for maximizing profits was to move manufacturing to a low-cost location in another country such as China or Malaysia. Would the United States have been better off than with a bankrupt Malden Mills?[49] Either way, the local jobs would have been lost and the community would have suffered. The tax base would have declined under either scenario. Consumers were largely unaffected by the bankruptcy, since there were other sources of supply for polar fleeces (indeed, that was one of Malden Mills's primary challenges). Suppliers as a class were likewise unaffected since the bankruptcy would not have changed consumer demand, though particular suppliers might have been better off had Malden Mills remained in business.

Overall, it seems that shareholders and bondholders were worse off because of the decision to rebuild the factory in Massachusetts. Consumers and suppliers were unaffected by the decision. Employees and the community gained a chance at a better situation but ultimately ended up with the same losses they would have suffered from the factory's move.

The empirical question becomes whether providing employees and communities with a chance to keep manufacturing jobs is worth the increased risk to shareholders and bondholders. The answer depends on how likely the company is to be able to make the business a success while also attending to the needs of other stakeholders. The better the odds of success, the better bet stakeholder theory seems for the United States as a whole. There is no answer that applies to these types of decisions across the board; they must be evaluated case by case. Under a utilitarian approach, then, the ethical issues are indeterminate; we cannot say which policy will best maximize social welfare.

Wealth generation as a rationale for shareholder primacy depends on an empirical question, as does the ethical argument for stakeholder theory. The evidence on both questions is decidedly mixed. The arguments mustered thus far for shareholder primacy are surprisingly weak either conceptually or empirically, or both. They do not justify the almost reflexive support for compensation plans that try to align executives' interests with those of shareholders. We should see a vigorous debate, not overwhelming consensus. But shareholder primacy has one last arrow in its quiver.

Implicit Bargaining

The final and arguably strongest argument in favor of shareholder primacy relies on the nature of corporate law as largely a system of default rules. Most of corporate law—in fact, most of contract law—consists of background rules that the parties can vary by agreement. The theory behind this system is that the parties are best positioned to craft the rules for their dealings with one another, and mandatory rules interfere with their ability to craft the most efficient exchange possible.

This structure could lead one to conclude that the content of the default rules is irrelevant, since the parties can change the rules at will. But this would be a mistake. It matters which rules the law picks because one of the key goals of transactional law is to help parties make deals while spending as little as possible on the deal-making process. Economists express this goal as "minimizing transaction costs." The law can help minimize the resources the parties have to devote to negotiating and drafting the transaction by choosing the default rules most parties would settle on anyway.

Choosing the correct default rule also matters because the endowment effect may make default rules "sticky." Numerous psychological experiments have demonstrated that under many conditions, people tend to prefer the option they already have above the value of its intrinsic merits, just because they already have it. The most famous experiments involved coffee mugs and a small sum of money. Subjects were given either coffee mugs or a small sum, such as $5. Then the experimenter permitted exchanges. Anyone with a coffee mug could exchange it for the cash and vice versa.

Remarkably little trading takes place in these experiments. This result seems odd. Either the mug is worth more than the money, less, or the same. If the mug is not worth precisely the amount of money offered, lots of trading should occur as the subjects trade up for the more valuable choice (the mug or the money). Many versions of this experiment have been conducted, and the amount of money given has been varied, so it is highly unlikely that the experimenters happened to choose the mug's precise value each time. Instead, the more likely explanation is the endowment effect: the subjects preferred whichever option they were given simply because they already had it.[50]

The same effect has been shown to apply to legal default rules, with subjects demonstrating a fairly strong preference for the default rule. For example, when New Jersey and Pennsylvania adopted opposite default rules for a term in a car insurance policy, citizens of both states overwhelmingly chose the default option. Perhaps New Jersey residents have markedly different insurance preferences than Pennsylvania residents, but the endowment effect seems a likelier explanation.[51]

Both because the law should be designed to minimize transaction costs and because the endowment effect makes initial choices somewhat sticky, default rules should be designed so that they reflect what the parties would have chosen themselves if they bargained over the issue.

Bainbridge has argued forcefully that corporate stakeholders would agree to shareholder primacy. In part, his argument relies on the indeterminacy and self-interest arguments I discussed earlier in this chapter, that stakeholder theory does not produce clear policy choices and that this indeterminacy leaves the door open to directors to make the decisions that further their own interests rather than the corporation's. But his most interesting argument addresses the degree of protection available to each type of stakeholder through contract.[52]

Bainbridge contends that shareholders have the weakest contractual protections and therefore the greatest need for the safeguards provided by the board's fiduciary duties. Since the other stakeholders can shield themselves through contract, shareholders will be willing (in our hypothetical bargain that tells us which default rules are optimal) to pay the highest price to secure the board's primary attention. Bondholders memorialize their agreement in a sophisticated and complex written contract called an indenture. Employees generally sign an employment agreement. Communities enter into agreements with companies before supplying them with special incentives or tax breaks to invest locally. Suppliers typically have written purchase orders and sometimes more detailed long-term supply agreements. Large customers similarly tend to have purchase orders or supply agreements, though consumers rarely do. In contrast, public shareholders almost never bargain with the corporation before purchasing shares on the open market.[53]

Bainbridge concedes that some of these groups—most notably employees—may not have the market power to exact many concessions. Factory floor workers, he agrees, are generally given nonnegotiable offers. But he argues that the competitive labor market protects employees, discouraging employers from offering contracts that will be rejected, even on a take-it-or-leave-it basis. Employees negotiate by seeking out the best possible terms and shunning employers who offer contracts that are too one-sided.[54]

Bainbridge's argument, while powerful, hangs on the outcome of a purely hypothetical bargain. No such bargaining among corporate stakeholders ever takes place, so we can only speculate about the likely outcome. And there are good reasons to question Bainbridge's conclusion that shareholders would value primacy more than other stakeholders would.

Shareholder primacy is not costless. For example, favoring shareholders may result in higher borrowing costs. Although shareholders could raise the costs of capital if they were denied shareholder primacy, lenders (such as bondholders and banks) are an equally important (and potentially expensive) source of capital. In exchange for shareholder primacy, lenders might demand higher interest rates or more extensive (and intrusive) capital protections and governance provisions to compensate them for the chance that shareholders' demand for high-risk investments will torpedo the company. Employees may similarly require higher wages to make up for the greater risk of losing their jobs after they have invested in acquiring firm-specific knowledge and skills. Communities may demand greater guarantees of protection before agreeing to tax credits or subsidies.

Shareholders would make similar demands for higher returns to give up shareholder primacy (assuming that is the current governing law, which as I argued above is not entirely clear). But the other stakeholders, especially in combination, might make this sacrifice worthwhile by granting concessions in exchange for a more balanced rule.

Plus, stakeholders enjoy less contractual protection than Bainbridge suggests. Employees below the executive level have little meaningful bargaining power, especially in workplaces that are not unionized. While Bainbridge is correct that the labor market provides some protection, that argument is effective only in times of relatively full employment. In times like these, when unemployment rates are high, workers with only fungible skills to offer have little choice but to accept the offered terms. And even when jobs are relatively plentiful, companies might rationally choose to compete on salary alone rather than job security or working conditions or other less salient provisions. If all companies offer equally undesirable terms, workers' power to say *no* is not terribly effective in influencing their contracts.

Bainbridge adds that federal and state laws exist to protect workers. But corporations are at least as effective in lobbying Congress as unions are, so there is no reason to think that workers have gotten a markedly better deal than shareholders in such legislation. Nor is there any guarantee that workers' legislative protections will not be undermined if their political fortunes deteriorate.

Most important, both the market and the statutory protection arguments are equally applicable to shareholders. Shareholders, too, have the power to go elsewhere when corporations treat them poorly. Their transaction costs for shifting allegiances are considerably lower than workers' are; shareholders only need to pay a broker's fee to sell their shares, while workers must give up a job and bear search costs to find another. And federal law offers shareholders substantial protection as well, in the form of disclosure rules enacted by the Securities Act and Securities and Exchange Act and remedies such as Rule 10b-5. Why should we assume that workers are better protected by the market and federal law than shareholders? The protections seem comparable, or at least analogous.

Communities may be the most vulnerable of all the corporate stakeholders. Corporations do not internalize the benefits they provide to communities in the form of employment and taxes, nor do they absorb the harms they inflict when they shift those jobs elsewhere. State and local governments can make up some of these incentives by providing subsidies to corporations to move into a community or to stay when thinking about departing.

But governments do not internalize all the benefits or harms to the community either and so will not be willing to pay corporations enough to fully internalize the impact of their actions on the community.

Governments benefit fully from any increase in taxes, but increased tax revenues represent only part of the benefit corporations provide. The community is enriched by the full amount of the salaries workers earn, not just the portion workers pay in taxes. Companies may also provide indirect benefits, such as rent to commercial real estate owners, demand for local services and products, and an enhancement of the community's reputation. Communities cannot protect themselves adequately through contract because there is no unified body or organization with the right incentives to bargain on their behalf.

Even bondholders, who enjoy the most contractual protection, should reasonably want fiduciary protections. Why does the law impose fiduciary duties, at least as a default rule, in contracts between sophisticated parties? Why not just let sophisticated parties bargain for the specific terms they want?

To answer these questions, we again have to think about the purpose of default rules in contract law. The goal of a good default rule is to minimize transaction costs, to adopt the rule the parties would choose if they bargained over this issue. Legal scholars typically explain that fiduciary duties are useful in long-term contracts where future issues are particularly difficult to predict. Rather than spend time and money providing for every possible contingency, the parties might reasonably opt for a general rule of decision, such as good faith or a duty of loyalty, that can be applied to any circumstance. Fiduciary duties are particularly useful when one party will have a lot of discretion. A duty of loyalty, for example, constrains managers' discretion and requires that they resolve conflicts in favor of the protected party.[55]

With this understanding, we can see that bondholders might want boards to owe them fiduciary duties even though they are already protected by a sophisticated contract. No matter how detailed bond debentures are, they still leave directors with enormous discretion in how they run the company. Bonds are usually either medium- or long-term debt, so the contract must cover contingencies that may arise over a number of years. This is precisely the sort of situation that calls for fiduciary duties.

We see, then, that contract law provides less protection to employees, communities, and other stakeholders than Bainbridge suggests and that there is good reason to think that many of these stakeholder groups would be willing to pay quite a bit for a rule that required management to consider their interests seriously.

There is also reason to think that shareholders might pay less than Bainbridge believes. His argument that shareholders would pay the most for protection is in part premised on shareholders' comparative inability to protect themselves through contract. But shareholders are more powerful than he depicts. While Bainbridge is correct that public shareholders have little formal power under state corporate law, they are more powerful now than perhaps ever before in the history of modern corporations. Institutional shareholders such as mutual funds, hedge funds, pension funds, banks, endowments, foundations, and insurance companies now own over 60 percent of all U.S. publicly traded stock.[56] This enormous block of stock votes with considerable unity, since many of these institutions follow the voting recommendations of proxy advisers such as Institutional Shareholder Services. Shareholders do not vote on important issues often, but when they do, their voices are increasingly important.

In addition to their formal legal power, shareholders exercise considerable informal power. Institutional shareholders exercise power by consulting with management, with the implicit threat that they will publicly air their concerns or even sell their shares (sinking the stock price) if their needs are not addressed. They also have the resources and organization to lobby Congress effectively for legislation that protects their interests.

These tools are incredibly effective. As Chancellor Strine of the Delaware Chancery Court has commented about institutional investors, "When they want something, they tend to get it."[57] He notes that institutional investors have successfully advocated for executive pay that is more closely tied to corporate performance, reductions in takeover defenses, the adoption of majority voting rules for board elections, and other policy objectives.[58]

Since shareholders often have the power to pursue their interests without the protection of management's fiduciary duties and since other stakeholders have much less power than suggested, the results of any hypothetical bargain among the parties with an interest in corporate policies are not determinable with any certainty. We should therefore hesitate to rely too heavily on the implicit contract argument to justify a shareholder primacy approach to corporate governance law.

HOW CAN WE DECIDE?

There is, when all is said and done, a reasonable case to be made for shareholder primacy. There is an argument that shareholder primacy minimizes agency costs by making it easier to prevent management from entrenching themselves or otherwise acting for their own benefit. Focusing primarily on shareholders' welfare may be the best way to maximize the wealth the corporation creates, which arguably is corporations' core purpose. And perhaps of all corporate stakeholders, shareholders most need the protections that come with shareholder primacy. If so, shareholder primacy might be the most efficient default rule, since all corporate stakeholders might agree to defer to shareholders to obtain the benefits shareholders would be willing to offer in exchange.

But none of these arguments—even in combination—is overpowering. Each has serious weaknesses. Shareholders' internal conflicts provide ample justifications for management to choose the policies that favor themselves. And management inevitably must also pay attention to the needs of other stakeholders in order to run the corporation effectively, so that shareholder primacy's monitoring advantages seem overstated. The evidence as to which rule better increases wealth is conflicted; groups like employees and customers are so critical to the company's success that instructing managers to pay attention to their needs may improve the bottom line. Plus, maximizing corporate wealth is not the same as maximizing social welfare, the true goal of a utilitarian policy. Corporations do not internalize all the harms or benefits they generate. A broader stakeholder rule might nudge executives toward behavior that maximizes social welfare rather than just corporate wealth. Finally, shareholders are not as helpless as some advocates of shareholder primacy have implied, nor are the contractual protections other stakeholders receive nearly as robust as some scholars have suggested.

My goal in this book is not to push for courts and legislatures to adopt mandatory stakeholder rules. My concern is with private ordering, and in particular with CEO compensation contracts. Since neither stakeholder theory nor shareholder supremacy has a clear claim as the socially superior policy, perhaps we should let boards decide how to balance the competing interests. In particular, boards might express their priorities through compensation design. Directors could encourage executives to take broader social concerns into account by adding features to their compensation contracts.

What would such an approach look like? I suspect boards could use the same techniques they currently employ to motivate executives to achieve other corporate goals. Suppose, for example, boards wanted their executives to try to minimize the company's impact on the environment. One way to make this clear to the senior managers would be to provide a bonus for reducing the company's carbon footprint by a set amount. As I argued in chapter 6, paying CEOs when the corporation achieves a performance goal may not be as effective a tool as is commonly believed. Still, incorporating pro-social goals into the CEO's compensation contract would send a strong message that the board values these goals.

The compensation contract would also allow the board to quantify the relative importance of its various ambitions for the corporation. Making 80 percent of the CEO's compensation turn on financial results, 10 percent on increasing employment numbers, 5 percent on customer satisfaction, and 5 percent on social goals tells the CEO very clearly how to weight each stakeholder's concerns. This idea solves the problem of balancing opposing concerns by encouraging the board to make its relative weightings explicit, through the executive compensation contract. Then the CEO's job becomes not the setting of priorities, which is properly left to the board, but implementing them.

Would any board be likely to adopt this approach? In regard to stakeholders whose satisfaction is closely tied to corporate profits, it might be appealing. Encouraging managers to pay close attention to the concerns of customers and employees has been shown to boost profits. The compensation contract might prove an effective tool to remind CEOs how critical these particular stakeholder groups are, and perhaps measures of success in these areas would be more difficult to manipulate than financial numbers. There is some evidence that supports the effectiveness of nonfinancial measures as bonus triggers.[59]

Boards seem less likely to include metrics of the contentment of stakeholders with less direct influence on the corporate bottom line, such as communities or the environment. For these stakeholders, the government might choose to try to persuade boards to include their concerns by providing tax benefits or regulatory relief. Such measures might well be justified and cost-effective for the government. Companies that provided internal incentives to do the right thing would impose fewer costs on the government such as environmental cleanup or unemployment insurance. These companies might also need less intrusive regulations and enforcement, since they would have internalized some desire to maximize social welfare.

I admit, though, to considerable discomfort at this level of governmental involvement in CEO pay. As Kevin Murphy has argued very persuasively, the history of governmental tinkering with executive compensation has been littered with failed experiments and unintended consequences.[60] Part of the reason for these failures may be that politicians and regulatory officials often lack relevant experience and so do not anticipate the strategic consequences of new legal rules. Part of the problem may also be that law, especially federal law, tends to be an all-or-nothing proposition. The government imposes a uniform rule on the entire state or country, which blocks companies from experimenting with different approaches to determine which works best. Board-initiated experiments, in contrast, allow for testing diverse approaches.

A number of states have just begun to authorize a new form of business organization that might permit the type of experimentation I am suggesting, at least to a degree. Beginning with Vermont, a handful of states have created new forms of business organizations that are devoted to *both* profits and some other (or set of other) goals.[61] The forms and details vary widely, including flexible purpose corporations, benefit corporations, and low-profit limited liability companies (L3Cs). I don't want to wade too deeply into this emerging area—and I certainly don't want to take you through the tax rules for foundations that originally motivated the creation of these new entities.[62]

The impulse behind them (other than the benefits to foundations looking for mission-related investments) is to create a hybrid organization that pursues both profits and other social policy goals, such as a cleaner environment. These organizations are specifically empowered to trade profits for other goals, and some of the statutes mandate annual audits to measure how effectively they are achieving their pro-social ends.[63] Those rules permit some experimentation, along the lines that I am advocating. But they probably do not provide enough flexibility for mainline, for-profit companies to dip their toes in the waters of prioritizing stakeholders other than shareholders.

They seem most useful for companies, like the clothing company Patagonia, that have always branded themselves as in some way pro-social. (Patagonia was one of the first companies to take advantage of California's new benefit corporations statute.)[64] These companies now have an additional tool they can use to bolster their pro-social images. More conventional companies that want to boost profits by making credible commitments to treat employees well, for example, are unlikely to find these new forms particularly helpful. But I'm reluctant to prejudge these new forms; they are too new to allow for any firm conclusions just yet.

If these new forms will not serve most companies' purposes, that leaves us again with the idea of pro-social incentive contracts. The maximalist vision of these contracts may prove impractical. Still, looking at the arguments explored in this chapter, it is hard to justify the broad support for shareholder primacy demonstrated by executive compensation contracts in the past two or three decades. There are evident weaknesses in the arguments for shareholder primacy, and the evidence about the impact of shareholder primacy on corporate wealth is conflicting. I would therefore expect at least some companies to try to raise share prices by experimenting with compensation packages that tried to focus executives on the stakeholders most likely to boost profits. At a minimum, boards should identify *which* shareholders' preferences they favor in terms of degree of risk acceptance and investment time horizon. The paucity of such experiments and self-conscious compensation design hints at the presence of some of the psychological dynamics I explored in chapter 8, such as groupthink and social cascades. Corporate directors should reexamine their acceptance of shareholder primacy in light of the arguments made in this chapter and reconsider whether aligning executives' interests *only* with those of shareholders is either feasible or desirable.[65]

CONCLUSION

We should consider the merits of a legal regime that emphasizes shareholder primacy (to the extent we have such a regime) from a social welfare perspective. Shareholders may not be the best guardians of social welfare. They are likely to pursue firm wealth but perhaps at much higher risk levels than are socially optimal given the externalities high-risk, corporate strategies impose on the rest of us.

Diversified shareholders may feel free to take risky bets, knowing that enough of them will pay off to make up for those that do not. But part of this freedom comes at the expense of the country as a whole, which must bear much of the costs of failure. Corporations are not liable for much of the damage they may cause, such as unemployment or loss of useful products. And they may escape paying for much of the damage they are liable for if they fail. Corporations are limited liability entities. Shareholders risk only the amount they have invested. If a corporation fails, its stock becomes worthless. But shareholders will not bear any additional costs beyond the loss of their investment. These costs are imposed on the corporation's creditors, who go undercompensated. We cannot trust shareholders to make socially optimal bets when they do not internalize the full expense of losing.

This is especially true today, as shareholders have become increasingly short-term in their orientation. While in 1960 investors held on to their stock in a company for an average of eight years, now the average holding period is down to four months.[66]

Who *can* we trust to make these decisions? Our best alternative is the board. I say this in the Churchillian sense of "worst except for all the others." We have no ideal choices here. As I explained in chapter 3, the directors' incentives are opaque. Plus, I suspect directors have mostly been socialized to prioritize stock price increases, which is good news for shareholders but not very comforting from a public policy standpoint.

Nevertheless, there is some room for optimism. The directors are apart from the corporation's daily management and lack the shareholders' intense financial interests in raising the stock price. They may have the psychological and fiscal distance to steer the corporation among the sometimes competing claims of profit and social good. But if we are to have any hope that directors will sometimes forgo the most immediately profitable strategies in favor of those most likely to build lasting, sustainable value, we must *tell* directors this is their job. We must end the shareholder primacy rhetoric and substitute a more balanced direction for corporate boards.

Even so, I do not—and we should not—expect too much from directors along these lines. The law dictates a corporate governance structure that sends a powerful message: shareholders matter, even if they have little real power most of the time. Shareholders elect the directors, at least technically, and are the residual claimants to corporate revenues. Directors are likely to judge their own performance (and expect others to judge it) by the advances and retreats of the stock price. But perhaps if we begin to tell directors we expect them to serve also as guardians of the broader social interest, and laud them when they do so, boards may at least soften some of the harshness of shareholders' ravenous quest for profits at any cost.

As of now, though, the dominant paradigm remains shareholder primacy. Although this is directors' avowed goal, they have not been pursuing it effectively when they decide how—and how much—to pay their CEOs. In the next chapter, I discuss some ways boards might pay CEOs more efficiently.

CHAPTER 10

Moving Forward

The chairman of a large, public company told me recently, "It's easy to criticize CEO pay. What we *need* is someone to tell us how to do it *right*."

That's a tall order, so maybe I should start by tamping down expectations a bit. In some ways the core problem with CEO pay is that directors have expected too much from it. Thanks to economists' theories about agency costs and the ways to reduce them, boards have looked to compensation as the dominant management tool for public company executives. Boards have relied too heavily on the structure of CEO pay to automatically monitor and manage their chief executives.

I have some bad news to deliver: pay isn't up to the job. There simply are no shortcuts when it comes to corporate governance. Paying for performance does not yield better performance, at least when we're dealing with the sort of high-level cognitive tasks we ask CEOs to perform.

The best solution would be to abandon the experiment with performance pay and go back to compensating CEOs as companies did before the 1970s: primarily using cash salaries. We could perhaps add some restricted stock as part of the package to help build a culture of ownership and responsibility, but the vast majority of CEOs' compensation should take the form of a guaranteed salary. Boards should also limit perks. There is no reason to provide perks for which there are no economic savings (e.g., because the company is buying items in bulk) or tax advantage (because the perk is tax deductible, such as health insurance).

There are several advantages to returning to guaranteed pay. First, it is cheaper (and often much cheaper) than performance pay. As I have explained, CEOs understandably demand higher expected pay to compensate them for taking on the risks associated with performance pay. That additional expense—combined with the historic bull market of the 1980s and 1990s and the behavioral dynamics explored in chapter 8—replaced three decades of stable CEO pay with a norm of real and often substantial increases each year. As a result, the largest U.S. companies now pay several times as much for leadership talent as they did in the 1960s in real terms. Because companies and executives mistakenly believe that there is an efficient market in CEO talent, it may prove difficult to bring compensation back to historic norms. At a minimum, though, switching to guaranteed pay should stop executive compensation's geometric rise. And over time, as norms shift, pay may even subside to some extent in real terms.

Second, awarding guaranteed pay should make executives more efficient. Performance pay has not bought companies better performance. On the contrary, there is substantial evidence that linking pay to certain metrics encourages at least some executives to cheat. In addition, performance pay—especially when it constitutes the bulk of an executive's compensation package—may focus executives on their chances of winning the pay lottery rather than on running the company. Guaranteed pay would avoid these problems.

Third and finally, guaranteed pay would provide boards with greater certainty and control over their executives' pay. With performance pay—especially with stock-based performance pay—companies hand over control of the amount boards end up paying the CEO to the unpredictable stock and product markets. But with salaries, directors know precisely how much they are committing the company to pay.

Switching back to guaranteed pay should yield substantial benefits—including ending executive compensation's dramatic increases, possibly lowering pay, helping executives work more honestly and efficiently, and providing directors with more certainty and predictability—and would mark a dramatic change from current practices. Nevertheless, some reform-minded readers will be disappointed in this solution. They might be hoping for something more radical than returning to older forms of compensation, something that would drastically cut the amounts CEOs are paid and help remedy the growing imbalance in wealth and income in the United States between those who have and those who lack.

There may be good reasons to be seriously concerned about this imbalance. The top 10 percent of income earners in the United States absorbed about 30 percent of total income during World War II and remained around that level until the 1970s. Since then, the top 10 percent has increased its share of national income to over 40 percent of the total (though this represents roughly a return to prewar levels).[1]

The root causes of this increase in income inequality are sharply debated. The Reagan administration's steep cuts in the top marginal income tax rate, the decline in unionization, advances in technology, changing social norms, and globalization have all been blamed for the increasing share of income enjoyed by the wealthiest. The rise in CEO compensation may also have played some role, at least in shaping social norms regarding what level of pay is appropriate.[2]

But regulating CEO pay is unlikely to make much of a dent in income equality, for at least three reasons. First and most obviously, the inequality problem is much deeper than the pay of public company CEOs. While changes have been more dramatic for those in the top fraction of 1 percent of the income scale,[3] they encompass at least the top 10 percent of income earners. Paring down the income of a few hundred (or even a few thousand) corporate chieftains would be unlikely to have much of an egalitarian impact on the hedge fund managers, investment bankers, corporate lawyers, entrepreneurs, professional athletes, rock stars, trust fund children, and others who top the income scale.

Second, government regulation has a very poor track record in controlling executive pay. As Murphy has written, "In most cases, companies and their executives have responded to the [government] interventions by circumventing or adapting to the reforms, usually in ways that increased pay levels and produced other unintended (and typically unproductive) consequences."[4] The government should accordingly tread carefully in this area as new legal rules are likely to have unforeseen (and undesirable) consequences.

Third, those reforms that intuitively seem most likely to reduce CEO pay quickly, such as mandatory caps, are also those least likely to be adopted. Corporate executives have not been shy about opposing measures that threaten their interests, especially in the pay arena. Dodd-Frank's requirement that public companies disclose the ratio of the CEO's pay to that of the worker at the company's median pay level, for example, has produced a firestorm of controversy.[5] One can only imagine how executives would react to a requirement that their pay be reduced by, say, half. The odds of Congress passing such a bill are prohibitively low. Even in Switzerland, a country where the population seems much more hostile to high pay than the population in the United States, voters shot down a referendum to cap CEO pay at twelve times that of the lowest-paid worker by a margin of 2 to 1.[6] (Caps are probably unwise as well as unlikely, but that discussion requires too much space to take up here.)

Other readers may feel my proposal to abolish performance pay goes too far. And even I recognize that the ideal solution will be challenging to implement under current conditions. There are at least four major obstacles to switching back to guaranteed executive pay.

The first problem comes from law. Federal tax law imposes substantial costs on companies that pay their senior executives more than $1 million in unconditional pay, so switching to cash compensation would result in a large corporate tax bill for CEO salaries that exceed $1 million per year.[7] Companies are going to be understandably reluctant to incur those costs.

The second problem comes from shareholders. Shareholders and analysts see performance pay as a mark of good governance (despite the lack of supporting evidence, discussed in chapter 6) and push hard for boards to make CEO pay as sensitive to corporate performance as possible.[8] Shareholders' new power to vote on executive pay packages makes their views more concrete, salient, and difficult to ignore. Directors therefore seem to care a great deal about shareholders' perceptions of the company's corporate governance and particularly about the views of shareholder advisory services such as Institutional Shareholder Services and Glass Lewis. The threat of a low rating from one of the advisory services or a negative shareholder vote on an executive pay package is likely to prove an insurmountable obstacle for most boards. As long as institutional shareholders and their advisers cling to the chimera of performance pay, reform will be very difficult to achieve.

The third problem lies with executives. Boards' experiment with performance pay has immensely improved CEOs' income in the past three decades. Median CEO compensation in large companies has more than tripled in real terms since the early 1970s.[9] Although performance pay comes with risk, that risk has richly paid off for CEOs as a class. We can therefore expect CEOs to resist a shift to a system that will cause their pay to stagnate or even decline. (Though a recent survey provides some hope that executives will put up less resistance than I fear. The survey found that executives seem to care more about *relative* pay—how much better or worse off they are than their peers—than they do about absolute pay and sharply discount long-term incentives over their risk-neutral expected value.)[10]

Boards themselves are the fourth and final major obstacle. The psychological dynamics I discussed in chapter 8 will make it very difficult to persuade directors that performance pay is ineffective. Worse, those boards that do try to reform executive compensation may risk losing their CEOs to competitors that remained wedded to performance pay. Because companies using performance pay must provide higher expected pay, boards willing to continue to shell out the extra money will have an advantage in executive recruiting and retention. The result may be a type of prisoner's dilemma problem, where all companies would be better off if they all abandoned performance pay, but an individual company could seize an advantage by continuing to embrace it.

The reality of this concern may be overblown. Charles Elson and Craig Ferrere have demonstrated that CEOs rarely move from one company to another.[11] But the *perception* that executives may leave for richer pastures may discourage boards from substituting cheaper guaranteed pay for expensive performance pay.

These obstacles should not prove insurmountable. Federal tax law can be changed to eliminate the provision privileging performance pay and to remove the cap on the deductibility of executive pay. Shareholders and boards might be persuaded that performance pay does not work. (I hope this book will help.) Companies might succeed in persuading CEOs that a smaller, guaranteed package is preferable to one that is richer but riskier, which would also lessen the risk (such as it is) of CEOs leaving for greener pastures. But none of this is certain, and all of it will take time.

In the meantime, there is a second-best alternative. Boards that feel they have no choice but to use performance pay for the bulk of their executive compensation packages can at least minimize the harm such pay can cause. To design more benign performance pay, boards should ensure that the triggers are (a) largely within officers' control; (b) hard to manipulate; (c) easy to measure; and (d) important to the corporation's long-term goals. When applying these triggers, directors should set targets that are reasonable rather than aspirational, with a sliding scale of benefits thereafter. And none of the payments should be so large that they reintroduce the lottery-type rewards that are one of the most destructive aspects of performance pay, even with the most optimistic performance projections. I explain each of these principles in more depth below, where I will also apply them to a case study.

Before I do, though, I think it would be helpful at this point to sum up what we've learned so far, so that the insights that drive these suggestions are fresh in readers' memories. Then I'll discuss a few competing reform proposals that have become popular recently and explain why they are unlikely to work. Finally, I'll conclude by setting out my suggestions for a type of performance pay that will soften its ill effects and demonstrate how to use these rules with a case study.

WHERE WE'VE BEEN

I started the book by reviewing the history of CEO compensation since World War II. In the past few decades, we have become accustomed to the specter of rapidly rising CEO pay and the widespread use of payment structures that link compensation to corporate performance (or at least appear to) such as stock options. But neither trend is inevitable. In fact, for the first few decades after World War II neither occurred. Instead, from the 1940s through the early 1970s, average CEO pay at large public corporations remained more or less flat in constant dollar terms and consisted primarily of salary and short-term bonuses.[12]

The history lesson furnishes both a caution and a puzzle. We should be careful not to assume that what seems normal now is necessarily inevitable. The country functioned quite well for decades without raising CEO compensation in real terms or tying executive pay to corporate performance. We need to explain why both these dimensions—the volume and structure of CEO pay—changed so starkly beginning in the 1970s. Explanatory theories of CEO pay that cannot help us understand this puzzle should be viewed skeptically.

I then tackled the black box that is the corporation. Who is the corporation? Who makes its decisions? What incentives do these decision makers have to act in the corporation's interests? The answers turn out to be surprisingly complex and do not fit well with the rhetoric that surrounds the executive labor market and its efficiency. Directors do not have any of the usual rational motives for acting in the shareholders' best interests. They are largely self-perpetuating and unlikely to be voted out by shareholders. They face little risk of personal liability if they make a poor decision, so long as they act in good faith and are disinterested and reasonably informed. And even if they are paid entirely in stock, the impact on their personal wealth of working hard to boost the company's stock price is almost certain to be trivial, especially in comparison with the net worth of the type of people who tend to land director jobs. In addition, directors face serious institutional constraints in terms of time, information, composition, and culture that impede their ability to manage the company effectively.[13]

How public corporations nevertheless seem not only to survive but also to thrive is something of a mystery under pure rational actor principles. We have to expand our understanding of human nature to encompass concepts such as role integrity and altruism to have any hope of understanding why directors take their jobs as seriously as I believe they do. But even with this broader view of human nature, we should be cautious about assuming that boards pursue shareholders' interests as platonic agents, acting precisely as shareholders would desire.

We should be correspondingly wary of arguments that justify CEO pay as the product of an efficient market, pointing to the sophistication of both buyers and sellers and the large stakes involved as proof. The buyers—corporate directors—have opaque motives and incentives when they act on the corporation's behalf. We should not blindly assume there is a perfect correspondence between the board's actions and the corporation's best interests. The results produced by negotiations between boards and CEOs may not mirror those that would be generated in a market less permeated with agency costs.[14]

There are additional reasons to be wary of those who justify CEO pay as the outcome of an efficient market. Scholars have devoted enormous creativity and ingenuity to developing theories that can explain how the radical changes CEO pay has experienced since the 1970s are consistent with an efficient executive labor market. Some of these theories include company size, advances in technology, company image and self-image, tournament competition, superstardom, government regulation, and behavior modification. But none of these theories convincingly explains the two shifts in CEO pay. Most don't even try. Instead, they justify the status quo—rapidly rising amounts of pay and companies' increasing efforts to tie CEO compensation to performance—without generally addressing why boards' current strategy to motivate their chief executives is so very different from their counterparts' tactics a few decades ago.[15]

We should not buy into the dominant paradigm. Defenders of the current state of executive compensation—whether they are participants, politicians, consultants, or academics—routinely, reflexively, and often condescendingly dismiss criticisms of CEO pay by referencing the market. The market in these discussions often takes on the overtones of a force of nature, or perhaps even something supernatural. CEO pay is correct because it *must* be; it is the product of unstoppable and efficient market forces. One cannot help but hear echoes of Voltaire's Dr. Pangloss telling us we live in the best of all possible worlds.[16] Efficient markets are powerful, and they can certainly produce amazing results when the circumstances are ripe. But the evidence strongly suggests that the executive labor market is *not* efficient. We should not accept its results unquestioningly.

Nor should we jump to the opposite conclusion, that the executive compensation system is the product of corrupt, backroom dealings or at least excessive deference to the CEO. Both scholars and the popular press have periodically—and sometimes quite eloquently—accused directors of overpaying CEOs in an either purposeful or unconscious effort to keep their board seats. But this seems an unlikely explanation for the alterations in CEO pay. What changed in the 1970s and subsequent decades when the two major shifts in CEO pay took place? Were directors in the 1960s less corruptible or less deferential than their contemporary counterparts?

Boards are at least formally much more independent today than they were in the 1960s or 1950s, yet pay continues to rise and boards continue to embrace problematic compensation mechanisms. Corruption seems an unlikely candidate to explain the changes in the compensation landscape. Managerial power may play an important role in setting CEO pay packages (though I am skeptical about the maximalist, corruption version of this theory), but it is not terribly promising as an explanation for why things have changed so radically. The theory does usefully emphasize the importance of focusing on the directors and their incentives and interests, though, rather than assume that boards will automatically pursue shareholders' welfare.[17]

Managerial power theory has also produced a very useful by-product with important lessons for us about a number of enormously popular compensation tools such as stock options and bonuses. To generate evidence of their managerial power theory, scholars such as Lucian Bebchuk and Jesse Fried have advanced powerful indictments of these devices, demonstrating convincingly that they do a lousy job of tying executives' pay to individual performance. Often they do not even manage to condition pay on the *corporation's* performance.[18] These critiques highlight the difficulty of using performance pay effectively, a point that ties in nicely with the broader arguments about performance pay that I review just below.

The account of what really has driven CEO pay is more complex than either the efficiency or the corruption stories and relies on a richer understanding of human nature. First, we have to realize that leaders' power to effect change is often overblown. Companies' success is the result of a host of factors, and only some of these are within CEOs' power to affect. The company's technology, the creativity and dedication of its employees, the competitiveness of its industry, the company's position within its industry, evolving market trends, and general economic conditions as diverse as prevailing interest rates and the price of oil combine to influence the company's degree of success (or failure). These variables separately or together will usually so confine the CEO's ability to act that their impact will swamp the effect of the company's chief executive.[19]

There are times and companies in which leadership becomes critical, and there seem to be some managers who are so talented that they transform their companies almost without regard to other influences. Steve Jobs and Warren Buffet are often put in this category. But these transformative CEOs are rare. On average, CEOs do not seem to control their company's fate, or even influence it very strongly, so long as they are competent. Most competent CEOs in the same position will do more or less the same things (perhaps in part because they are such a homogeneous group), or close enough that the differences have little ultimate impact on the company.[20]

Boards seldom realize this. Instead, they generally see picking and retaining the CEO as their most important job, a task on which the company's future hangs. With so much perceived to be at stake, directors invest a lot of faith in their ability to discern which candidate would do the best job leading the company. They also tend to exaggerate the differences among often quite similar candidates. Once they have found the champion who will save the company, directors pull out all the stops to get this paragon to accept the position.

Quibbling over pay at this stage seems shortsighted. Do you want to lose the best person for the job, someone who could drive sales (and the share price) into the stratosphere, because of a difference of a paltry couple of million in compensation? Pinching pennies on pay is a surefire way to lose the best leadership talent and ultimately grind the company into the dust. The best way to serve shareholders, says the conventional wisdom, is to hire the best person as CEO, even if that person is expensive. And directors can take considerable comfort in the knowledge that their strategy is embraced by almost all of their peers at comparable companies.[21]

Unfortunately, this line of thinking is deeply misguided. Truly transformative talent is rare. As importantly, it's unpredictable. Boards should resist the temptation to spend lavishly in an effort to land a CEO who is highly unlikely to prove as important to the company's future as the directors believe. Directors' misplaced faith in their own ability to recognize superstars is the product of a number of interrelated psychological phenomena. An executive's future performance is far less predictable than directors commonly think. They should therefore be skeptical of claims that a particular CEO is worth any price necessary; their second choice is about equally likely to excel.

Directors should also deemphasize comparisons to their peer companies when trying to decide how and how much to pay their CEOs. Competing companies are doing a poor job at making these decisions, so imitating other directors will only compound their mistakes. We have no objective measure of a CEO's value to the company, so there is no natural check against excessive pay. The only way to stop the social cascade in pay, then, is for boards to recognize that they all lack the relevant information, so there is no help to be gained by turning to their neighbors for answers. This is not a problem of agency costs or corruption. Even ideal directors, those who were perfectly motivated to pursue their shareholders' interests, would fall prey to the same overconfidence.[22]

Directors should try to break the mold not only in how much they pay their CEOs but also in *how* they pay them. During the 1970s, directors began dabbling in academic theories of paying CEOs based on how the company performed, under the rationale that this type of pay structure would motivate CEOs to work harder and smarter and ultimately generate higher returns for shareholders. What began as an experiment has transformed into corporate orthodoxy; today, directors, institutional shareholders, academics, and the financial press all agree almost unanimously that CEO pay should be tied to performance. Despite this remarkable consensus on the desirability of performance pay, there is no convincing evidence that paying for performance improves performance. To the contrary, there is substantial evidence that suggests that performance pay may actually undermine CEOs' intrinsic motivation and generate worse corporate outcomes.[23]

The adoption of performance pay—combined with the historic bull markets of the 1980s and 1990s—produced record growth in CEO pay. Boards' psychological dynamics (and academics' remarkable ability to keep coming up with new justifications) prevented them from applying the brakes. In the past decade, performance pay mechanisms stopped delivering such extraordinary returns to CEOs as the stock market struggled first with the Internet bubble and then with the financial crisis. But if nothing changes, the recovery—when it comes—will send CEO pay off to the races again.

We have given performance pay at least three good decades to prove itself. If it really worked, the evidence would likely be more conclusive. There are excuses for why the results might not be showing up on the kinds of tests we can do, but they are not terribly convincing, except to those who have a profound faith in markets' ability to do collectively what none of the investors can do individually.

What is more, even if we bought into the performance pay orthodoxy entirely, it's far from clear whose interests should matter. Performance pay is supposed to reduce agency costs by aligning the CEO's interests with those of important corporate stakeholders. But *which* corporate stakeholders? Employees? Customers? Suppliers? The communities in which the business operates? The country as a whole?

The standard answer is the shareholders, who are the closest analog to owners/principals we have in public corporations. From a social welfare perspective, however, it is not clear that shareholders are the best choice. Shareholders may want the company to do all sorts of things the rest of us would object to in the quest for greater profits: pollute the environment, dodge taxes, move production offshore, skimp on product safety, and so on.

And even if we could agree that shareholders are the most important constituents, we have to remember that shareholders are themselves a remarkably diverse group. They include young adults saving for retirement and hoping for the best long-term growth and also people who have already retired and are seeking safe returns. Shareholders are middle-class state employees, and they are wealthy professionals. They are Republicans, Democrats, Independents, and those who do not care about politics. They are individuals and banks, public pension funds and mutual funds, arbitrageurs and long-term investors. How are boards supposed to design CEO pay to line up executives' incentives with all these different groups?[24]

The current state of the research does not furnish any clear answers, which argues for experimentation. Rather than have states mandate certain solutions, the better approach at this early stage is to free up boards to make up their own minds. The role for law here is mostly enabling, but the law should also require disclosure. Boards should be very clear about what their goals are, so that the various corporate constituents can react appropriately. Boards that choose shareholders over all others should expect to have a harder time obtaining state and local subsidies for new operations than those who make communal welfare at least a partial priority. Similarly, those same shareholder primacy corporations may have an easier time finding equity investors but have a tougher row to hoe when selling bonds to lenders.[25]

The question of whose interests should matter is not strictly empirical or philosophical. To answer it, we need both empirical data and some consensus about policy. Let's allow boards to experiment transparently with different priorities for a decade or so before we consider locking them into one particular orientation. Does it increase or decrease profits to push CEOs to focus on maintaining high U.S. employment? Do sales increase from the good publicity enough to make up the difference? Does product quality increase and help make up for higher labor costs? What about the impact of having lower transportation costs? Greater employee loyalty? If keeping jobs in the United States hurts profits, by how much?

We could ask similar questions about environmental concerns, safe product design, or any other major question of corporate policy that boards face. Many steps taken for the good of some particular constituency may turn out to be good for profits as well. But if some of these steps typically hurt profits, we should then move on to the policy discussion about whether the trade-offs are worth it to the society as a whole. We cannot have the policy discussion until we know what the trade-offs are. If keeping jobs in the United States causes a company to go bankrupt, most people would probably agree that the policy's cost is too high. But if hiring more U.S. workers just decreases profit margins to some extent, the debate might look quite different. To get these data, we need to free up boards to experiment with setting different priorities, and directors should express those priorities in part through the executive compensation system.

POPULAR REFORM PROPOSALS

Now that we have a deeper and more accurate understanding of the forces that have shaped CEO pay, we're in a better position to evaluate reform proposals. It has not escaped general notice that there is something amiss with CEO compensation. On the contrary, it's difficult to go a week (or a day during proxy season) without some newspaper article trumpeting an example of apparently scandalous pay and clamoring for change.

Reformers have suggested a number of solutions, but these are generally based on the conventional assumptions about the underlying causes of the problem, the merits of performance pay, and the overall goals of shareholder welfare. Having unpacked these assumptions and exposed their substantial weaknesses, I would like to say just a few words about three of the most prominent of these proposals: relying more heavily on restricted stock, requiring boards to let shareholders have a vote on executive pay, and permitting at least some shareholders to nominate their own candidates to the board on the company's proxy form.

There are, of course, other proposals on the table—especially in Europe.[26] For example, in the United Kingdom, a report by the High Pay Commission (a think tank unaffiliated with the government) advocated for a number of reforms to bring down executive pay, many of which focused on increasing the transparency and salience of the total pay package.[27] (The High Pay Commission also argued for simplifying pay packages, a proposal that is quite compatible with mine.)[28] Similarly, in the United States, the Dodd-Frank Act included a provision requiring companies to disclose the ratio of the CEO's pay to that of the median worker in the company, presumably to pressure boards to bring this ratio down by cutting executive pay.[29] And in Switzerland, where voters recently granted shareholders a binding veto over executive compensation, the Social Democrats pushed for capping executive pay at an amount equal to twelve times the salary of a company's lowest-paid worker.[30]

I could easily spend a chapter or even an entire book writing about various suggestions to change the compensation system. I have chosen these three examples because they are either currently occurring or are authorized by statute. And I think they should suffice to demonstrate how our new understanding of CEO pay should transform how we think about reform.

Restricted Stock

The mildest reform proposal is to substitute restricted stock for stock options in CEO pay packages. Options have come under increasing fire over the past few years as scholars have drawn attention to their many flaws when used as a tool to align CEOs' incentives with those of shareholders. Some of these academics have called for replacing stock options to some degree with restricted stock.[31] They argue that restricted stock provides executives with incentives that better mirror those of shareholders. Other than the constraint on sale, restricted stock gives executives an investment vehicle that is essentially identical to the one held by shareholders. Options, in contrast, differ along a number of dimensions: their value declines sharply once the share price falls below the strike price; option holders typically do not participate in dividend distributions that occur before the option holder exercises the options; and options have to be granted in much larger numbers to make up for their greater risk, creating the potential for lottery-like results if the share price rises significantly.

Perhaps directors are again paying attention to academics. Restricted stock has made up an increasing share of executive pay packages in recent years, while options have been declining.[32] There are, however, other explanations for this shift. Due to recent accounting reforms, the cost of stock options may no longer be ignored when a company is tallying up the cost of executive pay; options now reduce the bottom line just as other forms of compensation do, and not just in the form of an obscure footnote to a financial statement.[33] Also, executives may be asking for more of their pay to be shifted from options to stock. While options are incredibly valuable during a bull market, the past decade has not been a strong period for stocks. Restricted stock holds much more of its value when share prices are declining, whereas options may easily become worthless. Executives may be asking for more restricted stock as a hedge against the risk of a bear market.

Whatever the cause, can we expect a shift to restricted stock to bring executive pay under control? Will restricted stock do a better job of motivating executives effectively? My suspicion is that restricted stock may do a somewhat better job along both dimensions than stock options do, but we should not expect any dramatic results.

Share for share, restricted stock is less risky and more valuable than options, so companies should be able to persuade executives to accept fewer shares of restricted stock than the executives give up in options. This shift may result in lower payments to CEOs. To see why this is so, imagine that a CEO is slated to receive one million stock options with a strike price of $10.00 per share (the market price at the date of the grant). If the share price declines to $9.99 and does not peek above $10.00 during the options' term, the options turn out to be worthless to the executive. There is no point in exercising a right to buy stock at $10.00 per share when it is worth less than that; who would buy a dollar for ninety-nine cents? One million shares of restricted stock, though, would still be worth nearly $10 million. If the share price instead rises to $11.00, then the options are worth $1 million, while the restricted shares are worth $11 million. Either way, the restricted stock is more valuable on a per share basis and far less risky.

Shifting from options to stock reduces the lottery factor in CEO pay. Because options are riskier, executives demand far more of them. For example, suppose again a company whose stock is trading at $10.00 per share and that the company's best estimate is that the price will increase to $12.50 per share over the options' life, say, three years. Valuing options is very tricky because it involves evaluating the likelihood of the stock climbing above the strike price over the option period, but let's simplify the problem and just assume that the current value of the options is $2.00 per share. Providing $2 million in equity pay would then require issuing one million options but only 200,000 shares of restricted stock. If the share price shoots up to $15.00 during the three-year life of the options, their value will skyrocket to $5 million (one million shares times the $5 by which the market price now exceeds the strike price). The 200,000 restricted shares, on the other hand, will only be worth $3 million. In this sense, options are a leveraged investment; the same value of options can produce much higher returns (or greater losses) than the equivalent value of restricted stock.

Boards may still end up paying their executives too much, even if they completely replace options with restricted stock. The switch to restricted stock will not address any of the psychological dynamics that lead to excessive CEO pay. And if share prices rise more than expected, CEOs may still take home far more in pay than directors intended. But because restricted stock is easier to value and reduces the lottery factor of options, it is less likely that boards will accidentally overcompensate their CEOs with restricted stock than with options.

Restricted stock may also do a better job of motivating executives than options do. A number of studies have associated negative executive behavior with the issuance of stock options. Options have been linked to the manipulation of financial statements, to companies issuing restatements, and to income smoothing (the practice of shifting corporate income into different years to make growth seem even).[34] They are also associated with lower dividend payments and more share repurchases, presumably because options' value depends on the price of shares; dividends decrease share prices, and stock repurchases increase them.[35] Because the potential rewards for these actions are lower with restricted stock, perhaps restricted stock will be less damaging to corporations than stock options.

On the other hand, options may play some role in incentivizing executives to make high-risk, high-reward investments, the kind diversified shareholders are presumed to want.[36] The risks options motivate may not always be the ones shareholders actually want, though. Options do not sufficiently expose executives to the costs if the investment goes awry but let them participate if the investment prospers, perhaps leading CEOs to overemphasize the positive and pay too little attention to the negative when calculating an investment's desirability.[37] Plus, options have been shown to increase executives' willingness to take risky strategies to avoid paying corporate taxes.[38] Ultimately, the effect of executives' options-induced risk taking on the corporation is unclear; options seem to have little positive impact on company performance, as far as the empirical studies can determine.[39]

Although restricted stock may not encourage corporate risk taking to the same degree as options do,[40] they may produce better overall results. Kevin Murphy has pointed out that one place we might test the effect of stock ownership is management-led leveraged buyouts (MBOs). When the senior executives take a company private, their ownership stake increases considerably. If equity ownership works well as an incentive, we should expect to see companies prosper after MBOs. MBOs serve as a good test because we have the same companies being operated by the same managers, so we avoid many of the confounding variables we usually face (though many still remain). The major change is the amount of equity owned by management. Murphy's study found that operating income goes up by some 20 percent three years after the managers take over.[41] These results seem promising, but we have no way of knowing how well the companies would have done without the MBOs.

More typical studies comparing the performance of companies whose executives own more stock to those whose executives own less confront the usual too-many-variables problem. They have also sometimes produced some rather strange results. One prominent study by Randall Morck, Andrei Shleifer, and Robert Vishny found that a company's performance increases when the senior executives own between 0 and 5 percent of the outstanding shares, then decreases moderately when the executive team's ownership rises above 5 percent, then increases slightly again when ownership exceeds 25 percent.[42] It is difficult to square this complicated relationship with our intuitive notions about ownership's impact on incentives. Other studies have found no relationship between a company's market capitalization and the amount of stock held by the senior executives.[43] Still others have traced a relationship to better company operating performance and better acquisitions but also to increased layoffs.[44]

In the end, restricted stock is still a form of performance pay, since it usually comes in the form of performance shares (stock that is conditioned on the company achieving certain performance targets). To the extent that the amounts at stake are lower with restricted stock than they are with options, the deleterious impact on executives' performance may be attenuated. (As I discussed in chapter 6, very high contingent payments tend to hurt performance.) If the law and institutional investors combine to require some form of performance pay, then restricted stock is perhaps a relatively benign form. But it is unlikely to curtail executive pay sharply or markedly to improve corporate performance.

Shareholder Say on Pay

A version of the second reform proposal has recently become the law in the United States—a shareholder vote on executive pay. At least every three years, shareholders must be given an up or down vote on the senior executives' pay packages. Under the current law, this vote is purely advisory; the board is legally free to ignore even an overwhelming repudiation by the shareholders.[45] Because the shareholder vote is only precatory, we might expect that it would have little effect on CEO pay. Moreover, so far the vast majority (some 98 percent) of executive pay packages that have come before the shareholders have been approved.[46]

Still, there is some anecdotal evidence that this high level of approval is in part due to boards making changes when they see trouble looming on the horizon, indicating the law is having an effect.[47] And since we are discussing reform efforts, we are not limited to the possibilities presented by existing law. There would be substantial political impediments to mandating a binding shareholder vote on CEO pay, but that is not to say that such a law would be impossible to pass. In fact, the United Kingdom is actively considering such a measure as of this writing.[48]

The question is whether either the existing, precatory vote or a possible binding vote will curb the growth of CEO pay or change its structure to better motivate executives. The answer depends on shareholders and what they believe. If shareholders—especially large, institutional shareholders—hold different views than boards do about the appropriate amount of pay and/or the way companies should design compensation packages, then a shareholder vote could change things significantly. A shareholder vote—even if advisory—represents an opportunity to introduce a new voice, breaking the self-reinforcing cycle in which boards, executives, and consultants give one another the same, affirming message about how they are handling CEO pay. The way to collapse a social cascade or to disrupt a groupthink dynamic is to break in with new information, with a strong, dissenting voice. Shareholders could provide that voice, forcing directors to rethink their views along both dimensions of CEO pay: amount and structure.

The statistics so far, though, tell a different story. As I mentioned just above, shareholders approved some 98 percent of executive pay packages in 2011 and a similar percentage in 2012.[49] That level of approbation strongly suggests that shareholders are drinking from the same well as directors and executives. Like directors, shareholders seem to believe that the level of pay is appropriate and that tying CEOs' pay to corporate performance is the best way to improve business outcomes (or at least share prices).

On structure in particular shareholders seem to have bought the conventional wisdom. Institutional Shareholder Services, the leading shareholder proxy advisory service (a company that tells institutional shareholders how to vote their shares), has adopted performance pay as the linchpin of its executive compensation strategy. Its proxy guidelines state, "Pay-for-performance should be a central tenet in executive compensation philosophy."[50]

As long as shareholders share directors' sense of what type and level of executive pay is desirable, granting shareholders an expanded voice in setting CEO pay will not result in major changes. The social cascade will only be strengthened by adding more voices to the chorus. Shareholder votes will not effect real change unless shareholders can be persuaded that the conventional wisdom is flawed. Until then, shareholders may actually cause some harm by pushing directors to tie executive pay even more closely to share price movements. Linking pay to stock prices will make it difficult to check CEO pay levels so long as markets continue their secular growth trends. Executives will continue to demand higher expected pay as a trade-off for accepting greater risk and will continue to reap lottery-like windfalls when share prices rise more than expected. Shareholder votes may curb particularly abusive compensation packages but otherwise seem unlikely to make much of a dent in either the structure or the amount of executive pay.[51]

Shareholder Nominees to the Board

The final popular reform proposal I want to discuss bears only indirectly on CEO pay. A number of commentators have argued for changes in how directors are selected. Right now, a board is basically a self-perpetuating body; in the absence of a takeover fight, the board's nominees are almost always elected (or, more likely, reelected). Shareholders have the technical power to elect whomever they wish, but the mechanics of the proxy voting process make it unlikely that they will have a choice other than the directors' nominees (again, in the absence of a takeover fight). As a result, directors have little electoral incentive to please shareholders; they will be reelected whether the shareholders are happy or not.[52]

The reform proposals would change this dynamic by forcing companies to allow at least some shareholders (generally those holding significant stakes) to place one or more of their own nominees on the corporation's proxy form. Shareholders would then have a choice between the board's nominees and those of major shareholders, without requiring the competing candidates to spend money on creating and mailing their own proxy forms. The expense of mailing a rival proxy form has been a major obstacle to shareholders who want to nominate a rival slate of directors.

One such proposal came close to becoming law. Acting under authority granted by the Dodd-Frank Act, the SEC passed a regulation in 2010 that would permit certain large shareholders to nominate their own candidates to the board on the company's proxy form. The rule was sharply limited: only very large, long-term shareholders (those who owned enough stock to make up at least 3 percent of the company's voting power and had held that stock for at least three years) could participate. Also, all shareholders together could nominate no more than 25 percent of the board (or one director, whichever was greater). Plus, shareholders who held their shares with the purpose of gaining control over the company could not use this new rule.[53]

Despite all these limitations, the rule aroused considerable opposition. Directors worried that having dissidents on their boards would harm the company, especially if the insurgent directors represented employee unions. Ultimately, the U.S. Chamber of Commerce and the Business Roundtable—an association of CEOs of major corporations—sued to overturn the regulation. The U.S. Circuit Court for the District of Columbia agreed that the new rule was invalid. The court found that the SEC had failed to consider sufficiently the economic costs and burdens imposed by the regulation. While the holding left the door open for the SEC to try again after investigating the rule's potential impact more thoroughly, the SEC has so far declined to reissue the rule.[54]

Shareholders or boards may adopt a rule granting themselves access to the corporate ballot even without further rule making by the SEC. Since the D.C. Circuit's decision, a few boards have adopted proxy access rules in order to forestall more expansive shareholder proposals. But it is too soon to say whether this will become a broad trend.[55] In 2012, shareholders proposed proxy access bylaws at twelve companies; only two passed.[56] If these proposals become more popular, or if the SEC promulgates a new version of its proxy access regulation, will granting shareholders some access to the corporate proxy for board elections have an impact on CEO pay?

As with granting shareholders a direct vote on pay packages, the effect will depend on which shareholders nominate directors and what those shareholders believe. Even if shareholders are limited to nominating a minority of the board, having dissenting voices present could help break the social cascade and groupthink that characterize executive pay. But it is far from clear that shareholder nominees will *be* dissenting voices on CEO pay.

All the proposals so far have limited access to very large shareholders—those who own at least 1 percent of the corporation's voting power—and most have mandated that these shareholders have held their stock for one to three years. Even these large shareholders, though, are a diverse group. Banks, mutual funds, and endowment funds seem likely to conform to directors' broad consensus about CEO pay—that the amount is market driven and therefore not open to debate and in form should be tied to corporate performance.

Public pension funds and employee pension funds may prove more aggressive about the amount of pay but are likely to join the chorus on the importance of performance pay. And even on the payment level question, their contribution is likely to be limited to tough questioning about which companies are considered "comparable" in compensation surveys. Though we have no data yet, even employee pension funds seem unlikely to engage in more fundamental skepticism about the existence of an efficient executive labor market. Unless shareholders adopt different views on performance pay and on the necessity to provide pay that is comparable to that paid by peer companies, empowering shareholders to nominate directors on the company's ballot is unlikely to have much impact on executive pay.

BENIGN PERFORMANCE PAY
Guidelines

If none of the current proposals are likely to do much good, is there anything the law, corporate boards, or shareholders can do to positively affect CEO pay without waiting for the major legal and cultural shifts required to abandon performance pay? Some improvements seem clearly warranted. The evidence that stock options do more harm than good is quite convincing, and there are no longer artificial incentives to use them based on accounting rules (though tax law still provides options with an unwarranted, privileged status as performance-based). It's time to put an end to executive stock options.

Instead, if boards or shareholders insist on performance pay, it should take the form of a bonus of either cash or restricted stock. The bonus triggers should be within executives' control or at least their strong influence.[57] Even the most passionate devotees of performance pay should realize there is little to be gained from tying pay to metrics executives cannot affect very much. Boards should stop relying on easy, bottom-line triggers such as stock price or earnings per share that are mostly determined by a plethora of external and internal factors beyond the CEO's control. Directors should instead use concrete measures that the CEO plays a powerful role in determining, which are easy to measure and hard to manipulate and which matter to the company's ultimate success.

The specific triggers will vary widely from company to company, and a positive factor for one business may be a negative one for another. There is some evidence that nonfinancial measures may prove particularly effective.[58] Examples that may work for some companies (again, depending on their particular goals and needs) include customer satisfaction, product innovation, workplace safety, product liability, environmental sustainability, and brand penetration. I explain how triggers should work in greater depth below, when I analyze the case study.

Once the directors have found appropriate goals for bonuses (whether in the form of stock or cash), there are two guidelines they should bear in mind when applying them. First, the threshold triggers for the bonuses should be reasonably attainable, and then the bonuses should increase as performance improves. I don't mean that the full amount of the bonus should be easy to earn. But part of the problem with performance pay is that it makes people feel controlled or compelled, reducing their intrinsic motivation. Putting at least some portion of the bonus pool comfortably within reach should ameliorate that effect.

Having relatively easy thresholds should not keep these bonuses from qualifying as related to performance for federal income tax purposes. (Remember that companies can only deduct CEO compensation over $1 million from their income to the extent the additional payments are related to performance.)[59] Federal regulations do not require that the performance goals be difficult to meet. To the contrary, they specifically authorize performance goals that ask the CEO only to keep things from getting worse, or even those that ask only that the company not suffer more than a certain amount in losses.[60]

The rest of the bonus pool should rise continuously as the performance metric improves to soften the incentives to cheat. Continuous does not mean proportionate; the amount of additional pay for each quantum of improved performance can decline as performance rises (a sort of logarithmic function rather than a straight line). What should be carefully avoided are discrete steps where large payments hinge on small differences in performance. Providing big stakes for small differences seems (and generally is) arbitrary. This sort of arbitrary distinction can serve as a rationalization to manipulate the outcome measures.

The second guideline is that directors should not make any bonus component—even with miraculous performance—too large in either absolute or relative terms. As I discussed in chapter 6, Ariely and colleagues performed a study in India where subjects could have earned up to six months' worth of expenses. The subjects' performance was much worse when the possible rewards were this high than when they were much lower.[61]

The lesson of this study is that very high rewards diminish people's ability to perform at the peak of their abilities. Such rewards should be avoided. When total pay must be a high number and when the bulk of this pay must be performance related, boards should break up the performance pay into many smaller, independent components. The key is to ensure that no action of the executive can result in enormous pay on its own. Although both absolute and relative pay are probably important here, the emphasis should be on relative pay. When a substantial percentage of an executive's compensation depends on a single metric, the executive is *less* likely to excel at the task being measured.

AutoZone, Inc.: A Case Study

How would these principles work in practice? I decided to use Auto-Zone, Inc., as a demonstration case study. AutoZone is a public company currently ranked in the low 300s in the Fortune 500 and is a member of the S&P 500 index. The company says it is the leading auto parts replacement retailer in the United States and is also a major player in the commercial auto parts market.[62] I picked AutoZone because although it is a very large, important company, its business model is relatively straightforward. The bonus triggers should therefore be easy to understand, and many of them will be applicable to a broad range of other retail businesses.

Let me start with a quick caveat. The process of designing a CEO's pay structure would ideally be conducted in conjunction with the directors and would require access to confidential information. Clearly it was not possible to use private information in a case study intended for publication. Instead, I have relied solely on public filings to learn about the company's business and to pick out appropriate bonus triggers. It's likely that some of my suggestions would change, perhaps quite a bit, if I consulted with AutoZone's board. But the public filings provide enough information that I believe I can give a fairly realistic sense of how my principles would work in practice.

In 2012, AutoZone paid its CEO, William C. Rhodes III, a little over $4.7 million. This was broken down (in rough numbers) into $1 million in salary, $90,000 in restricted stock, $2.1 million in options, $1.3 million in bonuses, and about $200,000 in other compensation (e.g., pension contributions and perks).[63]

For purposes of the case study, I'm not going to tinker with the total amount of pay. The point of the case study is to demonstrate a better way of structuring performance pay, not to choose the optimal level of pay, and I do not want to confuse my discussion about reforming compensation *structure* by intermixing the equally complicated arguments about pay *levels*. More fundamentally, reversing CEOs' gains from the past three decades would be extremely difficult. A more realistic goal would be to slow down the *growth* of CEO pay in real terms, preferably bringing it back to where it was for the first three decades after World War II: zero.

I do think median CEO pay is too high in large corporations (without saying anything at all about Rhodes's pay, which was well below the median for the S&P 500 in 2012), but trying to shrink it back to size would generate too much resistance from executives (and probably from many directors as well). Pushing to lower pay could torpedo the important structural reforms I am proposing. I don't want to make the perfect the enemy of the good.

Boards that follow my rules for performance pay will regain control over the growth of CEO compensation because they will be eliminating the possibility of pay packages that turn out to be much more valuable than intended. How they use that control is up to them. My recommendation is to start slowly, aiming to keep pay at current levels in real terms. Static executive pay would be a huge improvement over the current norm of significant growth. If corporate culture evolves the way I hope it will under the influence of these reforms, then perhaps boards may eventually be able to shrink CEO pay somewhat, though I doubt we will ever return to the days of $1 million in total pay for our largest companies (about $1.35 million in 2012 dollars).

Let's begin discussing AutoZone's structure with the salary component. Since I believe the best option is to get rid of performance pay altogether, let's keep AutoZone's salary number where it is. I won't suggest increasing it because Rhodes is already making the maximum salary that AutoZone can deduct from its taxable income under current law. Plus, the reason for this exercise is to demonstrate a better way of structuring performance pay; there's not much point in reducing the proportion of the package that is performance related. I've already said that my first choice would be to switch back to compensation packages that almost entirely consist of salaries; this section is for corporate boards that cannot or will not follow that recommendation.

I'm also not going to fiddle with the perks. They are clearly not intended to be linked to Rhodes's performance, and they don't make up a very significant percentage of the total package. I will say as a general matter that perks and retirement contributions should be sharply limited. There's no justification for a company to pay for an executive's country club membership, and I have trouble seeing a serious need for corporate jets or free spousal travel either. Perks are particularly dangerous from a publicity standpoint; they can easily be used to paint a portrait of an excessively lavish lifestyle lived at shareholders' expense, embarrassing the company. For example, Jack Welch, the legendary former CEO of General Electric, suffered a serious blow to his reputation when his postretirement perks (a luxury Manhattan apartment, use of the corporate jet, flowers, and sports tickets, all free of charge) were revealed during his divorce proceedings.[64]

Executives with seven- or eight-figure compensation packages can easily afford to pay their own rent, and companies are unlikely to derive much incentive benefit from providing these sorts of perks. Except to the extent specific perks have some tax advantage, or to the extent the corporation is able to supply them more cheaply than the executive could purchase them on his or her own (like health insurance), they should generally be avoided.

My focus is on the $3.5 million portion of Rhodes's package that is supposed to be linked to his performance—the stock, options, and bonuses. I would replace these with a carefully calibrated system of bonuses linked to a large number of metrics that meet the requirements of the guidelines I discussed above. AutoZone could pay some of these bonuses in restricted stock; executives' stock ownership has been linked to stronger company performance in some studies, and owning stock probably does help foster a culture of responsibility.[65] But the bulk of these bonuses should probably be paid in cash. Otherwise, too much of the CEO's pay will end up being deferred until after the ban on stock sales expires, potentially creating a serious cash flow problem for the executive (especially when it's time to pay income taxes).

What kind of metrics would work for AutoZone? I've come up with twenty-three, all of which are capable of being objectively measured. (Federal tax law currently requires that the criteria be objectively measurable for the payments to count as performance related.)[66] The bonus triggers fall into seven categories that AutoZone's public filings singled out as being important to the company's success. These include the company's brand value, its customer service, its expenses, its growth (especially in the number of stores), the value it provides to customers, its profitability, and its vulnerability to outside suppliers. I'll just discuss a few, but I've listed them all in table 10.1. (I've included the salary as well so that the chart includes the entire compensation package except for perks.)

AutoZone's public filings identified customer service as central to its business model.[67] Because customer service is so important to the company, I've allocated seven triggers to different components of customer service, for a total of 24 percent of the CEO's expected pay. In keeping

TABLE 10.1 AUTOZONE PROPOSED BONUS STRUCTURE

Category	Bonus Trigger	Threshold Payment (90% Likelihood)	Expected Payment (65% Likelihood)	Outer Limit of Payment (1% Likelihood)	Expected Percentage of Total
	Salary	*$1,000,000*	*$1,000,000*	*$1,000,000*	22%
Brand	Brand value (measured by consumer survey)	$112,500	$225,000	$281,250	5%
Customer Service	Employee retention (calibrated for average pay [reduce when pay goes up] and general unemployment rate [reduce when unemployment high]	$135,000	$270,000	$337,500	6%
	Customer service, retail (based on survey data)	$90,000	$180,000	$225,000	4%
	Customer service, retail (based on customers' return rate of products)	$45,000	$90,000	$112,500	2%
	Customer service, commercial (based on survey data only)	$90,000	$180,000	$225,000	4%
	Inventory availability (based on how often a part is out of stock when a customer wants one)	$45,000	$90,000	$112,500	2%
	Training of sales personnel (based on a written test administered to a random selection of sales personnel; at least five versions rotated at random)	$90,000	$180,000	$225,000	4%
	Growth in loyalty card programs (based on utilization)	$45,000	$90,000	$112,500	2%
Expenses	Debt rating	$112,500	$225,000	$281,250	5%
	Environmental liabilities (from preexisting conditions where locate new stores)	$45,000	$90,000	$112,500	2%
	Employment liabilities (from claims for violations of hours/work laws, sexual harassment, or other labor violations such as working conditions/safety, workers' compensation)	$67,500	$135,000	$168,750	3%
	Premises liability (slip and fall, etc.)	$22,500	$45,000	$56,250	1%

Category	Description				
Growth	New store location quality (based on new store ROI on a per-month open basis, indexed to national economic variables)	$90,000	$180,000	$225,000	4%
	Net store expansion (based on number of new stores opened minus those closed)	$90,000	$180,000	$225,000	4%
	New store concentration (average number of stores within 15 miles of each new store)	$22,500	$45,000	$56,250	1%
	Estimate of percentage of cars 7+ years old within area of new stores, controlled for national percentage)	$45,000	$90,000	$112,500	2%
Profits	Profit margin on goods sold	$112,500	$225,000	$281,250	5%
	Existing stores' ROI (indexed to national economic variables)	$135,000	$270,000	$337,500	6%
Value	In-house brand quality (based on warranty claims)	$90,000	$180,000	$225,000	4%
	External brand quality (based on warranty claims)	$67,500	$135,000	$168,750	3%
	Lowest prices compared to competitors (based on random checks of competitors' stores by an independent service)	$112,500	$225,000	$281,250	5%
	Quality measured by length of warranty of goods sold (both in-house brands and external)	$67,500	$135,000	$168,750	3%
Vulnerability	Inventory dependence (reduction in percentage of inventory from any one supplier)	$22,500	$45,000	$56,250	1%
	Totals	$2,755,000	$4,510,000	$5,387,500	100%

with the principles I explained above, all these triggers are (a) largely within officers' control; (b) hard to manipulate; (c) easy to measure; and (d) important to the corporation's long-term goals. I examine two of them in detail to provide a sense of what I mean.

One important measure of customer service would come from survey data. AutoZone does not say in its public filings whether it regularly conducts surveys of its customers to measure their satisfaction with their stores.[68] Given the strong emphasis the company places on the importance of customer service, though, if they're not already running such surveys, they probably should be. Customer service surveys clearly meet all four of my criteria for good bonus triggers. (Note that Auto-Zone has both retail and commercial operations; I have separate bonus triggers for each.)

Customer service is something the CEO can affect in a number of ways. CEOs can set hiring criteria that emphasize finding employees with good people skills, establish customer-friendly return policies, create training programs to ensure that sales representatives are knowledgeable, reward employees (with promotions, raises, bonuses, or recognition) for providing excellent customer service, and provide feedback through survey data and direct evaluations.

Survey data—especially if the surveys are conducted by an outside research firm—are not easy to manipulate by strategic actions that turbocharge the present at the expense of the future. Surveys can ask quantitative questions, such as requesting that customers rate the customer service on a numeric scale, that provide ready comparisons from year to year and make survey results easy to measure. They can also ask for general demographic information that makes it possible to control for variances in respondents' backgrounds.

And customer satisfaction is clearly critical to AutoZone's success, as the company has stated several times in its public filings. It would be hard to imagine any retail operation that would not benefit from making its customers happy.

Another useful measure of customer service is employee retention. Retention is an important factor for the company's costs, since it is expensive to find, hire, and train new employees. But I have categorized it as a customer service issue because experienced employees are likely to be more knowledgeable and helpful. Like customer service survey data, employee retention nicely meets my four criteria for bonus triggers.

CEOs can have substantial influence over employee retention. They can set salary and benefits levels to make jobs at AutoZone more attractive than other opportunities available to people with similar education and training. They can make the job more pleasant by training and hiring good managers and establishing pro-employee workplace policies. They can also give employees a sense that they have a future in the company, by promoting from within and making training available to employees who work hard and demonstrate potential to rise through the ranks. Conversely, CEOs can hurt employee retention by neglecting some or all of these steps.

Employee retention is a difficult statistic to manipulate. Employees either stayed or left. A CEO could implement temporary measures for a short-run improvement in retention, such as a boost to employee salaries. But such changes are hard to undo without causing serious harm to employee morale (with consequent drops in employee retention). Short of fraud, CEOs are unlikely to be able to change employee retention numbers through changes that help retention for a year or two but then fade when the gimmickry is revealed. Executives could boost retention more consistently by, for example, raising employee pay dramatically, but that would hurt other important bonus metrics like return on investment at stores and the company's debt rating and profit margins. To the extent performance pay works, the CEO should be appropriately motivated to balance the costs of employee retention measures against their probable benefits.

Retention is easy to measure. AutoZone must already track who works for it for multiple purposes, including knowing whom the company should pay and which stores need additional workers. Tracking the average tenure of employees or the percentage of employees who leave the company each year should be easy to do. (Either of these measures of employee retention should work well.)

Finally, employee retention is important to the company's success. As I mentioned above, hiring and training new employees is expensive. Harder to quantify but perhaps even more central to the company's bottom line, employee retention is key to the customer's experience. More senior employees should have greater knowledge about AutoZone's products and more experience with customers' reactions to them. Salespeople may also develop relationships with regular customers, building customers' trust that they will receive quality advice and excellent service. And employees should develop their sales skills over time, so employees with longer tenures should be better salespeople on average.

Once the directors have identified appropriate bonus triggers, they must then work out the details of how to apply them. As I mentioned above, I have two guidelines for boards here. First, the performance level that entitles the CEO to at least some amount of bonus for each trigger should be reasonably (even easily) attainable, with the bonuses then increasing as performance improves. The rate at which the bonus increases with improvements in performance should be higher at first, then decline to prevent CEOs from earning far more than planned if unanticipated conditions knock a metric out of the park. Second, no single component of the bonus should be very big in either absolute or relative terms.

Suppose, for example, that AutoZone decided to measure customer satisfaction using a survey question that asked customers to rank the overall quality of their experience on a scale of 1 to 10, with 10 being best. Let's further suppose that after a few years' experience with the survey, AutoZone found that the company-wide average score was typically around 7.8 and had never fallen below 7.2. AutoZone could set the threshold score for the CEO to receive any bonus at all under this measure at 7.0. That is just a bit below the lowest score AutoZone has had, so it seems very likely that the CEO will receive at least some payment under this measure. But since the company has experienced a score very close to this, a score below 7.0 is certainly possible.

To the extent the board can estimate the probabilities of hitting a certain target, the minimum measure to receive any part of the bonus should be about 90 to 95 percent likely. The point of setting a low minimum threshold, remember, is to ameliorate the tendency of performance pay to make its subjects feel controlled (and therefore resentful). Also, making at least part of the bonus very likely should help reduce the pressure CEOs might otherwise feel to meet their targets. As we saw from the studies in India, having too much money ride on performance tends to degrade performance.[69]

As shown in table 10.1, I've set the threshold reward for each bonus component at half the expected amount. That should be enough to reassure executives that they will receive substantial pay (especially when combined with their guaranteed salaries, which in AutoZone's case is over 22 percent of the total expected pay) while still leaving plenty of room to encourage superior performance.

The requirement to achieve the expected bonus amount should be somewhat tougher to achieve but still very likely. Boards should conceptualize this as quite likely but not certain, something they would expect the CEO to receive about 65 percent of the time. Since AutoZone's hypothetical customer service score is generally around 7.8, I might set the threshold for the expected bonus amount a bit below this, at around 7.6.

The bonus should rise continuously as performance improves according to a formula rather than in discrete steps. For our hypothetical survey results, for example, the formula for scores between the minimum threshold of 7.0 and the requirement for the full expected payment (7.6) would be this (with the bonus measured in thousands of dollars):

$$Bonus = 150^* \ [SurveyScore] \ -960$$

(I derived this formula by plugging in our desired outcomes (from table 10.1) into the general linear formula $y = mx + b$ and then solving using our two endpoints for x and y.) The formula does not have to be linear like this, just continuous. Linear formulas are simpler to design and implement, but more complicated formulas are certainly possible. The important point is that boards should avoid sharp differences in pay that stem from small differences in performance measures. (I recognize that the fact that there is a minimum score required for the CEO to earn *any* payment breaks this rule, but that is one of the reasons the threshold for the minimum payment should be set low enough that CEOs will almost always achieve it.)

Once the company has achieved the score needed for the full expected payment, the bonus amount should continue to rise continuously but more slowly. Every improvement in performance should garner an increase in pay, but the increases should become smaller to avoid ending up with unexpectedly large bonus payments if a performance measure wildly exceeds expectations. Boards can also use a cap to help prevent unexpectedly large payments, but they should be careful to set the caps at a performance level that is far above what they reasonably expect to occur. Caps come with a danger; studies have demonstrated that people often stop working as hard once they have achieved their goal.[70] But if the caps are associated with sufficiently high performance measures, this tendency should not come into play very often.

The simplest method is to set up another linear function with a shallower slope than the first one for performance results between the expected and the aspirational. I don't want to get too technical here, but the mathematically sophisticated might be tempted to use a single logarithmic function instead of two linear equations for this sort of structure. Note, though, that the logarithmic function likely will not fit the

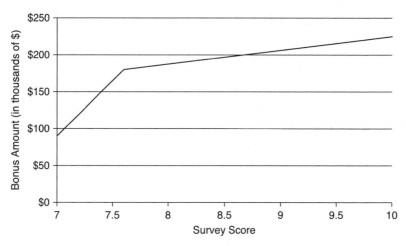

FIGURE 10.1. Model Bonus Formula for Customer Satisfaction

three points (threshold, expected, and cap) perfectly, the way the two linear functions do, and maybe not very well at all. For those who want more details about logarithmic formulas, please refer to note 71 below.[71] And again, linear formulas have the advantages of being simple to understand and easy to set up and are likely just fine for our purposes. In this case, we could use the same procedure as before but using the numbers for the expected and maximum bonuses to get this formula for the bonus (again measured in thousands of dollars):

$$Bonus = 18.75 * [Survey\ Score] + 37.5$$

Figure 10.1 shows what these two linear functions would look like (with the bonus given in thousands of dollars). No cap is necessary in this case, since the survey itself already provides us with one. The maximum score on the survey is 10.0, so there is no way for the bonus to exceed $225,000. But if we needed a cap, we could simply stipulate in the compensation contract that the maximum bonus payment would be subject to a cap.

The particular thresholds and limits I'm suggesting here are just guidelines. We need some experience with this new compensation system before we can begin to identify the sweet spots that provide the most powerful incentive at the lowest price. But the guiding principles are that the threshold triggers for the bonuses should be reasonably attainable, with the bonuses then increasing as performance improves, and that no single performance criteria be tied to a bonus payment that is particularly large in either absolute or relative terms.

The other variables can be easily set up with similar formulas. Some of the variables require a bit of fine-tuning, though, to compensate for external factors that are beyond the CEO's influence. For example, one of the bonus components in the growth category measures the quality of the locations AutoZone is choosing for new stores. AutoZone depends for its growth primarily on expansion to new areas, which is why another of the bonus components measures the net number of new stores. But it is also important to ensure that the new stores are chosen wisely, and not just to meet expectations about sheer numbers of openings.

For that reason, I'm proposing a variable that measures the most important determinant of the success of a new AutoZone store: the concentration of older cars in the neighborhood. AutoZone's primary customer base consists of owners of cars that are at least seven years old. These cars are generally out of warranty, so the owners are more likely to spend money on new parts. The more such cars (and owners) who live nearby, the more likely the new AutoZone store is to thrive.

This variable can be affected by national trends. During a recession, people are more likely to drive their cars longer, inflating this measure across the country. The CEO should not be rewarded for the recession's effect on how long people keep their cars. The point of the variable is to measure how well the CEO has chosen new store locations. So this variable also controls for the national average, by asking by how much the local average percentage of older cars *exceeds* the national figure. The bonus is proportional to the extent the new stores' neighborhoods have an unusually high concentration of older cars, which is precisely what the company should care about in choosing new store locations. Bonus targets may often require this sort of adjustment to account for factors outside the CEO's control.

I have one last clarification to make about my suggestions for better types of performance pay, and it has to do with timing. Some readers may have noticed in looking at table 10.1 that all the bonus measures I propose are based on a single year's results. I have limited the bonus triggers that way mostly for the sake of simplicity and clarity. Many of these triggers could easily have been set up with multiyear thresholds, and boards may often find such longer time horizons useful and appropriate. Boards should bear in mind, however, that executives heavily discount rewards they will not receive for several years, far beyond what economic models would predict.[72]

Unlike with the coarser measures of performance such as earnings or share prices, however, my more granular approach does not necessarily require that most of the bonuses be calibrated to long-term performance. Under my system, the criteria for bonuses are designed to reflect achievements that will *necessarily* build a strong foundation for the company's future success. They do directly what long-term earnings goals attempt to do indirectly: incentivize CEOs to build healthy, lasting businesses. And since the rewards occur more quickly, they do not have to cope with executives' tendency to underestimate the value of rewards they receive only after several years.

My incentive systems should have significant advantages over the current practices of relying mostly on stock options and a combination of performance shares and bonuses that are triggered by big-picture measures like stock price or earnings growth. My bonus criteria are more closely calibrated to what the CEO can actually affect and are much less susceptible to environmental effects. Even when environmental effects can have a large impact, boards can tailor the measures to reduce this influence when necessary.

Also, unlike measures like earnings per share, which are the product of the intersection of a vast array of factors, my narrower measures are harder for the CEO to game in the short run. In part this is simply because they *are* narrower; there just isn't as much play in the joints for the CEO to exploit. They also tend to act as checks against one another; CEOs who attempt to manipulate one of these measures are likely to see any gains offset by losses in other bonus measures. If the board chooses the bonus criteria wisely, setting targets one year at a time may often suffice.

My system also should reduce the negative effects of performance pay. Executives should be less prone to feel controlled (a feeling that has been shown to reduce intrinsic motivation); there are so many bonus factors that none of them should be particularly salient. Boards might further boost CEOs' sense of ownership over corporate strategy by involving them in choosing the bonus criteria (though involvement must not devolve into total delegation). This system also reduces the negative effects on performance that come from having huge payments depend on a single measure. No single measure can result in outsized payments, especially if boards carefully construct caps for each component. The small stakes (at least in relative terms) involved for each measure should also reduce executives' temptation to cheat.

This proposal should put directors more firmly in control of the pay executives actually take home. Under current practices, directors do set *expected* pay. But the forms of compensation they use—especially stock options—can easily end up being worth an amount very different from that the board initially intended (in either direction). The discrepancy occurs because the value of these compensation devices depends on the company's share price, and stock prices are difficult to predict.[73] (The same is true for bonuses tied to the company's earnings.) With the system I am proposing, boards can regain absolute control over the upper limits of the amounts CEOs actually collect. This system therefore has the potential to curb CEO pay growth, although the effect on growth will depend on what boards decide to do. Under my proposal, any increase in executive pay will be the result of a conscious decision by the board, not the effect of a capricious stock or product market.

Finally, this system may encourage boards to look at the company's business model from a different perspective. Directors will have to focus in considerable detail on the strategies that will make the business successful in order to figure out the performance measures that make most sense for their company. No doubt directors are already very aware of what the company has to do to succeed, but asking the question in a different context may yield insights that help make directors more effective monitors. Directors do not have to undertake this exercise when the key performance metrics they use are bottom-line figures like earnings per share.

Although the incentive pay system I'm proposing promises to produce many benefits, directors may be reluctant to make the transition, both because this is new and untested and because payments will no longer be tied directly to what shareholders care about most—share price. Any such reluctance is thoroughly understandable but misguided.

The system is new but sensibly rooted in empirical studies of human behavior. In contrast, the enormous volumes of data we have about current practices do not validate those practices; they indict them. If shareholders ultimately care about share price, then boards should pursue the strategy that is most likely to raise those prices. As I argued in chapter 6, tying executive pay to share prices has not turned out to be an effective way to boost shares (though it has worked wonders for executive pay growth). I hope that both directors and shareholders will be persuaded that the system I am proposing is more likely to have a positive long-term effect on earnings (and therefore share price).

There is a problem with this line of argument, however: shareholders may no longer be willing to wait for long-term benefits. In the first decades after World War II, shareholders typically adopted a buy-and-hold strategy, investing for the long term. They therefore had an interest in encouraging companies to invest in enterprises even when those investments might take a number of years to bear fruit. That is no longer the case for the average shareholder. While in 1960 investors held on to their stock in a company for an average of eight years, now the average holding period is a mere four months.[74] I have heard directors complain that as soon as an institutional shareholder buys a stake, it immediately begins to advocate for actions that will produce an instant profit, such as a share buyback (when the company buys its own shares in an effort to boost the stock price).

Investors with such a short time horizon for investment rationally lack the patience to nurture strategies that strengthen the company's prospects years in the future. But those are precisely the sorts of investments that produce strong, profitable companies. Shareholders antsy for a quick profit may resist tying CEO pay to metrics that have nothing to do with the company's immediate share price growth. This is a challenge that I hope can be overcome with the help of institutional investors that still do invest for the long term, such as public pension funds.

It's worth emphasizing again at this point that I see the performance pay system I am proposing as a second-best option. It would be better to abandon performance pay altogether, or at least to reduce boards' dependence on it. The research has generally failed to document that performance pay generates any real value to justify its enormous expense. At a minimum, boards should begin experimenting by cutting back on performance pay and reemphasizing straight salaries, as companies did for much of their (very successful) postwar history.

This will be hard to do. Federal tax law imposes substantial costs on companies that pay their senior executives more than $1 million in unconditional pay,[75] and shareholders and analysts see performance pay as a mark of good governance (despite the lack of supporting evidence).[76] Shareholders' new power to vote on executive pay packages makes their views more concrete, salient, and difficult to ignore. Amending the tax laws to remove the impediment to guaranteed pay would be helpful, but the more important and difficult task is to persuade shareholders of the futility of tying pay to performance. (One excellent step in this direction that directors should take: give your major shareholders copies of this book.)

CONCLUSION

What we really need is a cultural shift away from the myths that have brought us here. Companies are run by directors who have their own motivations and incentives, so we should not blithely assume companies will always act in their own rational interest. CEO pay changed radically after the 1970s in ways that are not explainable if we cling to the notion that the market for CEOs is highly efficient; it isn't. So we shouldn't rely on the market to produce good results or trust the results we have simply because the market produced them. But we shouldn't assume there is something nefarious going on either. There is little reason to believe in some conspiracy between CEOs and directors to siphon off corporate funds for their own benefit.

Instead, we should recognize that the changes in CEO pay occurred because of a combination of events. Academics proffered theories about the benefits of paying for performance. Directors then bought into these theories and began relying more and more heavily on performance pay, especially stock options. A historic bull market made these options unexpectedly valuable, resulting in much higher executive pay than directors had intended. Yet, because directors believed that the CEO was critical to the company's success (an importance that is probably exaggerated in most cases), they continued to justify spiraling pay levels as a good deal for the company. Social cascades, groupthink, and other social dynamics (helped along by a burgeoning consulting industry) prevented directors from reining in CEO pay and often even obscured the increasingly significant percentage of corporate profits the CEO was absorbing.

We should also recognize that performance pay is a mirage. The apparent relation between pay and performance has demonstrably increased executive pay, but it has not had a similarly concrete impact on corporate performance. Also, shareholder wealth and social welfare may not march together. If it turns out that they lead us in different directions, directors and the country generally should think seriously about reshaping corporations' goals. Even if we hold to shareholder wealth as corporations' central purpose, though, that goal can best be pursued by using the alternative compensation strategies I have put forward in this chapter.

Freed from these misconceptions, boards can begin developing and testing alternative means to motivate their senior management teams. Senior executives will always demand and should receive generous compensation packages; they are highly trained and specialized professionals who as a group add tremendous value. The question is once we get beyond a very comfortable guaranteed salary, how can companies best use their resources to get the most out of their leadership? The lessons Hewlett-Packard's managers learned should prove enlightening here:

culture, internal drive, and reputation are likely more effective motivators than conditional pay.[77]

We need to pay CEOs well, even handsomely. Compensation packages in the low seven figures may be perfectly appropriate. But we should stop treating high-powered managers like dogs we're teaching to salivate at the sound of a bell. If we pay them well and then build a supportive culture—one that encourages risk taking, innovation, and hard work and owning up to failures when they occur—the right kind of CEOs will deliver for us. The current cult of leadership and lottery-type compensation packages that can result in generational wealth foster precisely the wrong sort of culture for CEOs, one that encourages them to put their own interests first and the company's last. We want strong, healthy, innovative businesses that can create jobs that endure and products we are proud to buy. Getting there will require us to radically rethink how we structure pay and how we encourage our CEOs to lead our companies.

Notes

CHAPTER 1

1. Ben Rooney, "5 Most Overpaid CEOs," *CNN Money,* September 28, 2009, http://money.cnn.com/galleries/2009/news/0909/gallery.highest_paid_worst_CEOs/index.html.

2. See Sheryl Gay Stolberg and Stephen Labaton, "Obama Calls Wall Street Bonuses 'Shameful,'" *New York Times,* January 29, 2009, www.nytimes.com/2009/01/30/business/30obama.html.

3. "Past Leaders: John F. Welch, Jr.," *General Electric,* www.ge.com/company/history/bios/john_welch.html.

4. Robert Barker, "GE Stock: Cheaper, but Still No Bargain," *Bloomberg Businessweek,* September 10, 2001, www.businessweek.com/magazine/content/01_37/b3748131.htm.

5. Mark Lewis, "The Famous 15: America's Most Fascinating Tycoons," *Forbes,* December 13, 2001, www.forbes.com/2001/12/13/1213top15_print.html.

6. See Lucian Bebchuk and Jesse Fried, *Pay without Performance: The Unfulfilled Promise of Executive Compensation* (Cambridge, MA: Harvard University Press, 2004).

7. This book is about CEO pay in corporations whose stock is publicly traded. There are many large, important companies that are family owned or otherwise closely held; Cargill, Koch Industries, Pricewaterhouse Coopers, and Fidelity Investments are just a few examples. This book is not about them. Closely held companies are not generally required to disclose what they are paying their CEOs, and so they usually keep their executive pay a secret. The point of this book is to bring data to the debate about CEO pay, to pierce the mists of myth and conventional wisdom with facts about what companies actually have done and how their pay strategies have affected their performance. I can't do that for companies that keep their compensation practices secret. To the extent

that closely held companies use public companies' compensation practices as a model, their directors and officers should find this book a useful critique of those practices.

8. See Carola Frydman and Dirk Jenter, "CEO Compensation" (Working Paper 3277, Rock Center for Corporate Governance, Stanford University, 2010), 38, table 2, http://ssrn.com/abstract=1582232. In a recent article, Kevin Murphy has cited a 1968 study by Willbur Lewellen that found there were a few years during the 1950s when options were an important component of executive pay. See Kevin J. Murphy, "Executive Compensation: Where We Are and How We Got There," in Handbook of the Economics of Finance, ed. George Constantinides, Milton Harris, and René Stulz (North Holland: Elsevier, 2012), also available at SSRN: http://ssrn.com/abstract=2041679. As Carola Frydman and Raven E. Saks explain, Lewellen's study did not use the commonly accepted Black-Scholes method to value option grants. Instead, Lewellen measured options' value by the difference between their exercise price and the market price of the stock in each year, then dividing those potential gains over the length of the option. The Black-Scholes method measures the value of the options at the time they are granted. This is the method that therefore best reflects the board's intent at the time it issued the options. Depending on what happens in the stock market, the options may turn out to be worth more or less than the Black-Scholes estimate. Lewellen's method takes into account later changes in the stock price, changes the board did not know about when it granted the options. Because of how the market performed during the 1950s, Lewellen's method overstated the value of the options as boards could have evaluated them at the time of issue. Carola Frydman and Raven E. Saks, "Executive Compensation: A New View from a Long-Term Perspective, 1936–2005" (Working Paper 2007–35, FEDS, 2007; paper presented at the annual meeting of the AFA, New Orleans, 2008), 9, http://ssrn.com/abstract=972399.

9. Michael C. Jensen and William H. Meckling, "Theory of the Firm: Managerial Behavior, Agency Costs, and Ownership Structure," Journal of Financial Economics 3, no. 4 (1976): 305–60. At around the same time, other economists were also pushing for closer links between pay and performance under the "optimal contracting" label. See Murphy, "Where We Are," 132 and n. 157.

10. See Lynn A. Stout, Cultivating Conscience: How Good Laws Make Good People (Princeton: Princeton University Press, 2010), 42; Murphy, "Where We Are," 74 (mentioning his own, later work with Jensen that argued for using more stock options). See also Frank Dobbin and Jiwook Jung, "The Misapplication of Mr. Michael Jensen: How Agency Theory Brought Down the Economy and Why It Might Again," Research in the Sociology of Organizations 30B (2010): 29–64 (2010).

11. For example, Institutional Shareholder Services, the most influential shareholder advisory service in the United States, states, "Pay-for-performance should be a central tenet in executive compensation philosophy." Institutional Shareholder Services, "2012 Taft-Harley U.S. Proxy Voting Guidelines," January 2012, 21, www.issgovernance.com/files/2012ISSTaftHartleyAdvisoryServic esUSGuidelines.pdf.

12. See Frydman and Jenter, "CEO Compensation," 39, panel B.

CHAPTER 2

1. See Carola Frydman and Dirk Jenter, "CEO Compensation" (Working Paper 3277, Rock Center for Corporate Governance, Stanford University, 2010), 38, table 2, http://ssrn.com/abstract=1582232.

2. Ibid.

3. Ibid.

4. Ibid.

5. Ibid., 41, table 1.

6. Ibid.

7. See "The Wall Street Journal/Hay Group Survey of CEO Compensation," *Wall Street Journal*, May 8, 2011, http://graphicsweb.wsj.com/php/CEOPAY11.html; "The Wall Street Journal/Hay Group Survey of CEO Compensation," *Wall Street Journal*, May 20, 2012, http://online.wsj.com/article/SB10001424052702304019404577416861519464648.html?grcc=a642e7e468fde734843ea1bcfoed6827Z3ZhpgeZoZ114Z200Z56Z2&mod=WSJ_hpp_sections_management#articleTabs%3Dinteractive. Note that the samples for the Wall Street Journal surveys are slightly different from those in Frydman and Jenter, "CEO Compensation."

8. See Kevin J. Murphy, "Executive Compensation," in *Handbook of Labor Economics*, vol. 3, ed. Orley Ashenfelter and David Card (North Holland: Elsevier, 1998), 2485–563 (also available as Kevin J. Murphy, "Executive Compensation" [1998], 90, fig. 15, http://ssrn.com/abstract=163914); Kevin J. Murphy and Jan Zabojnik, "CEO Pay and Appointments: A Market-Based Explanation for Recent Trends," *American Economic Review* 94 (2004): 192.

9. See Murphy, "Executive Compensation" (1998), 90, fig. 15.

10. Ibid.

11. See Murphy and Zabojnik, "CEO Pay and Appointments," 192 n. 2.

12. See "Executive Paywatch: Trends in CEO Pay," *AFL-CIO*, 2012, www.aflcio.org/Corporate-Watch/CEO-Pay-and-the-99/Trends-in-CEO-Pay.

13. See "The State of Working America: Executive Pay," *Financial Times*, http://blogs.ft.com/businessblog/files/2009/01/state-of-working-america.pdf.

14. See Lucian Bebchuk and Yaniv Grinstein, "The Growth of Executive Pay," *Oxford Review of Economic Policy* 21 (2005): 283–303.

15. See Harwell Wells, "U.S. Executive Compensation in Historical Perspective," in *Research Handbook on Executive Compensation*, ed. Randall S. Thomas & Jennifer G. Hill (Northampton, MA: Edward Elgar, 2012), 41–57; also available as research paper 2011–19, Legal Studies, Temple University, 2011, 3, http://ssrn.com/abstract = 1775083.

16. Ibid., n. 13.

17. See Carola Frydman and Raven E. Saks, "Executive Compensation: A New View from a Long-Term Perspective, 1936–2005" (Working Paper 2007–35, FEDS, 2007; meeting paper, AFA, New Orleans, 2008), 9, http://ssrn.com/abstract=972399.

18. Ibid., n. 15.

19. See Frydman and Jenter, "CEO Compensation," 38, fig. 2.

20. Ibid., 39, panel B.

21. See U.S. Securities and Exchange Commission, *Release No. 34-1823*, 1938, 3 *Fed. Reg.* 1991.

22. See Nuno G. Fernandes, Miguel A. Ferreira, Pedro P. Matos, and Kevin J. Murphy, "The Pay Divide: (Why) Are U.S. Top Executives Paid More?" (Finance Working Paper 225, European Corporate Governance Institute, 2009), 1–2, http://radyschool.org/faculty/seminars/2010/papers/matos.pdf.

23. One notable exception comes from Fernandes and a number of coauthors, most notably Murphy (n. 22, above). More on this just ahead.

24. John M. Abowd and David S. Kaplan, "Executive Compensation: Six Questions That Need Answering," *Journal of Economic Perspectives* 13, no. 4 (1999): 145–68, fig. 1.

25. Ibid.

26. Ibid., fig. 2.

27. Fernandes et al., "The Pay Divide," 3.

28. See Randall Thomas, "Explaining the International CEO Pay Gap: Board Capture or Market Driven?," *Vanderbilt Law Review* 57 (2004): 1171–267, 1206.

29. Fernandes et al., "The Pay Divide," 3.

30. See Stephen H. Bryan, Robert C. Nash, and Ajay Patel, "The Structure of Executive Compensation: International Evidence from 1996–2004" (2006), http://ssrn.com/abstract=891207.

31. See Fernandes et al., "The Pay Divide," 18.

32. See Nuno G. Fernandes, Miguel A. Ferreira, Pedro P. Matos, and Kevin J. Murphy, "Are U.S. CEOs Paid More? New International Evidence" (May 22, 2012), EFA 2009 Bergen meetings paper; AFA 2011 Denver meetings paper; ECGI—Finance Working Paper No. 255/2009, available at http://ssrn.com /abstract=1341639.

33. See Home Depot, Inc., Schedule 14A, May 17, 2012, available at www.sec .gov/Archives/edgar/data/354950/000119312512146086/d277811ddef14a .htm#toc277811_23.

34. Ibid.

35. See Sarah B. Lawsky, "Probably? Understanding Tax Law's Uncertainty," *University of Pennsylvania Law Review* 157 (2009): 1036–42 (arguing that tax preparers cite probabilities of a position's success based on subjective beliefs and not mathematical probabilities because the uncertainties of tax law make mathematically correct statements difficult if not impossible).

36. See PWC, "Making Executive Pay Work: The Psychology of Incentives" (2012), available at www.pwc.com/gx/en/hr-management-services/publications /making-executive-pay-work-the-psychology-of-incentives.jhtml.

37. These data are derived from statistics produced by the U.S. Department of Commerce's Bureau of Economic Analysis. The data are available on the Bureau's website: www.bea.gov/national. The most helpful link is GDP "percent change from preceding period."

38. See Frydman and Jenter, "CEO Compensation," 39.

CHAPTER 3

1. See Philip Rucker, "Mitt Romney Says 'Corporations Are People' at Iowa State Fair," *Washington Post*, August 11, 2011, www.washingtonpost.com

/politics/mitt-romney-says-corporations-are-people/2011/08/11/gIQABwZ38I_
story.html.

2. Ibid. The full exchange can be seen at www.youtube.com/watch?v=
E2h8ujX6ToA.

3. Some payment decisions might also require shareholder approval, especially if they involve stock. For example, if the corporation does not have sufficient authorized but unissued shares, shareholder approval would be required
to authorize additional shares. See Delaware General Corporation Law, 8 Del.
C. § 242. But these circumstances are relatively unusual.

4. Although small in population and territory, Delaware is mightier than
California, New York, and Texas combined when it comes to corporate law.
For reasons too complex to go into here, Delaware law governs the internal
affairs of over half of all corporations in the United States.

5. 8 Del. C. § 141(a).

6. 8 Del. C. § 242(b)(1); 8 Del. C. § 251(c).

7. 8 Del. C. §§ 141(a), 142(b). See also Lucian A. Taylor, "Why Are CEOs
Rarely Fired? Evidence from Structural Estimation," *Journal of Finance* 65
(December 2010): 2051–87 (2 percent of S&P 500 companies fire their CEOs
each year).

8. See Corporate Board Member and PricewaterhouseCoopers, "What
Directors Think: Survey" (2008), 12, www.pwc.com/en_US/us/corporate-
governance/assets/what-directors-think-2008.pdf. Directors reported spending
20 hours per month on board business in 2008, up from 14 hours in 2002 (12).
Sarbanes Oxley was passed in 2002, and the next year the time directors spent
on board activities jumped to 19 hours per month (12).

9. 8 Del. C. § 220(d).

10. Ibid.; Kortum v. Webasto Sunroofs, Inc., 769 A.2d 113, 118 (Del. Ch.
2000).

11. Intrieri v. Avatex, C.A. No. 16335, 1998 WL 326608, at *1 (Del. Ch.
June 12, 1998).

12. See Kevin Roose, "The Invisible Hand Behind Bonuses on Wall Street,"
New York Times, January 16, 2012, www.nytimes.com/2012/01/17/business
/the-invisible-hand-behind-wall-street-bonuses.html?pagewanted=all.

13. See Lucian Bebchuk and Jesse Fried, *Pay without Performance: The
Unfulfilled Promise of Executive Compensation* (Cambridge, MA: Harvard
University Press, 2004).

14. For a recent discussion of this effect, see Charles M. Elson and Craig K.
Ferrere, "Executive Superstars, Peer Groups and Over-Compensation—Cause,
Effect and Solution" (August 7, 2012), available at http://ssrn.com/abstract=
2125979.

15. Keillor's radio show, *A Prarie Home Companion,* contains a Lake Wobegon segment that generally concludes, "That's the news from Lake Wobegon,
where all the women are strong, all the men are good-looking, and all the children
are above average." Garrison Keillor, *A Prairie Home Companion* (American
Public Media, July 16, 2011), 23 min., 3 sec., www.publicradio.org/tools/media_
player/popup.php?name=phc/2011/07/16/phc_20110716_64&starttime=
01:36:31.0&endtime=01:51:08.0.

16. Richard LeBlanc and James Gillies, *Inside the Boardroom: How Boards Really Work and the Coming Revolution in Corporate Governance* (New York: John Wiley & Sons, 2005), 51.

17. Marcel Kahan and Edward Rock, "Embattled CEOs," *Texas Law Review* 88 (2010): 987–1051, 996.

18. Adolf A. Berle and Gardiner C. Means, *The Modern Corporation and Private Property* (1932; rpt. Piscataway, NJ: Transaction Publishers, 1991).

19. See Kahan and Rock, "Embattled CEOs."

20. Ibid.

21. See Anup Agrawal and Gershon N. Mandelker, "Shark Repellents and the Role of Institutional Investors in Corporate Governance," *Managerial and Decision Economics* 13 (1992): 15–22; Richard Chung, Michael Firth, and Jeong-Bon Kim, "Institutional Monitoring and Opportunistic Earnings Management," *Journal of Corporate Finance* 8 (2002): 29–48; Stuart L. Gillian and Laura T. Starks, "Corporate Governance Proposals and Shareholder Activism: The Role of Institutional Investors," *Journal of Financial Economics* 57 (2000): 275–305.

22. See www.nasdaq.com/symbol/bac/ownership-summary (as of August 13, 2012).

23. See 8 Del. C. § 211(b). Delaware law does permit directors to be elected by written consent in lieu of an annual meeting, but such consent must generally be unanimous unless all the board seats are vacant and filled by written consent. As a result, written consent is not a practical electoral method for public corporations.

24. 8 Del. C. § 216.

25. Ibid.

26. 8 Del. C. § 212(b).

27. Securities Exchange Act of 1934, Rules 14a-1 through 14a-15, 17 C.F.R. 240.14a-1–15.

28. For example, Comtech Telecommunications Corporation spent $2.6 million on a contested proxy solicitation in 2012 that was later withdrawn. Comtech, "Investor Presentation: Q3 Fiscal Year 2012," 34, http://files.shareholder.com /downloads/CMTL/0x0x576407/fac55114-32d9-4db9-8b50-67e15ff393f7 /comtechInvestor_Presentation_FY12_Q3_rl.pdf.

29. See 8 Del. C. § 216(iii) ("Directors shall be elected by a plurality of the votes of the shares present in person or represented by proxy at the meeting and entitled to vote on the election of directors").

30. See 8 Del. C. § 216(iii) ("Directors shall be elected by a plurality of the votes of the shares present in person or represented by proxy at the meeting and entitled to vote on the election of directors"). For a discussion of the current trend of companies adopting majority voting rules, see Marcel Kahan and Edward Rock, "Embattled CEOs" (2009), 26, www.law.upenn.edu/academics /institutes/ile/CRTPapers/1209/Kahan&Rock_Embattled%20CEOs.pdf.

31. Nike, Inc., "Corporate Governance Guidelines," http://investors.nikeinc .com/Investors/Corporate-Governance/Guidelines/default.aspx.

32. See City of Westland Police & Fire Retirement System v. Axceliis Technologies, Inc., 1 A.3d 281 (Del. 2010).

33. See Ian Fried, "Costs Mount in HP Proxy Fight," *CNET News,* March 13, 2002, http://news.cnet.com/2100–1001–859261.html.

34. See SEC Rule 14a-11, 17 C.F.R. 240.14a-11; U.S. Securities and Exchange Comission, *Facilitating Shareholder Director Nominations,* Release Nos. 33–9136, 34–62764 (August 25, 2010), www.sec.gov/rules/final/2010/33–9136.pdf.

35. Business Roundtable and Chamber of Commerce of the United States of America v. SEC, 647 F.3d 1144 (D.C. Cir. 2011).

36. See Marcel Kahan and Edward B. Rock, "The Insignificance of Proxy Access," *Virginia Law Review* 97 (2011): 1347 (Research Paper 10–26, Institution for Law and Economics, University of Pennsylvania; Research Paper 10–51, NYU Law and Economics, December 9, 2011), http://ssrn.com/abstract=1695682.

37. See Bebchuk and Fried, *Pay without Performance.*
A stock option is the right to buy a share of stock at a set price, called the "strike price" or "exercise price." Corporations customarily set the strike price at the market price for the stock on the day the options are issued. Options come with a time limit; if the option holder does not "exercise" the option by buying the underlying stock before this time elapses, the options lapse. Options become more valuable as the market price rises above the strike price. Restricted stock shares are shares of the company's stock that cannot be sold for some period determined by the corporation. The idea of both options and restricted stock is to give the recipient an incentive to boost the stock price.

38. See Jeremy C. Owens, "Apple Chief Was Top-Paid CEO," *San Jose Mercury News,* May 22, 2012, 2D.

39. See Matteo Tonello, "The 2011 U.S. Director Compensation and Board Practices Report," November 11, 2011, http://blogs.law.harvard.edu/corpgov/2011/11/11/the-2011-u-s-director-compensation-and-board-practices-report/.

40. See Carmen DeNavas-Walt, Bernadette D. Proctor, and Jessica C. Smith, "Income, Poverty and Health Insurance Coverage in the United States: 2009," U.S. Census Bureau, September 2010, 40, www.census.gov/prod/2010pubs/p60–238.pdf.

41. See U.S. Securities and Exchange Commission, *Target, Inc. Proxy Statement DEF14A* (April 29, 2010), 16, www.sec.gov/Archives/edgar/data/27419/000104746910004446/a2198173zdef14a.htm.

42. Ibid., 5–10.

43. See U.S. Securities and Exchange Commission, *Wells Fargo & Company Proxy Statement DEF14A* (March 17, 2010), 64, www.sec.gov/Archives/edgar/data/72971/000119312510059552/ddef14a.htm.

44. See U.S. Securities and Exchange Commission, *Xerox, Inc. Proxy Statement DEF14A* (April 8, 2010), 38, www.sec.gov/Archives/edgar/data/108772/000120677410000874/xerox_def14a.htm.

45. See U.S. Securities and Exchange Commission, *Eli Lilly & Company Proxy Statement DEF14A* (March 8, 2010), 41, www.sec.gov/Archives/edgar/data/59478/000095012310021859/c55338ddef14a.htm.

46. See U.S. Securities and Exchange Commission, *Target, Inc. Proxy Statement,* 26.

47. See, e.g., *Aronson,* 473 A.2d at 812.

48. See 8 Del. C. § 141(a) ("The business and affairs of every corporation organized under this chapter shall be managed by or under the direction of a board of directors").

49. See Michelson v. Duncan, 407 A.2d 211, 217 (Del. 1979).

50. See Nixon v. Blackwell, 626 A.2d 1366, 1375–76 (Del. 1993) (entire fairness test applies when directors have a conflict of interest).

51. See Smith v. Van Gorkom, 488 A.2d 858, 873 (Del. 1985) ("We think the concept of gross negligence is also the proper standard for determining whether a business judgment reached by a board of directors was an informed one").

52. The facts in this paragraph are taken from the Delaware Supreme Court's opinion. In re Walt Disney Co. Deriv. Litigation, 906 A.2d 27, 35–46 (Del. 2006).

53. Ibid., 75.

54. See Federal Rule of Civil Procedure 23.1; Del. Chancery Rule 23.1; Grimes v. Donald, 673 A.2d 1207, 1217–1218 (Del. 1996); Aronson v. Lewis, 473 A.2d 805 (Del. 1984); Zapata Corp. v. Maldonado, 430 A.2d 779 (Del. 1981).

55. See 8 Del. C. § 107(b)(7).

56. See *In re Walt Disney Co. Deriv. Litigation.*

57. See 8 Del. C. § 145(g).

58. See 8 Del. C. § 145(a).

59. See 8 Del. C. § 145(g) (permitting insurance "whether or not the corporation would have the power to indemnify").

60. See 8 Del. C. § 145(c).

61. See Bernard Black, Brian Cheffins, and Michael Klausner, "Outside Director Liability," *Stanford Law Review* 58 (2006): 1055–158.

62. Smith v. Van Gorkom, 488 A.2d 858 (Del. 1985).

63. See Black, Cheffins, and Klausner, "Outside Director Liability," 1067.

64. Ibid., 1070.

65. The best overviews of this literature's insights are Russell B. Korobkin and Thomas S. Ulen, "Law and Behavioral Science: Removing the Rationality Assumption from Law and Economics," *California Law Review* 88 (2000): 1051; and Cass Sunstein and Christine Jolls, "A Behavioral Approach to Law and Economics," *Stanford Law Review* 50 (1998): 1471.

66. See Eric Posner, *Law and Social Norms* (Cambridge, MA: Harvard University Press, 2000): 49–67.

67. Ibid., 65.

68. See Heather Timmons and Vikas Bajaj, "Buffett and Gates Prod India's Wealthy to Be More Philanthropic," *New York Times,* March 25, 2011.

69. See Ian R. Macneil, *The New Social Contract: An Inquiry into Modern Contractual Relations* (New Haven, CT: Yale University Press, 1980), 40–44, 65–66. Relational contracting refers to Macneil's theory that contracts are not always formed based on discrete, one-time transactions. Some contracts are formed in the context of a long-term relationship. Contracts generally fit somewhere along a spectrum between discrete and relational. To the extent a con-

tract is more relational, it may have different characteristics from a discrete contract and should be interpreted differently.

70. Ibid.

71. Ibid., 129 n. 11 (quoting Dorothy Emmet, *Rules, Roles and Relations* [New York: Macmillan, 1966], 13–15).

72. Ibid., 40.

73. See Craig Haney, Curtis Banks, and Philip Zimbardo, "Interpersonal Dynamics in a Simulated Prison," *International Journal of Criminology and Penology* 1 (1973): 69–97.

74. Ibid.

75. See Phil G. Zimbardo, Craig Haney, W. Curtis Banks, and David Jaffe, "The Mind Is a Formidable Jailer: A Pirandellian Prison," *New York Times Magazine*, April 8, 1973, 36.

76. See J. Scott Armstrong, "Social Irresponsibility in Management," *Journal of Business Research* 5, no. 3 (1977): 185–213.

77. Ibid., 196–97.

78. Ibid., 199.

79. Ibid.

80. Ibid., 197–200.

81. See Charles Daniel Batson, *The Altruism Question: Toward a Social-Psychological Answer* (Hillesdale, NJ: Lawrence Erlbaum Associates, 1991), 109–74 (describing studies supporting the existence of empathy-driven altruism).

82. See Michael B. Dorff, "Softening Pharaoh's Heart: Harnessing Altruistic Theory and Behavioral Law and Economics to Rein in Executive Salaries," *Buffalo Law Review* 51 (2003): 811, 860 (adopting a similar definition). The famed sociobiologist Richard Dawkins adopted a similar strategy in discussing altruism: "It is important to realize that the above definitions of altruism and selfishness are *behavioural*, not subjective. I am not concerned here with the psychology of motives. I am not going to argue about whether people who behave altruistically are 'really' doing it for secret or subconscious selfish motives. Maybe they are and maybe they aren't, and maybe we can never know, but in any case that is not what this book is about. My definition is concerned only with whether the *effect* of an act is to lower or raise the survival prospects of the presumed altruist and the survival prospects of the presumed beneficiary." Richard Dawkins, *The Selfish Gene* (Oxford: Oxford University Press, 1989), 4; original emphasis.

83. See, e.g., Batson, *The Altruism Question*, 109–201; Nancy Eisenberg, *Altruistic Emotion, Cognition, and Behavior* (Hillsdale, NJ: Laurence Erlbaum Associates, 1986), 188–212; Alfie Kohn, *The Brighter Side of Human Nature: Altruism and Empathy in Everyday Life* (New York: Basic Books, 1990), 65–85; J. Philippe Rushton, *Altruism, Socialization, and Society* (Upper Saddle River, NJ: Prentice Hall, 1980), 38–57; Charles Daniel Batson and Jay S. Coke, "Empathy: A Source of Altruistic Motivation for Helping?," in *Altruism and Helping Behavior: Social, Personality and Developmental Perspectives*, ed. J. Philippe Rushton and Richard M. Sorrentino (Hillsdale, NJ: Laurence Erlbaum Associates, 1981), 167, 171–72, 180–85; Leonard Berkowitz, "Social Norms, Feelings, and Other Factors Affecting Helping and Altruism," in *Advances in*

Experimental Social Psychology 6, ed. Leonard Berkowitz (New York: Academic Press, 1972), 63; Gustavo Carlo et al., "The Altruistic Personality: In What Contexts Is It Apparent?," *Journal of Personality & Social Psychology* 61 (1991): 450; John F. Dovidio, "Helping Behavior and Altruism: An Empirical and Conceptual Overview," in *Advances in Experimental Social Psychology* 17, ed. Leonard Berkowitz (Orlando, FL: Academic Press, 1984), 361; Harvey A. Hornstein, "The Influence of Social Models on Helping," in *Altruism and Helping Behavior: Social Psychological Studies of Some Antecedents and Consequences,* ed. Jacqueline Macaulay and Leonard Berkowitz (New York: Academic Press, 1970); Rabindra N. Kanungo and Jay A. Conger, "The Quest for Altruism in Organizations," in *Appreciative Management and Leadership: The Power of Positive Thought and Action in Organizations,* ed. Suresh Srivastva and David L. Cooperrider (San Francisco: Jossey-Bass, 1990), 228–38; M. Audrey Korsgaard, Bruce M. Meglino, and Scott W. Lester, "Beyond Helping: Do Other-Oriented Values Have Broader Implications in Organizations?," *Journal of Applied Psychology* 82 (1997): 160; Shalom H. Schwartz, "Normative Influences on Altruism," in *Advances in Experimental Social Psychology* 10, ed. Leonard Berkowitz (New York: Academic Press, 1977), 221, 242–73; Shalom H. Schwartz and Judith A. Howard, "Internalized Values as Motivators of Altruism," in *Development and Maintenance of Prosocial Behavior: International Perspectives on Positive Development,* ed. Ervin Staub et al. (New York: Plenum Press, 1984), 229; Ervin Staub, "A Conception of the Determinants and Development of Altruism and Aggression: Motives, the Self, and the Environment," in *Altruism and Aggression: Biological and Social Origins,* ed. Carolyn Zahn-Waxler, E. Mark Cummings, and Ronald J. Iannotti (Cambridge: Cambridge University Press, 1986), 135; Lynn A. Stout, "On the Proper Motives of Corporate Directors (Or, Why You Don't Want to Invite Homo Economicus to Join Your Board)," *Delaware Journal of Corporate Law* 28 (2003): 10 n. 23 (citing studies that apply a game theory methodology).

84. See Dorff, "Softening Pharaoh's Heart," 861–77 (identifying and discussing these factors); Stout, "Proper Motives," 13–23.

85. See Dorff, "Softening Pharaoh's Heart," 861–62; Stout, "Proper Motives," 13–23.

86. See Carlo et al., "The Altruistic Personality"; Korsgaard, Meglino, and Lester, "Beyond Helping," 161–62; J. Philippe Rushton, "The Altruistic Personality: Evidence from Laboratory, Naturalistic, and Self-Report Perspectives," in Staub et al., *Development and Maintenance of Prosocial Behavior,* 271, 278–79; Staub, "Motives, the Self, and the Environment," 147; Herbert A. Simon, "Altruism and Economics," *American Economic Review* 83 (1993): 156, 157 (pointing to docility).

87. See Batson, *The Altruism Question,* 47–57; Dovidio, "Helping Behavior and Altruism," 361, 370–72; Staub, "Motives, the Self, and the Environment," 141–43.

88. For an excellent statement of why altruism might be relevant to directors' behavior, see Stout, "On the Proper Motives of Corporate Directors."

89. See Stephen Bainbridge, "Executive Compensation: Who Decides?," *Texas Law Review* 83 (2005): 1515, 1659–60 (quoting Bengt Holmstrom and

Steven N. Kaplan, "The State of U.S. Corporate Governance: What's Right and What's Wrong?," *Journal of Applied Corporate Finance* 16, no. 8 [Spring 2003]: 1).

90. See Taylor, "Why Are CEOs Rarely Fired?"

91. Public Law No. 111–203, § 951 (July 21, 2010).

92. See Emily Chasan, "'Say on Pay' Changes Ways—Companies Consult Investors, Stress Performance to Avoid Repeat of Negative Votes," *Wall Street Journal*, February 22, 2012, B4; Associated Press, "Say on Pay: Shareholders Rarely Reject CEO Pay," May 23, 2013, available at www.miamiherald.com /2013/05/23/3412742/say-on-pay-shareholders-rarely.html.

CHAPTER 4

1. See Steven Bainbridge, "Director Primacy and Shareholder Disempowerment," *Harvard Law Review* 119 (2006): 1735, 1939–40 (arguing that corporate governance law must be reasonably efficient since the U.S. economy has fared pretty well).

2. See Kevin J. Murphy, "Executive Compensation," in *Handbook of Labor Economics,* vol. 3, ed. Orley Ashenfelter and David Card (North Holland: Elsevier, 1998), 2485–563; also available as Kevin J. Murphy, "Executive Compensation" (1998), 90, fig. 15, http://ssrn.com/abstract=163914.

3. See Xavier Gabaix and Augustin Landier, "Why Has CEO Pay Increased So Much?," *Quarterly Journal of Economics* 123 (2008): 49–100. See also See Melanie Cao and Rong Wang, "Search for Optimal CEO Compensation: Theory and Empirical Evidence" (meeting paper, AFA, San Francisco, March 18, 2008), http://ssrn.com/abstract=972118.

4. Gabaix and Landier, "Why Has CEO Pay Increased So Much?"

5. See George-Levi Gayle and Robert A. Miller, "Has Moral Hazard Become a More Important Factor in Managerial Compensation?," *American Economic Review* 99, no. 5 (2009): 1740–69; Alex Edmans and Xavier Gabaix, "Is CEO Pay Really Inefficient? A Survey of New Optimal Contracting Theories," *European Financial Management* 15, no. 3 (2009): 486–96.

6. Gabaix and Landier, "Why Has CEO Pay Increased So Much?"

7. Benjamin E. Hermalin, "Trends in Corporate Governance," *Journal of Finance* 60, no. 5 (2005): 2351–84.

8. As I discuss later in this chapter, several scholars have attempted to create a measure of CEO talent. None of these measures, however, is remotely adequate.

9. See Gabaix and Landier, "Why Has CEO Pay Increased So Much?," 50.

10. See Carola Frydman and Dirk Jenter, "CEO Compensation" (Working Paper 3277, Rock Center for Corporate Governance, Stanford University, 2010), 38, table 2, http://ssrn.com/abstract=1582232.

11. See Charles M. Elson and Craig K. Ferrere, "Executive Superstars, Peer Groups and Over-Compensation—Cause, Effect and Solution (August 7, 2012), 33, available at http://ssrn.com/abstract=2125979.

12. Frydman and Jenter, "CEO Compensation," 21; Mark R. Huson, Robert Parrino, and Laura T. Starks, "Internal Monitoring Mechanisms and CEO

Turnover: A Long-Term Perspective," *Journal of Finance* 56, no. 6 (2001): 2265–97.

13. Frydman and Jenter, "CEO Compensation," 21; Steven N. Kaplan and Bernadette A. Minton, "How Has CEO Turnover Changed? Increasingly Performance Sensitive Boards and Increasingly Uneasy CEOs" (Working Paper Series 12465, NBER, August 2006), http://ssrn.com/abstract=924751.

14. Compare Dirk Jenter and Katharina Lewellen, "Performance-Induced CEO Turnover" (Working Paper, Stanford University, February 2010), www.stanford.edu/~djenter/Research.htm (arguing that CEO turnover is strongly related to company performance), and Murphy, "Executive Compensation" (arguing that CEO turnover is driven more by age than by performance in larger firms, though performance plays a larger role in smaller firms).

15. Frydman and Jenter, "CEO Compensation," 21.

16. Ibid.

17. See Carola Frydman and Raven E. Saks, "Executive Compensation: A New View from a Long-Term Perspective, 1936–2005," *Review of Financial Studies* 23, no. 5 (2010): 2099–138.

18. See Frydman and Jenter, "CEO Compensation," 22; Gregory L. Nagel, "The Effect of Labor Market Demand on U.S. CEO Pay since 1980," *Financial Review* 45, no. 4 (2010): 931–50.

19. Nagel, "The Effect of Labor Market Demand."

20. Ibid.

21. See Lucian Bebchuk and Jesse Fried, *Pay without Performance: The Unfulfilled Promise of Executive Compensation* (Cambridge, MA: Harvard University Press, 2004).

22. I am indebted to Jesse Fried for pointing out this argument to me.

23. Luis Garicano and Esteban Rossi-Hansberg, "Organization and Inequality in a Knowledge Economy," *Quarterly Journal of Economics* 71 (2006): 1383–435.

24. Ibid.

25. Ibid.

26. See Amotz Zahavi, "Mate Selection—A Selection for a Handicap," *Journal of Theoretical Biology* 53 (1974): 205–14.

27. See, e.g., Securities and Exchange Act of 1934, Rule 10b-5, 17 C.F.R. § 240.10b-5 (2010).

28. See Rachel M. Hayes and Scott Schaefer, "CEO Pay and the Lake Wobegon Effect," *Journal of Financial Economics* 94 (2009): 280–90 (proposing a model with this assumption to explain ratcheting CEO pay).

29. There is a huge literature on tournament theory, but the pioneering piece is Edward P. Lazear and Sherwin Rosen, "Rank-Order Tournaments as Optimum Labor Contracts," *Journal of Political Economy* 89 (1981): 841–64.

30. Ibid.

31. See Iman Anabtawi, "Explaining Pay without Performance: The Tournament Alternative," *Emory Law Journal* 54 (2005): 1557; Michael L. Bognanno, "Corporate Tournaments," *Journal of Labor Economics* 19 (2001): 290–315.

32. See Brian E. Becker and Mark A. Huselid, "The Incentive Effects of Tournament Compensation Systems," *Administrative Science Quarterly* 37 (1992): 336.

33. See Lazear and Rosen, "Rank-Order Tournaments."

34. See Becker and Huselid, "Incentive Effects."

35. See Jayant R. Kale, Ebru Reis, and Anand Venkateswaran, "Rank-Order Tournaments and Incentive Alignment: The Effect on Firm Performance," *Journal of Finance* 64 (2009): 1479–511.

36. Ibid. Compare Randall S. Thomas, "Should Directors Reduce Executive Pay?," *Hastings Law Journal* 54 (2003) (arguing that pay gaps hurt performance), and Kin Wai Lee, Baruch Lev, and Gillian Hian Heng Yeo, "Executive Pay Dispersion, Corporate Governance, and Firm Performance," *Review of Quantitative Finance and Accounting* 30, no. 3 (2008): 315–38 (arguing that pay gaps improve performance).

37. See U.S. Securities and Exchange Commission, *General Electric Company DEF14A* (March 14, 2011), 21, http://sec.gov/Archives/edgar/data/40545/000119312511065578/ddef14a.htm#tx122802_7.

38. See Lazear and Rosen, "Rank-Order Tournaments."

39. See Derek Bok, *The Cost of Talent: How Executives and Professionals Are Paid and How It Affects America* (New York: Free Press, 1993), 101.

40. See Anabtawi, "Explaining Pay without Performance," 1557.

41. See Ovid, *Metamorphoses XI,* trans. Brookes More (Theoi E-Texts Library, 2000), www.theoi.com/Text/OvidMetamorphoses11.html#2.

42. See Antonio Falato, Dan Li, and Todd Milbourn, "To Each According to His Ability? The Returns to CEO Talent" (2011), http://ssrn.com/abstract=1699384 (arguing CEO pay is correlated to several proxies for talent, such as frequency of press appearances, age at first CEO position, and selectivity of undergraduate institution). Khurana has written that the misguided quest to hire a superstar has played a key role in driving up CEO pay. Rakesh Khurana, *Searching for a Corporate Savior: The Irrational Quest for Charismatic CEOs* (Princeton, NJ: Princeton University Press, 2002).

43. See Kevin J. Murphy and Jan Zabojnik, "Managerial Capital and the Market for CEOs" (2007), http://ssrn.com/abstract=984376; Kevin J. Murphy and Jan Zabojnik, "CEO Pay and Turnover: A Market Based Explanation for Recent Trends," *American Economic Review* 94, no. 2 (2004): 192–96. See also Mariassunta Giannetti, "Serial CEO Incentives and the Structure of Managerial Contracts" (2009 meetings paper, AFA, San Francisco; 2008 meetings paper, EFA, Athens; Finance Working Paper 183/2007, ECGI; 2010), http://ssrn.com/abstract=889040 (arguing that many aspects of pay structure can be explained by the need to incentivize CEOs to acquire firm-specific skills).

44. The closest to direct evidence that I have seen is a recent (still unpublished) paper by three business school professors. See Claudia Custodio, Miguel A. Ferreira, and Pedro Matos, "Generalists versus Specialists: Managerial Skills and CEO Pay" (2011), www.sfs.org/Paper%20for%20Cavalcade%20website/Generalists%20versus%20Specialists.pdf. They find that CEOs with general skills, as measured primarily by past experience in another industry, command a pay premium of some $250,000. This amount seems relatively trivial when compared to total CEO pay, and unlikely to explain the large increase in pay observed since the 1970s. Also, this evidence does not reveal whether the cause of the premium is the *actual* increased utility of general managerial skills or

boards' *perception* of such utility. As we will see in the following chapters, there are strong reasons to suspect that boards' predictions of CEO talent are not accurate.

45. See Martijn Cremers and Yaniv Grinstein, "The Market for CEO Talent: Implications for CEO Compensation" (2008), http://recanati.tau.ac.il/vi/_Uploads/573Grintein.pdf.

46. See Elson and Ferrere, "Executive Superstars."

47. See Bebchuk and Fried, *Pay without Performance.*

48. See Khurana, *Corporate Savior.*

49. This quote is also sometimes attributed to Groucho Marx.

50. See Kevin J. Murphy, "Explaining Executive Compensation: Managerial Power versus the Perceived Cost of Stock Options," *University of Chicago Law Review* 69 (2002): 847; Kevin J. Murphy, "The Politics of Pay: A Legislative History of Executive Compensation," in *The Research Handbook on Executive Pay,* ed. Jennifer G. Hill and Randall S. Thomas (Cheltenham: Edward Elgar, 2012) (article also available at http://ssrn.com/abstract=1916358); Kevin J. Murphy, "Executive Compensation: Where We Are and How We Got There," in *Handbook of the Economics of Finance,* ed. George Constantinides, Milton Harris, and René Stulz (North Holland: Elsevier Science, 2013), available at http://ssrn.com/abstract=2041679.

51. See Murphy, "Explaining Executive Compensation."

52. See Financial Accounting Standards Board, *Financial Accounting Series: Statement of Financial Accounting Standards No. 123,* 2003, www.fasb.org/cs /BlobServer?blobkey=id&blobwhere=1175820918940&blobheader=application %2Fpdf&blobcol=urldata&blobtable=MungoBlobs.

53. See Murphy, "Politics of Pay," 29–30.

54. See 26 U.S.C. § 162(m).

55. See Treasury Regulations § 1.162–27(e)(2)(vi)(A).

56. See Gregg D. Polsky, "Controlling Executive Compensation through the Tax Code," *Washington & Lee Law Review* 64 (2007): 877 (citing numerous examples of experts expressing this belief but also casting doubt on the claim's empirical validity); Murphy, "Politics of Pay," 17–18.

57. Frydman and Jenter, "CEO Compensation," 38, table 2.

58. Ibid.

59. Ibid.

60. See Brian J. Hall and Jeffrey B. Liebman, "The Taxation of Executive Compensation," in *Tax Policy and the Economy,* vol. 14, ed. James M. Poterba (Cambridge, MA: MIT Press, 2000): 1–44, www.nber.org/papers/w7596; Nancy L. Rose and Catherine Wolfram, "Regulating Executive Pay: Using the Tax Code to Influence Chief Executive Officer Compensation," *Journal of Labor Economics* 20 (2002): S138–S175.

61. Those interested in a fuller discussion of Murphy's theory should read his excellent and thought-provoking articles, "The Politics of Pay" and "Executive Compensation: Where We Are Now and How We Got There."

62. See Murphy, "Where We Are Now and How We Got There."

63. There is also research suggesting that stock options encourage CEOs to innovate more, as measured by the number of patents taken out by the firm. See

Frederick L. Bereskin and Po-Hsuan Hsu, "New Dogs New Tricks: CEO Turn-over, CEO-Related Factors, and Innovation Performance" (2011), http://ssrn.com/abstract=1684329; Josh Lerner and Julie Wulf, "Innovation and Incentives: Evidence from Corporate R&D," *Review of Economics and Statistics* 89 (2007): 634–44.

64. The expected return is what an investor would earn *on average* from an opportunity if she or he invested in the same opportunity multiple times, each time facing the same odds of earning a return. This is easier to understand if we think of a coin toss. Imagine you bet me the next time you flipped a coin it would come up "heads." (This is a fair coin, and you cannot manipulate the coin toss through sleight of hand.) We agree that if the coin comes up heads, I'll pay you a dollar. If the coin comes up tails, you'll pay me a dollar. There is a 50 percent chance that either of us will win; there are only two possibilities, and each outcome is equally likely. The expected return to you for entering this wager is the amount you would earn *per game* if we played this game an infinite number of times. That's an important caveat. If we only played a few times, anything could happen. You might have a winning streak and produce heads five or even ten times in a row. Assuming the coin toss is fair, though, over time these sorts of streaks will pretty much even out; the coin will come up heads and tails with roughly equal frequency. The amount you would expect to earn on average is: (odds of heads) × (return if heads) + (odds of tails) × (return if tails). In this case, that would amount to $(.5) \times (1) + (.5) \times (-1) = 0$. This is just what we would expect from a fair bet; the expected return for each of us is zero. Compare this, by the way, to a typical lottery. The lottery might offer a $10 million prize and sell tickets for $1. If more than ten million tickets are sold, the expected return is less than the price of entry. That is the definition of an unfair wager, and most lotteries are unfair. They can still be fun, though, especially for the lucky person who actually wins. Note that the expected return is not the *actual* return unless we play the game many times. On a single coin toss, someone will win a dollar, and someone will lose a dollar. Only if we play many times will our actual results approach our expected returns.

65. Even noted critics of the executive compensation system agree. See Bebchuk and Fried, *Pay without Performance.*

66. See Ingolf Dittmann and Ko-Chia Yu, "How Important Are Risk-Taking Incentives in Executive Compensation?" (2010), http://ssrn.com/abstract=1176192.

67. See Murphy, "Explaining Executive Compensation," 847.

68. These statistics all derive from Frydman and Jenter, "CEO Compensation."

69. Ibid.

70. See Frydman and Jenter, "CEO Compensation," 18.

71. See Khurana, *Corporate Savior,* 27–50.

CHAPTER 5

1. See Renee Adams, Benjamin E. Hermalin Jeanette and Michael S. Weisbach, "The Role of Boards of Directors in Corporate Governance: A Conceptual

Framework and Survey," American Economic Association, *Journal of Economic Literature* 48 (2010): 96, note 46 (citing Adam Smith, *Of the Publick Works and Institutions Which are Necessary for Facilitating Particular Branches of Commerce*, bk. V, pt. III, art. I, para. 18 of *An Inquiry into the Nature and Causes of the Wealth of Nations* [New York: P. F. Collier & Son, 1909–14]).

2. See Adolf A. Berle and Gardiner C. Means, *The Modern Corporation and Private Property* (1932; rpt. Piscataway, NJ: Transaction Publishers, 1991).

3. Ibid., 115.

4. Ibid., 116.

5. Joseph A. Livingston, *The American Stockholder* (Philadelphia: J. B. Lippincott, 1958), 227.

6. See Eugene F. Fama, "Agency Problems and the Theory of the Firm," *Journal of Political Economy* 88 (1980): 288, 293.

7. Ibid.

8. Graef Crystal, *In Search of Excess: The Overcompensation of American Executives* (New York: W. W. Norton, 1992).

9. Charles Elson, "Executive Overcompensation—A Board-Based Solution," *Boston College Law Review* 34 (1993): 937, 942.

10. Ibid., 943–44.

11. Derek Bok, *The Cost of Talent: How Executives and Professionals Are Paid and How It Affects America* (New York: Free Press, 1993).

12. Ibid., 224–26.

13. Ibid., 98.

14. Ibid., 99.

15. Ibid., 114–18.

16. For a nice list of some relatively recent examples, see Lucian Bebchuk and Jesse Fried, *Pay without Performance: The Unfulfilled Promise of Executive Compensation* (Cambridge, MA: Harvard University Press, 2004), 3, n. 6.

17. See Lucian Bebchuk, Jesse Fried, and David Walker, "Managerial Power and Rent Extraction in the Design of Executive Compensation," *University of Chicago Law Review* 69 (2002): 751; Bebchuk and Fried, *Pay without Performance*.

18. See Bebchuk and Fried, *Pay without Performance*, 25.

19. Ibid., 25–27.

20. Ibid., 27–31.

21. Ibid., 31–33.

22. Ibid.

23. Ibid., 34–36.

24. Ibid., 37–39.

25. Crystal, *In Search of Excess*, 12.

26. Ibid., 42–50.

27. See Bebchuk and Fried, *Pay without Performance*, 37–39.

28. Ibid., 45–48.

29. Ibid., 48–51.

30. See Joann S. Lublin, "Pay Starts to Bend to Advisory Votes," *Wall Street Journal*, July 29, 2011, http://online.wsj.com/article/SB10001424053111903635604576474231868112632.html.

31. See E. Scott Reckard, "Citi Vote Sends Pay Message," *Los Angeles Times*, April 19, 2012.

32. Ibid.

33. I am indebted to Jesse Fried for this point.

34. See Fabrizio Ferri and David A. Maber, "Say on Pay Votes and CEO Compensation: Evidence from the UK," *Review of Finance* 17, no. 2 (2013): 527–63.

35. See Bebchuk and Fried, *Pay without Performance*, 51–52.

36. Ibid., 53–54.

37. Ibid., 54–55.

38. Staggered boards operate something like the U.S. Senate. The directors are divided into two or (more commonly) three groups, with each group serving staggered three-year terms. Staggered boards help defend against a hostile takeover because they delay by about a year the buyer's ability to gain control of the company. The hostile acquirer can replace the outgoing one-third of the board very quickly once it owns a majority of the outstanding shares of stock. But the other two-thirds of the board will have either one or two years remaining in their terms. It is not until a year after the acquisition, when the next group's term ends, that the acquirer can truly gain control. There are also a host of other antitakeover measures available, and many of them are quite popular and effective. But this is beyond my scope.

39. See Anup Agrawal and Ralph A. Walking, "Executive Careers and Compensation Surrounding Takeover Bids," *Journal of Finance* 49 (1994): 985–1014.

40. See Bebchuk and Fried, *Pay without Performance*, 55–56.

41. Ibid., 56–57.

42. Ibid., 57–58.

43. Ibid., 61–63.

44. Ibid., 64–66.

45. On this last point, see Bebchuk and Fried, *Pay without Performance*, 66–67.

46. Bebchuk and Fried, *Pay without Performance*, 67.

47. Ibid., 68.

48. Ibid.

49. Ibid., 67.

50. See Erik Lie, "On the Timing of CEO Stock Option Awards," *Management Science* 51 (2004): 802–12, www.biz.uiowa.edu/faculty/elie/Grants-MS.pdf; Jesse M. Fried, "Option Backdating and Its Implications," *Washington & Lee Law Review* 65 (2008): 853.

51. See, e.g., Boyer v. Wilmington Materials, 754 A.2d 881 (Del. Ch. 1999) (directors held liable for selling corporate assets to another company in which they owned an interest).

52. See John E. Core, Robert W. Holthausen, and David F. Larcker, "Corporate Governance, Chief Executive Compensation, and Firm Performance," *Journal of Financial Economics* 51 (1999): 372 (cited in Bebchuk and Fried, *Pay without Performance*, 81).

53. Core, Holthausen, and Larcker, "Corporate Governance."

54. Bebchuk and Fried, *Pay without Performance,* 80–82.

55. Ibid., 82–83.

56. Ibid., 83–84.

57. Ibid.

58. See Kevin J. Murphy, "Explaining Executive Compensation: Managerial Power versus the Perceived Cost of Stock Options," *University of Chicago Law Review* 69 (2002): 847, 850.

59. See Elson, "Executive Overcompensation."

60. See Bebchuk and Fried, *Pay without Performance,* 72.

61. I am indebted to Jesse Fried for this argument.

62. See Stephen M. Bainbridge, "Executive Compensation: Who Decides?" [Review of Bebchuk and Fried, *Pay without Performance*] *Texas Law Review* 83 (2005): 1615, 1628–29.

63. Ibid., 853.

64. See Rachel Graefe-Anderson, "CEO Turnover and Compensation: An Empirical Investigation" (PhD diss., Pennsylvania State University, 2009), 4, www.smeal.psu.edu/csfm/turnovers_compensation_rgraefeanderson.pdf.

65. See Bebchuk and Fried, *Pay without Performance,* 39–41, 84–85.

66. Ibid., 85.

67. Ibid.

68. See Stefan Winter and Philip Michels, "The Managerial Power Approach—A Tautology Revisited" (November 1, 2012), available at http://ssrn.com/abstract=2179036.

69. Ibid.

70. Ibid. Winter and Michels also claim that Bebchuk and Fried's argument is a tautology. I'm afraid this point is quite clearly wrong, the result of Winter and Michels conflating a term they invent—"power based pay"—with total pay. The critical move occurs at p. 13: "To summarize, if U and C are held constant, power based pay Y must increase in power P. This follows directly from the definition of power. It is therefore neither possible nor reasonable to try to establish a functional relationship between power and pay empirically."

The first sentence is correct, based on the authors' definition of "power based pay." The second sentence expands the conclusion about power based pay to *all* pay, which is a move that is unwarranted. Their alleged tautology is a result of conflating power based pay with total pay; it has little to do with Bebchuk and Fried's argument. Bebchuk and Fried argue that managerial power has an important effect on *total* pay, resulting in pay that is higher than the market would otherwise command. That is, they implicitly divide total pay into pay determined by the market (which the company would have to pay the CEO even if the CEO did not have any undue influence over the board) and pay that is the product of corruption. Winter and Michels find a tautology here only by expanding the definition of "power" to include the influence of both corruption and the market. It may be true that in some sense both the market and corruption exercise "power" over the board, but that does not transform the thesis that CEOs effectively bribe directors to overpay them into a tautology. From a policy standpoint, market power is very different from power that stems from corruption. Lumping them together serves only to confuse the issue.

71. They also point to evidence that directors respond to negative publicity. See Bebchuk and Fried, *Pay without Performance,* 68–70. But this result is hardly surprising and would likely hold true even if the pay packages being criticized were optimal. Directors understandably care about their reputations, just as we all do. We might expect them to respond to public criticism of packages that are difficult to explain as optimal, even if they are.

72. Bebchuk and Fried, *Pay without Performance,* 87–94.

73. See Crystal, *In Search of Excess,* 195–99.

74. Starting in 2006 (a few years after the publication of Bebchuk and Fried's *Pay without Performance*), the SEC issued regulations requiring companies to report pension benefit details for each named executive officer, including the value of all pension benefits earned during the year and the value of pension benefits earned to date. Public companies must now disclose these figures in the compensation tables. See United States Securities and Exchange Commission, *Executive Compensation and Related Person Disclosure,* Release Nos. 33–8732A, 34–54302A, IC–27444A, Section II(C)(1)(d), (November 7, 2006), www.sec.gov/rules/final/2006/33–8732a.pdf; United States Securities and Exchange Commission, *Executive Compensation,* Regulation S-K, Item 402(c) (2)(viii) (August 8, 2007), www.sec.gov/divisions/corpfin/guidance/execcomp-402interp.htm.

75. See Joseph Gerakos, "CEO Pensions: Disclosure, Managerial Power, and Optimal Contracting" (2010), http://faculty.chicagobooth.edu/joseph.gerakos /PDFs/Gerakos_PensionDisclosure.pdf.

76. See Bebchuk and Fried, *Pay without Performance,* 122–27.

77. See Carola Frydman and Dirk Jenter, "CEO Compensation" (Working Paper 3277, Rock Center for Corporate Governance, Stanford University, 2010), 39, panel B, http://ssrn.com/abstract=1582232.

78. See Bebchuk and Fried, *Pay without Performance,* 139 (citing a study by SCA Consulting).

79. Ibid., 137–46.

80. Ibid., 140–43.

81. Ibid., 154; Ingolf Dittmann and Yu Ko-Chia, "How Important Are Risk-Taking Incentives in Executive Compensation?" (2010), http://ssrn.com /abstract=1176192.

82. See, e.g., Wenli Huang and Hai Lu, "Timing of CEO Stock Option Grants and Corporate Disclosures: New Evidence from the Post-SOX and Post-Backdating-Scandal Era," (2010), http://ssrn.com/abstract=1463823; David Aboody and Ron Kasznik, "CEO Stock Option Awards and the Timing of Corporate Voluntary Disclosures," *Journal of Accounting and Economics* 29 (2000): 73–100; David Yermack, "Good Timing: CEO Stock Option Awards and Company News Announcements," *Journal of Finance* 52 (1997): 449–77. Similarly, executives may manipulate the precision of the information they disclose to manipulate stock prices in their favor. See Qiang Cheng, Ting Luo, and Heng Yue, "Managerial Incentives and Management Forecast Precision" (2013), http://ssrn.com/abstract=2202064 or http://dx.doi.org/10.2139 /ssrn.2202064.

83. See Lie, "On the Timing of CEO Stock Option Awards."

84. See Securities and Exchange Act of 1934, Rule 16a–3(g)(1), 17 C.F.R. § 240.16a3–(g)(1) (2006); David I. Walker, "Unpacking Backdating: Economic Analysis and Observations on the Stock Option Scandal," *Boston University Law Review* 87 (2007): 561.

85. See Fried, "Option Backdating and Its Implications," at 883–84.

86. See John E. Core, Wayne R. Guay, and David F. Larcker, "Executive Equity Compensation and Incentives: A Survey," *Economic Policy Review* 9 (2003): 27–50; Bebchuk and Fried, *Pay without Performance*, 152–58.

87. See Bebchuk and Fried, *Pay without Performance*, 144–46.

88. Ibid., 74–76.

89. Ibid., 76–79.

90. Ibid., 77 ("Under one version of this explanation, all those involved in the pay-setting process—including executives, their advisers, and compensation consultants—make mistakes. But this is a highly implausible explanation for the persistence of the inefficient practices we will be discussing").

CHAPTER 6

1. See Michael Beer and Mark D. Cannon, "Promise and Peril in Implementing Pay-for-Performance," *Human Resource Management* 43 (2004): 7.

2. Even as recently as 2008, Forbes Magazine listed HP as one of the best-managed large companies in the world. See Steve Kichen, "In Pictures: America's Best-Managed Companies," *Forbes.com,* www.forbes.com/2008/12/22/managed-companies-best-bigcompanies08-cz_sk_1222bestmanaged_slide_24.html.

3. See Ben Worthen, "Defending H-P in Age of Tablets," *Wall Street Journal,* June 5, 2012, http://online.wsj.com/article/SB10001424052702303506404577 448673337730172.html?mod=WSJ_hpp_MIDDLENexttoWhatsNewsTop.

4. See Edward L. Deci, "The Effects of Contingent and Noncontingent Rewards and Controls on Intrinsic Motivation," *Organizational Behavior and Human Performance* 8 (1972): 217–29.

5. Burrhus F. Skinner, *The Behavior of Organisms* (New York: D. Appleton-Century, 1938).

6. Adolf A. Berle and Gardiner C. Means, *The Modern Corporation and Private Property* (1932; rpt. Piscataway, NJ: Transaction Publishers, 1991).

7. Michael C. Jensen and William H. Meckling, "Theory of the Firm: Managerial Behavior, Agency Costs, and Ownership Structure," *Journal of Financial Economics* 3, no. 4 (1976): 305–60.

8. See 26 U.S.C. § 162(m).

9. If this was the rationale, it was not executed very effectively. For example, the Treasury Regulations that implemented this section declared stock options could qualify as performance-related pay even without any performance condition. See 26 C.F.R. Sec. 1.162–27(e)(2)(vi).

10. See Beer and Cannon, "Promise and Peril."

11. Ibid.

12. See Institutional Shareholder Services, "2012 Taft-Harley U.S. Proxy Voting Guidelines," January, 2012, 21, www.issgovernance.com/files/2012ISS TaftHartleyAdvisoryServicesUSGuidelines.pdf.

13. Lucian Bebchuk and Jesse Fried, *Pay without Performance: The Unfulfilled Promise of Executive Compensation* (Cambridge, MA: Harvard University Press, 2004)

14. John M. Abowd, "Does Performance-Based Managerial Compensation Affect Corporate Performance?," *Industrial and Labor Relations Review* 43, no. 3, Special Issue: Do Compensation Policies Matter? (1990): 52S–73S.

15. Barry Gerhart and George T. Milkovich, "Organizational Differences in Managerial Compensation and Financial Performance," *Academy of Management Journal* 33, no. 4 (1990): 663–91. There are other studies with similar results. See, e.g., David F. Larcker, "The Association between Performance Plan Adoption and Corporate Capital Investment," *Journal of Accounting and Economics* 5 (1983): 3–30; Jonathan S. Leonard, "Executive Pay and Firm Performance," *Industrial and Labor Relations Review* 43, no. 3 (1990): 13S–29S; and Robert T. Masson, "Executive Motivations, Earnings, and Consequent Equity Performance," *Journal of Political Economy* 79, no. 6 (1971): 1278–92.

16. C. Bram Cadsby, Fei Song, and Francis Tapon, "Sorting and Incentive Effects of Pay for Performance: An Experimental Investigation," *Academy of Management Journal* 50, no. 2 (2007): 387–405.

17. See, e.g., Michael J. Cooper, Huseyin Gulen, and Raghavendra Rau, "The Cross-Section of Stock Returns and Incentive Pay" (2011), http://ssrn.com/abstract=1572085 (CEO incentive pay, especially stock options, has a strong negative relationship with future stock performance); Jesse F. Dillard and Joseph G. Fisher, "Compensation Schemes, Skill Level, and Task Performance: An Experimental Examination," *Decision Sciences* 21 (1990): 121–37 (no relationship between merit pay and performance); Joan L. Pearce, William B. Stevenson, and James L. Perry, "Managerial Compensation Based on Organizational Performance: A Time Series Analysis of the Effects of Merit Pay," *Academy of Management Journal* 28 (1985): 261–78; and H.L. Tosi and L.R. Gomez-Mejia, "The Decoupling of CEO Pay and Performance: An Agency Theory Perspective," *Administrative Science Quarterly* 34 (1989): 169–89 (concluding that even among studies that found a relationship between incentive pay and company performance, the relationship was small, with performance explaining less than 15 percent of the variance in executive pay).

18. Harald Dale-Olsen, "Executive Pay Determination and Firm Performance—Empirical Evidence from a Compressed Wage Environment," *Manchester School* 80, no. 3 (2012): 355–76.

19. H. Young Baek and José A. Pagán, "Executive Compensation and Corporate Production Efficiency: A Stochastic Frontier Approach," *Quarterly Journal of Business and Economics* 41, nos. 1–2 (2002): 27–41.

20. Matt Bloom and George T. Milkovich, "Relationships among Risk, Incentive Pay, and Organizational Performance," *Academy of Management Journal* 41, no. 3 (1998): 283–97.

21. Kevin J. Murphy, "Executive Compensation," in *Handbook of Labor Economics,* vol. 3, ed. Orley Ashenfelter and David Card (North Holland: Elsevier, 1998).

22. See, e.g., Michael Beer and Nancy Katz, "Do Incentives Work? The Perceptions of a Worldwide Sample of Senior Executives," *Human Resource*

Planning 26, no. 3 (2003): 30–44; Derek Bok, *The Cost of Talent: How Executives and Professionals Are Paid and How It Affects America* (New York: Free Press, 1993); Alfie Kohn, "Why Incentive Plans Cannot Work," *Harvard Business Review* 71, no. 5 (1993): 54–61; Susan J. Stabile, "Motivating Executives: Does Performance-Based Compensation Positively Affect Managerial Performance?," *University of Pennsylvannia Journal of Labor and Employment Law* 2 (1999): 227; Lynn A. Stout, "Killing Conscience: The Unintended Behavioral Consequences of 'Pay for Performance,'" unpublished MS, version available at www.law.leeds.ac.uk/assets/files/research/cblp/conf-jan13/killing-conscience .pdf.

23. See Beer and Katz, "Do Incentives Work?"

24. See, e.g., Carola Frydman and Dirk Jenter, "CEO Compensation" (Working Paper 3277, CESifo, 2010) ("Because of the lack of credible instruments, this literature has been unable to identify the causal effects of managerial incentives on firm value").

25. Tobin's Q is the market capitalization of the firm divided by the asset value.

26. ExecuComp is available at www.compustat.com/products.aspx?id= 2147492873.

27. Murphy, "Executive Compensation."

28. Ibid.; see also John M. Abowd and David S. Kaplan, "Executive Compensation: Six Questions That Need Answering," *Journal of Economic Perspectives* 13, no. 4 (1999): 145–68.

29. See Murphy, "Executive Compensation."

30. See Bebchuk and Fried, *Pay without Performance*. See also Trevor Buck, Alistair Bruce, Brian G.M. Main, and Henry Udueni, "Long-Term Incentive Plans, Executive Pay, and UK Company Performance," *Journal of Management Studies* 40, no. 7 (2003): 1709–27 (criticizing U.K. long-term performance plans as subject to manipulation by executives and as actually decreasing pay-performance sensitivity).

31. See Bok, *The Cost of Talent*; Jaap W. Winter, "Corporate Governance Going Astray: Executive Remuneration Built to Fail" (Policy Paper 5, Duisenberg School of Finance, 2011), http://ssrn.com/abstract=1652137 (arguing that for this reason, when times are good, companies feel they should reward executives for their success, but when times are bad, companies reward executives for their efforts in trying times).

32. There is some dispute as to whether executives and other employees overestimate or underestimate options' value as compared to their value as measured by the standard Black-Scholes method. Either way, my point here is that they value contingent pay less than they value guaranteed pay. As a result, they will bargain for higher expected pay in exchange for agreeing to accept the risk that the company's performance will fall short of the payment triggers. For some leading studies in the undervaluation/overvaluation debate, see, e.g., John E. Core and Wayne R. Guay, "When Efficient Contracts Require Risk-Averse Executives to Hold Equity: Implications for Options Valuation, for Relative Performance Evaluation, and for the Corporate Governance Debate," University of Pennsylvania Institute for Law and Economics Research Paper 03–32 (July 2003), available at http://ssrn

.com/abstract=429301 (executives undervalue options relative to Black-Scholes but only by about 6 percent); Brian Hall and Kevin Murphy, "Stock Options for Undiversified Executives," *Journal of Accounting and Economics* 33, no. 2 (2002): 3–42 (cost of options to companies exceeds value to executives because executives cannot diversify against risk of options); Kevin Hallock and Craig A. Olson, "The Value of Stock Options to Non-Executive Employees," NBER Working Paper No. W11950 (January 2006), available at http://ssrn.com/abstract=877455 (nonexecutive employees' valuations vary widely, but most value options higher than Black-Scholes); Lisa K. Muelbrook, "The Efficiency of Equity-Linked Compensation: Understanding the Full Cost of Awarding Executive Stock Options," *Financial Management* 30, no. 2 (2001): 5–44 (executives may discount options value as much as 47 percent because of diversification limits).

33. I am indebted to Jesse Fried for pointing out that many people would make this argument.

34. Daniel H. Pink, *Drive: The Surprising Truth about What Motivates Us* (Edinburgh: Canongate Books, 2011).

35. See Sam Glucksberg, "The Influence of Strength of Drive on Functional Fixedness and Perceptual Recognition," *Journal of Experimental Psychology* 63 (1962): 36–44.

36. See Karl Duncker, "On Problem Solving," *Psychological Monographs: General and Applied* 58 (1972).

37. See Glucksberg, "The Influence of Strength of Drive"; Winter, "Corporate Governance Going Astray."

38. See Deci, "The Effects of Contingent and Noncontingent Rewards."

39. Ibid.

40. Ibid.

41. See Edward L. Deci, Richard Koestner, and Richard M. Ryan, "A Meta-Analytic Review of Experiments Examining the Effects of Extrinsic Rewards on Intrinsic Motivation," *Psychological Bulletin* 125, no. 6 (1999): 627–68; Amy Rummel and Richard Feinberg, "Cognitive Evaluation Theory: A Meta-Analytic Review of the Literature," *Social Behavior and Personality* 16 (1988): 147–64; Shu-Hua Tang and Vernon C. Hall, "The Overjustification Effect: A Metaanalysis," *Applied Cognitive Psychology* 9 (1995): 365–404; Uco J. Wiersma, "The Effects of Extrinsic Rewards in Intrinsic Motivation: A Meta-Analysis," *Journal of Occupational and Organizational Psychology* 65 (1992): 101–14. But see Judy Cameron and W. David Pierce, "Reinforcement, Reward, and Intrinsic Motivation: A Meta-Analysis," *Review of Educational Research* 64 (1994): 363–423.

42. See Deci, Koestner, and Ryan, "A Meta-Analytic Review."

43. Ibid.

44. Ibid.

45. Ibid.

46. See Anton Souvarov, "Addiction to Rewards" (2003), www.nes.ru /public-presentations/suvorov_js-08-12-03.pdf.

47. See Colin F. Camerer and Robin Hogarth, "The Effects of Financial Incentives in Experiments: A Review and Capital-Labor-Production Framework," *Journal of Risk and Uncertainty* 19 (1999): 7–42 (a review of 74 studies).

48. See Dan Ariely, Uri Gneezy, George Loewenstein, and Nina Mazar, "Large Stakes and Big Mistakes," *Review of Economic Studies* 76, no. 2 (2009): 451–69.

49. Ibid.

50. Ibid.

51. Ibid.

52. Ibid.

53. See Smith v. Van Gorkom, 488 A.2d 858 (Del. 1985).

54. See Daniel J. Simons and Christopher F. Chabris, "Gorillas in Our Midst: Sustained Inattentional Blindness for Dynamic Events," *Perception* 28, no. 9 (1999): 1059–74; Lisa Ordonez, Maurice Schweitzer, Adam Galinsky, and Max Bazerman, "Goals Gone Wild: The Systemic Side-Effects of Over-Prescribing Goal Setting" (Working Paper 09–083, Harvard Business School, 2009), http://papers.ssrn.com/sol3/papers.cfm?abstract_id=1332071.

55. See Mei Cheng, K.R. Subramanyam, and Yuan Zhang, "Earnings Guidance and Managerial Myopia" (Working Paper, Northwestern University, Kellogg School of Management, 2007), www.kellogg.northwestern.edu /accounting/papers/k.r%20subramanyam.pdf.

56. See Ariely et al., "Large Stakes and Big Mistakes."

57. See Teresa M. Amabile, Elise Phillips, and Mary Ann Collins, "Person and Environment in Talent Development: The Case of Creativity," in *Talent Development: Proceedings of the 1993 Henry B. and Jocelyn Wallace National Research Symposium on Talent Development*, ed. Nicholas Colangelo, Susan G. Assouline, and DeAnn L. Ambroson (Unionville, NY: Trillium Press, 1994).

58. See John R. Deckop, Robert Mangel, and Carol C. Cirka, "Getting More than You Pay For: Organizational Citizenship Behavior and Pay-for-Performance Plans," *Academy of Management Journal* 42, no. 4 (1999): 420–28.

59. Stout, "Killing Conscience."

60. Ibid.

61. See Richard M. Titmuss, *The Gift Relationship* (London: Allen and Unwin, 1970).

62. See Dan Ariely, *Predictably Irrational: The Hidden Forces That Shape Our Decisions* (New York: HarperCollins, 2008).

63. See Winter, "Corporate Governance Going Astray."

64. See Stout, "Killing Conscience."

65. For a nice discussion of some of this evidence, see Qiang Cheng and David B. Farber, "Earnings Restatements, Changes in CEO Compensation, and Firm Performance" (Working Paper, Sauder School of Business, 2008), http:// ssrn.com/abstract=808344; Frydman and Jenter, "CEO Compensation."

66. See Paul M. Healy, "The Effect of Bonus Schemes on Accounting Decisions," *Journal of Accounting and Economics* 7 (1985): 85–107.

67. See Jared D. Harris and Philip Bromley, "Incentives to Cheat: The Influence of Executive Compensation and Firm Performance on Financial Misrepresentation," *Organization Science* 18, no. 3 (2006): 350–67, http://ssrn.com /abstract=1010197. See also John C. Coffee, "What Caused Enron? A Capsule Social and Economic History of the 1990's" (Working Paper 214, Columbia

Law and Economics), http://ssrn.com/abstract=373581 (attributing increase in earnings restatements to dramatic rise in use of stock options).

68. See Beer and Cannon, "Promise and Peril."

69. For example, in 1994, HP paid its CEO, Lewis Platt, about $1.1 million in salary, $90,000 in bonuses, nearly $1.7 million in restricted stock, and 70,000 options. These amounts rose the next year to about $1.4 million in salary, $150,000 in bonuses, $2.1 million in restricted stock, and 80,000 options. See Hewlett Packard Company Definitive Proxy Statement, January 12, 1996, available at www.sec.gov/Archives/edgar/data/47217/0000898430-96-000110 .txt. SEC rules did not require companies to estimate the value of stock options at the time, but since the options lasted ten years and HP's stock skyrocketed during that period, the options turned out to be worth millions.

CHAPTER 7

1. See Jeanne W. Ross and Cynthia M. Beath, "Building Business Agility at Southwest Airlines" (Research Paper 4664-07, MIT Sloan; Working Paper 369, CISR, 2007), http://ssrn.com/abstract=1020963.

2. See Staff, Bloomberg News, Reuters, Associated Press, "Year to Be Profitable, Routes to Be Added," *Houston Chronicle,* May 15, 2003, B2 (in Business Briefs/Houston & Texas).

3. See Kerry E. Grace, "Southwest Airlines Posts $56 Million Loss," *Wall Street Journal,* January 23, 2009, B6.

4. Ibid.

5. See Bill Hensel Jr., "Southwest Reworks Top Positions: A Department of Labor Relations Will Be Created," *Houston Chronicle,* August 5, 2004, B9, www .chron.com/business/article/Southwest-Airlines-reworks-top-positions-1991496 .php.

6. See Melanie Trottman, "Big Fuel-Hedging Call Is Paying Off—Carrier Was Able to Protect Itself against Soaring Energy Prices in Second Half," *Wall Street Journal,* January 16, 2001, B4.

7. See Loren Steffy, "Airline Industry: Low-Fare Reputation Worth Lots," *Houston Chronicle,* September 30, 2011, B1.

8. See Dave Carter, Dan Rogers, and Betty Simkins, "Fuel Hedging in the Airline Industry: The Case of Southwest Airlines" (2004), http://ssrn.com /abstract=578663.

9. See James R. Meindl, Sanford B. Ehrlich, and Janet M. Dukerich, "The Romance of Leadership," *Administrative Science Quarterly* 30 (1985): 78–102.

10. See Derek Bok, *The Cost of Talent* (New York: Free Press, 1993), 103; Franklin G. Snyder, "More Pieces of the CEO Compensation Puzzle," *Delaware Journal of Corporate Law* 28 (2003): 129, 153–60.

11. See Snyder, "More Pieces of the CEO Compensation Puzzle."

12. See Stanley Lieberson and James F. O'Connor, "Leadership and Organizational Performance: A Study of Large Corporations," *American Sociological Review* 37 (1972): 118.

13. See Bok, *The Cost of Talent,* 103.

14. Ibid.

15. See Snyder, "More Pieces of the CEO Compensation Puzzle."

16. Ibid.

17. See Donald C. Hambrick and Phyllis A. Mason, "Upper Echelons: The Organization as a Reflection of Its Top Managers," *Academy of Management Review* 9, no. 2 (1984): 193–206.

18. See Bok, *The Cost of Talent*, 105.

19. See Market Data Center, "Commodities & Futures Overview," *Wall Street Journal*, http://online.wsj.com/mdc/public/page/mdc_commodities.html?mod=mdc_topnav_2_3028.

20. See Michael T. Hannan and John Freeman, "The Population Ecology of Organizations," *American Journal of Sociology* 82 (1977): 929–64; Sydney Finkelstein, Donald C. Hambrick, and Albert A. Cannella Jr., *Strategic Leadership: Theory and Research on Executives, Top Management Teams, and Boards* (New York: Oxford University Press, 2008).

21. See Finkelstein, Hambric, and Cannella, *Strategic Leadership*, 21.

22. Lieberson and O'Connor, "Leadership and Organizational Performance."

23. Ibid.

24. Ibid., 122.

25. See Gerald R. Salancik and Jeffrey Pfeffer, "Constraints on Administrator Discretion: The Limited Influence of Mayors on City Budgets," *Urban Affairs Quarterly* 12, no. 4 (1977): 475–96 (studying big city mayors' impact on the city's budget); Nan Weiner and Thomas A. Mahoney, "A Model of Corporate Performance as a Function of Environmental, Organizational and Leadership Influences," *Academy of Management Journal* 24 (1981): 453–70 (finding the same results with a similar, refined methodology but different results with a different procedure); Alan Berkeley Thomas, "Does Leadership Make a Difference to Organizational Performance?," *Administrative Science Quarterly* 33, no. 3 (1988): 388–400 (finding similar results but arguing for a different interpretation).

26. See Weiner and Mahoney, "Model of Corporate Performance," 456. Weiner and Mahoney argued that profitability (profit relative to assets) is a better performance measure because it accounts for company size. Using that measure, they found that leadership (which they call "stewardship") accounted for 43.9 percent of variance. But the authors felt little could be concluded from these results. Their entire model only accounted for 54.5 percent of variance, and stewardship's influence was measured indirectly, from the residuals following estimation of the regression model. Other, unmeasured variables may therefore have accounted for some or all of the variance attributed to stewardship. Ibid., 465.

27. See Richard H. Hall, *Organizations: Structures, Processes and Outcomes*, 5th ed. (Upper Saddle River, NJ: Prentice Hall, 1991), 145.

28. Marianne Bertrand and Antoinette Schoar, "Managing with Style: The Effect of Managers on Firm Policies," *Quarterly Journal of Economics* 118, no. 4 (2003): 1169–208.

29. David J. Denis and Diane K. Denis, "Performance Changes Following Top Management Dismissals," *Journal of Finance* 50, no. 4 (1995): 1029–57.

30. See Finkelstein, Hambric, and Cannella, *Strategic Leadership.*

31. Ibid., 26–35. See also Hall, *Organizations,* 146.

32. Noam Wasserman, Nitin Nohria, and Bharat Anand, "When Does Leadership Matter? A Contingent Opportunities View of CEO Leadership," in *Handbook of Leadership Theory and Practice,* ed. Nitin Nohria and Rakesh Khurana (Cambridge, MA: Harvard Business Publishing, 2010); also available as "When Does Leadership Matter? The Contingent Opportunities View of CEO Leadership" (Working Paper 02–04, Strategy Unit; Working Paper 01–063, Harvard Business School, 2001), http://ssrn.com/abstract=278652.

33. See Morten Bennedsen, Fracisco Pérez-González, and Daniel Wolfenzon, "Do CEOs Matter?" (Working Paper FIN-06–032, NYU, 2006), http://ssrn .com/abstract=1293659. The authors have since performed a similar study on the impact of CEO hospitalizations, with similar results. See Morten Bennedsen, Francisco Pérez-González, and Daniel Wolfenzon, "Estimating the Value of the Boss: Evidence from CEO Hospitalization Events" (Working Paper, Stanford University, 2011), www.stanford.edu/~fperezg/valueboss.pdf.

34. See Antonio Falato, Dan Li, and Todd Milbourn, "To Each According to His Ability? The Returns to CEO Talent" (Working Paper, Washington University, 2010), http://apps.olin.wustl.edu/faculty/milbourn/CEOAbilitySep24.pdf.

35. See Meindl, Ehrlich, and Dukerich, "Romance of Leadership," 78–102.

36. See Xavier Gabaix and Augustin Landier, "Why Has CEO Pay Increased So Much?," *Quarterly Journal of Economics* 123 (2008): 49–100.

37. See Marko Terviö, "The Difference That CEOs Make: An Assignment Model Approach," *American Economic Review* 98, no. 3 (2008): 642–68.

38. See Hall, *Organizations,* 146.

39. Seoyoung Kim, "The Role of Luck in CEO Performances" (2011), http:// ssrn.com/abstract=2026589.

40. See Lieberson and O'Connor, "A Study of Large Corporations," 123.

41. See Weiner and Mahoney, "Model of Corporate Performance," 453–70. See also Alison Mackey, "How Much Do CEOs Matter—Really?" (Working Paper, 2005), http://ssrn.com/abstract=816065 (finding that leadership accounts for 29.2 percent of the variance in corporate performance).

42. See Randall Morck, Andrei Shleifer, and Robert Vishny, "Management Ownership and Market Valuation: An Empirical Analysis," *Journal of Financial Economics* 20 (1988): 293–315.

43. See Finkelstein, Hambrick, and Canellela, *Strategic Leadership,* 38–39.

44. See Jeffrey Pfeffer and Gerald R. Salancik, *The External Control of Organizations: A Resource Dependence Perspective* (New York: Harper & Row, 1978), 7.

45. Richard J. Connors, *Warren Buffett on Business: Principles from the Sage of Omaha* (Hoboken: John Wiley & Sons, 2010), 143.

CHAPTER 8

1. See Azam Ahmed, Ben Protess, and Susanne Craig, "A Romance with Risk That Brought on a Panic," *New York Times,* December 11, 2011, available at

http://dealbook.nytimes.com/2011/12/11/a-romance-with-risk-that-brought-on-a-panic/.

2. Ibid.

3. Ibid.

4. Ibid.

5. See Hal R. Varian, "Economic Scene: Observe, Theorize, Measure, Test, and Don't Overlook What Goes Wrong," *New York Times,* October 24, 2002, C2.

6. See Thomas S. Ulen, "Firmly Grounded: Economics in the Future of the Law," *Wisconsin Law Review* (1997): 433, 457.

7. See Richard Posner, "Rational Choice, Behavioral Economics, and the Law," *Stanford Law Review* 50 (1998): 1556–57; see also Stephen M. Bainbridge, "Mandatory Disclosure: A Behavioral Analysis," *University of Cincinnati Law Review* 68 (2000): 1035 n. 54 ("Standard economic analysis recognizes that individual decisionmakers may depart from rationality, but assumes that such departures come out in the wash—they cancel each other out so that the average or equilibrium behavior of large groups will be consistent with rational choice"); Donald C. Langevoort, "Theories, Assumptions, and Securities Regulation: Market Efficiency Revisited," *University of Pennsylvania Law Review* 140 (1992): 851, 862.

8. See Christine Jolls, Cass R. Sunstein, and Richard Thaler, "Theories and Tropes: A Reply to Posner and Kelman," *Stanford Law Review* 50 (1998): 1593, 1599.

9. See Russell Korobkin, "Aspirations and Settlement," *Cornell Law Review* 88 (2002): 1, 13–14 ("Studies have shown that fans of competing football teams believed that their team committed significantly fewer infractions than the fans of the opposing team perceived; that nearly all drivers believed they were better than average; that people engaged to be married believed their chances of getting divorced were close to zero [although most knew the base rate is approximately 50 percent]; that married couples' estimates of the percentage share of the household chores that they perform routinely exceeds 100% when added together; and that people believed there was an above-average chance for positive events to occur to them, but a below-average chance they would experience negative events" [footnotes omitted]).

10. Ibid., citing David M. DeJoy, "The Optimism Bias and Traffic Accident Risk Perception," *Accident Analysis & Prevention* 21 (1989): 333, 338–39.

11. See Robert Prentice, "Whither Securities Regulation? Some Behavioral Observations Regarding Proposals for Its Future," *Duke Law Journal* 51 (2002): 1397, 1463 n. 307; Amos Tversky and Daniel Kahneman, "Judgment under Uncertainty: Heuristics and Biases," in *Judgment under Uncertainty: Heuristics and Biases,* ed. Daniel Kahneman, Paul Slovic, and Amos Tversky (Cambridge: Cambridge University Press, 1982), 3, 9.

12. See Prentice, "Whither Securities Regulation?"

13. See Hillel J. Einhorn and Robin M. Hogarth, "Confidence in Judgment: The Persistence of the Illusion of Validity," *Psychology Review* 85 (1978): 395, 396 (noting that experience can enhance the illusion of validity through confirmatory bias); A.V. Muthukrishnan, "Decision Ambiguity and Incumbent

Brand Advantage," *Journal of Consumer Research* 22 (1995): 99–100; Prentice, "Whither Securities Regulation?" ("People will be confident in the prediction that a person is a librarian when a description of that person matches a stereotype of a librarian, even if the information contained in the description is scanty, unreliable, or outdated"); Susanna Kim Ripken, "Predictions, Projections, and Precautions: Conveying Cautionary Warnings in Corporate Forward-Looking Statements," *University of Illinois Law Review* (2005): 929, 960 (noting that the illusion of validity causes people making judgments under uncertainty to experience excessive confidence in fallible choices); Tversky and Kahneman, "Heuristics and Biases," 9 (describing the illusion of validity).

14. See Tversky and Kahneman, "Heuristics and Biases," 9 ("An elementary result in the statistics of correlation asserts that, given input variables of stated validity, a prediction based on several such inputs can achieve higher accuracy when they are independent of each other than when they are redundant or correlated").

15. Ibid. between ("The internal consistency of a pattern of inputs is a major determinant of one's confidence in predictions based on these inputs").

16. See Leon Festinger, *A Theory of Cognitive Dissonance* (Stanford: Stanford University Press, 1957). See also C. Daniel Batson, "Rational Processing or Rationalization? The Effect of Disconfirming Information on a Stated Religious Belief," *Journal of Personality and Social Psychology* 32 (1975): 176; C. Daniel Batson, "Experimentation in Psychology of Religion: An Impossible Dream," *Journal for the Scientific Study of Religion* 16 (1977): 413, 416; Alafair S. Burke, "Improving Prosecutorial Decision Making: Some Lessons of Cognitive Science," *William & Mary Law Review* 47 (2006): 1587, 1593–602; Matthew D. Lieberman et al., "Do Amnesiacs Exhibit Cognitive Dissonance Reduction? The Role of Explicit Memory and Attention in Attitude Change," *Psychological Science* 12 (2001): 135.

17. See Amos Tversky and Daniel Kahneman, "Causal Schemas in Judgments under Uncertainty," in Kahneman, Slovic, and Tversky, *Judgment under Uncertainty*, 117, 126–28.

18. As Kahneman and Tversky have written, "Redundancy among inputs decreases accuracy even as it increases confidence, and people are often confident in predictions that are quite likely to be off the mark." "Heuristics and Biases," 9.

19. See Burke, "Improving Prosecutorial Decision Making," 1594–98 (discussing confirmation bias and selective information processing).

20. See Xavier Gabaix and Augustin Landier, "Why Has CEO Pay Increased So Much?," *Quarterly Journal of Economics* 123 (2008): 50.

21. L. Ulrich and D. Trumbo, "The Selection Interview since 1949," *Psychological Bulletin* 63 (1965): 100–116.

22. See Richard E. Nisbett et al., "Popular Induction: Information Is Not Necessarily Informative," in Kahneman, Slovic, and Tversky, *Judgment under Uncertainty*, 101, 113–15.

23. See Richard D. Arvey and James E. Campion, "The Employment Interview: A Summary and Review of Recent Research," *Personnel Psychology* 35 (1982): 281–322; Michael M. Harris, "Reconsidering the Employment Interview:

A Review of Recent Literature and Suggestions for Future Research," *Personnel Psychology* 42 (1989): 491–726 (interview has moderate validity); John E. Hunter and Rhonda F. Hunter, "The Validity and Utility of Alternative Predictors of Job Performance," *Psychological Bulletin* 96 (1984): 72–98; Eugene C. Mayfield, "The Selection Interview—A Reevaluation of Published Research" *Personnel Psychology* 1 (1964): 239–60; G. C. Milne, "The Interview: Let Us Have Perspective," *Australian Psychologist* 2 (1967): 77–84; Richard R. Reilly and Georgia T. Chao, "Validity and Fairness of Some Alternative Selection Procedures," *Personnel Psychology* 35 (1982): 1–62; A. Rodger, "The Worthwhileness of the Interview," *Occupational Psychology* 26 (1952): 101–96; P. M. Rowe, "The Employment Interview: A Valid Selection Procedure," *Canadian Personnel and Industrial Relations Journal* 28 (1981): 37–40; N. Schmitt, "Social and Situational Determinants of Interview Decisions: Implications for the Employment Interview," *Personnel Psychology* 29 (1976): 79–101; Ulrich and Trumbo, "The Selection Interview since 1949"; Ralph Wagner, "The Employment Interview: A Critical Summary," *Personnel Psychology* 2 (1949): 17–46; Edward C. Webster, *The Employment Interview: A Social Judgment Process* (Schomberg, ONT: SIP Publications, 1982); Orman R. Wright Jr. "Summary of Research on the Selection Interview Since 1964," *Personnel Psychology* 22 (1969): 391–413. But see Michael A. McDaniel et al., "The Validity of Employment Interviews: A Comprehensive Review and Meta-Analysis," *Journal of Applied Psychology* 79 (1994): 599, 610 (even an unstructured interview has a "respectable" level of validity); Willi H. Wiesner and Steven F. Cronshaw, "A Meta-Analytic Investigation of the Impact of Interview Format and Degree of Structure on the Validity of the Employment Interview," *Journal of Occupational Psychology* 61 (1988): 275, 286, 289 (interviews have satisfactory to modest validity, depending on the type of interview, and produce better results than random selection).

24. For books, see, e.g., Tino Gambino, *The Mad Professor's Crapshooting Bible* (Las Vegas, NV: Pi Yee Press, 2006); Frank Scoblete, *Golden Touch Dice Control Revolution! How to Win at Craps Using a Controlled Dice Throw!* (Daphne, AL: Research Services Limited, 2005); Stanford Wong, *Wong on Dice* (Las Vegas, NV: Pi Yee Press, 2005). For websites, see, e.g., Dice-Play, "Rhythm Rolling Dice Control—Craps," *ntlworld.com*, http://homepage.ntlworld.com /dice-play/RollRhythm.htm; Guide Bill Burton, "Casino Gambling: Rhythm Rolling the Dice," *About.com*, http://casinogambling.about.com/library /weekly/aao31101b.htm; "The Soft Touch: Playing with the Cause," *Dice Coach*, www.dicecoach.com/ladiesonlysept09.asp. There is even an online newsletter for dice setters: "Newsletter," *Dice Setter.com*, www.dicesetter.com /newsletter/Newsletter_toc.htm.

25. See James M. Henslin, "Craps and Magic," *American Journal of Sociology* 73 (1967): 316.

26. Erving Goffman, *Interaction Ritual: Essays in Face-to-Face Behavior* (New Brunswick, NJ: Transaction Publishers, 1967).

27. See Ellen J. Langer and Robert P. Abelson, *The Psychology of Control* (Los Angeles: Sage, 1983), 59–90.

28. Ellen J. Langer, "The Illusion of Control," in Kahneman, Slovic, and Tversky, *Judgment under Uncertainty*, 231.

29. Ibid., 238.

30. See Langer and Abelson, *The Psychology of Control*, 62.

31. Ibid., 62–63.

32. Stephen Schwartz and Roger O. Hirson, *Pippin* (New York: Drama Book Specialists, 1975).

33. The common misperception that past luck will repeat itself leads to the "hot hand" phenomenon. See Guillermo Baquero and Marno Verbeek, "Do Sophisticated Investors Believe in the Law of Small Numbers" (2006), http://papers.ssrn.com/sol3/papers.cfm?abstract_id=891309 (sophisticated investors display a belief that money managers have a "hot hand"); Thomas Gilovich, Robert Vallone, and Amos Tversky, "The Hot Hand in Basketball: On the Misperception of Random Sequences," *Cognitive Psychology* 17 (1985): 295–314.

34. Seoyoung Kim, "The Role of Luck in CEO Performances" (2011), http://ssrn.com/abstract=2026589.

35. See Solomon E. Asch, *Social Psychology* (New York: Prentice-Hall, 1952), 450–59. See also Solomon E. Asch, "Opinions and Social Pressure," in *Readings about the Social Animal*, ed. Elliot Aronson (New York: Worth, 1995), 13; Solomon E. Asch, "Effects of Group Pressure upon the Modification and Distortion of Judgments," in *Group Dynamics*, 2nd ed., ed. Dorwin Cartwright and Alvin Zander (Trowbridge: Redwood Press, 1960), 189–99; Solomon E. Asch, "Studies of Independence and Conformity," *Psychological Monographs: General and Applied* 70 (1956), 1; Solomon E. Asch, "Studies of Independence and Conformity: A Minority of One against a Unanimous Majority," *Psychological Monographs: General and Applied* 416 (1956): 69–70; Abraham S. Luchins and Edith H. Luchins, "On Conformity with True and False Communications," *Journal of Social Psychology* 42 (1955): 283; Stephen P. Robbins, *Organizational Behavior*, 8th ed. (Upper Saddle River, NJ: Prentice Hall, 1998), 257 (citing studies by Asch about group conformity).

36. For a treatment of this idea in corporate contracts more generally, see Marcel Kahan and Michael Klausner, "Path Dependence in Corporate Contracting: Increasing Returns, Herd Behavior and Cognitive Biases," *Washington University Law Review* 74 (1996): 347–66.

37. See Irving L. Janis, *Groupthink: Psychological Studies of Policy Decisions and Fiascoes*, 2nd ed. (Boston: Houghton Mifflin, 1983).

38. See Donald C. Langevoort, "The Human Nature of Corporate Boards: Law, Norms, and the Unintended Consequences of Independence and Accountability," *Georgetown Law Journal* 89 (2001): 797, 799.

39. Janis, *Groupthink*, 247.

40. Ibid., 250.

41. See Korn/Ferry Institute, "34th Annual Board of Directors Study" (2003), 6–8 (finding that in 2002, 83 percent of boards included a CEO or COO of another company, while only 44 percent included even one African American board member and only 17 percent included at least one Latino board member).

42. See Stephen M. Bainbridge, "Why a Board? Group Decisionmaking in Corporate Governance," *Vanderbilt Law Review* 55 (2002): 32; Langevoort, "The Human Nature of Corporate Boards," 810–11 (boards naturally trend toward collegiality and hence groupthink). See also Marleen A. O'Connor,

"The Enron Board: The Perils of Groupthink," *University of Cincinnati Law Review* 71 (2003): 1233, 1261–69 (arguing the Enron board suffered from groupthink).

43. See Janis, *Groupthink*, 9–10.

44. See James Fanto, "Whistleblowing and the Public Director: Countering Corporate Inner Circles," *Oregon Law Review* 83 (2004): 435, 463–64; Janis, *Groupthink*, 255–56. See also John M. Levine and Lauren B. Resnick, "Social Foundations of Cognition," *Annotated Review of Psychology* 44 (1993): 585, 601 (pointing out that groupthink is particularly present in cohesive groups with strong leaders).

45. See Joseph E. Bachelder III, "Executive Employment Agreements: Selected Issues and Developments," *Practicing Law Institute/Tax* 824 (2008): 143 (citing surveys showing that the portion of S&P 500 companies splitting the roles of CEO and chairman of the board rose from 21 percent in 2001 to 37 percent in 2007).

46. We start with the premise that the first student drew a light ball and then guessed Mostly Light. We then ask what the odds are that the second student drew a dark ball but guessed Mostly Light. There is an equal chance that the instructor chose Mostly Light versus Mostly Dark. If the instructor chose Mostly Light, there is a 1 in 3 chance that the second student drew a dark ball and then a 1 in 2 chance that the second student randomly chose to guess Mostly Light. This amounts to a 1 in 12 chance that the instructor chose Mostly Light and the second student drew a dark ball and then guessed Mostly Light. If the instructor chose Mostly Dark, there is a 2 in 3 chance that the second student drew a dark ball and then a 1 in 2 chance that the second student randomly chose to guess Mostly Light. This yields a 2 in 12 chance that the instructor chose Mostly Dark and the second student drew a dark ball and then guessed Mostly Light. In sum, then, there is a 3 in 12 (or 1 in 4) chance that after the first student drew a light ball the second student drew a dark ball but guessed Mostly Light. Conversely, there is a 3 in 4 chance that the second student drew a light ball given the observation that the second student guessed Mostly Light.

47. The chances of drawing two lights and a dark are 4 in 27 ($2/3 \times 2/3 \times 1/3$) if the balls came from the Mostly Light urn but only 2 in 27 ($1/3 \times 1/3 \times 2/3$) if the balls came from the Mostly Dark urn. To allow for the 25 percent chance that the second ball was dark, despite the second student guessing Mostly Light, we need to discount these possibilities by 25 percent (multiplying them by .75) and then add back a 25 percent chance that the second ball was actually dark under both the Mostly Light and Mostly Dark cases. The result is about a 9 percent chance that a Mostly Dark urn would produce these draws, compared to a 13 percent chance that a Mostly Light urn would produce them.

48. See Lisa R. Anderson and Charles A. Holt, "Classroom Games: Information Cascades," *Journal of Economic Perspectives* 10 (1996): 187. See also Lisa R. Anderson and Charles A. Holt, "Information Cascades in the Laboratory," *American Economic Review* 87 (1997): 847; Abhijit V. Banerjee, "A Simple Model of Herd Behavior," *Quarterly Journal of Economics* 108 (1992): 797, 798; Sushil Bikhchandani, David Hirshleifer, and Ivo Welch, "Learning from the

Behavior of Others: Conformity, Fads, and Informational Cascades," *Journal of Economic Perspectives* 12 (1998): 151, 154; Cass R. Sunstein, "Deliberative Trouble? Why Groups Go to Extremes," *Yale Law Journal* 110 (2000): 71, 82.

49. See Anderson and Holt, "Classroom Games," 189 (describing game); Anderson and Holt, "Information Cascades in the Laboratory," 847 (describing experimental results).

50. Anderson and Holt, "Information Cascades in the Laboratory," 851–52.

51. See Sunstein, "Why Groups Go to Extremes," 78.

52. See Miriam A. Cherry and Robert L. Rogers, "Markets for Markets: Origins and Subjects of Information Markets," *Rutgers Law Review* 58 (2006): 339, 345–47 (discussing information markets such as the Iowa Electronic Markets and the Hollywood Exchange Markets); Saul Levmore, "Simply Efficient Markets and the Role of Regulation: Lessons from the Iowa Electronic Markets and the Hollywood Stock Exchange," *Journal of Corporate Law* 28 (2003): 589, 594.

53. See Sunstein, "Why Groups Go to Extremes," 76.

54. See U.S. Securities and Exchange Commission, "SEC Votes to Adopt Changes to Disclosure Requirements Concerning Executive Compensation and Related Matters," July 26, 2006, www.sec.gov/news/press/2006/2006–123.htm (announcing the new rules).

55. See Edward Herlihy et al., "Current Developments on the Financial Institutions Landscape," *Practicing Law Institute/Corporate* 1467 (2005): 115, 129 (deriding the current trend of hiring multiple compensation consultants to double-check executive compensation proposals).

56. See Graef Crystal, *In Search of Excess: The Overcompensation of American Executives* (New York: Norton, 1992).

57. Ibid.

58. Ibid.

59. See, e.g., Carly Fiorina, "Government Shouldn't Decide Executive Pay," *CNN Politics*, February 5, 2009, www.cnn.com/2009/POLITICS/02/05/fiorina.pay/index.html.

60. See M. Todd Henderson, "Paying CEOs in Bankruptcy: Executive Compensation When Agency Costs Are Low," *Northwestern University Law Review* 101 (2007): 1543.

61. See Susan Carey, "Judge Approves UAL's Managers Incentive Plan," *Wall Street Journal*, January 19, 2006, A2.

62. See Lynn Stout, *Cultivating Conscience: How Good Laws Make Good People* (Princeton: Princeton University Press, 2010), 42. See also Frank Dobbin and Jiwook Jung, "The Misapplication of Mr. Michael Jensen: How Agency Theory Brought Down the Economy and Why It Might Again," *Research in the Sociology of Organizations* 30B (2010): 29–64.

63. See Thomas Piketty and Emmanuel Saez, "Income Inequality in the United States, 1913–1998," *Quarterly Journal of Economics* 118 (2003): 34–35 (arguing that social norms shifted during the 1970s to make greater income inequality more acceptable).

64. See discussion in chapter 3.

CHAPTER 9

1. Dodge v. Ford Motor Co., 170 N.W. 668 (1919).

2. See M. Todd Henderson, "Everything Old Is New Again: Lessons from *Dodge v. Ford Motor Company,*" in *Corporate Law Stories,* ed. J. Mark Ramseyer (New York: Foundation Press, 2009), 37–75.

3. Ibid.

4. Ibid.

5. See Henderson, "Everything Old Is New Again"; D. Gordon Smith, "The Shareholder Primacy Norm," *Journal of Corporate Law* 23 (1998): 277.

6. The classic defense of shareholder primacy is Adolf A. Berle, "Corporate Powers as Powers in Trust," *Harvard Law Review* 44 (1931): 1049.

7. See Lucian Bebchuk and Jesse Fried, *Pay without Performance: The Unfulfilled Promise of Executive Compensation* (Cambridge, MA: Harvard University Press, 2004).

8. The classic advancement of the stakeholder view is E. Merrick Dodd Jr., "For Whom Are Corporate Managers Trustees?," *Harvard Law Review* 45 (1932): 1145.

9. See Lynnley Browning, "Fire Could Not Stop a Mill, but Debts May," *New York Times,* November 28, 2001, C1.

10. Ibid.

11. See Gretchen Morgenson, "GE Capital vs. the Small-Town Folk Hero," *New York Times,* October 24, 2004, C5.

12. "See In Brief: Malden Mills Drops Plan to Auction Assets," *Wall Street Journal,* February 21, 2007, B4.

13. See Browning, "Fire Could Not Stop a Mill."

14. Ibid.

15. See Berle, "Corporate Powers" (advancing shareholder primacy); Dodd, "Trustees" (arguing for stakeholder position).

16. See Brett H. McDonnell, "Corporate Constituency Statutes and Employee Governance," *William Mitchell Law Review* 30 (2004): 1227.

17. See Stephen M. Bainbridge, "Director Primacy: The Means and Ends of Corporate Governance," *Northwestern University Law Review* 97 (2003): 547.

18. See Citron v. Fairchild Camera and Instrument Corp., 569 A.2d 53, 64 (Del. 1989).

19. See William T. Allen, "Our Schizophrenic Conception of the Business Corporation," *Cardozo Law Review* 14 (1992): 261.

20. Delaware law does permit the certificate of incorporation—roughly analogous to the corporation's constitution—to exempt directors from liability "for any breach of the director's duty of loyalty to the corporation or its stockholders." Delaware General Corporation Law § 102(b)(7). As David Yosifon has pointed out, although a duty to the "corporation" might include other stakeholders such as bondholders or employees, there is no explicit reference to any other stakeholder than shareholders. See David G. Yosifon, "The Law of Corporate Purpose" (Santa Clara Univ. Legal Studies Research Paper No. 14-12, September 28, 2012), available at http://ssrn.com/abstract=2154031. Still, it is hard to make very much of this absence. The statute could be reasonably read to favor either interpretation.

21. Some notable voices arguing that Delaware law endorses the stakeholder theory are former Delware chancellor William T. Allen, former Delaware Supreme Court chief justice Norman Veasey, Harvard law professor Einer Elhauge, and Cornell law professor Lynn Stout. The other side counts current Delaware chancellor Leo E. Strine Jr., UCLA law professor Stephen Bainbridge, and Santa Clara law professor David Yosifon among its champions. See Allen, "Schizophrenic Conception"; E. Norman Veasey and Cristine Di Guglielmo, "How Many Masters Can a Director Serve? A Look at the Tensions Facing Constituency Directors," *Business Law* 63 (2008): 761; Einer Elhauge, "Sacrificing Corporate Profits in the Public Interest," *New York University Law Review* 80 (2005): 733; Lynn Stout, *The Shareholder Value Myth: How Putting Shareholders First Harms Investors, Corporations, and the Public* (San Francisco: Berrett-Koehler, 2012); Leo E. Strine Jr., "Our Continuing Struggle with the Idea that For-Profit Firms Seek Profit," *Wake Forest Law Review* 47 (2012): 135–72; Stephen M. Bainbridge, *The New Corporate Governance in Theory and Practice* (New York: Oxford University Press, 2008), 53; Yosifon, "The Law of Corporate Purpose."

22. Ebay Domestic Holdings, Inc. v. Newmark, 16 A.3d 1, 34 (Del. Ch. 2010).

23. See Bainbridge, "Director Primacy."

24. See Dodd, "Trustees."

25. See Thomas Donaldson and Lee E. Preston, "The Stakeholder Theory of the Corporation: Concepts, Evidence and Implications," *Academy of Management Review* 20 (1995): 65–91 (citing surveys from 1968, 1977, and 1984).

26. See D. Gordon Smith, "The Shareholder Primacy Norm," *Journal of Corporation Law* 23 (1998): 277, 290 (discussing studies). Bainbridge argues that the evidence is to the contrary but cites in support only two studies, one of which (by Korn/Ferry) found that directors acknowledged their subsidiary obligation to other constituencies. Bainbridge, "Director Primacy." The dispute, though, does not undercut Bainbridge's argument about how we ought to view corporate governance.

27. Milton Friedman, "The Social Responsibility of Business Is to Increase Its Profits," *New York Times*, September 13, 1970, 32, 33.

28. The property scholar David Fagundes calls this sort of rhetorical move "property romance" when used in the intellectual property context. See David Fagundes, "Property Rhetoric and the Public Domain," *Minnesota Law Review* 94 (2010): 652.

29. See Bainbridge, "Director Primacy"; Lynn A. Stout, "Bad and Not-So-Bad Arguments for Shareholder Primacy," *Southern California Law Review* 75 (2002): 1189.

30. See James E. Penner, "The 'Bundle of Rights' Picture of Property," *UCLA Law Review* 43 (1996): 711.

31. See Donaldson and Preston, "Stakeholder Theory."

32. See Daniel R. Fischel, "Organized Exchanges and the Regulation of Dual Class Common Stock," *University of Chicago Law Review* 54 (1987): 119, 134. Fischel argues that one way to ensure that shareholders' interests prevail is to give them the exclusive right to elect the corporation's directors.

33. See Stout, "Arguments for Shareholder Primacy."

34. See Bainbridge, "Director Primacy"; Anant K. Sundaram and Andrew C. Inkpen, "The Corporate Objective Revisited," *Organization Science* 15, no. 3 (2004): 350–63.

35. See Stout, *The Shareholder Value Myth*, 69–71.

36. Ibid., 107–9.

37. See Sundaram and Inkpen, "Corporate Objective."

38. See Bainbridge, "Director Primacy."

39. See R. Edward Freeman, Andrew C. Wicks, and Bidhan Parmar, "Stakeholder Theory and 'The Corporate Objective Revisited,'" *Organization Science* 15, no. 3 (2004): 364–69.

40. See Sundaram and Inkpen, "Corporate Objective."

41. Ibid.

42. See Frank Levy and Peter Temin, "Inequality and Institutions in 20th Century America" (Working Paper 07–17, Department of Economics, MIT, 2007), http://ssrn.com/abstract=984330.

43. See Margaret M. Blair and Lynn A. Stout, "A Team Production Theory of Corporate Law," *Virginia Law Review* 85 (1999): 247.

44. Ibid.

45. See Shawn L. Berman, Andrew C. Wicks, Suresh Kotha, and Thomas M. Jones, "Does Stakeholder Orientation Matter? The Relationship between Management Models and Firm Financial Performance," *Academy of Management Journal* 42, no. 5 (1999): 488–506.

46. See Amy J. Hillman and Gerald D. Keim, "Shareholder Value, Stakeholder Management, and Social Issues: What's the Bottom Line?," *Strategic Management Journal* 22, no. 2 (2001): 125–39.

47. See Donaldson and Preston, "Stakeholder Theory"; Freeman, Wicks, and Parmar, "Stakeholder Theory."

48. Here I am making several deeply problematic assumptions about our ability to craft a social welfare function that treats all people's utility equally and somehow manages to add up different people's "utiles" even though utility is an ordinal—not cardinal—function. I make these assumptions for the sake of narrative clarity. But my underlying point here—that there are opposing interests that must be balanced—does not depend on these assumptions. For a more in-depth discussion of the problems inherent in social welfare functions, see Michael B. Dorff and Kimberly Kessler Ferzan, "Is There a Method to the Madness: Why Creative and Counterintuitive Solutions Are Counterproductive," in *Theoretical Foundations of Law and Economics,* ed. Mark White (Cambridge: Cambridge University Press, 2009).

49. I assume here it is the interests of the United States that matter because this book's goal is to improve U.S. policy and law. A more universalist conception might argue that off-shoring jobs is of net benefit to the world's population and that it is the *world's* welfare that matters, not just that of the United States. While I am sensitive to these humanitarian concerns, they range far beyond the scope of this book.

50. See Daniel Kahneman, Jack L. Knetsch, and Richard H. Thaler, "Experimental Tests of the Endowment Effect and the Coase Theorem," *Journal of Political Economy* 98, no. 6 (1990): 1325–48.

51. See Daniel Kahneman, Jack L. Knetsch, and Richard H. Thaler, "Anomalies: The Endowment Effect, Loss Aversion, and Status Quo Bias," *Journal of Economic Perspectives* 5 (1991): 193–206.

52. See Bainbridge, "Director Primacy." Although Bainbridge is not the only scholar to make this argument, his is the most legally sophisticated articulation I have seen. See, e.g., Sundaram and Inkpen, "Corporate Objective."

53. See Bainbridge, "Director Primacy."

54. Ibid.

55. See Henry N. Butler and Larry E. Ribstein, "Opting Out of Fiduciary Duties: A Response to the Anti-Contractarians," *Washington Law Review* 65 (1990): 28–30; Frank H. Easterbrook and Daniel R. Fischel, "Contract and Fiduciary Duty," *Journal of Law and Economics* 36 (1993): 425, 427.

56. See Arthur R. Pinto, "The European Union's Shareholder Voting Rights Directive from an American Perspective: Some Comparisons and Observations," *Fordham International Law Journal* 32 (2009): 587, 594 n. 26.

57. See Leo E. Strine Jr., "One Fundamental Corporate Governance Question We Face: Can Corporations Be Managed for the Long Term Unless Their Powerful Electorates Also Act and Think Long Term?," *Business Lawyer* 66 (2010): 14.

58. Ibid., 14–15.

59. See Rajiv D. Banker, Gordon Potter, and Dhinu Srinivasan, "An Empirical Investigation of an Incentive Plan That Includes Nonfinancial Performance Measures," *Accounting Review* 75 (2000): 65–92.

60. See Kevin J. Murphy, "The Politics of Pay: A Legislative History of Executive Compensation" (Marshall School of Business Paper FBE 01.11, 2011), http://ssrn.com/abstract=1916358.

61. See Mark Lifsher, "Firms File for Do-Good Status," *Los Angeles Times*, January 4, 2012.

62. For those interested in reading more about them, I recommend Usha Rodriguez, "Entity and Identity," *Emory Law Journal* 60 (2011): 1315–19, as a good introduction.

63. For a list of low-profit, limited liability company statutes, see Daniel S. Kleinberger, "A Myth Deconstructed: The 'Emperor's New Clothes' on the Low-Profit Limited Liability Company," *Delaware Journal of Corporate Law* 35 (2010): 879, 880 (notes 1 and 2).

64. See Lifsher, "Do-Good Status."

65. Lynn Stout has made a similar plea. Stout, *Shareholder Value Myth*, 110–15.

66. See Jesse Eisinger, "Challenging the Long-Held Belief in Shareholder Value," *New York Times*, June 27, 2012, available at http://dealbook.nytimes.com/2012/06/27/challenging-the-long-held-belief-in-shareholder-value/.

CHAPTER 10

1. See Thomas Piketty and Emmanuel Saez, "Income Inequality in the United States, 1913–1998," *Quarterly Journal of Economics* 118, no. 1 (2003): 1–39.

2. Ibid.

3. Ibid.

4. Kevin J. Murphy, "Executive Compensation: Where We Are and How We Got There," in *Handbook of the Economics of Finance,* ed. George Constantinedes, Milton Harris, and René Stulz (North Holland: Elsevier, 2012).

5. See Pub. Law No. 111–203, Title IX, § 953(b), July 21, 2010, 124 Stat. 1904 (2010).

6. See Caroline Copley, "Proposal to Cap Executive Pay Rejected by Swiss Voters," *Huffington Post,* November 24, 2013, available at www.huffingtonpost .com/2013/11/24/executive-pay-switzerland-proposal_n_4333376.html.

7. 26 U.S.C. § 162(m).

8. See Institutional Shareholder Services, "U.S. Corporate Governance Policy 2014 Updates (November 21, 2013), available at http://www.issgovernance .com/files/2014USPolicyUpdates.pdf.

9. See chapter 2.

10. See PWC, "Making Executive Pay Work: The Psychology of Incentives" (2012), available at www.pwc.com/gx/en/hr-management-services/publications /making-executive-pay-work-the-psychology-of-incentives.jhtml.

11. See Charles M. Elson and Craig K. Ferrere, "Executive Superstars, Peer Groups and Over-Compensation—Cause, Effect and Solution (August 7, 2012), 33, available at http://ssrn.com/abstract=2125979.

12. See chapter 2.

13. See chapter 3.

14. See chapter 3.

15. See chapter 4.

16. See Voltaire, *Candide* (New York: Simon & Brown, 2011).

17. See chapter 5.

18. See chapter 5.

19. See chapter 6.

20. See chapter 6.

21. See chapter 7.

22. See chapter 7.

23. See chapter 8.

24. See chapter 9.

25. See chapter 9.

26. Stefan Lange and James Angelos, "Germany Weighs Pay Curbs: Legislation Would Give Shareholders More Say over Executive Compensation," *Wall Street Journal,* March 12, 2013.

27. High Pay Commission, *Cheques with Balances: Why Tackling High Pay Is in the National Interest* (2013), available at http://highpaycentre.org/img /Cheques_with_Balances.pdf.

28. Ibid.

29. Pub. Law No. 111–203, Title IX, § 953(b), July 21, 2010, 124 Stat. 1904 (2010).

30. See Emma Thomasson, "Swiss Citizens Voted on Sunday to Impose Some of the World's Strictest Controls on Executive Pay, Forcing Public Companies to Give Shareholders a Binding Vote on Compensation," *Reuters* (March

3, 2013), available at www.reuters.com/article/2013/03/03/us-swiss-regulation-pay-idUSBRE92204N20130303.

31. See Ingolf Dittman and Ernst Maug, "Lower Salaries and No Options? On the Optimal Structure of CEO Pay," *Journal of Finance* 62 (2007): 303–43; Brian J. Hall and Kevin J. Murphy, "Stock Options for Undiversified Executives" *Journal of Accounting and Economics* 33 (2002): 3–42. But see Richard A. Lambert and David F. Larcker, "Stock Options, Restricted Stock, and Incentives," (April 2004), available at SSRN at http://ssrn.com/abstract=527822.

32. See chapter 2.

33. See FAS Statement of Financial Accounting Standards No.123R, *Share-Based Payment,* December 2004, available at www.fasb.org/pdf/fas123r.pdf.

34. See Qiang Cheng and David B. Farber, "Earnings Restatements, Changes in CEO Compensation, and Firm Performance" (Working Paper, Sauder School of Business, 2008), http://ssrn.com/abstract=808344; John C. Coffee, "What Caused Enron? A Capsule Social and Economic History of the 1990's" (Working Paper 214, Columbia Law and Economics), http://ssrn.com/abstract=373581 (attributing increase in earnings restatements to dramatic rise in use of stock options); Carola Frydman and Dirk Jenter, "CEO Compensation" (CESifo Working Paper 3277, 2010); Jared D. Harris and Philip Bromley, "Incentives to Cheat: The Influence of Executive Compensation and Firm Performance on Financial Misrepresentation," *Organization Science* 18, no. 3 (2006): 350–67, http://ssrn.com/abstract=1010197; Julia Grant, Antonio Parbonetti, and Garen Markarian, "CEO Risk-Related Incentives and Income Smoothing" (AAA Financial Accounting and Reporting Section [FARS] Paper, 2009), http://ssrn.com/abstract=1106096.

35. See Markus C. Arnold and Robert M. Gillenkirch, "Stock Options as Incentive Contracts and Dividend Policy" (Finance & Accounting Working Paper Series, University of Frankfurt, 2002), http://ssrn.com/abstract=303242.

36. See Stephen H. Bryan, Lee-Seok Hwang, and Steven B. Lilien, "CEO Stock-Based Compensation: An Empirical Analysis of Incentive-Intensity, Relative Mix, and Economic Determinants," http://ssrn.com/abstract=177490; Shivaram Rajgopal and Terry J. Shevlin, "Empirical Evidence on the Relation between Stock Option Compensation and Risk Taking" (2001), http://ssrn.com/abstract=172689; Melissa A. Williams and Ramesh P. Rao, "CEO Stock Options and Equity Risk Incentives" (2000), http://ssrn.com/abstract=239640.

37. See Calvin H. Johnson, "Stock and Stock-Option Compensation: A Bad Idea," *Canadian Tax Journal* 51, no. 3 (2003).

38. See Sonja O. Rego and Ryan J. Wilson, "Equity Risk Incentives and Corporate Tax Aggressiveness," *Journal of Accounting Research* 50, no. 3 (2013): 775–810.

39. See Shivaram Rajgopal, Michelle Hanlon, and Terry J. Shevlin, "Large Sample Evidence on the Relation between Stock Option Compensation and Risk Taking" (2004), http://ssrn.com/abstract=427260.

40. See Bryant, Hwang, and Lilien, "CEO Stock-Based Compensation."

41. See Kevin J. Murphy, "Executive Compensation," in *Handbook of Labor Economics,* vol. 3, ed. Orley Ashenfelter and David Card (North Holland: Elsevier, 1998).

42. Randall Morck, Andrei Shleifer, and Robert Vishny, "Management Ownership and Market Valuation: An Empirical Analysis," *Journal of Financial Economics* 20 (1988): 293–315.

43. See Carola Frydman and Dirk Jenter, "CEO Compensation" (Working Paper 3277, Rock Center for Corporate Governance, Stanford University, 2010) (citing studies).

44. Ibid.

45. United States Securities and Exchange Commission, *Shareholder Approval of Executive Compensation and Golden Parachute Compensation,* Release Nos. 33–9178; 34–63768, Final Rule, 33–9178, www.sec.gov/rules /final/2011/33–9178.pdf.

46. See Emily Chasan, "'Say on Pay' Changes Ways—Companies Consult Investors, Stress Performance to Avoid Repeat of Negative Votes," *Wall Street Journal,* February 22, 2012, B4; Sam Liu, "The Impact of the Dodd-Frank Act on Executive Compensation" (2012), http://ssrn.com/abstract=1996257.

47. See Randall S. Thomas, Alan R. Palmiter, and James F. Cotter, "Dodd-Frank's Say on Pay: Will It Lead to a Greater Role for Shareholders in Corporate Governance?," *Cornell Law Review* 97 (2012): 1213.

48. See Robert Hutton, "U.K. Shareholders to Get More Control over Executive Pay," *BloombergBusinessWeek,* June 20, 2012, www.businessweek.com /news/2012–06–19/u-dot-k-dot-to-give-shareholders-votes-on-top-pay-boost-disclosure.

49. See Chasan, "'Say on Pay' Changes Ways"; Associated Press, "Say on Pay: Shareholders Rarely Reject CEO Pay," May 23, 2013, available at www.miamiherald.com/2013/05/23/3412742/say-on-pay-shareholders-rarely .html.

50. See Institutional Shareholder Services, "2012 Taft-Harley U.S. Proxy Voting Guidelines," January, 2012, 21, www.issgovernance.com/files/2012ISS TaftHartleyAdvisoryServicesUSGuidelines.pdf.

51. See Fabrizio Ferri & David A. Maber, "Say on Pay Votes and CEO Compensation: Evidence from the UK," *Review of Finance* 17, no. 2 (2013): 527 (finding that U.K. corporations reacted to shareholder rejections of CEO pay packages by tying executive pay more closely to the company's performance).

52. See chapter 3.

53. See "SEC Adopts New Measures to Facilitate Director Nominations by Shareholders: SEC Release No. 2010–155," August 25, 2010, www.sec.gov /news/press/2010/2010–155.htm.

54. Business Roundtable v. SEC, 647 F.3d 1144 (D.C. Cir. 2011).

55. See Ning Chiu, "And Then There Were Sixteen . . . A Rundown on Proxy Access Shareholder Proposals," *Davis Polk Briefing: Governance* (2012), www.davispolk.com/briefing/corporategovernance/blog.aspx?entry=149.

56. See Ben Fritz, "Disney Shareholders Defeat Governance Proposals," *Wall Street Journal,* March 6, 2013.

57. See Susan J. Stabile, "Motivating Executives: Does Performance-Based Compensation Positively Affect Managerial Performance?," *University Pennsylvania Journal of Labor & Employment Law* 2 (1999): 227.

58. See Rajiv D. Banker, Gordon Potter, and Dhinu Srinivasan, "An Empirical Investigation of an Incentive Plan That Includes Nonfinancial Performance Measures," *Accounting Review* 75 (2000): 65–92.

59. 26 U.S.C. § 162(m).

60. "A performance goal need not, however, be based upon an increase or positive result under a business criterion and could include, for example, maintaining the status quo or limiting economic losses (measured, in each case, by reference to a specific business criterion)." 26 C.F.R. § 1.162–27(e)(2).

61. See Dan Ariely, Uri Gneezy, George Loewenstein, and Nina Mazar, "Large Stakes and Big Mistakes," *Review of Economic Studies* 76, no. 2 (2009): 451–69.

62. See AutoZone, Inc. Form 10-K, October 22, 2012, available at www.sec.gov/Archives/edgar/data/866787/000119312512430271/d404388d10k.htm.

63. See AutoZone, Inc. Definitive Proxy Statement, October 22, 2012, available at www.sec.gov/Archives/edgar/data/866787/000119312512430155/d425096ddef14a.htm.

64. See Ben White, "On Exhibit: Executives' Pay and Perks; Tyco, Adelphia Trials Highlight What Company Heads Received," *Washington Post,* April 7, 2004, E1.

65. See chapter 6.

66. 26 U.S.C. § 162(m).

67. See AutoZone, Inc., Form 10-K ("Customer service is the most important element in our marketing and merchandising strategy").

68. Ibid. AutoZone's 10-K does say it conducts consumer marketing research, but doesn't specify what form this takes.

69. See Ariely et al., "Large Stakes and Big Mistakes."

70. See chapter 6.

71. Logarithmic functions have the right shape to begin with; they rise steeply at first, then curve toward the horizontal without ever quite reaching it. It is possible to pick our three points—the threshold amount, the expected amount, and the maximum amount—and then find the logarithmic formula that comes closest to hitting all three. (Not to worry, we don't have to do the calculations ourselves. There is very good software available for free that will do the heavy lifting for us. For example, the program Graph is available at www.padowan.dk/download/. Microsoft Excel can also do this.) Unless we chose the points with a particular formula in mind, though, the formula we get is unlikely to fit well enough for our needs. In our customer service survey example, our three points would be (7, 9), (7.6, 18), (10, 22.5), where the *x*-coordinate represents the survey score and the *y*-coordinate represents the bonus payment (in $10,000 units). When we plug those numbers in, Graph or Excel gives us the formula:

Bonus=32.4432 * ln(Survey Score)—51.3781

But when we plug our survey scores into the formula, we find some serious discrepancies from our desired points. The formula tells us to award a survey score of 7.0 with a bonus of $117,000, quite a bit above our desired value of $90,000. Similarly, a score of 7.6 comes back with a bonus of $144,000, not our desired $180,000, and a score of 10.0 would garner a bonus of $233,000, a bit over our cap of $225,000. Given the difficulties of fitting a logarithmic function precisely to our three points, I recommend just using two linear functions, as I advised in the text.

72. See PWC, "Making Executive Pay Work: The Psychology of Incentives" (2012), available at www.pwc.com/gx/en/hr-management-services/publications /making-executive-pay-work-the-psychology-of-incentives.jhtml.

73. Boards could ameliorate this problem even with stock options by imposing caps on their value, but this is seldom done.

74. See Jesse Eisinger, "Challenging the Long-Held Belief in Shareholder Value," *New York Times,* June 27, 2012, available at http://dealbook.nytimes .com/2012/06/27/challenging-the-long-held-belief-in-shareholder-value/.

75. 26 U.S.C. § 162(m).

76. See Institutional Shareholder Services, "Proxy Voting Guidelines."

77. See Teresa M. Amabile, "How to Kill Creativity," *Harvard Business Review* (September–October 1998): 76–87, available at http://gwmoon.knu .ac.kr/Lecture_Library_upload/HOW_TO_KILL_CREATIVITY.pdf; Alfie Kohn, "Why Incentive Plans Cannot Work," *Harvard Business Review* 71, no. 5 (1993): 54–61; Jaap W. Winter, "Corporate Governance Going Astray: Executive Remuneration Built to Fail" (Policy Paper 5, Duisenberg School of Finance, 2011): 1521–35, http://ssrn.com/abstract=1652137.

Index